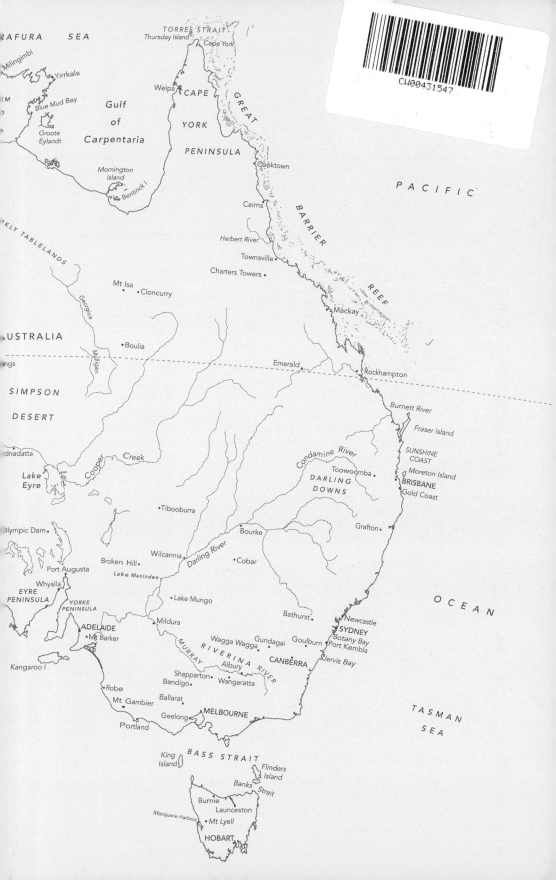

THE STORY OF AUSTRALIA'S PEOPLE

THE RISE AND RISE OF
A NEW AUSTRALIA

ALSO BY GEOFFREY BLAINEY

The Peaks of Lyell
The University of Melbourne: A Centenary Portrait
Johns and Waygood, 1856–1956
A Centenary History of the University of Melbourne
Gold and Paper: A History of The National Bank of Australasia
Mines in the Spinifex: The Story of Mount Isa Mines
The Rush That Never Ended: A History of Australian Mining
A History of Camberwell
The Tyranny of Distance: How Distance Shaped Australia's History
Wesley College: The First Hundred Years (with S. E. K. Hulme and J. H. Morrissey)
The Rise of Broken Hill
Across a Red World
The Steel Master: A Life of Essington Lewis
The Causes of War
Triumph of the Nomads: A History of Ancient Australia
A Land Half Won
Our Side of the Country: The Story of Victoria
All for Australia
Making History (with C. M. H. Clark and R. M. Crawford)
The Great Seesaw: A New View of the Western World, 1750–2000
A Game of Our Own: The Origins of Australian Football
Odd Fellows: A History of IOOF Australia
Blainey, Eye on Australia: Speeches and Essays of Geoffrey Blainey
Sites of the Imagination: Contemporary Photographers View Melbourne and Its People
(with Isobel Crombie)
Jumping Over the Wheel
The Golden Mile
A Shorter History of Australia
White Gold: The Story of Alcoa of Australia
In Our Time
A History of the AMP 1848–1998
A Short History of the World
This Land is All Horizons: Australia's Fears and Visions (Boyer Lectures)
A Very Short History of the World
Black Kettle & Full Moon: Daily Life in a Vanished Australia
A Short History of the Twentieth Century
A History of Victoria
Sea of Dangers: Captain Cook and His Rivals
A Short History of Christianity
The Story of Australia's People: The Rise and Fall of Ancient Australia

THE STORY OF AUSTRALIA'S PEOPLE

THE RISE AND RISE OF A NEW AUSTRALIA

GEOFFREY BLAINEY

VIKING
an imprint of
PENGUIN BOOKS

VIKING

UK | USA | Canada | Ireland | Australia
India | New Zealand | South Africa | China

Penguin Books is part of the Penguin Random House group of companies
whose addresses can be found at global.penguinrandomhouse.com.

First published by Penguin Random House Australia Pty Ltd, 2016

Cover design by John Canty and Alex Ross © Penguin Random House Australia Pty Ltd
Text design by John Canty © Penguin Random House Australia Pty Ltd
Maps by Guy Holt © Penguin Random House Australia Pty Ltd
Cover image: *The Bathers*, by Anne Zahalka (© Anne Zahalka/Licensed by Viscopy)
Typeset in Adobe Caslon Pro by Samantha Jayaweera, Penguin Random House Australia Pty Ltd
Colour separation by Splitting Image Colour Studio, Clayton, Victoria
Printed and bound in Australia by Griffin Press, an accredited ISO AS/NZS
14001 Environmental Management Systems printer.

National Library of Australia
Cataloguing-in-Publication data:

Blainey, Geoffrey, 1930–
The story of Australia's people: the rise and rise
of a new Australia / Geoffrey Blainey.
9780670078028 (hardback)
Includes bibliographical references and index.
Australia – History – 1851-1901.
Australia – History – 20th century.
Australia – History – 2001-
994

penguin.com.au

For Australia and its civilisation,
the time is still 'early morning'…

CONTENTS

PART THREE
The Ascent of Another Australia

Maps

PREFACE

The first volume in this history traced the story of the Australians from their discovery of the land at least 50 000 years ago. Much later, the great rising of the seas – before the peoples' eyes – gave the country its present size, shape and coastline.

The first volume tried to piece together the Aboriginal peoples' way of life – often ingenious – that changed slowly in the course of thousands of years before the arrival of the British in 1788. Then came the swift decline and disarray of the Indigenous peoples, as the more fertile parts of Australia became a British land. The book ended in 1851 with the whispers and news of gold, discovered on the far side of the Blue Mountains. This second volume carries the story through momentous changes, many being unexpected, into the twenty-first century.

The two books give less space to political history than is normal, and more attention to how people worked and lived, played and prayed, travelled or were unable to travel. Sometimes notable political leaders walk into these pages, less because of specific achievements or national crises than because their religious or social views or personal backgrounds typify their era. Some important politicians receive less space than individuals who typify an era, or mirror another facet of our history: Catherine Spence, who nervously overcame the obstacles faced by public speakers in an era when women rarely spoke in public, or Jimmy Governor, who during three months of 1900 was a kind of Aboriginal Ned Kelly, or Don Bradman, who was worshipped by perhaps the first nation in the world to be obsessed with spectator sport.

The book is comprehensive by most standards, but the space allocated to events and trends since the 1990s is rationed. In a story covering such a long period it is vital that the very recent past should be seen in perspective: it is only one loud tick of the clock. The early chapters in this volume are drawn from a section of my book *A Land Half Won*, published in 1980; most have been updated, heavily condensed, rearranged or rewritten. The bulk of the book is new. While working on it, I was often surprised that so much research on ancient and new Australian history was completed in each modern decade. Alas, I have not read it all.

In a long lifetime as a historian I have come to accept – and regret, too – that errors quietly creep into one's books. As historians we busily chase errors away but others take their place. Writing history remains a hard and precarious task, but always fascinating.

Geoffrey Blainey
Melbourne, September 2016

crossed earlier by land explorers and by shepherds and
ks; and some places rich in gold had been camped upon
rs, shepherds, farmers, mail deliverers, dray-drivers and
They kept their eyes open for Aborigines, for pastures and
es and snakes and a multitude of things, but few looked
because they had no reason to believe that it existed here.
ver valleys concealed, just below the grass or river gravels,
antity of alluvial gold dispersed in small grains, flakes and
e and small nuggets.

irst rush would begin when somebody, by intent or acci-
mpsed gold and applied efficient methods of separating
gold from the masses of gravel and clay. In the late 1840s
ost happened. Near the present town of Beechworth a
vas digging a water race or ditch near the waterwheel of
our mill when he saw grains of gold. 'Master, this looks
,' said the worker eagerly to his employer. Thinking it was
s mica, the master said, 'No.' Two years later, far away in
ills of the Californian mountains, an identical event – the
of a channel near a waterwheel – yielded the gold that
e greatest rush the world had seen. But for a little igno-
e Australian gold rushes would probably have preceded the
ian, and the waterwheel mill at Beechworth would have
famous in international history.

sands of Australians sailed to California to dig for gold,
ay returned to view their own valleys and creeks with
knowledgeable eyes. In 1851 a returning digger, Edward
nd Hargraves, visited the Bathurst district where shep-
d been known to find gold and requested to be taken to
site. With his simple Californian skills of how to look and
nine, he found four or five grains of gold in the summer-
. He continued the search, persuaded others to search, and

PART ONE

A Land
Half Won

CHAPTER (

Rush t
the goldfi

The stampede for gold began in May 185
a few women and children set out from
Mountains to the new goldfield straddl
creek. The search spread southwards, an
was dug in Victoria than in New South
first year a long chain of goldfields had
ports the tall ships loaded with intendi
sail for Melbourne.

For decades, settlers had been walking
ing it, but that was not surprising. In a
their eyes on the grass and do not easily
more precious than grass. Most of the

had bee
their flo
by drov
shearers
waterho
for gold
In fact r
a vast q
even lar
The
dent, gl
grains o
that aln
worker
a little
like gol
worthle
the foot
digging
began t
rance, t
Califor
become
Tho
and ma
new an
Hamme
herds h
one suc
how to
dry cree

by May hundreds of ounces of gold had been found in that place that Hargraves named Ophir, after the Biblical place of gold. The news created amazement, and the newly arrived diggers repeatedly had to assure themselves that the incredible was true.

The wool industry and its roads and tracks aided discovery. Gold-bearing ground is more likely to be discovered if people happen to cross that ground in the course of their daily work. Understandably, the first discoveries in Victoria in 1851 were close to sheepfolds, pastoral huts and up-country roads. The first gold of Warrandyte was found near a hut. The first gold of Clunes was found in a quartz reef virtually in the backyard of a squatter's homestead; the reef was so handy to the squatter's vegetable garden that it had been originally considered more valuable as a source of gravel for the garden paths. At Buninyong, which was perhaps the largest inland village in Victoria, the first gold was found close to a road by the village blacksmith, who had walked only 1.6 km from his forge. The first gold of Castlemaine – the heart of the famous Mount Alexander field – was found in a bough yard where the shepherds kept their sheep at night. The first gold of Bendigo was found in a chain of waterholes near a shepherd's hut and stockyard. The first gold at Ballarat was found near an up-country road. Hitherto travellers had passed by these riches without seeing them.

The sheep-owners were disturbed by these events taking place close to where their flocks of sheep grazed. In the face of the rush of workingmen to the newest gold diggings, could enough shearers and shepherds be recruited? 'The gold mania is still raging,' wrote William Lewis, the Scottish manager of a sheep run near the new Ballarat gold diggings, on 13 October 1851. Riding his horse to inspect the discovery, he found hundreds of men working beside a flowing creek. Some dug up the gold-bearing gravel and earth, others carried or wheeled it to the creek, and others rocked to and fro the large wooden 'cradles' that, full of gold-bearing gravel shovelled in, allowed the heavy grains of gold to wriggle their way to the bottom and there be collected.

'The ground', wrote Lewis, 'is covered with tents, and the scene very much resembles some of the large fairs' held in Scottish cities. It was also like a gypsy camp and could vanish at any moment, for all the shallow gold might be worked out or the creek might dry up. On Christmas Day Lewis again wrote home to explain that the pay of reapers and all kinds of rural labourers was soaring but the profitable wool industry was surviving. And he was thinking, 'What if no further goldfields were discovered?' All would return to normal.

But there was no returning. Gold was a beacon and also a barrier that separated Australia from its previous history.

By the law of England all gold belonged to the Crown, and that had been one reason why the shepherds who found gold in the 1840s had not publicised what they found. The law enabled the Australian governments to regulate the new goldfields minutely. Faced with the prospect of unimaginable chaos as people left their jobs in 1851 and hurried to the goldfields, the government in Sydney ruled that every digger must buy a licence at the exorbitant fee of thirty shillings a month, and the licence then entitled him to dig for the Crown's gold. The high licence fee was ingenious. It was intended to tax heavily those who found gold but to drive back to their normal jobs those shepherds, clerks and road-menders who were unable to find it. Devised on the spur of the moment to meet social dislocation of an extent that perhaps even Britain had not suddenly had to face in the previous century, the tax remained in Victoria and New South Wales even after the scarcity of labour had been turned into glut by the gold-seekers coming across the seas. A sensible tax in the crisis of 1851, it was to become a major cause of another crisis in 1854 after thousands of people, having crossed the world to dig for gold, had trouble finding it. They were compelled to pay the tax even if they found no gold.

3

Victoria produced more than nine-tenths of the gold mined in the 1850s. It attracted the majority of overseas immigrants, most of whom had paid their own fare for the long sea voyage. Nearly half a million arrived, mostly males, and the Victorian government set out to find them wives by paying the fares of women from the British Isles. In Liverpool the gold-seekers boarded sailing ships freshly built in Boston, and these 'clipper' ships rarely exceeded 2000 tonnes but jammed in the passengers. Commanded by captains who were determined to make fast times, they usually sighted no land between the British Isles and the Victorian coastline. Displaying such dashing names as *Lightning* and *Champion of the Seas*, they were among the fastest ships built up to that time.

When gold-seekers came in sight of the Victorian coast they had been at sea for ten or fifteen weeks of idleness and therefore were not yet fit for the hard life that lay ahead. As soon as they landed at Melbourne or Geelong – the main ports for the gold-fields – they gathered equipment and set out to walk. Of those who went from a port to the goldfields in the early 1850s, perhaps ninety-five of every hundred walked the whole way.

They carried as much as their arms, shoulders and backs would bear. Loading themselves with a small tent, blankets, pick and shovel and pan, cooking implements and perhaps a little flour, sugar and tea, they sometimes staggered along the road. If they had little strength, and a little money to spare, they sometimes bargained with the owner of a slow-moving bullock dray or faster horse-cart to carry much of their load. Many travellers were really hitchhikers who walked alongside a dray or cart and took advantage, when the dray halted at nightfall, of making their bed beneath the shelter of the dray and sharing the camp fire of the drayman. Others erected tents or built tiny huts of bark or slept on the ground or on a mattress of gum leaves. A horseman who rode after dark might pass, in the space of one hour, eighty or a hundred camp fires where groups of gold-seekers were cooking or keeping warm.

On new-found goldfields each digger was allowed only a small plot of ground in which to search for gold. With such a rule more diggers could be crammed into a golden valley here than in California, where the mining claims were large. On the typical Victorian fields in the early 1850s one man received a square mining claim no larger than the floor of a moderate suburban bedroom or dining room. He dug down with his pick, and the earth and gravel he threw up with his long-handled shovel formed a mound around his claim. If he was lucky enough to discover gold he carried the gold-bearing clay or gravel down to the nearest creek or waterhole, where he washed away the waste and collected the gold. In a typical shallow field, a digger exhausted his ground in a few weeks and then looked for another claim. Distant fields were often enticing, and news of a discovery in a new region could draw ten or twenty thousand people, all rushing to select the most promising ground. Inevitably the majority arrived too late or, taking up inferior ground, spent sweat and capital in finding little or nothing.

The diggings were a casino but the prizes went more to men of strength and stamina. The acclimatised colonial was more likely to find gold than a migrant fresh from England; a barrel-chested labourer was more likely to succeed than a weedy clerk. Here was one of the rare instances in modern history where a great natural resource was more freely available to the poor than to the rich, for the poor were more accustomed to hard work, and only hard work could harvest the diggings. Whereas the first vital natural resource – the grasslands – had been apportioned in huge lots to sheep-owners, the second vital natural resource was apportioned more equally among tens of thousands of diggers. The democratic flavour of the 1850s came partly from this wide dispersal of wealth and the widespread hopes of finding it.

Aborigines coming to inspect the new towns found gold nuggets. Even boys and girls had success. William Howitt, a sixty-year-old English author who arrived in Melbourne in 1852, marvelled at the young Australian lads who 'are doing business on their own before they have a trace of beard on their chins'. A boy of fourteen or fifteen had found enough gold to finance the purchase of a horse and cart. One young teenager, enriched by gold, bought a flock of sheep; another owned a shop that sold sly grog. In the forest near golden Bendigo in 1853 lived three girls from Hobart Town – Lizzy aged six, Kitty aged nine and Jenny aged eleven – and they earned money by preventing workhorses from wandering away in search of green grass.

In appearance the busier diggings were a foretaste of the European battlefields of 1915. They resembled lines of trenches and clusters of foxholes. Many diggings were long lines of shallow holes surrounded by fresh piles of clay and soil. Nearby straggled the encampments of thousands of tents and huts. Like a military camp the first diggings consisted mainly of men wearing a uniform of serge shirt, moleskin trousers and knee boots: 'thousands of the finest men I had ever seen'.

Meanwhile, gold was the craze. Almost every Australian woman in the countryside learned how to identify it and thousands of schoolchildren could tell a small piece of gold from mica or something else that was shiny and valueless. Gold could be recognised by its heaviness and softness and usually by its colour. Even a small nugget no larger than a halfpenny felt strangely heavy in the cup of the hand.

The most exciting finds were the bigger nuggets of gold. At Ballarat in 1858 the 'Welcome' nugget was found by Cornishmen in a shaft 55 metres deep. Probably the largest nugget so far found in the world, it was surpassed eleven years later when the wheel of a cart rubbed the top of an even larger lump of gold near the Victorian gold town of Dunolly. When rid of impurities in a small furnace, the so-called Welcome Stranger weighed 2284 ounces (64 750 grams). It earned a sum of money that would have been sufficient, at ruling prices, to buy eight or ten farms, each with live-stock and fences and buildings already in place.

Monuments were erected later on the site of these two remark-able discoveries. It is a commentary on the allure of gold that people should have erected monuments to these inanimate nug-gets at a time when they had erected few monuments to their most celebrated citizens. And yet the massive nuggets symbolised the excitement of an era when nearly all gold-seekers had their oppor-tunity. These were monuments to everyman. They were emblems of hope.

4

In the first three years of the gold rush, the cost of living in Melbourne must have increased by at least 200 per cent. Daily life seemed to sway on the brink of chaos. Between January 1851 and January 1854 the price of flour and bread more than doubled, that of poultry and fresh butter trebled, the price of hay for the cows quadrupled, the price of eggs and green onions was multiplied by six, that of carrots by twelve and that of cabbages by thirty. Cabbage soup had become almost a luxury. The inflation of prices – more rapid even than the inflation of the 1970s – created intense distress for new migrants who mistakenly imagined that they had enough money to buy food and blankets before walking to the diggings.

In Ballarat many of the underground mines were beginning to differ from those in other Australian goldfields. They were deeper and usually more hazardous. Heavy pieces of timber were lowered down the shaft to support the workings, for a miner could easily be buried by a fall of clay or rock. At the end of the day many of the miners, in order to reach the surface, had to climb ladder-ways as tall as a fifteen-storey building. The Victorian taxes and regula-tions penalised rather than encouraged this risky form of mining; after all, a new mine could be explored and developed for six or eight months – each of its miners paying monthly taxes – before it yielded its first gold. Or it could yield nothing.

In the face of such an influx of people and their demand for more services, the government needed more revenue. The goldmin-ers were expected to provide it. In September 1854 the hunt for the tens of thousands of unlicensed miners was increased dramatically from one inspection a month to about eight a month. The rift with the government widened. Each angry episode stirred up the next.

Sir Charles Hotham, a high-ranking British naval officer, had become governor of Victoria earlier in that year. Inheriting the troubles on the goldfields, he was determined to solve them. Any hint of a popular uprising alarmed him, for law and order were his speciality. He had commanded a British naval squadron on the West African coast in the late 1840s and in less than two years he captured more than 130 slave ships and liberated more than 11 000 slaves.

His knowledge of the uprisings in European cities in 1848, the 'year of revolutions', was also foremost in his mind. He was told that some of the European enthusiasts of 1848 were now digging for gold in Victoria. On his first visit to the goldfields he gained the strong impression that the rough bushy terrain, the thousands of abandoned and worked-out mines and the myriad shallow prospecting holes would favour guerilla warfare – an innovation practised effectively by Spaniards during the war against the Emperor Napoleon just over forty years earlier. He feared that if the miners eventually adopted this form of warfare against the British soldiers in Victoria they could ultimately be victorious.

The unrest on the goldfields sometimes burst into flames, and they were fanned by the behaviour of several of Ballarat's senior public officials. On 7 October 1854 a drunken miner named James Scobie was murdered at Bentley's Hotel. James Bentley, a former Tasmanian convict, was rightly suspected but quickly acquitted by his friend, the local magistrate. As the acquittal was seen as corrupt, indignation in parts of Ballarat grew intense. A crowd numbering maybe 8000 gathered on the afternoon of 17 October, and suddenly the large glass lamp outside the hotel and then the windows were smashed. Soon the wooden hotel was on fire, with a brisk breeze to fan the flames. Soldiers were sent for: they were too late. It was a sign of the isolation of Ballarat that almost one week passed before the burning of the hotel was reported in the main Melbourne daily. On Hotham's own instructions Bentley was arrested, and he was eventually convicted of manslaughter.

Meanwhile, meetings of protest were held to persuade the government to redress grievances, the list of which grew longer. In the presence of huge crowds, a Ballarat Reform League was launched. Its republican manifesto announced boldly that 'it is not the wish of the league to effect an immediate separation of this colony from the parent country'. Hotham responded by setting up investigations into grievances, but voices in the crowd demanded action at once. Many remembered the events of six years before in Europe, when rebellious crowds took up arms even against the army, and in England where crowds, more peaceful, demanded that the parliament should be elected by all the people.

Governor Hotham sent more soldiers from Melbourne in an attempt to maintain public order, but by the end of November the tension was acute. At a dinner held in Ballarat in honour of the visiting American consul the 'loyal toast' to the Queen was proposed, but the diners at first responded with a stubborn silence. Before long a republican flag, coloured dark blue and white and called 'the southern cross', was about to be unfurled on the most prominent flagpole on the goldfield. 'The Australian flag shall triumphantly wave in the sunshine of its own blue and peerless sky over thousands of Australia's adopted sons,' predicted the *Ballarat Times*.

Miners were active in amassing armaments; and the eloquent, educated young Irish miner Peter Lalor belatedly became the leader of the armed and many of the unarmed. On 30 November at a mass meeting a minority of miners deliberately burned gold licences in an illegal act of defiance that Lalor encouraged. Numerous miners – but perhaps not a majority – believed Lalor's promise that they would achieve much more by a display of arms than by continuing to negotiate. When the news of the latest protests reached Melbourne, Hotham privately reported that 'a riot was rapidly growing into a revolution'. He rushed reinforcements up the long road towards Ballarat, but their arrival was in doubt because the rebels and their sympathisers were in control of many entry points to the widespread goldfield.

The rebelling miners had hastily built a stockade or fortress with wooden walls enclosing a large rectangle of ground in which stood huts, tents, abandoned holes, a blacksmith's forge, and enough space for armed men to parade. The hundreds who intermittently

manned the stockade carried weapons ranging from the latest rifles
to sharp iron pikes. In fact they were armed physically rather than
mentally. Unwisely on the afternoon of Saturday 2 December 1854
many miners left the stockade in order to spend the night with
friends or family. Other protesters were absent on duty, concealed
near the main roads so that they could intercept further soldiers or
supplies coming from Melbourne.

The peaceful campaign in Ballarat formed probably the best-
organised and most articulate protest movement seen in Australia
in the nineteenth century. But the confident call to arms by Lalor
and the erecting of the Eureka stockade were almost certain to lead
to retaliation; in that era almost every government in the Western
world would have retaliated. Hotham and his officials resolved to
regain control of the goldfield as soon as their spies learned that
most of the armed rebels were absent for the weekend.

On the Sunday morning, with the light of the full moon to guide
their marching steps and the horses too, soldiers and police moved
towards the stockade. At daybreak they broke through the wooden
wall and, employing bayonets and swords as well as guns, ended the
rebellion. At least thirty miners and five soldiers were killed, and a
few innocent spectators who lived nearby were wounded or bullied.
'I must protest against the barbarities practised by the mounted
troopers,' wrote a reporter from the *Geelong Advertiser*. During the
confusion the miners' leader, Peter Lalor, escaped capture. He was
severely wounded, however, and his left arm had to be amputated
while he lay in hiding.

Lalor had held a strong position, in military strength and
in public support, at the end of November. By the early morning of 3 December 1854, however, his position was pitifully weak,
with many of his men killed, wounded, captured or in hiding. If,
instead, he had succeeded in maintaining his whole army on the

alert that Sunday morning, and if he had also employed guerilla warfare near the roads and in the potholed diggings, he might have defeated Hotham's forces or compelled them to retreat. The miners, with reinforcements from Bendigo and other goldfields, might even have marched on Melbourne. That, in fact, had been one of Hotham's earlier fears.

If the miners had marched on Melbourne, what could Hotham have done? Where would he have found reinforcements for his small force? He could hardly have requested support from regiments in Tasmania, because that would have heightened the chance of an uprising there; convicts and former convicts inhabited Tasmania in superior numbers. He could have called on naval support from Sydney, which was Britain's main naval base in the Pacific Ocean, but New South Wales itself had to be defended. Russia's navy, too, had to be watched. Britain was still waging war with Russia on land and sea, and in the main Australian ports the sea-captains and merchants held a reasonable fear that some day Russian warships could arrive without warning, bombard the wharves and even capture ships about to carry gold bars to England. It was the genuine fear of a Russian attack on Sydney Harbour that led to the erecting, a few months later, of the tower and gun emplacements at Fort Denison (alias Pinchgut), close to the site of the present Opera House.

So, if Lalor had been more experienced, and all his miners had remained in the stockade on that first weekend in December 1854, his forces probably would not have been routed. The result of the rebellion would have been undecided and postponed. Perhaps the two leaders would have found a compromise, or perhaps they would have fought another battle in Ballarat or elsewhere. It is not easy to assess whether the Ballarat revolution would have evaporated or triumphed, and whether the miners' republic ultimately stood or fell. No matter which side finally won, the intervening period might well have included months of chaos and confusion.

Hotham had won, and swiftly he set out to exploit his victory. He was not equipped, however, for such a task. His decision to charge a group of thirteen rebels with treason proved to be a mistake. Most Victorians, hoping that Hotham would be magnanimous, expected peace and an end to the long dispute. In Melbourne early in 1855 the jury refused to convict the rebels, a refusal that had the result of enhancing the legitimacy of their rebellion.

Hotham remained the governor. Unexpectedly he died just one year after Eureka; and the Victorian parliament, realising that he had been diligently performing what he insisted was his duty, resolved to commission in his memory an elaborate monument by Sir Gilbert Scott, one of England's leading cathedral architects. Only the mining representatives in parliament opposed the gesture. The tall column of coloured stone and the ornamental wrought-iron fence were duly shipped to Australia and erected over Hotham's grave, only a short walk from the place where Lalor himself was to be buried three decades later. The leaders' graves are not the scene of pilgrimages. In the annual celebration of Eureka the ordinary miners buried at Ballarat remain the public's heroes.

In reshaping politics the miners' protests affected Victoria rather than Australia as a whole. Democratic ideas were invading the main cities and settled districts of the country. It was like an incoming tide that could be temporarily halted but not defeated. The tide came from Britain, from its authors and journalists and parliamentarians and from the migrants who carried modern ideas in the sailing ships that poured into Australian ports in the 1850s. Britain was not yet willing to implement at home the idea of a vote for every man – in this reform it would lag more than half a century behind Australia – but it was willing to allow Australian parliaments to experiment and to shape their own form of government. Ruling opinion in Britain no longer saw the more advanced colonies as existing simply to enrich the homeland. The revolt of the American colonies three-quarters of a century earlier had taught Britain's rulers a lesson. The recent uprisings in many European cities in 1848 taught the same lesson.

In England in the 1840s the Chartist movement won a host of converts, many of whom could be found later in the tents and mines of Ballarat. With the help of the Ballarat Reform League they called for a new kind of parliament that sat for only one or two years before again facing the electors. At each election every man should be entitled to vote, and every man should be free to stand for parliament. And their astonishing new concept of 'payment of members' would enable miners, ploughmen and blacksmiths to give up their normal work and be paid a salary while they attended parliament.

In contrast the reigning idea of British democracy was that the owners of property should elect the members of parliament. The owners had a special stake in the nation; they were likely to be educated, to be experienced in business, and to maintain the established order. The British government intended to apply this rule to Australia, not fully realising that here the property and wealth, especially the new-found gold, was very widely shared. Thus, when the British government approved of the new constitutions for Victoria and New South Wales it stipulated, among many clauses, that a man earning a salary of £100 a year was entitled to a vote. That sum, while impressive in London, was commonplace in Sydney and Melbourne. Even before the new Australian parliaments began to liberalise their own constitutions they were far advanced by the standards of their homeland and indeed of most countries in Europe.

The incentives and fears promoting democracy in Australia were already high before the Eureka Stockade quickened the movement towards popular control of Victoria's new parliament, which first met in 1856. In that year the democratic movement was even more influential in South Australia's new parliament and owed nothing to the events in Ballarat. Together Victoria and South Australia shared at least one political innovation that eventually rolled around the world. Together they introduced the secret ballot on a national election day and made it work.

The idea of a secret ballot was shunned by most English politicians as cowardly and even revolutionary. The normal practice on the day of a parliamentary election was for the electors – and they were few – to declare publicly for whom they were voting. Accordingly a progress count of the votes was available to the public throughout polling day, and if the contest was close the rival candidates were tempted to use bribes to persuade voters to hurry forward and cast their vote. It was practicable to bribe a voter, because the briber could stand at the polling place and see how the voter actually cast his vote. The practice of public voting also encouraged landlords to intimidate their tenants, or employers to intimidate their skilled workers who possessed a vote.

Most Victorian democrats thought the secret ballot was vital. What was the point of pleading for a widening of the franchise if many of those new voters, either through fear or bribery, did not vote for their favoured candidate? In Victoria an ardent but belated enthusiast for the secret ballot was William Nicholson who, arriving from the north of England in 1842, soon became a rich grocer and, at the age of thirty-four, the mayor of Melbourne. Many of his supporters came from the goldfields. By a narrow majority, the secret ballot became law in Victoria in March 1856 and in South Australia just a fortnight later. Three of the other self-governing colonies, including the new colony of Queensland, had adopted the secret ballot by 1859. Before the end of the century it was sweeping the democratic world, where it was generally called the Australian or Victorian ballot.

Many Australians were intensely proud that their land was becoming a political laboratory. Ballarat's protests also led to the bold rewriting of Victoria's mining laws and taxes. The expensive miner's licence was replaced by a cheap miner's right – one small piece of printed paper replaced another. The tax collected from the goldmines now came in the form of a tax on gold exports: if you dug no gold you paid no tax. Above all, the miners were allowed to make the mining laws for each district – a vital responsibility because the shallow and deep mines, and the hard-rock and alluvial mines, needed different laws and regulations for the sake of efficiency, fairness and safety. In each district the miners elected the members of local courts, which in turn made the detailed laws and even adjudicated in mining disputes. Here was a startling triumph for the democratic colony called Victoria.

5

Ships carrying Chinese gold-seekers arrived just when the Victorian government was trying to cope with a thorny dilemma: how to manage new-found goldfields and the foreigners and locals pouring in. Chinese immigrants were not a novelty. Since the 1840s they had worked as shepherds in new pastoral territory where their work ethic, with some exceptions, was said to outshine that of the ex-convicts. On the Darling Downs in Queensland in 1852 more than half of the sheep were shepherded by newly arrived Chinese. As the squatter Patrick Leslie observed in a letter to a brother in Scotland, his six Chinese employees were 'most excellent servants'. The cook, so clean and eager, was 'a perfect treasure'; the two

Chinese gardeners were preferable to the Englishman who had often been drunk; and another Chinese driving the water cart soon made the bullock respond to orders given in the Cantonese rather than the English language.

Chinese diggers arrived steadily in 1852 and then poured in, a total of about 18 000 reaching Melbourne in the space of eighteen months. The reaction among Victorian diggers was the same as that of the diggers in California who were already trying to expel the Chinese. It was hard enough finding gold – even finding enough gold to pay for the monthly licence – without the energetic Chinese competing side by side with them. After a tax was imposed on Chinese immigrants at the port of entry in 1855, the foreign shipowners simply sailed around the new law by landing their Chinese passengers at the lonely South Australian port of Robe, after which they set out to walk the 300 kilometres to the nearest Victorian goldfield. Of the square-rigged ships that carried Chinese passengers from Hong Kong in 1857 to Singapore, San Francisco, Havana, Madras and various other destinations, more probably sailed to the little-known port of Robe than to any other. Mainly British, American and Dutch ships, five sailed for Robe in January, six in February and eleven in March, and from the beach at Robe the Chinese, with their belongings carried on long shoulder poles, jogged to the unguarded Victorian border and so to the diggings. Late in that decade more than 40 000 Chinese lived on the diggings and did business with Chinese general stores, joss houses, herbalists and doctors, opium dealers, gambling-house keepers and, in the town of Guildford, a Chinese circus and horse-and-coach company. Their way of life had little influence on the English-speaking diggers, with two strong exceptions: they sold them fresh vegetables, and their acupuncture needles were used to treat the sciatica of men who worked in damp mines.

The two cultures clashed, resulting in riots at Buckland in Victoria and Lambing Flat in New South Wales in the years 1857–61. European miners tried to drive out the Chinese gold-diggers, storekeepers and tradespeople. Many Chinese were manhandled and abominably treated. Soldiers and police had to march or ride long distances to impose order. In the following ten years relations were improved, especially in Victoria. The fear that the Chinese and especially Cantonese might dominate Australia did not occur, and towards the close of the century their share of the total population declined. They were not expelled; rather, they simply ceased to come ashore in such numbers. The decline of the rich and shallow goldfields – once the magnet for the Chinese – did as much as immigration laws to curb their inflow.

Most Chinese were looked down upon or criticised because of their opinions and habits. Perhaps half were opium-smokers and, according to the official Chinese interpreters, most were heavy gamblers. As gambling and alcohol gave pleasure to English-speaking Australians, these charges against the Chinese were not entirely consistent. On the other hand the popular economic argument that most Chinese did not spend much of their money in the land where they had found their gold had some merit.

It was the custom more than a century ago to place nearly all blame on the Chinese, but now, as if in guilt, it is increasingly the custom to place no blame on the Chinese and to view them as simply the innocent victims of racism. The Chinese, however, had their prejudices, including their intense pride in their race and their civilisation, which they saw as decidedly superior to those of Britain and Europe.

Understandably they held their own suspicion of strange, foreign ways. In their opinion the British wore clothes that no self-respecting Chinese would wear, did not wash themselves often, worshipped a heathen god, did not honour their ancestors, and drank themselves under the table. Quong Tart, leaving Canton as a boy of nine to work on the Braidwood goldfield near Canberra, later confided that the Chinese believed the British were red-headed savages.

6

Throughout the 1850s, gold was the craze. It transformed the land. From 1851 to 1870 gold supplanted wool as the leading export. Gold accentuated the dominance of the south-east corner of the continent. It spurred the inflow of free immigration and ended the shipments of British convicts to Tasmania. It made the Australian mood more democratic and optimistic. In fact, a surfeit of optimism was to be a dangerous legacy of the 1850s.

Gold enthroned Melbourne over Sydney. In the first twenty years of the gold rushes Melbourne's population increased nine times over, whereas Sydney's increased by less than three. Young cities, they already had slums. In summer many lanes smelled strongly of sewage, which seeped or trickled from the holes in the ground that served as lavatories in a typical backyard. Later came a new respect for hygiene, aided by cheap soap and plentiful supplies of running water.

Infectious diseases spread in the crowded inner suburbs, where one in every ten children did not reach their fifth birthday. In Victoria outbreaks of smallpox – attributed to Chinese immigrants – broke out in 1857, and diphtheria and influenza were a menace in 1860. Sydney in 1867 suffered from a major outbreak of measles and in 1875 most cities suffered from scarlet fever. Typhoid was common. The local undertakers could vouch for the waves of infectious diseases. Though Australia was viewed in Europe as enjoying a healthy climate, the city cottage and the tent or bark hut on the gold diggings was not a healthy dwelling.

Eyes were alert for other minerals, and goldfields were now harder to find. Between 1860 and 1870 the rich copperfield of Wallaroo and Moonta was found near the sea in South Australia; the Queensland fields of Peak Downs and Cloncurry and Mount Perry yielded their first copper; and far inland the shallow copper of Cobar (New South Wales) was discovered by Danish settlers sinking a well, for this was arid sheep country.

In the 1870s, tin became a target for some prospectors. The thoughtful, rarely smiling bushman 'Philosopher' Smith found a massive lode of tin at Mount Bischoff in Tasmania, and the shepherd Joseph Wills found the first payable tin in New England. Rich tinfields were also opened at Stanthorpe and tropical Herberton in Queensland, and in the cold valleys of north-eastern Tasmania. By the end of the decade Australia was briefly the world's main miner of tin.

Meanwhile, the spearhead of the gold rushes thrust its way into remote places. The main movement was in the form of a long anticlockwise loop that ran for some 20 000 kilometres. The rushes that began in the south-east corner of Australia in 1851 were repeated in the South Island of New Zealand one decade later. Queensland, which had just become an independent colony, yielded rich gold in 1867 at Gympie, not far from the Pacific Ocean, and at Charters Towers and the steamy Palmer River far to the north in the early 1870s. Simultaneously gold was found near the Darwin end of the Northern Territory. There the movement of prospectors around the continent halted for more than a decade, before leaping across to Western Australia in the mid-1880s.

In the next decade came a sequence of western rushes culminating in Kalgoorlie and the dry mulga country beyond. The circular movement of gold prospectors was virtually over. From Ophir to Kalgoorlie – from the south-east around to the south-west of the continent – the rushes had occupied a span of a little over forty years. It was therefore conceivable for one man to have taken part in most of the main rushes that marked that anticlockwise march, if only any man could have persisted so long in the face of so many obstacles and hardships and disappointments.

The mighty men were those who prospected in rainforest or desert. They had to carry their own supplies, cut their own tracks through forest and find their own water in the near-desert. Their victories were in the mountain forests of Gippsland in the 1860s, in the heat of Cape York Peninsula in the 1870s, in the cold rainforests of western Tasmania in the 1880s, and in the dry interior of Western Australia between 1886 and 1895. In forbidding terrain they pushed inland with the aid of a series of stepping stones of their own making. Thus when gold was found in 1887 at Southern Cross in Western Australia it became the supply base for excursions to the east. Eventually, in 1892, rich gold – often set like precious stones in the white-quartz rock – was found at Coolgardie, and that became the supply base from which bold prospectors probed further east, and so the gold of Kalgoorlie became the stepping stone from which prospectors moved even further into the interior. What lay in the centre or core of the continent? The puzzle intrigued or excited more and more official explorers and private searchers.

7

If a European sea power had decided to create a colony on that isolated Australian coastline – say at the present Cairns or Darwin – it could have annexed a a hinterland of rich materials with ease. In the late 1820s the British, fearing that the French would make a colony in Western Australia, founded a small settlement at Albany and another in Perth. In the admiralty headquarters in London, British statesmen continued to fear the rival French. Their opinion was that it was not enough for Britain to claim formally the whole continent, a claim it finally made in 1826. Real sovereignty depended on actually occupying part of the coast with people, as well as a proclamation on paper. In effect the British loosely applied to themselves – or thought that they had – the very principle that, for their own benefit, they had applied to the Aborigines.

Occasionally worrying news or rumours crossed the Channel from France. In 1836 it was understood that in the Mediterranean port of Toulon the French were equipping a foreign expedition. North-west Australia – namely Dampier's Land, whose huge deposits of rich iron ore were not yet discovered – was said to be the goal. Another rumour pointed to the ambitious Americans, now a rising sea power. In London, Sir John Barrow, secretary to the admiralty, threw up his hands: 'it would be a most humiliating mortification, to witness the tri-coloured flag, or that of the stripes and stars, waving on Dampier's Land'.

In the early 1840s the French occupied the Marquesas and Tahiti and nearby South Pacific islands; they had been claimed by British navigators in the late eighteenth century. There was no international uproar. If they had then peacefully annexed a small region of Australia, an area consisting of no more than one-tenth of the continent, they might have aroused a diplomatic incident, and perhaps a short time of international tension. But chances of such a loud but peaceful uproar diminished. In the 1850s for the first time in centuries France became a friend and ally of Britain, and they fought on the same side in the Crimean War. Moreover the British attitude to empire was no longer so possessive, and one stream of British opinion even assumed that the Australian colonies would, like Massachusetts and Virginia and the early colonies that created the United States of America, eventually follow a similar road to independence.

France was now eager to find a new and remote colony, possibly a place to which it could send convicts. In 1853 it began to occupy New Caledonia – an island about the size of the present Israel and discovered nearly a century earlier by Captain Cook. In selecting that Pacific island on the eastern shores of the Coral Sea, France thereby shunned one of its last opportunities to snatch a small remote portion of this dry continent. Indeed, if the Aborigines even in one region had been more united and less debilitated by diseases, and if they had begun to understand the politics and rivalries of the barely comprehensible world that was half-swallowing them, they could have informally invited the French, thereby conferring on them some legitimacy.

France's decision to ignore Australia was understandable. Even colonial Australians took little interest in most parts of their own land, and hardly a soul in Melbourne or Sydney thought kindly of the idea of setting up any kind of business in that far diagonal, especially on the shores of the Indian Ocean or Arafura Sea. The effects of this decision, or default, were far-reaching. The huge continent became the sole possession of Britain. Few decisions have had more influence on Australia's modern history.

CHAPTER TWO

A never-never land

In 1860 the exploration of the land was still an exciting topic. Vast areas had been seen by no European. In the far north the mosaic of gorges and tropical forest was untouched by roads but criss-crossed by various narrow Aboriginal pathways. On sweeping plains the native grasses and shrubs knew no hoofmarks. Most of the landmarks in the centre were still unknown to Europeans: the monumental Uluru was on no map, and the scalloped tops of the Petermann Ranges had not been sighted through a telescope. The coloured map in the best guidebook to Australia entirely excluded the northern third of the country. Large areas in the interior were inscribed with not one place name.

Long stretches of the Australian coast had attracted not one port. In 1860 it was possible to travel in a steamship from Perth nearly all the way to the mangroves on the bay at Cairns – it was not yet a township – and see no other ship except perhaps in the narrow sea lane of Torres Strait. Half the length of Australia's coast could be traversed without coming across one town with 1000 people. The entire northern coast of the continent held not one British harbour or village. The ports founded there in the 1820s in the hope that at least one would become a rival to Singapore had been soon abandoned.

2

We now know that most of Australia's real interior, through defects of climate and terrain and soil, cannot be ploughed or even sown with pasture. This arid heartland stretches from the coastlands of the Indian Ocean in the west to the plains near the Pacific Ocean in the east. It extends from the cliffs of the Great Australian Bight in the south to the edge of Arnhem Land. This area has no name; but from the 1870s parts of it were colloquially called the Outback and from the 1880s the Never-Never. In 1906 one part was called the Dead Heart by the Melbourne geologist Professor J. W. Gregory. Vast and oval-shaped, and occupying more than half of Australia, it still holds only a tiny fraction of the people; but it was seen as promising and even enticing in 1860, and in some ways it still is.

In 1860 it produced virtually nothing worth exporting. The weight of opinion suggested then that most of it was barren, arid, very hot. Charles Sturt in 1845 had encountered barren ground and high temperatures near the border of Queensland, South Australia and the Northern Territory, and had turned back in disappointment. Edward Eyre had travelled close to the shores of the Great Australian Bight and seen parched hungry land stretching north. Some explorers had come to the edge of a furnace-like interior and turned back. Augustus C. Gregory, chewing over the available evidence in 1856, decided that 'the remainder of the unexplored interior is a desert, or at least unfit for the habitation of civilized man'.

For every experienced person who envisaged a rolling desert in the centre, at least another hoped that out there, beyond the dancing heat, lay provinces of well-grassed land. 'As big as Denmark,' said the cautious; 'bigger than France,' said the optimists. There was even space for that permanent inland sea that for decades had been one of the magnets of the explorers: an Australian Caspian Sea. As late as 1865 the South Australian priest Julian Tenison-Woods concluded the second volume of his history of Australian exploration with the hope that the inland sea, if it existed, might become the centre of an empire. There actually is an inland sea, Lake Eyre, which is far north of Adelaide and is by far the largest lake on the Australian map; but its surface is normally a kind of mud sprinkled or crusted with dry salt. None of the celebrated Australian explorers ever saw it filled or even one-quarter-filled with water, but we now know that for just a few months the water can not only exist but be deep, the result of unusually heavy rains falling on lands embracing one-sixth of the continent and finding their way far to the south. Lake Eyre – lying below sea level and indeed the lowest land in the continent – was an immense bowl or sump waiting to catch the water. It was a source of hope as well as disappointment. Perhaps another Lake Eyre might be found far inland, a permanent sheet of fresh water replenished in summer by the melting of snow on high mountains nearby.

The idea has arisen in certain circles that it was easy to be a land explorer and therefore that Burke and Wills, because they failed, must have been dunces. Most major explorers in this period, however, could not be adequately prepared for the long journeys they made. They set out with much less knowledge than we now can acquire by spending a day in a library with maps and meteorological records. There was no explorers' club where leaders could meet to exchange information. Most of the ambitious Australian explorers of the time did not once meet each other. But most kept journals of their expeditions and most wrote books.

By 1860 the senior explorers usually concluded that it was valuable to employ an Aboriginal guide. He indicated where water might be found; he searched for straying horses and camels. And yet Burke and Wills did not have an Aboriginal guide for most of their long journey across Australia; nor did John McDouall Stuart. At times such a guide would have helped, but then again he would be one more mouth to feed. Most Aboriginal guides did not live off the land, preferring instead the flour and sugar and other supplies carried for them.

Every explorer learned that in dry country the first task was to look for water. It was Charles Sturt who in the 1840s thought that a horse needed 6 gallons (27 litres) of drinking water a day – until he discovered in the very hot days of the inland that it drank 20 gallons (91 litres) a day. Where was the next drink to be found? The search for water became crucial in later periods when most explorers were in arid territory. It was not readily understood that camels were superior to horses for an exploring party in very hot weather, and in rocky or bushy country.

A decision whether to employ camels or saddle horses, packhorses or bullock teams, wagons or drays, or a combination of the six was not easy. Europeans and Australian-born bushmen preferred horses – they knew more about them – but sometimes their preference was mistaken. Robert O'Hara Burke was provided with both camels and horses, but for the hazardous part of his journey across Australia he chose six camels and one riding horse. New to camels, he realised that they had a freakish ability to travel far without a drink of fresh water, but he was not informed that a load-carrying camel could regularly travel only about 25 kilometres a day. Burke had been misinformed by an Indian expert that it could travel 32 in

a day, and that error proved to be a tragic step in the chain of mishaps that led to his death in 1861 near Cooper Creek, by the border
of Queensland and South Australia.

Stuart was to be penalised because he selected horses. Once
they had to endure four days and nights, travelling 180 kilometres,
without water. Later they had to cross a long stretch of stony country, without iron horseshoes for part of the way. Horses as well as
men were heroes of exploration.

Stuart's choice of animals was a vital decision in Australian
history, for his journey indirectly opened up a new line of communication to Europe. Already the new electric telegraph stretched
overland from England to its greatest possession, India; and the
Indian mutiny of 1857 showed the potential value of a telegraph
for summoning ships and troops during a military crisis. A telegraph line from Britain to Europe and then to Asia and Australia
would strengthen the military security of Sydney and Melbourne
and Adelaide and enable them to call on Britain for naval reinforcements in the event of war – the Russian war scare in the
mid-1850s had provoked that sense of insecurity. The telegraph
might also enrich the Australian colony that became its terminus.
South Australia was determined to be that terminus. It sent forward the gritty Scottish explorer Stuart on a series of journeys that
ultimately led him to the warm waters of the Arafura Sea – east of
the site of Darwin – where he washed his hands and raised a British
flag on 24 July 1862. A year later South Australia took over the big
region through which he had passed, and for almost half a century
it was to be governed from Adelaide and known formally as the
Northern Territory of South Australia.

Stuart's journeys provided a route for the overland telegraph. By
1872 the continent was spanned by a long north–south line of wire,
suspended between tall poles spaced sixteen to the mile. A chain of

telegraph stations, and the parallel cart track by which each isolated station was supplied, provided bases for the last of the explorers who set out to investigate the unknown space stretching between the telegraph line and the Indian Ocean far west. Here lay one of the largest tracts of land not yet known to Europeans. Between 1872 and 1876 it was a magnet for explorers.

Wonderful sights and dismal sights were seen by these explorers of the Western Desert. W. C. Gosse, the South Australian, saw one of the most astonishing views less than 320 kilometres from the telegraph line. Travelling with his camels through the spinifex and the sandy rises in 1873, he could see in the distance a high rocky hump. Suddenly, from the top of a hill, the red hump was set out before him: 'what was my astonishment', he wrote, 'to find it was one immense rock rising abruptly from the plain'. He called it Ayers Rock, after an Adelaide politician, but its ancient Aboriginal name was Uluru, and that name has returned to favour. Gosse did not realise that technically it was an inselberg rather than a rock, for it was the remnant – wind-smoothed and water-carved – of a tableland. On Sunday 20 July 1873, Gosse and his Afghan companion Hamran looked for a way up its steep sides. Together they climbed and scrambled and puffed. Gosse took off his boots so that he could gain more grip, but his feet blistered. The view and the exhilaration were compensation. 'This rock,' he exclaimed when he returned a week later, 'appears more wonderful every time I look at it.'

The elderly commandant of South Australia's volunteer army, Colonel Peter Warburton, set out from the telegraph station at Alice Springs in 1873 in the hope of crossing the wilderness to Perth. With three Europeans, two Afghan camel drivers, an Aborigine named Charley, and seventeen fat camels, he thought he was prepared for a parched land. But he was not prepared for the extent of the dryness or for the time required to penetrate unknown country.

Fortunately there was no war scare in Adelaide during his absence, because the colonel was away from his post in the city for a year and a half, and for part of that time he was 'missing'.

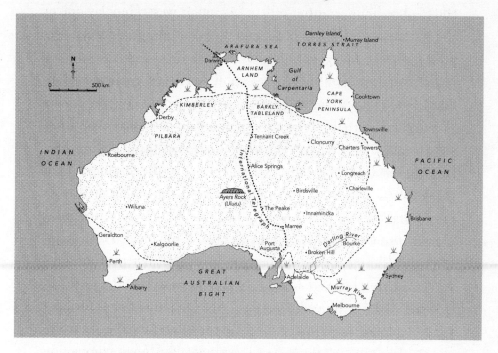

The Never-Never, 1900 – a vast area that can produce neither crops nor sown pastures.

Warburton was driven off course by the scarcity of water. His long string of camels became shorter. One ate a poisoned plant, three became so weak that he had to abandon them, four ran away, and seven were killed to provide meat for the hungry men. Only two camels finished the journey, and on them Warburton heaped praise. Exhausted and ill, he reached the Oakover River in Western Australia and eventually the tiny port of Roebourne in January 1874. He completed his journey but had found nothing. The first half of his journey, to the north-west of Alice Springs, can now be glimpsed by hundreds of thousands of people yearly on the flight between Sydney and Singapore. About three hours after leaving Sydney they reach his route; and in one effortless hour they cross the country on which Warburton and his camels laboured for four months.

'No horses could have lived with us,' said Warburton emphatically. John and Alexander Forrest would have agreed. They set out from Geraldton with twenty horses in 1874 in the hope of travelling east to the overland telegraph line. Using their two Aborigines as waterfinders, they rarely rode ahead unless they knew that water was awaiting them. So they moved slowly east, passing between the later goldfields of Peak Hill and Wiluna but seeing no gold. Briefly they clashed with Aborigines. Finally, they came to the Peake telegraph station, exactly six months after leaving the Indian Ocean. They had travelled nearly 3000 kilometres, most of them on foot, while their horses carried the baggage and supplies.

At last they reached Adelaide where people lined the roadside, crowded the balconies and rooftops, rang church bells and cheered as the explorers rode their horses slowly towards the heart of the city. At the town hall the brass band played 'The Song of Australia' and the Aboriginal explorer Tommy Pierre made one of his short racy speeches. This enthusiastic welcome was for bravery. The Forrests had found nothing of value.

If only one of the explorers could find, between the overland telegraph line and the pastoral country on the west coast, a grassy corridor along which cattle and sheep could move between Perth and the eastern cities! Even if wells had to be sunk in the dry stretches of the track, even if the track were open only for four months of the year, it would break the isolation of Western Australia.

Ernest Giles was one who sought that track. He had gone to the fashionable London school Christ's Hospital, where Coleridge

of 'The Rime of the Ancient Mariner' had studied. Giles himself
became a dusty kind of mariner, navigating the Australian sandy
deserts. He dreamed what might lie in that sparsely explored terrain: 'There was room for snowy mountains, an inland sea, ancient
river, and palmy plain, for races of new kinds of men inhabiting a
new and odorous land, for fields of gold and golcondas of gems,
for a new flora and a new fauna.' He also exulted that 'there was
room for me!'

On his second journey, in 1873, he was alone and far from help.
Walking in intense heat, he was saved by his own stamina and a
mouse-sized wallaby that had been thrown from its mother's
pouch: 'I pounced upon it and ate it, living, raw, dying – fur, skin,
bones, skull, and all.' He never forgot the delicious taste of the animal. Only when Giles brought camels to that harsh country did he
succeed in conquering the wide spaces.

3

It was now three-quarters of a century since the British first settled
in Sydney. And yet in vast expanses of the centre and north of the
continent the way of life went on with not much change in the past
thousand years – the births, the fondness of the people for their
children, their systematic moving from camp to camp, the making
of their wooden weapons and implements, the command of languages and the gift of mimicry, and the skilled lighting of the grass
in such a way as to enlist smoke and wind as offensive weapons.

Many Aborigines had already heard by word of mouth that
strange men and animals were passing through other tribal lands;
but when at last the horsemen came into clear view the effect was
still overpowering. Boys blinked with puzzlement when they saw
men on horseback. They marvelled at the heaviness and the feel of

articles made from iron, copper or tin; metalwork was unknown to them. The temptation to steal them was intense, though sometimes they probably thought that they were entitled to carry them away in return for gifts of food which they had already deposited, noticed or unnoticed, near these strangers. Misunderstandings were inevitable.

Aborigines, when alarmed or threatened, applied their own warnings. The explorers on horseback would notice a grass fire quickly burning in their direction, and hurriedly retreat through the approaching smoke. Or they would see an armed band of Aborigines swiftly place themselves in a strategic position where they could defend the nearest waterhole. In dry country the drinking water was a military asset. It was also a matter of life and death, for twenty thirsty horses – unless driven away – might drink all the water available that day.

In this sparsely peopled region the exploring party would travel for many days without seeing one Aborigine. And then surprisingly large numbers would appear, even a hundred or more men but rarely a woman or child. Most men, whether displaying the painted stripes of red and white on their chest or quite naked except for a cap topped with feathers, were physically impressive. Some were so confident that they jeered and laughed at the intruders.

The semi-desert Aborigines could be charming as well as defensive. Stuart was once approached by Aborigines who offered him a present of birds and parrots and four dead possums – highly edible when cooked that night. Two of the visitors he described as 'tall, powerful, well made, and good-looking', and as impressive as any natives he had seen. Their father was old and talkative. Several times he gave what Stuart called 'one of the Masonic Signs', and then patted him on the shoulder and stroked his beard in a friendly way.

Explorers had gained experience in how to fight Aborigines effectively. Riding a horse or occasionally a camel, they had speed

as well as a high observation tower. Aided by a recent and more
accurate brand of revolver, they gained a military and psychological advantage over Aborigines on foot. But every now and then,
far inland, a large Aboriginal group seized the initiative. In June
1860, Stuart, eager to become the first person to cross the continent,
was suddenly surrounded near the present Tennant Creek, about
2200 kilometres north of Adelaide. His morale was slipping, his
team of three was short of food, and the tired and frightened packhorses had to be defended too. Moreover the military skills of the
Aborigines – their ability to advance in two columns – alarmed him:
'If they had been Europeans they could not better have arranged
and carried out their plan of attack.' A few days later he realised
that his one course of action was to commence the long trek back
to Adelaide.

Of the infectious diseases that had already made havoc in coastal
districts no signs could be seen here. The explorers' journals kept in
the Never-Never do not often express a belief that the Aborigines
were dying out. Most of those living in the far interior were fit, alert
and confident.

4

The outward spread of the squatters before 1850 was remarkable, but
the later invasion of grasslands, saltbush and mulga country covered an even larger area, embracing nearly all the Never-Never that
could be occupied and some that couldn't. The expansion called for
courageous stockmen and shepherds, hardy mailmen, blacksmiths,
well-sinkers and the women who ran self-sufficient households and
served also as padres, nurses, schoolteachers and sewing mistresses.
Financiers living in the safety of cities often backed these remote
ventures. So too did individual Aborigines who served as guides,

waterfinders, interpreters, finders of straying horses and bullocks, and searchers after lost white people. Anybody who was thinking of settling in the outback was firmly advised by the popular manual of 1881, the *Australian Grazier's Guide,* to hire a 'smart black boy', if one can be got'. The manual is said to have been written by the novelist Rolf Boldrewood.

The procession of sheep and cattle moving slowly towards the Never-Never was so continuous that by the late 1880s most of the occupiable land in the eastern half of Australia was taken up. Virtually the entire route followed by the explorers Burke and Wills in their journey between Melbourne and the Gulf of Carpentaria was now grazed by sheep or, in the far north, by cattle. Not far from the place where they died a town called Innamincka was born, and streets were optimistically laid out by surveyors in 1890. The plains of the Gulf of Carpentaria, the Barkly Tableland and the Channel Country were occupied, and a few pastoralists even lived in the vicinity of Alice Springs, which was not yet a proper village.

The masterminds of the Never-Never were the drover and the head stockman. Much of the interior formed a chain of intersecting drovers' routes. On most nights of the 1880s a map of the drovers' camps – if such a map could have been compiled – would have shown an irregular chain of firelight stretching from the Kimberley to Camooweal and Cloncurry and across to Longreach and Bourke and Wilcannia and Port Augusta and Oodnadatta. In hot weather or when waterholes were far apart, cattle travelled at night, but normally they were halted near nightfall; and in watches of two to four hours the drovers took turns to keep awake, the red embers in front of them, the polished horns of the cattle occasionally reflecting the light, the strange moaning noise of the resting cattle rising and falling like the sound of distant surf. Overhead the black sky was dusted with stars. Like Clancy of the Overflow, as thousands once recited, they saw the sunlit plains extended and at night 'the wondrous glory of the everlasting stars'.

Sheep in almost uncountable numbers were driven – at 10 kilometres a day. Cattle from the Barkly Tableland in the Northern Territory would walk slowly, painfully slowly, down the Birdsville Track to the settled districts of South Australia. Cattle from the Gulf Country of Queensland would be driven in slow stages to the Wodonga saleyards in Victoria. The long Canning stock route in the interior of Western Australia was soon to be surveyed, linking distant cattle runs with goldfields displaying a huge appetite for fresh beef.

The skilled drovers were widely known. Nat Buchanan was a name known to nearly everyone in Never-Never land. In 1878 he drove 1200 cattle all the way – about 2400 kilometres – from Aramac in central Queensland to the Daly River in the Northern Territory, passing through difficult country in the late stages of the journey; his cook was killed by Aborigines while making damper. In 1880 he made the long journey from St George, near the border of New South Wales and Queensland, all the way to Glencoe station, not far from Darwin. He reached his destination with 20 000 cattle – perhaps more than any man had previously driven on a long trip.

In drought a stretch of 90 kilometres without water was frequent, and thirsty cattle were not easily managed. 'They smell water from a long distance,' wrote one drover, and when they smelled it they were likely to break into a mad rush towards it. In their thirst they might knock over a wagon or charge into a horse and rider. Wonnaminta waterhole became notorious after that night of 1883 when 1300 bullocks rushed its water. In the stampede about 600 bullocks were smothered by the weight of bodies and the sticking mud.

5

The movement into parts of the interior was sometimes aided by steam, iron and steel. In 1859 Francis Cadell, a South Australian who had been the first to voyage up the Murray a few years earlier, steamed 800 kilometres up the Darling in his paddle-steamer *Albury* and tied up beside a stout gum tree near the Mount Murchison sheep station. After unloading flour and stores he carried away 100 bales of wool. In the same year Bourke, 1450 kilometres up the Darling, was reached by steamer and became the port for a wide sweep of pastoral country that was opened in the 1860s. Whereas the opening-up of the Murray to steamers was valuable for commerce, the opening of the Darling River was indispensable because its steamers penetrated further inland. This narrow, tree-lined river was the first steam highway to the dry country.

Paddle-steamers, gathering their wood fuel from the steep banks of the river, provided the cheap transport so essential for remote country. Steam engines also worked the machines that bored for underground water. In 1879, on the million-acre (400 000-hectare) sheep station Kallara, not far from the Darling River and the wool port of Bourke, a drilling or 'boring' machine discovered artesian water. The water, rising from far below the surface of the ground, gushed high into the air and kept on gushing.

The exciting news spread up and down the Darling and ran inland by electric telegraph and that word-of-mouth called the bush telegraph. In the following decade, further drilling located a vast artesian basin. Small Queensland outback towns began to draw their water from artesian bores, stock routes at the back of Bourke were provided with precious water, and many pastoral stations filled dams and troughs with the water that gushed up – sometimes luke-warm or even hot – from the boreholes. The finding of artesian and other underground waters began to generate overconfidence, and the day would come when large sheep-owners could point to dams full of bore water and surrounding plains eaten bare by sheep.

Corrugated iron – now a familiar part of Australia's human-made landscape – began to meet a demand. It had first been used on arched roofs in the London docks in the 1830s, and the iron was made more durable by the galvanising technique invented in France in the same decade. By the 1850s it was being used sparingly in Australia. In the outer outback it offered clear advantages, being relatively cheap to carry, durable as a building material, easily dismantled in a dying town or deserted outstation, and versatile in areas where building timbers were rare. In dry country those settlers who lived beneath a shingle or bark roof with no spouting and who collected their water in an old wooden barrel or a heavy square iron tank (usually a second-hand tank in which malt had come from England) realised quickly another benefit in corrugated iron. The iron roof and spouting collected rainwater and a round iron tank at the side of the house stored it. The new outback towns of the 1880s gleamed from afar, their 'tin' roofs and walls shining across the tree-less plains.

Iron and then steel began to provide the outback with many of its fences. At first there had been shepherds or stock workers instead of fences, but the high cost of labour and often the desire to keep out straying stock increased the demand for fences in the middle-distance country. As early as 1861 a sheep station in the Riverina built 87 kilometres of wire fence, stringing the wire between stout posts.

One decade later, long wire fences could be seen on huge sheep runs towards Barcaldine and Longreach, and boundary riders who patrolled the fences on horseback replaced the shepherds who had followed the flocks on foot. Wire fences were more popular in sheep country but were less favoured by cattle farmers because the heavy cattle could lean against the wires and break or bend them. After barbed wire was invented in the United States in the early 1870s, it was tried in Australia. It was stronger than plain wire and the pointed barbs discouraged cattle from leaning against the fence.

For the kangaroos that had grazed on the plains for thousands of years the wire fence was both prison and trap. Whereas they jumped the formidable log fences of the old days, they hesitantly approached the thin strands of wire and halted. Red kangaroos that found themselves locked in a huge paddock would turn back and speed across the plains, sometimes in the formation of a great fan a kilometre wide. Many ran headlong into the wire fence or tried to step under, entangling themselves. One nature writer of the 1880s thought that in the Riverina the wire fences were as deadly as the professional hunters of kangaroos.

For years most stations in the Never-Never were barely touched by the era of steam; and yet they came to depend on the steam water-boring machines and – from the 1880s – the coastal refrigerating plants that at last enabled Australia's surplus meat to be frozen and exported. And increasingly they depended on wire for fencing, corrugated iron for roofs and water tanks, and on the nearest railway terminus, no matter how far away at an inland town. For in 1890 a few long inland railways were approaching the edge of the Never-Never.

6

Many people now vowed that the remote inland country was the real Australia. It had huge pastoral runs and few fences and fewer places that could even be called 'townships' – a favoured word of that era. Few of the small townships had a clergyman, and the hotels were the main meeting places and their main drinks were brandy, rum or other spirits. Men far outnumbered women, and the working horses must have outnumbered the people. Hardly a newspaper was published in the entire Never-Never but in the cities by the 1890s more and more was written about these hot places where so few people lived amid adversity.

The life there was distinctive; it harnessed the heroic virtues and some of the mean as well. It was a life in rhythm with the gallop of a horse at a time when city people more and more obeyed the hands of the clock. The most popular writers of the 1890s – Henry Lawson and Banjo Paterson – wrote about the Never-Never or the outback. And what is now called 'the Australian Legend' began to depict noble qualities – loyalty and mateship and courage – in the life and attitudes of the swagmen, shearers, stockmen, windmill repairers and boundary riders who lived out there.

The Never-Never was lonely and remote, but it also provided the narrow corridor or telegraph route that did more than any event of the century to ease the people's sense of isolation. Before 1872 the very latest news from London had come out by the mail-steamship but thereafter it came by the electric telegraph and was not much more than twenty-four hours old. Unlike the international telephone call initiated more than half a century later, the impersonal telegraph message was conveyed by operators sitting up day and night in a chain of telegraph stations spaced all the way from London through Calcutta to Jakarta, Darwin, Alice Springs and Adelaide. The telegraph cable went, when necessary, along the bed of the sea as well as over the land; and the sea was its vulnerable connection. When at last on 22 August 1872 the worldwide line was completed and the first message was eagerly awaited in Australia, a silence ensued. The undersea copper cable extending from Java to Darwin had accidentally been severed, and the first message did not arrive for two months. Breaks in the cable were frequent, and in 1976 the cable was silent for nearly six months.

Even a simple message of ten words was so expensive that the average Australian family did not think of using it even to convey news of the death or birth of a loved one. But it brought quickly to Australia the news of the latest war in Europe, a sudden financial crisis in New York, and the death of a star of opera or sport.

In the following century the first sound of a radio and the first glimpse of a television picture were to give a sense of wonder to adults and children, but that wonder could hardly have exceeded the excitement felt by those who had stood in the street outside a newspaper office and read in the window a news item, freshly telegraphed across land and sea from the British Isles.

CHAPTER THREE

Rabbits, wattles and Paterson's curse

The land explorers had almost finished their work. By 1890 only a few areas of central or mid-western Australia had still not been seen by a European. Some of these areas, admittedly, were as large as an English county but on a map of Australia they seemed insignificant.

There was a slower form of discovery than the physical discovery of Australia and its resources. The continent had to be discovered emotionally. It had to feel like home for Europeans as it did for Aborigines. All those plains, those rocky slopes and shiny-leafed trees had to become familiar. The bright light and the sense of space and the heat of summer – qualities that at first bewildered most new-comers – had to be tamed or accepted. The abnormal had to become normal, but the process of acclimatisation was slow. Every immigrant who arrived in Australia carried preferences about landscape, colours, climate, vegetation, distances and culture that Australia could rarely meet. Most of the child migrants carried personal memories, songs, stories and pictorial images that symbolised the British Isles, and later they passed on those memories to their own children who perhaps knew only the new land. Every woman who came ashore carried a cultural litmus paper that, when she looked about her, often turned red when it should have turned blue.

2

Writers and painters, more than any other group, shaped the attitudes and emotions of Australians to and about their land. Their power to shape, however, was limited by the tastes of their audiences. The influence of such poets as Kendall and Gordon and such artists as S. T. Gill and Louis Buvelot depended on their success in striking echoes and responses in an increasing population of native-born Australians or those migrants who were influenced not only by memories of the British Isles but by the sense that their own future lay here.

Adam Lindsay Gordon, poet and horseman, was the most influential of the early poets and painters. Indeed it is doubtful whether, in the first century of any European colony in the new world, any artist more quickly won such influence. He died in 1870, and was then known more widely as a steeplechase rider than as a poet, but after his death his poetry outdistanced every Australian rival for at least a generation.

Gordon had spent the first seven years of life in the Azores, in the warmer zone of the North Atlantic, and he was perhaps mentally acclimatised to the hot summers and strong light of Australia. As his father had served in the Bengal Lancers and was a scholar of Hindustani, the family presumably did not view the tropics or hot climates with that nervousness that permeates most other immigrants. Soon after arriving in Adelaide in 1853, Gordon wrote: 'In this climate anyone can sleep in the open.' And anyone, he thought, could work harder than in England, for here 'the air is so clear and fresh that if you perspire as I do profusely you do not feel the heat'.

After serving for several years in the Mounted Police, with his carbine and pistol and long sword, Gordon took to the horse trade, breaking in horses, training them, and buying and selling them. In 1861 he inherited money from his mother's estate but it trickled away. He sat briefly in the South Australian parliament and his speeches tell more about his knowledge of Latin and of classical mythology than of the political controversies of the day. He rode in countless steeplechases in Victoria and South Australia, a lean courageous rider. At Mount Gambier, high above the blue lake, a strong wooden fence ran along the escarpment; and once Gordon jumped his horse over the fence and down to a narrow ledge and then back over the fence. If his horse had slipped Gordon would have fallen to his death or to a crippling injury.

He was 183 centimetres tall, skinny and light, a little stooped, short-sighted and not always observant. An Englishman who admired Gordon marvelled that the poet in his travels saw hardly a snake or lizard, hardly a white cockatoo, let alone a flock, and no koala, emu, pelican or black swan. As he rode across country he recited the poetry of Browning, Byron, Scott, Swinburne and T. B. Macaulay. An admirer of Latin authors, he borrowed books by Horace, Virgil and Ovid and translations of Homer from a rural Catholic priest. The frequent Latin allusions and quotations in Gordon's Australian poems helped to attract a large educated audience in England but puzzled part of his massive Australian audience.

He was not a businessman by aptitude. He lost money in livestock in Western Australia and in running a livery stable behind the main street of Ballarat. One of his ventures was to finance the publishing of his own anonymous verses. Melbourne publishers brought out two volumes, largely at Gordon's expense, in June 1867. One book was a dramatic lyric set in France. The other, bound in mauve cloth and titled in gold letters *Sea Spray and Smoke Drift*, included many of the verses he had sent to sporting journals. Fewer than 100 copies were bought by the public, and only one review appeared in the press, and that was in a sporting newspaper. His third volume, *Bush Ballads and Galloping Rhymes*, appeared in Melbourne bookshops in June 1870. On the day when the first copies were for sale, Gordon was found 10 kilometres away, in the tea-tree scrub near the beach at Middle Brighton, shot dead through the mouth by his own rifle.

Several poems in that last volume were to make him famous. 'The Sick Stockrider' was to be a national anthem for several decades. Most schoolchildren and adults could recite how the dying stockrider looked back over his life, how he recalled the sound of stockwhips as he wheeled around the wild scrub cattle, and the dry crackling sound of the reed beds as the galloping horses brushed by. Readers loved to recite the hazards of the stockmen: one ripped by a steer, another breaking his neck, and poor Frank Mostyn dying in 'the horrors' of alcohol. Now rarely recited in public, the verses once conveyed the scents, sounds, excitement, violence, camaraderie and harshness of bush life to thousands of reciters.

The poem, and the sick stockrider, helped to make the wattle blossom a symbol of Australia:

> *Let me slumber in the hollow where the wattle blossoms wave*
> *With never stone or rail to fence my bed;*

Again and again Gordon painted the dry heat and the full voltage of the summer light, and the gold of the wattle blossoms. To our eyes he does not capture the dry interior, but to the eyes of an earlier generation he did. His verses late in the century affected the sight of the Australian impressionist painter Arthur Streeton, who painted what Gordon called the 'burnished blue' of the skyline and the 'dreamiest distance'. Whereas the hot winds – often called brickfielders or siroccos – were feared even by the early European settlers who lived in coastal cities, Streeton's landscapes actually celebrated the 'hot trying winds and slow immense summer'. He and his fellow painters were heralding a new Australian attitude to climate. Likewise in the early 1900s Dorothea Mackellar wrote her poem 'My Country' with its famous first line, 'I love a sunburnt country'. With the new attitude to climate, which of course was an Aboriginal attitude, most Australians probably did not yet agree. Certainly most farmers preferred green grass, as did the bank managers who lent them money.

In the long coastline between Brisbane and Adelaide there is perhaps only one place where the arid country and the hungry scrubland extend right to the ocean; and there a tongue of arid land divides the mouth of the Murray River from the fertile southeastern corner of South Australia. Gordon often crossed that dry tongue of land, for it was his riding road between his home and Adelaide. Here were Gordon's 'sere woodlands and sad wildernesses'.

3

Adam Lindsay Gordon tried to make the new colonists feel at home. The colonists on the other hand tried to transplant their old home to their new. Almost everywhere could be seen signs of their success or (modern commentators would say) their failure. In their zeal to import grasses, flowers and vegetables, fruit trees and shade trees and hedges, they also imported weeds. Some weeds came as stowaways and some as assisted immigrants. They came in the hair and tails of imported animals. They came in packing materials, they came accidentally in packages of seeds, and they came in the ballast that sailing ships brought out and then unloaded on wastelands near ports. Some of these exotic plants were deliberately imported and tended with care: there was no thought that they might some day be called weeds.

A weed was more likely to arrive if it originally flourished near a foreign port on a route to Australia. Cape Town was a frequent port of call for early ships, and moreover its climate was not unlike that of Perth and Melbourne. From South Africa came the boxthorn, originally favoured as a hedge because its sharp thorns would keep cattle and sheep from straying. From South Africa came the boneseed plant and probably the onion grass; only a few tiny bulbs at first, the onion grass then multiplied by the billion and took over pastures and garden plots. The yellow-flowering capeweed was first noticed near the West Australian port of Albany in 1833, and it covered the paddocks with gold in spring and died away in midsummer, leaving paddocks almost bare. As its name suggests, it came from the Cape of Good Hope or Cape Town and was originally given the courtesy of a capital C. Later the courtesy was withdrawn.

Poisonous weeds arrived and a few spread like an infection. The Cape tulips – naturally from South Africa – were carried to Perth and Adelaide and planted in home gardens where their orange and rose flowers could give pleasure. With their large bulbs they spread to the pastures where they ceased to give pleasure: they poisoned the livestock. Similarly in the 1870s a German woman living in the goldfields of north-east Victoria planted innocuous German seeds in her garden. The seeds flourished, and everyone admired her display of St John's wort. The plant spread to the Bright racecourse,

covered nearby hills and half a century later brightened patches
of ground in five states, its deep roots defying cheap methods of
eradication.

Almost any weed with a pretty flower was petted and favoured,
transplanted and watered, and so given opportunities to find the
soil and climate and botanical niche where it might eventually run
wild. The Mediterranean herb known in England as viper's bugloss
had bell-shaped flowers of vivid purple. Finding its way to a few
Australian flower gardens, it became a runaway weed in many parts
of the temperate zone from Holbrook in New South Wales to the
Great Southern Railway in Western Australia. In mid-spring it
spread itself like a rich purple mat, a glorious sight on the grasslands. In Victoria and New South Wales it came to be known as
Paterson's curse – the accursed Paterson is said to have been a home
gardener in Albury – and in South Australia it was called Salvation
Jane and in Western Australia it was the Lady Campbell weed. It
ruined nutritious pastures and could not easily be rooted out.

As ships called at South Africa on their way here and at South
American ports on the way to England, the South American
plants were less likely to arrive here accidentally. But there was
some direct trade with the Americas. The Bathurst burr is said to
have come from Chile in the 1840s, its seeds clinging to the tails
of imported horses. It soon ran wild, especially on the grasslands
around Bathurst, and by the 1850s was a pest. One decade later the
Noogoora burr of North America was also common, and its sharp
spines stuck to the wool and lowered its value.

Plants from tropical America seemed to be even slower to take
root in Australia, partly because our subtropical and tropical regions
were settled late. The decorative plants were the most troublesome
once they had arrived. The lantana was tended carefully in gardens
all the way from Sydney to the furthest tropical ports but eventually

it escaped and strangled vast areas of countryside, its berries attracting birds that spread and fertilised the seeds. The water hyacinth
and its shiny leaves and mauve flower attracted gardeners. It was
soon floating on the warm rivers and in January 1911 the Clarence
River at Grafton – one of the few important navigable rivers in
Australia – was closed to steamships by the pontoon of hyacinths.

An early prickly pear from the Gulf of Mexico is known to
have grown in a plant pot near Scone in New South Wales as
far back as 1839. Its tough prickles made it a promising hedge in
the days when, the cattle and sheep being so plentiful, the 'living fence' or hedge was eagerly cultivated. By the mid-1880s the
prickly pear, in many Queensland districts, formed a straggly for-
tification extending far. By 1925 the patches of prickly pear covered
more land than all the cultivated crops and orchards in Australia.
Fortunately in the next ten years the prickly pear (*Opuntia inermis*)
was conquered by the introduction of an Argentinian tunnelling
caterpillar, *Cactoblastis*.

Certain diseases usually died during the long voyage to
Australia in the era of the slow sailing ship. Distance served as a
form of quarantine, but some diseases and insects evaded it. The
vineyards of Victoria had become almost as extensive as those of
the other colonies combined when in 1887 the phylloxera insect was
detected in a vineyard near Geelong. Thereafter, as in France, vineyard after vineyard had to be destroyed in the hope of eliminating
the insect; and Victoria was quickly outstripped by South Australia
in the production of wine.

Even the sheep, whose coming to this country proved one of the
most successful transplants in recorded history, altered the vegetation. They competed with native animals for the same grasses and
shrubs. Some species of kangaroo suffered, while others flourished
and multiplied into a high population not known in Aboriginal

eras. Bandicoots, rodents and wallabies nested and foraged in the coarse grasses, but their native home was soon overturned to provide, in effect, woollen singlets for Europe. The squatter pigeon was decimated in the eucalyptus woodlands of the outback and the flock pigeons that at times flew in myriads on the Barkly Tableland suffered from changes in the pastures. In Tasmania certain of the larger creatures of the open country were hunted to extinction. The Tasmanian emu, which laid a dark-green egg that weighed as much as a dozen hen's eggs, was soon extinguished. The Tasmanian tiger – the striped, meat-eating marsupial – was hunted by the sheep-owners and was extinct probably by the 1930s.

Cages of English birds were imported. Hutches and deck-pens of foxes and deer and other animals were brought out in the hope that they would multiply for the delight of the homesick hunter.

The 1860s was a busy decade for acclimatisation societies, which met in the cities and planned the introduction of all kinds of useful creatures. Through the work of these societies the house sparrow, the English starling and the Indian myna arrived and soon they prospered. The mania for acclimatising was in one sense a reflection that people themselves were still unacclimatised and longed for reminders of home. Victoria had the most vigorous Acclimatization Society partly because it held the highest proportion of foreign-born adults in the 1850s and 1860s. Facing rural problems – plagues of grubs or caterpillars – they thought of the remedies of home, not realising that one fine remedy often created a new ill.

4

On Christmas night of 1859 the elegant Liverpool clipper ship *Lightning* reached Melbourne with passengers and a small consignment of livestock. It is doubtful whether any cargo loaded at any port in recorded history was to prove more fecund than the small animals that were carried ashore.

The twenty-four wild rabbits – along with five hares and seventy-two partridges – had been shipped from Liverpool to the English-born squatter Thomas Austin, and were promptly carried past Geelong to his estate at Winchelsea, on the undulations of the Western District. Austin was a sportsman and employed his own gamekeeper to care for the consignment. The partridges were placed in an aviary and later they were joined by English blackbirds and thrushes. At least thirteen of the rabbits were imprisoned inside a paling fence and they too began to multiply. Though the popularity of the phrase 'to breed like rabbits' belonged to the future, it really commemorated the activities of Austin's rabbits.

Soon, so many rabbits ran about his sheep run near Winchelsea that he invited friends to join him on shooting excursions. His hunts followed the English country tradition, and he employed men as beaters to frighten the rabbits and drive them within range of the hunters' guns. In the year 1866 he and his guests shot 448 hawks, 622 native cats, 32 tame cats and a total of 14 253 rabbits. Austin now lived in a hunter's paradise of his own making. The rabbits were established securely on the grasslands that seemed heaven-made for them, and the grasslands ran without a break or barrier to South Australia and New South Wales and even to Queensland.

Years later, when the rabbits had become a plague in about half of the continent, the popular belief was that Austin was solely to blame for the terrible invasion. He had been a squatter, and so he was a suitable target. His elaborate shooting parties had been described in the newspapers almost shot by shot, and it was common knowledge that he had bred thousands of rabbits, so he was more conspicuous than other landholders who had quietly imported or bought rabbits in South Australia as well as Victoria. It was also the popular belief that the rabbits – by then respected as a foe of herculean strength and fertile mind – had spread of their own will all the way from Austin's land to new warrens as far as 3200 kilometres away. Recent investigations suggest that the rabbits possessed many other human allies in their first years. Other English people nostalgic for home applauded their appearance, and both landowners and rural labourers carried the rabbits in baskets and boxes to their own homes and gardens and hoped that they would multiply. That they did multiply was aided by a succession of favourable seasons: droughts were infrequent during the rabbits' initial decades of rapid advance.

The rabbits in lush years now spread at lightning speed. One or two could suddenly appear as if making a reconnaissance, and yet the nearest known colony of rabbits might be 80 kilometres away. Along the Darling River in the early 1880s the unexpected arrival of the first few rabbits made some pastoralists wonder whether they had been deliberately released by passengers travelling in the paddle-steamers.

'The rabbits are coming, the rabbits are coming' became a familiar warning in dozens of districts in the last third of the century. Many flock-owners who were warned of the coming horde made their own precautions. George Riddoch, a South Australian with sheep runs in three colonies, lost so much money when the rabbits overran his land near Swan Hill that he took pains to defend another of his sheep runs north of the Darling River about 1883. He knew the nearest rabbits were still 160 kilometres away and so he gave orders that men were to be employed on his boundary as patrollers. Their task was to watch for any trace of rabbits – any dung, fur or scratchings in the ground.

And then the rabbits came, a wide grey tide. By the first month of 1887 Riddoch employed 125 rabbiters. More of his employees were now catching rabbits than were, presumably, carrying out all the station's other tasks put together. By the end of the year on that one property, his men had caught more than a million rabbits.

All the time the search went on for the remedy that would sweep the species from the land. In the hope of reducing the pest, they used iron traps, cats and ferrets, hunting dogs, guns, nets, fumigants, and all kinds of concoctions and devices. Bushmen soon had as many recipes for poisoning rabbits as housewives had for cooking them. A mixture of phosphorus and sugar and cold water was added to bran and left on the ground as bait. Another tempting mixture contained phosphorus, flour, and wheat or oats. Many farmers mixed baits of chaff and arsenic, or quinces and strychnine, or arsenic and carrots.

5

By the early 1890s the rabbits were thriving in most parts of Australia south of the tropics. They were at home in the hot half-deserts where a furry creature seemed the most unlikely inhabitant. They flourished on the riverbanks and in the sandhills. They revelled in the plains and ran on to the colder tablelands. Even where the grass was scarce they could flourish because they ate the saltbush and other low plants or the bark from mulga, sandalwood and stunted trees, effectively ringbarking and slowly killing these trees. As the leaves of these trees were a reserve of fodder for sheep and stabilised the soil, their destruction was costly.

In the hope of containing the rabbits, long rabbit-proof fences were built by governments. Among the longest fences in the world, one was built across a vast tract of Western Australia. It stretched for 1833 kilometres, from the Southern Ocean near the port of

Esperance, to a tropical beach beyond Port Hedland. That fence was begun too late, and when the wooden posts were in place the rabbits had already slipped by and were feeding in the fertile strip of Western Australia.

How the rabbits reached Western Australia was a puzzle. The evidence is powerful that their ancestors came west across the dry Nullarbor Plain, not far from the ocean. On several of the harsh stages of that journey, kitten rabbits had probably been carried in an empty billy by travellers, to be released by a waterhole and a patch of green grass, there to multiply – while the grass lasted.

Almost everywhere, the rabbits indirectly became a form of social welfare. They transferred money from wealthy squatters to rural labourers. Thousands of professional rabbiters with their dogs, traps, nets and poisons made a high monthly income by destroying rabbits on the large pastoral stations. Hundreds of these rabbiters then turned from poisoning the rabbits to trapping them for the English market, and in the year 1906 Australia was to earn more by shipping away rabbit meat and skins than by shipping frozen beef. In that year 22 million frozen rabbits were exported, mostly to London, and rabbit pies were probably eaten in cottages close to the English woods where the progenitors of the pie had run wild only half a century previously.

In many years perhaps one-twentieth of Australia's potential income from wool was devoured by rabbits, and even more in bad years. One sheep-owner in the Cobar district began with 16 000 sheep but in the year 1892 his flocks were reduced to a mere 1600. Asked for the explanation, he replied in three simple words: 'the rabbit invasion'. On scores of large sheep stations the rabbit trappers made a living in nearly every year until the 1950s, when the deliberate spread of the myxomatosis disease began to decimate the population of rabbits.

6

Much of the early history of Australia is a story of the lottery of transplanting. The Austin family, of rabbit fame, knew the variations that this theme could play. The first Austin to arrive was a young Somerset convict, who had stolen beehives and honey. In Tasmania, after his sentence expired, he acquired farms, a big orchard, an inn, and a most profitable river ferry. He was childless and his nephews who came out inherited his money, and James and Thomas Austin moved to Victoria with the first sheep and prospered.

James Austin returned to England and bought the abbey house and the famous ruined abbey at Glastonbury. He presided over the place where King Arthur was said to have been buried and where pilgrims came in medieval times to see the famous thorn tree that they believed had been planted by Joseph of Arimathea. According to legend, Joseph had come to England as a missionary and had placed his priestly staff in the ground at Glastonbury and it had sprouted as a thorn tree, flowering twice a year – the symbol of the miraculous. On this sacred site James Austin, returning from Australia in 1856, had settled down as proprietor.

It was he who arranged, three years later, that the cargo of English rabbits be sent to Liverpool for shipment to the Victorian estate of his brother. When as an old man he made a final visit to Australia he must have been astonished to see how these furry 'thorns' had multiplied.

CHAPTER FOUR

The long honeymoon

The male migrants arriving in Australia strongly preferred the cities. Coming mainly from English cities, they had no intention – after leaving the ship – to travel by horse-coach or train and settle down in the inland mining and farming towns. The wives too liked the cities and their amenities, and often they selected the suburb where a circle of old family friends had made their home. By 1890 at least six of every ten Australians lived within sight of a public clock or street lamp. Even in Tasmania most of the increase in population was in towns.

Some politicians deplored the growth of the cities, but they were a reflection of economic success. The inland industries and the transporting of their products were becoming so efficient that they required a smaller part of the workforce, thus leaving the rest of the population free to produce other goods and services. The rising standard of living increased the demand for biscuits, hats and other manufactured goods, which, of course, were made in the towns; and increasingly they were made in Australia rather than imported from British towns. The mechanisation of farms and inland transport increased the demand for ploughs and railway locomotives and other equipment, and they were made in cities. Commerce boomed, and it created work for bank clerks, stockbrokers, merchants and warehouse workers.

The size of the capital cities puzzled many travellers arriving from England. The statistician Timothy Coghlan said almost annually in the 1890s that the progress of our chief cities 'has no parallel among the cities of the old world'. Here, 'perhaps for the first time in history,' he argued, 'is presented the spectacle of magnificent cities' growing not only with dazzling rapidity but embracing within their own suburban boundaries one-third of the population of the colony they governed. After his annual huffing and puffing he added quietly that he disapproved of this spectacle. Most people, however, were probably proud of their city. It was a symbol of what the settlers had so quickly achieved. It was a boast in brick and stone.

2

The capital city of each colony usually grew faster than any rival city. To possess a parliament house and a civil service was to possess the hormones of growth. By the late 1880s Adelaide and Melbourne were more than ten times larger than the largest rival town in their own territories. Sydney and Brisbane were more than seven times larger than their nearest rivals. Occasionally the second-largest city of a colony would challenge the capital, but the challenge rarely lasted long.

A capital city was aided by geography. While the atlas shows the continent is rather square in shape, the inhabitable Australia is a long ribbon of land, occasionally bulging but nearly always near the sea. Australia was thus designed for coastal cities, and the capital of a colony usually sat on a central part of the coast. Far inland, Australia had no wide navigable rivers and lakes on which a rival commercial city – a Chicago or Minneapolis – could grow. Once a capital city had arisen it could use its political power – and its railways – to retard rivals.

When manufacturers decided to set up a factory or mill or foundry, most chose the coastal capital. It had more customers than any other town, and was convenient to several railways pushing inland as well as to the local wharves. By 1891 Melbourne and Sydney were the dominant factory cities. Likewise nearly all immigrants came ashore at a capital city; and when too many migrants landed in Brisbane or any other capital the government often undertook public works near the city in order to give them work. So a city grew.

Such were the influences that combined to build one dominant city in each colony. Tasmania was the exception, and there Launceston in the north tried to rival Hobart in the south. Developing countries today often produce the same dominant city.

3

Melbourne and Sydney were far and away the largest cities. Their rivalry was almost neurotic. Those observers who ridicule the rivalry perhaps do not realise in how many ways those cities differed late in the nineteenth century. The differences between their institutions and ideologies were probably deeper than the contrasts between the Liberal and Labor parties in the nation today.

While Sydney had been founded as a place for convicts, and Melbourne newspapers often felt pleasure in recalling that 'mishap',

Melbourne was essentially a free city. And yet thousands of former convicts had flocked to Victoria during the gold rushes and had remained there. While the politics of Sydney in 1880 were largely in the hands of men who were born in Australia or had lived here for decades, the parliament in Melbourne was ruled more by British migrants who had arrived during the gold rushes. This contrast of origins was reflected in March 1856 in the first cricket match played between the two colonies: the winning team from New South Wales, with one exception, consisted of the Australian-born, but all the Victorian players were migrants. By the end of the century a Victorian group of politicians, sportsmen and schoolteachers were the more likely to be Australian-born.

In an era when the climate was viewed as energy-sapping, Melbourne had the more bracing climate; and alert European visitors sometimes contrasted its 'Yankee-like' energy with the easygoing pace in Sydney. In religion the rival colonies and cities were also dissimilar. In Victoria the Presbyterians and Methodists and other nonconformist churches were popular and, in total, had slightly more adherents than the Anglican church, but in New South Wales they were only half as numerous as the Anglicans. And in political theology the colonies were far apart, the free traders ruling in New South Wales and the protectionists in Victoria.

The economic differences between New South Wales and Victoria were also wider than now. The pastoral industry was perhaps three times as important in the wide grasslands of New South Wales. On the other hand the farmers who ploughed the land were far fewer in New South Wales; and the area of sown crops was dwarfed by Victoria's until the end of the century. Likewise Victoria was much richer in gold, and sometimes displayed economic bravado.

The smell of wet ink on the prospectus of a new goldmining company, or the sight of a land auctioneer's marquee in an outer suburb, invigorated many middle-aged and old Victorians. They had paid their own fare to cross the world to take part in an enormous lottery in the 1850s and it would be surprising if such adventurous people kept their savings, nearly a generation later, in the form of a bag of sovereigns in a pit dug in the backyard. Melbourne had a higher ratio of speculative investors, and they sometimes infused the city streets with the ozone of recklessness.

The rivalry between Melbourne and Sydney impeded early hopes that the six colonies would federate into the one nation or commonwealth. Even those politicians who in spirit saw themselves as Australians were often caught in the undertow of animosity. Alfred Deakin, the young Melbourne politician who perhaps more strenuously than any other in that city was to campaign for a federation, noted how James Service as premier of Victoria attended an intercolonial conference in Sydney in 1883, and on his return gave a banquet in the new Queen's Hall in Parliament House. In his speech at the banquet he announced how 'he had found Sydney asleep and how with the help of friends who rallied around him he had awakened the slumberers'. When the speech was tapped along the telegraph to Sydney, politicians there were angry – all the more angry, confided Deakin mischievously, because Service had spoken the truth. In retaliation the politician Sir John Robertson said Victoria was a mere cabbage garden – obviously an allusion to its small area.

A welcome prize for Victoria was the silver-lead lode of Broken Hill, which actually lay in New South Wales. A long, deep and – near the surface – dazzlingly rich ore deposit, it was discovered in 1883 by Charles Rasp, a German working as a boundary rider on the sheep station of Mount Gipps. He had actually been an

officer fighting in the Franco-Prussian War but deserted the battlefront near Paris, changed his name, and migrated to Australia.
He was well educated, intelligent; he sensed that the heavy mineral specimen he found on the surface of the hard dry ground was a
herald of wealth lying below, and eventually became one of the few
major prospectors in Australia to make a fortune from his discovery. Usually a mining claim or lease in Australia was small, but Rasp
was optimistic enough to purchase from the New South Wales
government for the trifling sum of five shillings an acre (0.4 hectares) an oblong block of ground 3 kilometres long and covering
virtually all the rich silver, lead and zinc in the mining field. He
formed a little syndicate of co-owners, most of whom worked in
the local sheep stations as managers or dam sinkers, or doing other
pastoral tasks. They paid small sums for their shares, and the money
went into sinking the shallow shafts that soon revealed masses of
silver – sometimes in exquisite shapes and colours and displaying
minerals never before seen in the world. At that time silver was,
for each ounce, second only to gold in value; and indeed in some
nations the refined silver as well as gold was held in the bank vaults
in order to underpin the business.

How could these sheep men develop and manage such a rich
and complicated mine and smelter far from the coast? They sent
one of their fellow directors to Nevada and Colorado and recruited
two outstanding experts, paying them high salaries. When these
experts saw the bleak new township and the dusty treeless streets
and the little iron houses, with the broken hill in the background,
they knew why they were paid so much.

The new public company, floated in 1885 under the name of
the Broken Hill Proprietary Company Limited, set up its head
office in Melbourne, the city to which most of its directors and
big shareholders retired. The company formed the habit of hiring

the best managers and advisers. It could afford to – for about ten years it made in total by far the highest profits hitherto recorded in Australia. By 1940, no longer working its exhausted mine at Broken Hill, it was primarily a steelmaker on the coast and the largest and most diversified firm in Australia, and by 2010 – under the name of BHP Billiton – was the largest mining company in the world. Other powerful companies emerged at Broken Hill, including Zinc Corporation which, under the later name of Rio Tinto Zinc Corporation, was on its way in the 1970s to becoming a world giant with operations in many countries and a head office in London.

4

Sydney financiers were vexed to see Melbourne extending its claws to faraway places. Melbourne capital was busy in Fijian and north Queensland sugar plantations, New Caledonian nickel mines, the kauri forests of New Zealand, sheep stations in most parts of the country, and the mines on the west coast of Tasmania. Melbourne was also the main tap through which British capital flowed. In Melbourne were the main offices of English-owned banks and pastoral-finance firms and the busiest stock exchange in the country. As Melbourne was the main port of call for the European mail steamers and a central place from which wholesale merchants distributed imported goods to many parts of Australia and New Zealand, its role as a commercial and financial depot was vital.

A simple way to describe the Melbourne sphere of influence, as distinct from the Sydney sphere, is to map those towns and regions that adopted Australian Rules football rather than rugby, soccer or other winter games. By 1890 that code of football – invented in the Melbourne parklands during the gold rushes – was played in Victoria, Tasmania, the Riverina and Broken Hill districts of New

South Wales, South Australia and, after a slow start, in Western Australia. Those were, presumably, the regions where Melbourne wholesale merchants and their commercial travellers did business, where Melbourne banks were more likely to open branches, where its mining interests were, and where its various coastal-shipping companies operated. That Sydney and its commercial hinterland did not take to Australian Rules football was partly a reflection of its suspicion of a game concocted in Melbourne.

5

The prosperity that had prevailed since the gold rushes reached a gilded crest in the 1880s. Melbourne's population soared: it was 268 000 in 1881 and 473 000 in 1891. In that year a few women and men, still walking the streets, could remember the Melbourne of their childhood: a new village with green hills running down to the clear River Yarra. Few cities in the world had grown so swiftly. In 1885 the visiting English journalist George Sala named it 'Marvellous Melbourne'.

Melbourne's population also gained through the strange delayed effect of the gold rushes. For in the late 1850s, the main rush for gold being over, the single men who were the typical gold-diggers tended to settle down and marry. The result was a strong increase in the birthrate in the late 1850s and early 1860s, a token increase in the 1870s, and another dramatic increase in the 1880s when the gold-rush children reached marriageable age. There were about 5000 marriages in Victoria in the year 1879, but about 9200 in 1889. The children of the late gold era were marrying, and as they needed houses the building industry boomed. The suburbs fanned out to Malvern and Camberwell, Preston and Moonee Ponds and Footscray, and steam railways were built to serve them. From 1885

Melbourne built a suburban web of cable tramways, like those in the hilly cities of San Francisco and Dunedin. As the population increased, the price of city property jumped, doubling in the decade to 1885 and continuing to rise. In the main streets, baby skyscrapers were built: eight storeys, ten storeys, and even one of thirteen storeys. No city in Europe had such tall office buildings.

The flurry of building extended to everything – factories, wharves, railways, mansions, terrace houses, suburban villas and bungalows, schools, churches, town halls, grandstands, banks and shops. The building industry was the largest employer in the city; and in the mornings one saw the carpenters, bricklayers, tilers, slaters, tuck-pointers, plasterers, wallpaperers, house-painters and all the tradesmen carrying their tools to work, for work tools were too precious to be left overnight on a building site. In the outer suburbs one saw the 'For sale' signs on rows of new houses standing on the edge of paddocks, and on Saturdays the flags of the auctioneers and the white marquees signified where subdivisions would be auctioned. The land sales went on at such distances from the heart of the city that even in London, the world's largest city, the 30 or 50 kilometres from the city would have seemed too far. There were subdivisions at places as far away as Frankston, Ferntree Gully, and the plains near Laverton where one land-alligator spoke of building a pier to enable intending residents to travel to the city by fast steamer. Some of these building sites were not exploited for another century.

The optimism made the stock exchange a symbolic institution of the 1880s. In the first three months of 1888 – until the Stock Exchange of Melbourne called for a long Easter break – the buying of Broken Hill silver shares verged on lunacy. Fortunes were made with ease: the losing of them would be just as easy. In the space of twelve months sixty-two new silver companies were floated.

And yet the boom in mining shares was initially justified. Broken Hill and Mount Morgan and several other dazzling mines, which were undiscovered when the decade commenced, were paying a larger sum in annual dividends than the richest Victorian goldmines had paid in their whole lifetime. The names of Broken Hill companies were bandied about in thousands of households as if they were family friends. The share mania continued. The volume of business on the main stock exchange in Melbourne was at its peak in 1890.

One year later the silver shares were sagging. Everything in Melbourne – the price of every asset – was sagging. Sydney, not usually seen as such a spectacular or sensational city, was growing at a faster pace than Melbourne. In the decade to 1891 Sydney's population almost doubled to 400 000. The sight and smell of black coal smoke from tugs, launches, ferries, wharf cranes, and coastal and ocean steamships pervaded the harbour, for Sydney was now a city of steam. Cheap coal was one of those advantages that enabled New South Wales to overtake Victoria until, in 1890, they were almost level in population. That Sydney would become the victor seemed almost certain to observers – except those in Melbourne.

Brisbane almost trebled its population in the 1880s and was now the fourth-largest city in Australia with close on 90 000 people. In the one decade it had passed Ballarat, Newcastle, Bendigo and Hobart and its city streets were reminiscent of New Orleans with their wide verandas, colonnades and airy promenades, and the slow fans or punkahs on the ceilings of the larger hotels, clubs, offices and banking chambers. Adelaide was the other large city, with nearly 120 000 people, but in the 1880s it had grown only by one-third. That rate of growth, spectacular if it had happened in a European capital city, seemed paltry in Australia.

And yet Adelaide, alone, had the crucial amenity of a modern city. Whereas elsewhere the night carts clattered along the streets, removing the nightsoil even from city hotels and baby skyscrapers, in Adelaide the main suburbs were sewered in the 1880s. The typical capital city was unhealthy and babies and young children had a higher chance of remaining alive if they lived in the country, with its poor medical services, its scatter of small hospitals, and the hazards of the bush. In New South Wales between 1871 and 1886 the death rate of children under the age of five was twice as heavy in Sydney's suburbs as in the country. In the heart of Sydney the death rate of children under five was even higher. Here was a sunny, well-drained site for a city, but on the healthy site sat an unhealthy city. In one sad year, 1875, the city lost one in every eleven children under the age of five through diarrhoea, pneumonia, bronchitis, measles, scarlet fever, diphtheria and other illnesses and mishaps.

Sydney began driving sewerage tunnels in the early 1880s, following the example of Adelaide, but the work was slow and the city spread out far ahead of the new tunnels. The septic tank was still untried in the suburbs. Sydney, at least, was a decade ahead of Melbourne where the underground mains of the sewerage system were not commenced until 1892. Melbourne held a population of half a million when, five years later, its first house was sewered. Melbourne could boast of its high skyline and its healthy sea winds and spacious parks and wide streets, but the deaths from typhoid suggested that sewerage tunnels should have preceded skyscrapers.

CHAPTER FIVE

Cutting down
the tall poppies

In London, Berlin and Brussels those editors and politicians who wondered about the world's future watched nervously the experiment with democracy in Australia. What kind of candidate would voters elect? What crazy laws would their parliaments pass? Some observers feared that the rights of private property would be endangered by a form of government that entrusted ultimate power to people of whom many could not write, and many owned no property or savings.

The last of the convict colonies were slow to become democratic; Western Australia did not even have a fully elected parliament until 1890 and Tasmania's older parliament did not grant every man the vote until 1900. Already in several other colonies the lower houses or assemblies were among the most democratic in the world. Since 1860 the colonies holding more than 90 per cent of the continent's people offered almost every European man the right to vote at elections for the lower house. Aboriginal men had the same right though rarely used it.

2

The novel form of democracy was not snow-pure. In theory almost every man could vote, but owners of property exercised that right more diligently than the wandering shearer. The businessman in the city used his vote more than the digger on the goldfields. Votes were available only for those who registered themselves on the electoral roll, but many citizens did not bother to pay the few pennies that the act of enrolling demanded. Others had trouble in reaching a polling booth on election day, for the polling booths were far apart and closed early. There was another unfair law. Though nearly every man over the age of twenty-one had the right to vote, those who owned property had the right to cast one vote in every electorate in which they owned property – so long as they could personally visit an electorate on the day or days of polling. Postal votes did not exist. Known as plural voting, it remained normal in most colonies until the end of the century; and in the swinging seats the plural vote could be decisive.

The lower house was elected on the popular vote but there was also an upper house – a legislative council – that was elected on a narrower franchise. The upper houses were places for reviewing new laws: they were like a House of Lords without the lords. An upper house could occasionally thwart or impede the lower house. In most colonies the upper houses were elected only by the professional and propertied people. In New South Wales and Queensland the members of the upper house were nominated for life, and in Victoria and South Australia their initial term was ten or twelve years, and so they were less sensitive to rapid changes in public opinion. Whereas the lower houses were to become more democratic, the upper houses were slower to change. As late as 1960 in the states three of the five surviving upper houses did not acknowledge adult suffrage, whereas in the federal parliament the upper house or senate had been popularly elected for more than sixty years.

In the new democratic era the governor, residing in his mansion in the capital city, no longer governed but he did restrain the rash acts of a parliament. Infrequently he did reserve his assent to a bill that had been passed by both houses of parliament. Even if he assented, the government in London had the right – infrequently used – to disallow the bill at any time in the following two years. Moreover the governor was not entitled to assent to colonial bills that legislated on such topics as divorce and coinage, or that contradicted England's treaties with foreign nations or facets of its commercial policy. Such bills he had to send to London where they might or might not receive the royal assent. The bills passed by the new colonial parliaments were, after the 1860s, not often deferred or challenged by the governor or by the British parliament in distant London.

3

Those conservatives who wondered how Australia could ever be governed effectively when the miner, boot-repairer and wood-cutter could vote, might have been slightly reassured if they had known that in the first forty years of self-government most of the cabinet ministers were men of property. The typical premier of a colony was likely to be a self-made, self-employed man of moderate wealth though – to critical English eyes – of scant polish. He was likely to be a merchant, general businessman, landowner or lawyer. As members of parliament in most of the colonies were not paid until the 1880s, only men of independent means could afford to sit in parliament. Moreover there was a belief, expressed at election meetings, that a man who had proved successful in business was more likely to succeed in conducting the larger business of the government. Before 1890 the city merchants and businessmen were most likely to provide the premier. They were developers in the age when national development was a magic phrase.

4

People strolling past the various parliament houses did not necessarily think that they were the highest seat of power. Some thought more power lay inside the newspaper offices. A city daily not only told the public what the politicians said: it increasingly told the politician what they should say.

Even in 1850 the newspapers numbered about fifty and extended from Perth to Brisbane. They had a freedom that was wider than that enjoyed by the press in many of the leading nations of Europe. In France, Austria, Russia and Prussia the governments frequently censored newspapers, taxed them, hounded them and closed them. England collected a tax on every copy of every newspaper until 1855. Australia, in contrast, usually imposed no newspaper taxes and even in the convict era its governors gradually ceased to interfere with newspapers unless the editor was, in their eyes, totally out of hand. On the other hand the only person sent to gaol after the leaders of the Eureka rebellion were tried in court in 1855 was Henry Seekamp, the editor of the *Ballarat Times*. He was found guilty of seditious libel but his wife, Clara, an actress, carried on the newspaper in his absence.

There was money in news, both for those who reported it and those who read it. Between 1854 and 1856 the Fairfax family's *Sydney*

Morning Herald and its rival *The Empire* were quick to send small boats out to intercept deep-sea ships arriving at the Heads with the latest English news. Aboard they would buy British newspapers from officers or passengers, race back to the port, and issue an 'extraordinary edition' – sold in the streets by newsboys calling out 'Extra, extra!' – that printed almost word for word the latest news from the British newspapers carried aboard the ship. That the news was eighty or ninety days old made it no less exciting. Moreover merchants possessing the latest news might make quick money or avoid financial losses.

The electric telegraph, the steam printing press, and a new kind of printing paper – made cheaply from wood pulp instead of old rags – were transforming the city newspapers. More up-country readers were attracted as the railways and the fast coaches of Cobb & Co. carried the newspapers to their district on the same day. In several colonies the post offices became the ally of the city editor; by the early 1860s several million newspapers annually were carried free by the post offices. In some colonies postage was eventually charged but as late as the 1890s three colonies allowed newspapers to pass free through the post. New South Wales went further and allowed people who had read their newspaper to wrap it up again and post it, without affixing a stamp, to friends within the colony.

Most newspapers were sombre by present standards. The pages were large and headlines were small. The front page was jammed with small advertisements and often the shipping news, for the departure of a large ship carrying the mail to England was a stirring event. An editorial was long and written in such a tone as to suggest that it should be read only in a room where the half-drawn blinds provided a funereal light. Even in 1880 an illustration rarely appeared in daily newspapers. They carried no comics or cartoons, no crosswords, no page for women or children, no chatty comments on restaurants, and few notices of births, deaths or marriages. Sometimes the Monday newspaper – there was no Sabbath edition – carried as much reportage of Sunday sermons as Saturday sport.

The typical reporter kept in the background, shunning the word 'I'. Here is a report of a massive flood drowning parts of Brisbane in February 1893: 'On looking over the city and down upon the flood one felt utterly sick at heart. Dozens of houses could now be counted that had either collapsed or were aslant. The rate of the river's race to the sea could be easily gauged as house after house was seen to float down. Through a powerful glass one after another was watched as it struck the bridge, the roofs being crumpled up like paper in a strong man's hand.'

Political news attracted readers. Whenever Parliament was sitting, the main daily newspapers in Sydney and Melbourne employed a small team of reporters in the press gallery where they wrote in relays, and messengers carried their reports down the hill to the printery where a row of compositors stood ready in the late hours of the night. The compositors painstakingly picked the various metal letters of the alphabet from the tray in front of them and so – like an eternal game of Scrabble – set up the speech in cold type. It is fair to say that Australia could not have succeeded with its bold concept of a vote for every man but for the role of the newspapers in informing and educating most of those who cast a vote on election day. A serious tone pervaded most newspapers but in 1886 the advertisements for *The Echo* – the evening version of the *Sydney Morning Herald* – proclaimed that the paper tried to be 'bright, racy, outspoken, and entertaining'.

The newspaper editors tried to shape as well as to express public opinions. David Syme, a lean young Scot who mined for gold in California and Victoria, joined hands with his brother Ebenezer who in 1856 had just bought at auction the insolvent *Age* newspaper in Melbourne. Ebenezer died young, his widow, Janet, taking over his shares before retiring to England, and David became the dynamic leader. In the mid-1860s, in a time of unemployment in Victoria, he preached the need for a protective tariff against nearly all imports, whether from England or Tasmania, and was later acclaimed as the 'Father of Protection' in Australia. The circulation of his daily increased steadily. Politicians began to realise the power of this man who was rarely seen at a political gathering, was unknown to almost every person in the street, spoke at no public rally, and was rarely seen in church on Sunday. How much power he possessed over politicians is difficult to gauge but it was large. In 1877 he regularly proclaimed that his penny newspaper sold twice as many copies as any other daily paper in Australia. In 1890 he boasted that *The Age* sold more copies than any other daily in the British Empire, except a few famous newspapers in London. Syme believed that newspapers should be educators of the people more than voices of the people. As instructors, wrote Syme, the public meeting and the press had no rivals: 'But for the platform and the press not one of the great reforms of recent times would have been carried.'

The scholar and politician Viscount Bryce, who served Britain as ambassador in Washington, assessed in his massive book *Modern Democracies* the role of the Australian press towards the end of the nineteenth century: 'the three or four greatest newspapers in Sydney and Melbourne exercised more power than any newspapers then did in any other country, being at times stronger than the head of the political parties'.

By 1890 the large newspapers were possibly reaching the peak of their political influence. They were not yet forced to compete strenuously with racy tabloids for whom politics was only one course in the daily banquet of news. And they did not yet face competition from radio and television whose main news often was to come in the form of quick snapshots.

Most of the powerful proprietors and editors took an intense interest in religious topics. The Fairfaxes of Sydney were ardent Congregationalists and employed as editor the Reverend John West, a talented clergyman in their own sect and at one time the eloquent spokesman of the anti-transportation movement in Tasmania. Two of the Syme brothers had been nonconformist clergymen before turning to printer's ink and printing paper. In Melbourne in 1908 the graveside service for David Syme was conducted by the Reverend Patrick Murdoch, who had arrived from Scotland a quarter of a century earlier as a Free Presbyterian. He was the father of Sir Keith and the grandfather of Rupert – newspaper magnates. In the nineteenth century the editor's chair and the clergyman's pulpit had both been crusading branches of the media.

5

Of the richest people in Australia, most were large landowners. Originally called squatters, the name persisted even after they owned their lands or held them from the colonial governments on long-term lease. Most owned sheep though many owned cattle. As wool was the country's main export these men – and a few women – were vital to economic life. Politically they were powerful, and their stronghold was the legislative councils, which formed the house of review in the political system. With the mass of the people they were not very popular: the main source of unpopularity was that they were rich. It was also believed, at times with full justification, that when the public lands from the 1860s onwards were thrown open for sale, the squatters sometimes used unfair methods to obtain possession of lands on which their livestock grazed.

In bidding for land their main rivals were the small-scale farmers, known as selectors. They too were not averse to using unfair methods of gaining land that they wanted.

The conflict between squatters and selectors was one of the fiercest political and economic struggles in Australian history, and the struggle was at its height in the years 1860 to 1914. Oddly it was resolved more satisfactorily than would have been predicted. The squatters won possession of most of the land that was suited for grazing, and the selectors won most of the land that was suited for either ploughing or a mixture of ploughing and grazing. This solution did not bring any popularity to the squatters. They were not equal enough in a society that was increasingly devoted to equality. As Australia became more egalitarian the pastoralists were viewed in populist circles as tall poppies who should be cut down.

The squatter – 'pastoralist' was now the favoured name – usually stood on the top of the social ladder. He may have begun his career in a hut with an earthen floor and a bark or shingle roof, but by the 1880s he – or his oldest son – owned a grand house in the midst of his lands and often a notable mansion in the nearest capital city. The English historian James Anthony Froude, visiting Australia in the course of a world tour in 1885, visited Ercildoune, a squatter's home beyond Ballarat, and expected to find a wooden hut in a wild tract of forest inhabited by 'semi-savages'. Instead he was driven in a horse-drawn vehicle through a gateway slightly reminiscent of the entrance to 'a great English domain' and past avenues of trees and 'high trimmed hedges of evergreen' and then at last came a glimpse of a large granite dwelling with small diamond-shaped windowpanes. Surrounded by 'clean mown lawns', a croquet ground and lawn-tennis court, and flowerbeds, it resembled 'an English aristocrat's country house reproduced in another hemisphere'. To his surprise he was welcomed by an Australian-born family displaying cultivated manners and tastes: 'The contrast between the scene which I had expected and the scene which I found took my breath away.'

Marriage was a vital topic for these pastoralist families – and those who hoped to join them through marriage. The absentee owner of Ercildoune, near Ballarat, was Samuel Wilson who lived in style in England, where he gained satisfaction when his daughter married an earl while a son married the daughter of a duke. The pastoralists who stayed in Australia – especially the first generation – faced a restricted choice of brides. Quite a few married cousins, and others married into other pastoral families. A historian of such families observed that by 1900 'whole districts were interlinked by marriage', so that an outsider who married one of the daughters instantly 'acquired an entire neighbourhood of connections'.

One of the heartlands of this elite were the plains extending west from Melbourne and Geelong all the way to the South Australian border and just beyond. Many were lowland Scots, though the next generation were native-born. Originally Presbyterian, the later generations of these families tended to be Anglican – a church slightly more fashionable and inclined to rule people's daily lives with fewer restrictions. The Geelong Grammar School, mainly for boarders, became one of their favoured schools. If their sons were sent to Britain for the last stage of their education they preferred Cambridge. There one of the most inventive oarsmen in the whole history of the sport of rowing, Steve Fairbairn, came from a Victorian squatting family.

In social life these families were sometimes lampooned, and it was even said that they were devoid of talent; but for such a small group of the population they displayed talent or ability that shone in many fields, including business. Patrick White, the only Australian to win the Nobel prize for literature, was a member of a pastoral family from the Hunter Valley. Many of the well-known names in politics came from such families. They tended to dominate the upper houses in each colony, and even in the lower house of the federal parliament they were to be very influential.

6

By 1875 dozens of trade unions were active in Australia, but most were exclusive clubs rather than big unions that preached the brotherhood of all workers. Many coalminers of the Hunter Valley and goldminers in Victoria were unionists. In the printing shops, in iron foundries, and among the stonemasons and bricklayers, trade unions could be found. A unionist passing along a city lane and suddenly detecting the sour smell of colonial leather in the large workshop of a saddle-maker or bookbinder could expect to find a few unionists inside.

In the countryside a trade unionist was a rarity. If he existed he told nobody: he might be sacked. Among women who worked in factories or as servants in homes and boarding houses, a trade union was unknown. Among the white-collar men, among the clerks and officials in banks and government offices, the very thought of joining a union would have been almost as rash as the thought of arriving at work without a hat.

Most unionists in Australia in 1875 were craftsmen or tradesmen. They had served an apprenticeship and had learned a skilled trade. Their trade union was not only a defence league but also a social club and minor welfare agency. Before the governments began to provide social welfare functions, most unions collected a weekly due from their members and so accumulated a small kitty of money that might help a member who was too ill to work or might help his widow on burial day. Occasionally a trade union conducted a strike in pursuit of shorter hours of work or to prevent wages from falling, but the strikes rarely lasted long. Few union leaders could foresee the day when a strike could dislocate a city or a whole industry. Few leaders of unions could probably conceive of the day when unionists would be the most powerful group in a strong political party.

The trade unions in the 1870s embraced only a small fraction of the employees. No leaders of unions were national or colonial figures. It is likely that in Adelaide or Sydney in the 1870s an adult, if asked for the name of a prominent unionist or a prominent preacher, would have selected a preacher with greater ease.

William Guthrie Spence was probably the first unionist to become a national name. He had come to Victoria as a six-year-old from an island in the Orkneys – 60 kilometres beyond the tip of Scotland – and on the goldfields he lived in a tent with his parents. In the early years of the rushes he was a child shepherd, a gold-digger and a butcher. His formal education was brief but he read resolutely and gained a fluency in writing and in public speaking. Most of his early years he spent around Creswick, a gold town that lay on the fringe of bare green volcanic hills to the north of Ballarat.

In July 1878 Spence decided to form a trade union on the new deep alluvial goldfields near Creswick. Other unions had been formed on Australian goldfields and coalfields, but most of their branches were ailing. Provoked by the attempt of the mining companies to cut wages from seven shillings to 6s.6d a day, Spence called a meeting of miners one winter's night at Thomas Dibdin's wooden hotel in Broomfield Gully, a town today almost deserted. Guided along dark tracks by lanterns, 150 miners crowded into the hotel, heard Spence speak of the advantages of forming a union, and elected him secretary and the publican as treasurer. President of the union formed that winter in the nearby town of Creswick was

John Sampson, a Cornish miner whose grandson, Robert Menzies, was to become the prime minister of Australia.

Spence, then in his early thirties, became a missionary for the union. He encouraged the opening of new branches or the revival of old branches in many other Victorian goldfields. He had an instinct for strategy and tactics. Wisely his union set up accident funds whereby members or their widows could receive compensation in the event of accidents in the mines; and mine-owners applauded the accident fund, especially as they did not have to finance it. Perhaps they also realised that so long as the accident fund dominated the finances of the miners' union, the union could not afford long strikes: a long strike used up so much money that it robbed the accident fund. In fact, in its first two decades the Amalgamated Miners' Association throughout Australia spent more than nine-tenths of its revenue on compensating the victims of accidents or their families.

Spence knew how far he could squeeze the shareholders of the mines. Unlike many men who later were to lead unions, he knew minutely the economics of industry. It has long been forgotten that he was not always a miner working for his daily wage. Soon after the union was formed he and some mates took over a goldmine under the tribute system and worked it for three years on a profit-sharing basis with the owners. He was thus a shareminer, the underground equivalent of a sharefarmer. Likewise, scores of members of his union were share speculators who used their inside knowledge of particular gold reefs to buy and sell shares on the stock exchanges that then flourished in the mining towns. They knew therefore that if wages were unrealistically high the low-grade mines would have to close, thus depriving unionists of work.

The miners' union flourished. It linked up with the coalminers in New South Wales and formed branches on the goldfields of

New Zealand. By 1890 its members probably exceeded 23 000, the biggest union in Australasia.

If travellers happened to see Spence standing on a railway station during one of his journeys as an organiser, they would have noticed nothing unusual in his appearance, manner or speech. Spence's indignation might run hot but it rarely approached boiling point. A negotiator, he was inclined to see a strike as a last resort. His appearance, like his speeches, aroused few emphatic comments. The painter Tom Roberts observed simply that Spence's head had 'more height above the eyes than the average'.

Though he travelled far as an organiser and negotiator in the 1880s, Spence spent most days in his hometown where the Amalgamated Miners' Association had its headquarters. In Creswick he drilled with the volunteer militia, sat on the town council, and spoke at meetings of the debating society. On Sundays he stood on the platform of the Presbyterian Sunday school, and on some evenings he preached in the local chapels of the Primitive Methodists and Bible Christians, who found most support from working people.

The miners' union became so powerful by 1886 that a few shearers wondered whether William Spence might be the crusader who could organise shearers into a union that spanned the continent. The larger pastoralists ran sheep on a colossal scale. Their woolsheds, some of which were noble buildings of bluestone and sandstone, could easily have been mistaken for the civic hall of a flourishing town.

In discipline some of these shearing sheds were like factories. Here scores or more shearers began work on the stroke of six in the morning, halted for meals and the regulation smokos, and worked exactly nine hours on every day except Saturday. Nearly every shed imposed fines on shoddy workmanship: a foreman observed any sheep that was carelessly shorn and marked it with a 'raddle' of red ochre, and for that sheep the shearer was not paid and might even be fined.

It is not necessarily poverty or a deep sense of injustice or poor living conditions that leads to a revolt by workers. The shearers slept in rough huts and ate large but rough-cooked meals and worked until the sweat could be wrung from their clothes. And yet they were paid more than the larger army of rural labourers who worked as ploughmen, fencers, potato diggers or haymakers. Moreover shearers worked a shorter week, especially in summer, than the farm labourers. What distinguished the shearers from other rural workers was an ability to organise themselves. They were also distinguished by the belief – usually but not always true – that their employers could afford to pay them more.

Many sheep-owners in the mid-1880s were no longer so prosperous. The price of wool had fallen, the seasons were less reliable, and in the dry interior many of the big pastoral runs were sliding deeply into debt. They had borrowed too much, and the annual interest owed by many individual sheep stations now equalled one-third or even one-half of the value of their annual wool clip. The sheep-owners naturally searched for savings, and in some districts they tried to lower their payments to shearers.

At Creswick, the unionists' mecca, a young goldminer named David Temple was accustomed to go shearing each winter; and when he heard that a shearer's pay was to be reduced, he wondered whether all his travelling from shed to shed, his back-stiffening work with the shears and the petty rules devised by some of the owners, made the job worthwhile. When he told his mother, a level-headed Scot, she said simply: 'Why don't you go to Mr Spence?' Temple spoke to Spence and explained his grievances as a shearer. Spence decided that he would back the forming of an

Amalgamated Shearers' Union. An inaugural meeting was held at a hotel in Ballarat on a cold Saturday night in June 1886, and with Spence as president the union began to enrol members on the eve of the new shearing season. Organisers were sent around the countryside. Others went to New Zealand and, printing the union rules in Maori as well as English, enlisted more than 2000 shearers by the end of the year. The union enrolled Aborigines as well as Maori.

The union tried to be dominant in each district. Pastoralists who refused to give in to Spence's demands were deprived of shearers. In response some pastoralists recruited non-union shearers in country towns and gave them free tickets to the railhead nearest their woolshed. The union, however, was often waiting for the arrival of the tainted shearers. Spence's men would camp by the road leading to the sheep station and refuse to allow shearers to pass along that road. Sometimes Spence's men arrived in force at the shearers' huts and kidnapped those who did not belong to the union. Many found it expedient to join.

Distance was the main obstacle facing Spence's lieutenants as they rode their horses from shearing shed to shearing shed in the far outback. Distance, however, was also their ally. The big sheds, being far from the railway lines and the big towns, were also far from the large police stations and soldiers' barracks. At times, when hundreds of unionists assembled in an outback town and defied the local police, reinforcements of police or soldiers were sent by train from the coast; but that happened only in a grave emergency. In the cities the police were numerous and were usually on the side of the employers during industrial skirmishes, but in the outback the unionists held the advantage. Far outnumbering the police and the volunteer militia of the bush towns, the union could quietly impose its own law and order.

Spence's union did not insist that all shearers should earn alike. His union did not penalise the shearers who set a fast pace and earned far more money than their workmates. The 1890s were to become famous for shearing records. In some districts small crowds gathered at out-of-the-way shearing sheds to see the champions display their remarkable stamina and dexterity. The daily tallies of the best shearers were discussed in hotel bars, argued about and fought over. One of Australia's new folk heroes was the shearer and unionist Jackie Howe, and in October 1892 at Alice Downs station in Queensland he shore a daily average of 259 sheep during a five-day run, and on the sixth day he shore 321 ewes in less than eight hours – the most remarkable burst of blade-shearing so far seen in the world.

The shearers' demands for more money seem to have encouraged the creation of the first shearing machines. Frederick Wolseley had come to Australia as a seventeen-year-old during the gold rushes and had become an employee on a sheep station and then an owner. With financial help from his brother, Field Marshal Sir Garnet Wolseley, he developed a shearing machine that could be powered by shafting from a steam engine. His machine was shearing sheep at Walgett in New South Wales with some success in 1885. Three years later a woolshed near the Darling River installed forty machines, and more of the big stations installed Wolseley machines in the hope of cutting costs and in the belief that a semi-skilled man could handle the machine shears more easily than the hand blades. The machine would thus weaken the bargaining position of the unionists by opening the work to thousands of newcomers.

The shearing machines affected another machine. Wolseley set up a factory in Birmingham to make shearing machines on the large scale, and in 1895 he diversified and made the first Wolseley motor cars. The young Melbourne engineer who managed his factory decided to make his own car, the Austin, and it became one of the most popular of the English-made cars.

Spence's union spread far outback and as far north as the shearers travelled in their annual circuit. Under the new name of the Australian Workers' Union, adopted in 1894, it was to be the largest union in the land for about three-quarters of a century. Spence was first its chief executive and then its president, giving him a high status in the infant Labor Party, but in national politics he could never attain the influence he wielded in the workplace.

He saw the union not only as a means of sharing more of the wool industry's profits among the shearers but as an instrument of moral change. Membership of the union, wrote Spence, makes a man a 'better husband, a better father, a better and more active citizen'.

Few, if any, union organisers in the world had created two big trade unions that successfully marshalled workers from so many isolated places. The great man in the early history of the labour movement, Spence's fame seemed imperishable but was not. In the First World War, when Australians were divided on whether young men should be compelled to join the army and go overseas to fight, Spence decided as a minister in a Labor federal cabinet that he should place the interests of the nation, as he perceived those interests, above the commands of his party. He was not forgiven.

7

At first the rising power of unions in Australia seemed to have no limit. In 1889, when about 150 000 dock workers in London went on strike, the financial aid that came from Australia was virtually sufficient to enable the dockers to remain on strike until they won their dispute. Here were the carriers and the heavers of the world's largest port, carried to victory by donations that came from every large town in Australia, from lord mayors and judges, from workingmen who sent around the hat, from the gate receipts of football matches and music recitals, from stock exchanges and scores of conservative members of parliament, as well as from trade unions.

In August 1890 the upheaval was transferred from the waterfront of the Thames to wharves in Australia. The officers of coastal ships, the seamen and wharf labourers went on strike in Sydney and Melbourne. The Maritime Strike eventually embraced shearers far inland – those from Spence's big union and those from the small Queensland shearers' union – and the coalminers of Newcastle and the silver-lead miners of Broken Hill. Here was a trial of strength between big unions and strong employers.

The strike provoked dramatic episodes that were talked about for a generation. In Melbourne at the end of August 1890 the government feared disorder, partly because the erratic supply of coal for the gasworks could snuff out the streetlights but more because a mass meeting of strikers and sympathisers had been called for Sunday 31 August. As a precaution the government mustered the volunteers of the militia in Melbourne, and in the barracks Lieutenant-Colonel Tom Price told a section of the Mounted Rifles that if a riot occurred and it was ordered as a last resort to fire at a crowd: 'Fire low and lay them out.' His men did not have to lay them out – they did not even leave the barracks – but Price's instructions were engraved so deeply into the minds of people that folklore sometimes recalled mistakenly that the troops had actually confronted the masses and threatened to fire.

On 19 September 1890 in Sydney, employers and their supporters took the reins into their own hands by driving drays and wagons of wool to the deep-sea berth at Circular Quay. The strikers who declared the wool to be black lined the route and several tried to halt the procession of wool carters. At Circular Quay, just a century after the first convicts had been taken ashore, many of the descendants of those convicts were now insisting that in this land the master was no longer the master. At the quay the crowd seemed so huge and menacing that the Riot Act was read aloud to them and they were told to disperse. It was like ordering the salt water to run out of the harbour. Accordingly the constables on horseback scattered the people.

The blades were silenced and the country's main export was endangered. But the unions – even the shearers' union – were not yet powerful enough, and economic conditions were not buoyant enough, to favour the strikers. Moreover the strikers received no generous flow of funds from English sympathisers, nor from many of those Australians who only a year ago had gladly supported the striking dockers of London.

Everywhere the strikers were defeated. Unionism declined sharply, and in the 1890s the number of union members in Australia fell to perhaps one-quarter of the former tally. The next advance in the strength of unionism had to wait until the following decade.

One far-reaching effect, however, is attributed to the strike. The entry of the labour movement into parliament is said to have sprung partly from the defeat in 1890 and the realisation that labour would always be struggling in industrial disputes unless it could enlist police, soldiers and statute book on its side. There might be some truth in this argument. And yet it is also plausible that, had the unions won their strike in 1890, they might have entered parliamentary politics with even more energy and the confidence that in unity lay strength.

8

There were already signs that the labour movement would show its strength in parliaments as well as in workplaces. Charles Jardine

Don, an Australian stonemason, was perhaps the first workingman to take his seat in a parliament in the British Empire, but he was a generation ahead of his time. As a young Scot he had educated himself at night in debating clubs and mutual improvement societies, had read widely and learned apt quotations from William Cobbett, Tom Paine and Adam Smith, and taught himself how to speak in public. Migrating to the Victorian goldfields at about the age of thirty-three, he dug for gold at Ballarat and became a stonemason in Melbourne. He also chiselled away at society, campaigned for the eight-hour day and for the opening of lands that squatters occupied. In 1859 he won the seat of Collingwood in the legislative assembly, and is said to have worked as a stonemason on the walls of the new Parliament House in the day and to have spoken inside at night. Charles Don could not tap any deep sense of solidarity among working people, for society was still mobile and optimistic.

In his five years in parliament Don received no payment as a member; this vital innovation came to most colonies only in the period 1887 to 1890. As a politician Don therefore had to keep himself partly from his earnings as an inner-suburban publican, and his death at the age of forty-six was probably hastened by occupational hazards faced as a stonemason and publican. He deserves to be remembered, but has no memorial.

Twenty years after Don was dead, few workingmen sat in the colonial parliaments. And then in the early 1890s, almost overnight, they became prominent in the legislative assemblies, first in New South Wales in a season of prosperity and then in other colonies as the depression deepened. Payment of members now enabled workmen and small employers to give up their normal jobs and sit in Parliament. There was increasing unease with the performance of the self-employed, middle-class politicians who traditionally held workmen's electorates, and in January 1890 the Trades and Labor Council in Sydney voted overwhelmingly to campaign in the hope of winning seats for their allies and members. New ideologies from the northern hemisphere increasingly favoured the redistribution of wealth from rich to poor, and Parliament was the place to organise this transfer. In New South Wales in June 1891, to the astonishment of many experienced politicians, the new Labour Electoral Leagues won thirty-five of the 141 seats in the Legislative Assembly.

The platform on which Labor fought that first election was, by the standards of the time, quietly radical. It promised to fight for free education beyond the primary schools – a fight that it was eventually to postpone for many years. It promised to fight for the eight-hour day as the maximum workday in all occupations, and kept the promise more in the cities than in the country. It called, often with success, for safety in mines and factories. It successfully called for a fair electoral system in which no man could vote more than once, in which policemen and soldiers could at last be permitted to vote, and shearers, sailors and other wandering workers could have a chance of registering an absentee vote on election day. It resolved that the people should elect their own magistrates, an idea that was not adopted. Economic nationalism flavoured Labor's policy. The government should buy only goods made in New South Wales. White labour was preferred. Thus any of the local Chinese who made furniture would be compelled to stamp their timber with a confession that it was made by Chinese labour.

Most unionists, after the strikes of 1890, believed strongly that the armed forces should not be the special instruments of employers in settling industrial disputes. Hence the Leagues sought to confine professional soldiers to the manning of the forts. Presumably a 'purely volunteer' army was unlikely to march against workers engaged in demonstrating or striking.

If we had to seek the philosophers whose thoughts underlay that first Labor platform, the finger would initially point to the populist American Henry George, who had spoken to vast crowds in Australia only the previous year. This San Francisco messiah argued in his famous book *Progress and Poverty* that governments should impose a single tax on land and that the tax should be based on the fact that the market value of most land grew largely as a result of the increase of population, the building of railways and public works, and other indirect improvements for which the owner of the land could take no credit. There was merit in George's scheme, especially for a new country where the price of land quickly multiplied. And in the 1880s, during that bellowing boom in which real estate soared in price, the Australian governments could in fact have abolished all taxes and concentrated their taxation on that 'unearned increment' that the rising value of land provided.

George's main idea was not new to Australia and versions of it had been shaped and popularised here in the 1870s, especially by William H. Gresham, a Yorkshireman who worked as a ship chandler and merchant at Port Melbourne. In spare hours Gresham lectured on land reform and wrote pamphlets. He was also owner of a small boat that he called *Felix Holt*, in honour of the radical hero of George Eliot's new novel, and in that boat he set out from Port Melbourne before dawn on 13 May 1875 to make sales to incoming ships. The vessel ran into a fierce bay storm, and he and his two boatmen were not seen again. One of Gresham's pamphlets on taxing the land was read by Henry George himself with approval before he published *Progress and Poverty*, his own book on taxing land, in 1879.

George's ideas had a brief vogue in South Australia and then swept through New South Wales, influencing a string of inland towns extending from Lithgow to Wagga Wagga. There his ideas had a broad appeal, for he supported free trade and private enterprise while believing in what that first Labor platform described as 'the natural and inalienable rights of the whole community to the land'. George's influence presumably explains why the Labor Party did not at first believe in the income tax. He insisted that only one tax was needed – a tax on land.

The sudden arrival of Labor as a prominent party in New South Wales in 1891 was followed by success in other colonies. Labor won ten seats in Victoria in 1892 and eight in South Australia a year later. In Queensland in 1893 it won nearly one-quarter of the seats in the assembly. Most were seats in the outback and in the tropical gold towns where trade unions backed the party.

In December 1899 in Queensland, the party briefly tasted power. Probably the first Labor government in any country, it ruled for a total of six days. Its 36-year-old leader, Anderson Dawson, did not accept the rising Labor axiom that members of the parliament should largely control the leader, and he himself chose his cabinet ministers. The story of his courageous ascent from a Brisbane orphanage and the goldmines of Charters Towers to the front bench of parliament was to be repeated many times in the early history of the labour movement. His ultimate quarrel with the Labor Party was also a story repeated often.

In time to come the emergence of the Labor Party would be seen by many as the most important event in Australian political history and the main source of the wellbeing of several generations of working people and their families. The party had fine achievements but prosperity was not necessarily one of them. The favourable standard of living of the average Australian was visible long before a Labor Party was visible. Indeed the first half-century of the party's existence achieved – for a variety of reasons – little improvement in the prosperity of the average Australian.

CHAPTER SIX

In hot pursuit
of a 'pure world'

South Australia was in many ways an exceptional colony. Its migrants were different; its mix of Christian religions was unusual; and its own soil missed the excitement and wealth of the gold rushes. The strongest in agriculture, it suffered from periodical droughts. Unusual too was its phase of radical politics, which began about 1884 and continued for just over a decade. South Australia was the first to open children's courts and the first to attempt the compulsory arbitration of industrial disputes. It was the first place in the world to apply Henry George's simple taxation reforms and the first in Australia to place a tax on income earned from personal exertion. It was an early crusader against excessive alcohol, and it led Australia and almost every part of the world in the vital democratic reform of granting the vote to women.

The early democratic reforms had largely ignored Australian women. The privileges of the 1850s were not for them. They did not vote or sit on juries. They rarely wrote to or for the main newspapers and magazines. They had no hand in the learned professions. Speakers looking down from the platform at a public meeting did not often see a woman's hat in the rows of bare male heads. Women were paid less than men even when they did exactly the same work; and the costly task of providing a school place for every child in the main colonies in the 1870s, when education became compulsory, was therefore financed in part by the lower salaries of women teachers.

2

The names given to plants illustrated a prejudice against women. An inferior Australian beech was called a she-beech and the timber cutters called an inferior native pine the she-pine. The casuarina tree was called the she-oak, for its grain was like English oak but its timber was deemed inferior. There was a time when the beer brewed in the colonies was mockingly called she-oak to indicate its inferiority to English beer, which presumably came in oak kegs. Once colonial beer became respectable it was usually given masculine names: it was often called shearer's joy, and in Sydney's hotels the tallest glass of beer was known as a Bishop Barker, after the Anglican bishop who arrived in 1855 – a very tall man of 198 centimetres.

In a few matters women were the privileged ones. They were not numerous in the back-breaking occupations. The harsh life in the outback was imposed on relatively few women. The divorce laws, viewed from some angles, were extremely unjust to them, but in Australia in the 1870s only one divorce or judicial separation was granted each fortnight, and even by the 1890s they were uncommon.

A few laws were clearly unjust to women but were modified in practice. Under the English law still ruling in Australia a married woman's grip on her own property and income was precarious, but according to a well-informed Melbourne merchant in the 1860s 'hardly a marriage takes place without a summons to the lawyer – from all at least who can afford the cost': the lawyer then drew up a document that circumvented the law. Soon the marriage lawyer was redundant. Between the 1860s and the early 1890s each colony passed its own Married Women's Property Act, which gave women virtually the same property rights as men. The British mode of government assumed that ownership of property conferred political rights. Since many married women now owned property and paid rates and taxes, it seemed that their full political rights would soon be conceded.

And yet to possess no voting rights was seen as hardly a serious deprivation. Some Australian men were deliberately excluded from the vote not because they were insignificant but because they were so influential. New South Wales in its electoral law of 1858 precluded all members of the army, navy and police force from voting and even from attempting to persuade an elector how he should vote. In some colonies a clergyman could not stand for parliament. In such a mental climate it was possible for politicians to agree upon the importance of women and still deny them the vote. Their vital role, it was said, was as a mother in the family home; and rarely had the home been so venerated as in the last decades of the reign of Queen Victoria.

The educational reforms of the 1870s also hinted that women would soon receive the vote. When education was made compulsory for most Australian children, girls and boys were treated equally. Perhaps the schoolroom would transform the polling booth. A democracy that called itself enlightened could hardly continue to give the vote to illiterate men who had no stake in the country and had lived here only one year, but refuse the same vote to educated women, some of whom were born in Australia, owned a stake in the country, paid taxes and played an intelligent part in the controversies of the day.

3

In national life in the 1880s more and more women were becoming prominent. While hundreds of thousands kept house with skill and fed and clothed their children and guided and encouraged them, and while thousands more women excelled in teaching, nursing and the few professions yet open to them, some were starting to shine in other fields. The first female doctors graduated from the universities, of which Australia had only three, and a small cluster of female poets, novelists and painters reached a discerning audience. Jane Sutherland painted landscapes with the new Heidelberg School of artists, and Alice Cornwell floated goldmines near Ballarat and then voyaged in the mail steamer to London where in 1887 she bought the *Sunday Times* and made it an even more influential newspaper. She was a forerunner of the Western Australian mine-owner Gina Rinehart, who more than a century later was one of the richest women in the world.

Famous in her era was Nellie Mitchell of Melbourne, later Dame Nellie Melba, who studied at the new Presbyterian Ladies' College when it was one of the best girls' schools in the land, played when very young the pipe organ in the Town Hall, took singing lessons from talented teachers, lived briefly with her new husband on a sugar plantation in north Queensland and – high with ambition and determination – went with her Scottish father, a builder, to Europe where she made her operatic debut in Brussels in 1887. Less than twenty years later, thanks to the new gramophone, she became, except for a few members of royal families, the most celebrated

woman in the world. Female pop stars and film stars, female prime
ministers and chief justices were still unknown.

When Melba became a professional singer, no woman held a
seat in parliament, no woman sat as a judge, no woman was a university professor, and no woman chaired a big public company. Even
the right of women to attend a university was a battle still being
fought, and in 1880 the universities at Auckland, Christchurch and
Melbourne had only recently won that right. At the University
of Sydney women were not yet seen, and at Adelaide their official presence had been delayed by the intervention of the colonial
secretary in London who baulked at South Australia's parliament
approving such a topsy-turvy idea.

Inside the main churches the dictum of St Paul the Apostle still
prevailed. Women listened; they did not speak. In only a few minor
Protestant sects were women even allowed to make an address
or sermon from the pulpit. One sect, sympathetic to women as
preachers, was a Methodist offshoot called the Bible Christians,
and it was stronger in South Australia than in any other part of the
world except perhaps Cornwall. Mrs Serena or 'Serrie' Lake was
one of its part-time preachers. Known in England as 'the sweet girl
gospeller', she migrated to Queensland and then moved in 1870
to Adelaide where in her late twenties she delivered Sunday sermons. The town hall was crowded with nearly 2000 people who
listened, it was said, with 'breathless attention'. The births of her
seven children, of whom six died in infancy, merely interrupted
her preaching. Women were often the unobtrusive allies in secular
campaigns. They made the rebellious blue and white flag that flew
at the Eureka rebellion in 1854. At rallies in favour of higher wages
or safe working conditions they could be prominent – for the sake
of their husbands and children. At the South Australian copper-
fields of Moonta and Wallaroo in 1874 a major strike by miners was

supported publicly by 100 or more women. Armed with poles and brooms made from lengths of Mallee tree, they were soon 'charging in all directions'. In the terminology of the time they were called women, not ladies.

The political movement that drew women conspicuously into public life in Australia was the crusade against alcohol. It was not that the consumption of alcohol was soaring. The drinking of brandy, rum and other spirits had been more damaging before 1850, when Australia was more masculine. Thirty years later, men ceased to outnumber women by such a large margin and the number of drinkers for each thousand people declined, and beer and wine challenged spirits. Nonetheless in town and country the inns and hotels were widespread and were, alongside the churches, the main places for social gatherings. The standard of living of many of the poorer families clearly suffered because the husband spent too much of the family's small income on his alcohol. In such a household, violence was probably more likely, and the neglect of children – through a parent's drunkenness or poverty – more apparent. Their daughters and sons, too, when they joined the workforce, were more likely to drink alcohol. If the number of hotels could be reduced, the temptation to drink would be reduced, though eager drinkers could still buy a bottle of sherry or brandy at the licensed grocer. It was widely believed that a contented and Christian family life was certainly not aided by alcohol.

In Victoria in 1885 many Christian women began a systematic doorknock in the hope of persuading adult females to sign a petition calling on Parliament to empower ratepayers to vote against any new hotels proposed for their neighbourhood and even to close existing hotels. The women's petition grew and grew. If all the pages were arranged in a single line, it would have extended for half a kilometre. Eventually Victoria's parliament granted this right – it was called local option – for a vote of ratepayers to close hotels. Mainly as a result of a series of local polls, the number of hotels in Victoria was to be halved during the next generation.

It so happened that when the crusade was just under way, a wealthy American woman called at several Australian ports while making a world cruise. A divorcee – a rarity in Australia – and an excellent public speaker, she was an active member of an organisation founded in Ohio eleven years previously, the Woman's Christian Temperance Union. Just as many American women had been leaders in the crusade against slavery in mid-century, they now led a crusade against what she called another, more insidious form of enslavement – alcohol. The WCTU was the spearhead of this campaign for a 'sober and pure world'. Believing that it could only achieve victory if women were given the right to vote, and believing that women must first learn to be effective campaigners in public, it disseminated a new attitude to public speaking. In the space of a few months Mary Leavitt spoke in many Australian and New Zealand towns, attracting men as well as women to her audience, and creating branches of the WCTU wherever she spoke. Leavitt's speeches were a revelation for men who had not previously heard a woman speak in a public hall. She displayed charm, intellect and sheer fluency.

4

The career of Catherine Helen Spence, who became the first female political candidate in the British Empire, showed the hazards of learning to speak in public. The daughter of an unsuccessful Scottish banker, she had sailed as a teenager in 1839 for Adelaide, where she spent the remainder of her life. Twice marriage was proposed to her but she said firmly, 'No'. One reason for her firmness was her Calvinistic fear that children whom she brought into the world might have no hope of eternal salvation. By the time she was thirty her religious gloom had evaporated but her prospects of marriage and perhaps her desire for marriage had also faded: 'People married young if they married at all in those days.' Instead Miss Spence had work to do, a talent to use. In 1854 a London firm published *Clara Morison*, her two-volume novel. Though she was the first woman to write a novel about Australia she at first earned little public praise, for a woman usually wrote in disguise.

This nameless inhabitant of a man's world thought women should serve in public life. In her quiet ambition Spence was aided by unusual advantages: a critical mind, a clear style of writing, wide intellectual interests, and a small private income. She spent time and money in assisting to create the Boarding-Out Society, which supervised families who took poor or orphaned children into their homes.

It was difficult for women to acquire experience in that quintessential task of public life, the making of speeches. When Catherine Spence returned to Adelaide in 1866 from an overseas tour she was invited to give a lecture on her impressions of England, but the idea that she herself should deliver the lecture did not occur to the organisers. She did not even attend the meeting and instead her friend, a newspaper editor, read her script. Five years later, when she was in her mid-forties, she decided that she should personally read aloud the lectures she had been invited to write on the poets Elizabeth and Robert Browning. On the chosen day she was nervous. She had received no tuition in elocution and no lessons in that gesturing that was an important part of platform speaking. 'I never speak in public with gloves on,' she wrote later. 'They interfere with the natural eloquence of the hand.' She could not call on other women for advice, for she knew no woman in Adelaide who had spoken formally to a large mixed audience. Nor could she feel sure that her natural voice was strong enough to reach the back seats of the hall.

Fortunately the young barrister Samuel Way offered to sit in the back row and raise his hand if her voice became indistinct. The lecture began, and Spence felt very nervous but showed no outward sign of her apprehension. What the women in the audience thought of the fact that she was performing a man's role, she herself did not reveal. Many women were among the staunchest enemies of women's liberation.

Originally a Presbyterian, Spence became a Unitarian. That most intellectual of all the sects was not averse to women preaching. In Melbourne, Miss Martha Turner was elected by the wealthy Unitarian congregation as one of its pastors in 1873, and for about seven years she conducted most of the duties of the ministry, performing marriages, and preaching from time to time in a clear bluestocking style from a raised desk in the church. Twice she visited Adelaide to conduct a series of Sunday services in the Unitarian church in Wakefield Street. There in the congregation sat Spence, all ears and eyes, for she had not heard a woman preach in that city of churches. 'I was thrilled', wrote Spence, 'by her exquisite voice, by her earnestness, and by her reverence.' Suddenly she thought how much the world had lost, through so many centuries, by its refusal to allow women to preach. She resolved, if the chance arose, to become an occasional preacher. At first she was merely invited to read a printed sermon but later she wrote her own. She began to enjoy the drama and theatre of the pulpit and public meeting, and her delight is visible in her autobiography.

Most Australians as late as 1890 had not heard a woman preach in church or even speak from a political platform. Even the idea of women writing political letters to the editors of newspapers was seen as uncomely, and so for thirty years Spence published her political letters under the name of her brother. Her controversial book of 1884, *An Agnostic's Progress from the Known to the Unknown*, was also anonymous. Here was one of Australia's most thoughtful citizens, conscious that in assessing the serious issues of the day she had to disguise herself because she was female.

5

A woman speaking in a public hall or in the open air was viewed as bringing all women into disrepute. Moreover in a public place any speaker, especially a woman, was exposed to interjections; and these were more frequent and abusive than they are today. Women faced another obstacle in the era before the electric microphone: speaking often to a noisy crowd could permanently strain the voice. And should a woman take the chair of a public meeting? The answer was usually no. Often a man was invited to take the chair even at the early Australian meetings organised by the WCTU.

The branches of the WCTU, mostly small, tended to consist primarily of the evangelicals called dissenters or nonconformists. Wesleyans, Congregationalists, Baptists, Primitive Methodists, Bible Christians, Quakers and members of the Church of Christ and the new Salvation Army could be found in a typical branch. To attack the makers and sellers of alcohol far more than the victims who drank it was the aim of the WCTU. Surprisingly the actual churches to which most of its members belonged were not yet forthright opponents of alcohol. At Holy Communion or the Lord's Supper, alcoholic wine was still served in nearly all churches, though that traditional drink was to be abandoned by several of the larger dissenting churches before the end of the century.

The WCTU was the first big women's group in Australia
and New Zealand to devote itself to social reform. In calling for
women to receive the vote, it knew that they were more likely
to oppose the alcohol industry. Hitherto small groups of men
had led the campaign for the female franchise. Foremost was Sir
Julius Vogel, who had edited newspapers on the Victorian goldfields before migrating to New Zealand. A Jew, he believed that
just as the recent emancipation of the Jews in the Western world
had liberated talents for the public's gain, so would the emancipation of women. In 1887 he actually introduced a bill to give
women the vote, and almost succeeded. The rise of the WCTU
bolstered his campaign.

In 1893 New Zealand became the first country in the world to
enfranchise women. In the following year, with the powerful aid of
the WCTU, South Australia also succeeded. There women not only
won the right to vote but to stand for parliament. They first voted at
a general election on 25 April 1896.

Though Catherine Spence was not a member of the WCTU
she became the first woman in Australia to stand for a seat in a
major legislative body. In 1897 South Australia set out to elect ten
citizens who would sit in the national convention set up to debate
the federation of the Australian colonies; and Spence stepped forward as a candidate. In her early seventies, white-haired and plump
and benevolent in appearance, she presented her case in her distinct
Scottish accent. Though she was not among the ten leading candidates, she polled more than 7000 votes.

Much of the general opposition to women participating in politics was simply a belief that marriage and the family were more
important than public meetings and parliament. Australia in
1902 became the first country to allow women to stand for parliament, but year after year no woman gained election. At last in 1921

Mrs Edith Cowan, in her sixtieth year, won a seat in the Western Australian lower house. South Australia, the pioneer, did not elect a woman to its state parliament until 1959.

6

Schools and churches were crucial to the female world. More women than men went to church. In the popular Sunday schools run by Protestant churches, women ran many of the classes. In day schools run by the government close to half of the teachers employed in 1890 were women, and in Catholic schools the nuns did much of the teaching. It is likely that after school, when young children were at home, a mother rather than a father encouraged them to read and taught them how to spell and pronounce difficult words.

In 1873 Victoria become one of the few parts of the world where attendance at school was free and compulsory. New South Wales soon followed and in 1900 Queensland became the last. Children from the age of six or seven had to attend for a certain number of days or weeks annually – a rule that allowed for periods of absenteeism. It was considered unfair on the parents to enforce compulsion when the harvest was being brought in and a child's labour was needed. Tasmania was less diligent and in 1886 perhaps half of the children enrolled did not attend school regularly.

In most schools the discipline was strict. Corporal punishment, with a cane or stick or leather strap or a firm flat of the hand, was normal. Many lessons, especially the multiplication tables and the spelling, were often learned by chanting – an effective method now out of fashion. Children were taught to write by practising on a thin piece of slate or stone until finally they were given pen, ink and paper. A form of apprenticeship prevailed in teaching as in butchers' and carpenters' shops, legal offices, and even in schools.

The pupil-teachers learned their skills in the classroom – the big specialist teachers' college came later.

In Victoria the free government schools charged no fees except for optional subjects such as needlework and music tuition. New South Wales, however, charged a general tuition fee until 1906. Parents paid the small sum of threepence a week for each child but for poor parents an exemption was possible. In an unusual rule introduced in 1880, students could travel free of charge by the normal government train to the nearest school; but not many rural students lived close to a railway station, let alone one where a timetable was favourable to their coming and going.

Outside the cities the common kind of school was small with only one teacher, usually a woman. A typical bush school of the 1870s was just a framework of timber roofed with slabs of bark. We know that in the declining New South Wales goldfield of Eurunderee (sometimes known as Pipeclay) the tall, gaunt male teacher could not adequately spell – 'anxiety' was one of the words that troubled him. Textbooks were often inappropriate. He taught geography from a popular book produced for the national schools of Ireland, but for young Australians one page created puzzlement: it pronounced that when 'you go out to play at 1 o'clock' the sun will be lying in the south. One student, Henry Lawson, revelled in the excitement when on hot days a black goanna lay on the large beam of wood near the ceiling 'and improve[d] his mind a little'. In contrast the new city schools of the time were handsome two-storeyed structures with perhaps 500 or more children studying under a strict silence imposed from above.

Everywhere the governments gave large subsidies to primary schools run by the main religious groups but this aid was phased out, especially from the 1870s. It was cheaper to operate a system of government schools. But if religion was also to be part of the curriculum in government schools, which branch of Christianity should be taught? The Catholics resolved to finance their own schools. Decade after decade until the 1960s, education was their financial burden, especially as many of their parents were relatively poor. Fortunately unpaid religious teachers eased the burden. The arrival in Ballarat in 1875 of Mother Gonzaga Barry and the sisters of the Loreto order attracted a crowd that filled the main railway platform and tumbled into the passenger carriage where the new nuns were seated. On the shores of the local lake they began to teach the Latin motto that read: 'Mary, Queen of the Angels. As long as I live I put my faith in Christ who died for me.'

A running quarrel was conducted between government and Catholic schools. Bishops sometimes denounced the state or secular schools. In New South Wales in June 1879 they were called 'seed-plots of future immorality, infidelity, and lawlessness'. It was believed that Catholic children who went to government schools were weaker in Christian faith, laxer in morality: 'their manners are rough and irreverent; they have little sense of respect and gentleness; they have no attraction for prayer or for the Sacraments'. These warnings came primarily from the new Catholic archbishop of Sydney, the 45-year-old Roger Vaughan.

The primary schools could teach lessons up to Form 8; after the age of thirteen or fourteen attendance was not compulsory. Secondary education, only for the few, was the home of Latin and almost the only gateway to university. Most of the secondary colleges were owned by the churches and financed largely by the fees paid, three times each year, by parents; they could be found in every capital city and in most of the provincial cities. The boys' colleges were widely criticised as being obsessed with competitive sport, but their impact on national life was to be high. In the new Commonwealth of Australia, the post of prime minister was to be held for almost half of the first eighty years by former students of Melbourne Grammar and Wesley College – schools that were separated by only ten minutes' walk along the tree-lined St Kilda Road.* As late as 1900 the colonial governments provided only a few secondary or high schools, an exception being New South Wales. Its Fort Street High School in the heart of Sydney is famous.

All over Australia the gains from public education were apparent. Those who had to sign the marriage register, on the day of their wedding, provided firm evidence. In 1857 about 30 per cent were incapable of signing their own name, but thirty years later the percentage had fallen to 4 per cent. The illiterate signified their consent by drawing a cross on the paper. Illiteracy was probably higher than the marriage register indicated, for many illiterate people were capable of writing a signature of sorts.

A vast effort went into the building of churches, especially from the 1840s. In the space of one decade, more than 1000 churches, chapels and Sunday schools were built across the country. People who were poor gave their sixpenny coin. Women baked scones and cakes for fetes; a farmer might donate a fat lamb and three dozen eggs or lend a shearing shed for a country dance, which raised useful money. Women, though possessing no official role in most congregations could dominate an organising committee; in Western Australia in 1927 the Catholic church at the port of Onslow was planned by a committee of six women and no men.

In new towns, people lent their dining room, shop or storeroom for the first congregation. Public schoolrooms were used on Sunday, with the teacher's permission. On the west coast of Tasmania in the 1880s one mine manager provided a shed, and the Sunday service

---

* In sequence the prime ministers were Alfred Deakin, Stanley Melbourne Bruce, Robert Menzies, Harold Holt and Malcolm Fraser. While Menzies and Holt came from Wesley, the other three were from Melbourne Grammar. Three studied at Melbourne University and two at Cambridge and Oxford.

was interrupted by horses neighing in the stable next door. When the small boys naturally laughed at the noise, the mine manager, himself the preacher, spoke sternly: 'Have silence, boys, in the House of the Lord.' In country districts when Houses of the Lord were specially built, they were often made of cheap materials such as corrugated iron, which was immune to white ants.

At first governments offered subsidies and a block of land for new church buildings, but eventually the churches fended for themselves. In the big cities Gothic cathedrals or large handsome churches with internal balconies were built. Churches that could seat 800 or 1200 people were not rare. Small towns occasionally afforded a handsome church. In the 1840s Tasmanians built several of the most nostalgic country churches in the English-speaking world. Augustus Pugin, designer of the interior of the new Houses of Parliament in London and the details of the Big Ben clock, was a friend of Tasmania's first Catholic bishop, Robert Willson, for whom he designed every detail of two entrancing churches still standing in the tiny towns of Oatlands and Colebrook.

Australia, unlike the British Isles, kept detailed tallies of the number of worshippers in each denomination, and by the end of the nineteenth century the religious ladder was stable. Anglicans were about 40 per cent of the population, Catholics 25 per cent, Presbyterians and Methodists each 12 per cent, followed at a distance by Baptists, Congregationalists and many of the smaller nonconformist sects. All religions were equal in the eyes of the law. A few atheists, rationalists and other secularists could be found but most did not advertise their whereabouts. Australians, except for most of the Chinese, were overwhelmingly Christian in 1901, and it is probable that, compared to Britain, a slightly higher proportion of the people went regularly to church. On Sunday afternoon, for an hour or more, a high proportion of Protestant children attended

Sunday school. The social rule had become strict: you wore your neatest, cleanest and best clothes on Sunday, and those who lacked such clothes tended not to attend church at all.

The churches also were tribes or clans. They were distinctive, ethnically. Catholics were most likely to be of Irish descent, though in Sydney their early bishops were English Benedictines. Anglicans tended to be of English descent, Presbyterians were of Scottish or Northern Irish descent, while Methodists were overwhelmingly from England, especially from Cornwall. What is now identified as religious intolerance in old-time Australia was partly a form of ethnic rivalry.

A 'mixed marriage' was considered risky. The riskiest mix was one part Catholic and one part Protestant. Between Catholics also stood barriers. The Jesuits, Marist Brothers and Christian Brothers, all of whom specialised in teaching, could be like rival teams playing in the same league. So too were many of the convents. Mary MacKillop, an Australian-born nun who in 1866 became the first Superior of the Sisters of St Joseph of the Sacred Heart, fell out with the Bishop of Adelaide and took refuge in Sydney. Within the Church of England the barriers could be just as high, and an Anglican family from one town might blink when encountering a cloud of incense in another Anglican church they visited.

While church rivalry was intense the exceptions were numerous. A large slice of public opinion tolerated a mixed marriage. Two respected prime ministers, Joseph Lyons and Ben Chifley, were Catholic boys who had married Protestant girls. Chifley's wedding in 1914 to Elizabeth McKenzie was, at her firm request, in a Presbyterian church; and thereafter they went to their separate churches. In contrast the religious friction was absent in many activities. Sport was the busy leveller, especially in a country town, and the same team could field members of many faiths.

Funeral tributes, during the heyday of religious intensity, defied the prevailing sectarian prejudices and loyalties. In 1897 the funeral of Sir William Clarke, one of Melbourne's richest men, left the new Anglican cathedral with a remarkable variety of clergy – including Jewish – walking in the rain-swept procession. A tribute to Clarke had already been given in a rural Catholic church that many of his household servants attended – a church to which he had been a generous donor.

In numerous towns the deep religious chasm lay not so much between Catholic and Protestant as between rival Protestants. Thus the Methodists, until 1902, were divided into five sects; and preachers from, say, the Primitive Methodists were rarely if ever invited to speak from a Wesleyan pulpit, while the Bible Christians and the United Free Methodists and the Methodist New Connexion also went their separate ways. The arrival of the Salvation Army in Australia in the 1880s led to more rivalry – indeed, most of its converts came from other evangelical churches. Earlier the Presbyterians were divided into three main competing sects, but they were informally united by their belief in education, the fact that their clergy were well educated, and by their activities in philanthropy – a role taken over in recent decades by Jews.

More than today, there was earnest discussion of what could make Australians more virtuous. Many applauded the views of John West, a Congregational minister who became the editor of the *Sydney Morning Herald*. He warned that people deserved to be despised 'if they grasped at wealth to the neglect of their social and political duties' and if they neglected their duty to educate 'the rising generation and the working classes'. The duty to educate heathen people abroad, especially about Christianity, was also a goal. Between 1870 and 1900 many hundreds of Australian women and men went as Christian missionaries to Fiji, Tonga, New Zealand, the New Hebrides (now Vanuatu), Papua and New Guinea, India and China. Perhaps one-quarter of the black population in South Africa now belong to the Zion Christian sects, the founding of which owed much to John Alexander Dowie who was earlier a Congregational minister in rural South Australia and Manly, and then a Charismatic in Collingwood and Chicago. Many of the overseas districts where Australian missionaries worked are, today, more Christian than the Australian towns from which they came.

In 1900, opponents of Christianity were still few. Atheists, agnostics, rationalists and freethinkers were fewer than 1 per cent of the people counted in the census. There was some acceptance of the theory – circulating even before 1859 when Charles Darwin published his book *On the Origin of Species* – that all the different forms of human life had evolved over a vast period of time rather than been created by the hand of God. Most Christians, however, were not worried by such ideas.

7

Family life, still central in national life, was affected by the sharp decline of the birthrate. The Sydney statistician Timothy Coghlan lamented the decline with the warning: 'No people has ever become great under such conditions.' For many years the colonies had been proud of their favourable birthrate. A bandage for wounded pride, it had been a rebuke to those English commentators who implied that a society founded on convicts was unlikely to multiply and that a warmer climate was not healthy for British people.

Many politicians thought the long-term decline in Australia's birthrate stemmed from the drift to the cities and what they thought was a less uplifting way of life there. They knew too that birth control was practised by more and more Australians. The discovery of the process of vulcanising rubber in the 1840s had led to a quiet revolution; and the man's condom or French letter and the woman's pessary were increasingly used. Possibly abortions of unwanted babies became more frequent; and by the 1890s 'penny royals' and 'steel drops' and other advertised concoctions were widely used to induce abortions. But these pharmacy items were often neglected by courting couples. Thus in 1905 in New South Wales a survey of married couples over the past twelve years revealed one irrefutable fact: one-third of all the first-born children had been conceived before marriage.

While moralists clicked their tongues in dismay at the fall of the birthrate, they found a cheering statistic: the death rate was falling. Between the 1860s and the early 1900s it fell by one-third. Deaths became less common in childbirth, though one of every ten children died in infancy. A purer milk supply, careful quarantine regulations at the ports, and the belated sewering of sections of large cities helped to curb infectious diseases. It was ironical that most of the Australian cities had long given priority to building railways and grand hotels and town halls. The people's health often came second. In Melbourne, a city with half a million people, not one house was sewered until the year 1897. The decline in the death rate was not sufficient to compensate for the decline in the birthrate.

8

In economic life women were far more important than the statistics indicated. Their contribution was rarely measured in money, but they dominated a sector of the economy that added immensely to people's wellbeing.

In women's main workplace, the kitchen, occurred many economic activities that are now confined to factories. A married woman usually did not work outside the home but found work inside it. She cooked all the meals eaten in the house and made many of the ingredients. The main streets then were not lined with cafes or takeaway food shops, and the private house served as the main eating place. Many housewives baked their own bread, and most baked their own cakes and tarts, biscuits and scones, and those puddings and sweets with which each meal was concluded. Most housewives, when summer came, sealed freshly cooked fruit in bottles, to be eaten when fresh fruit was no longer available. They made their own plum or apricot jam and apple or quince jelly, their own chutneys and tomato sauce, and summer soft drinks. On the farms, women made butter and cheese for their own table. In the cities more dripping than butter was spread on hot toast at break-fast time, and the dripping was not bought at the butchers' shops but was the hot fat collected from the cooking of meat at home. A thrifty housewife – thrifty was a word of praise – saved a large sum by carrying out these manufacturing tasks.

The catering industry was dominated by housewives who – usually without payment – provided the food, plates and cutlery for most of the weddings, reunions, church dinners, Sunday-school picnics, sporting suppers and other social functions held across the land. Of the large sums raised privately for charity in a typical year, a large but hidden component was this contribution from the family's kitchen.

Many wives or their servant – if they could afford one – made soap and candles and herbal medicines. Dresses and shirts and underclothes were made in the home, and socks and jumpers and skirts were knitted. A sewing machine, not requiring electricity or steam, turned a house into a small garment factory. And of course the repairing of clothes – by patching or darning – was a major activity. In most households was a large darning bag full of socks and dresses and shirts that were waiting to be repaired or rejuvenated. Numerous children wore clothes that had been made at home.

Labour-saving devices and machines were few. Not yet invented were the washing machines for dishes and clothes, the house refrigerator and coffee-making machine, the electric toaster and electric jug and hotplate, and other household devices and mechanical aids. In 1890 more than half of the houses in Australia did not use electricity, though in cities most houses had gas pipes that served to provide energy for lighting the rooms.

Cleaning was a major week-long task. Windows were washed, though the typical cottage did not have large windows. Floors and wooden eating tables had to be scrubbed with warm soap and a brush. Mats had to be taken outside and thumped to eliminate the dust. Rooms had to be swept and dusted, for dust and ash appeared more frequently inside a house than they do today: the daily wood fires created ash, while the dust crept in from the unmade streets on windy days. In the unmechanised era the most useful device in the home was a busy pair of hands.

In 1890 a minority of homes employed one or more domestic servants. Hotels too were large employers of women. Indeed many of the owners and managers of hotels were women. Another major employer was the private houses that took in boarders and provided each one with a room or a shared room, and a communal bathroom and lavatory. Their boarders received a hot breakfast and hot dinner on each working day, and three meals on Sunday. Some boarding houses – especially a terrace house that had once belonged to a wealthy family – might hold ten or fifteen boarders.

While no hard statistics are available, perhaps 3 per cent of the workforce of a large city lived in boarding houses at the end of the century. Most were single men who had come from country towns or interstate cities to take on jobs. Bank clerks and office workers might live in one boarding house, skilled workers in another. Country parliamentarians whose income was small preferred to live in a boarding house; and when the first federal parliament met in 1901, the Labor members coming from distant electorates were said mostly to board in East Melbourne or other inner suburbs. A few superior boarding houses took in married couples or single men who held managerial positions. John Monash and his wife were once listed as residing in a boarding house in East Melbourne, perhaps because their own house was being sold or renovated.

For single women, domestic tasks formed the largest source of paid work. A young woman reaching Sydney in 1896 and looking in the front window of a labour or employment office – all were private and not government offices – would see a list of positions and their weekly wage, which usually included free 'board and lodging'. She could apply to be a cook, general servant, housemaid and parlourmaid, kitchenmaid or pantrymaid, laundress, waitress, needlewoman or general housekeeper. A few rich households might employ a governess to teach the children. Early in the 1900s the growth of factories with their higher pay and shorter hours and no weekend work were to attract many women who once would have worked as domestic servants.

CHAPTER SEVEN

Rich and poor:
the economic whirlpool

In Australia the rich were not so conspicuous as in the British Isles and the United States. They did not travel around the city in carriages whose drivers were gaudily dressed or hire their own Pullman carriage when they travelled by rail. The relative scarcity of capable domestic servants, male and female, tended to limit the number of rooms in the mansions. Many of the rich men were pastoralists whose main house was in the country, and either was not in sight of railways or main roads or, if within sight, was shielded by avenues of English trees and tall gums. In Australia another social custom hid the very rich from the public gaze in the nineteenth century: many of the rich returned home and spent their last years in the British Isles. Perhaps they held property here but spent the income overseas. In 1880 a small *Who's Who* could have been compiled of the wealthy Australians who now lived in England and Scotland.

In Europe only a young man with capital, a trusted surname, and thrift, energy and commercial acumen had a chance of making a small fortune by the age of sixty. In Australia, however, a young migrant family could land with no money, a name so disreputable that they changed it, and a feckless improvidence that seemed a liability; but even they had an opportunity of attaining some wealth.

2

If we could piece together a history of the host of people who failed in business ventures and then started again, starting even a third and fourth time, their history would explain – more than the successes – the persisting optimism in the air. So many of the insolvent and the impoverished, the bruised and the pummelled, believed that by their own efforts they would rise again; and we have the opportunity to meet two of them, in their latter years, on the plains of the Wimmera.

Thomas Williams was born in 1826 at Ryde, less than three hours' walk from inner Sydney. After working for twelve years as a carpenter, boy and man, on sheep and cattle stations as remote as the Clarence River in the north and the Canberra district in the south, he set out for California. He spent twelve months on the gold diggings where, he said later, he did 'well'. That poker-faced adverb was often an understatement. Back in Sydney in 1851 he crossed the Blue Mountains to the first gold rushes before becoming one of the first diggers in Bendigo where gold gleamed in shallow holes. He earned the handsome sum of £3000 in the space of seven weeks.

As more fortunes were made from buying and selling than from gold, Williams next became a merchant, buying farm produce in Sydney and selling it in Melbourne. Perhaps even more money could be extracted from fortunate diggers squandering gold

sovereigns in hotels and saloons, and so he opened the Golden
Fleece Hotel. In one year Williams made at least £10 000 – more
than a carpenter could have hoped to earn in three lifetimes.

This quick movement from one occupation to another was typical of the times. Williams moved to a wine and spirits business,
where his run of luck ceased. He lost £14 000 – a fortune – in two
years. The buffetings of his career, however, were far from over.

Meanwhile, a young English immigrant was passing through a
similar apprenticeship of success and failure. Edward Usher was a
Kentish man who migrated to Adelaide in 1849. He set up a brick-
yard and baked bricks, at first with some success. In his own guarded
reminiscences he did not mention what happened to the brick-
yard, but it seems likely that so many builders went to the Victorian
goldfields in the early 1850s that nobody wanted new houses or new
bricks. He too set off for the Victorian goldfields where during
seven months he did 'fairly well'. We would actually need to hear
him speak that phrase to know what was 'fairly well'. He returned
to Adelaide, to learn that his wife had died.

Buying a wagon and team, he loaded it with South Australian
butter, cheese, bran and oats, and travelled the 600 kilometres to
Bendigo. There he learned so many miners had just left for the
Ovens gold rush that the market for his goods was weak. How much
he lost on that speculation he did not reveal. Back in Adelaide he
found another wife and made bricks again. He cannot have prospered because again he set out for the Victorian diggings, that place
of perpetual hope. 'And how did you get on, Mr Usher, in your four
years on the Maryborough gold-field?' His answer, not recorded,
was probably: 'Not quite so well.'

Usher was next heard of, living about 150 kilometres to the
south, at the farming towns of Birregurra and Colac where he followed his old trade as a brickmaker. Once more he fell on poor

times. Injuring his knee and unable to make bricks, he took up shoemaking to support his growing family. How does a brickmaker take readily to shoemaking? One can only marvel at colonial ingenuity. Eventually he turned to that panacea, the small farm. He took up land towards the Otway Ranges and also made boots and shoes in his spare time. Like many farmers he moved to new districts, for the soil, deficient in phosphate, was soon exhausted by several successive years of crops. In 1877 he decided to find a larger farm, and at Peppers Plain in the new wheat belt near Jeparit, with not a high hill in sight, he and his sons grew wheat on the large scale. Being an experienced jack-of-all-trades, he presumably made boots for the children, bricks for the fireplaces and, of course, carted his own bags of wheat to the nearest railway station. By the late 1880s, justifiably proud of his success as a colonial battler, he paid a small fee – along with thousands of other Victorians – for his life story to be published briefly in a massive *Who's Who* of Victorian citizenry, a volume as heavy as a family Bible and still to be found in second-hand bookshops.

There, on the same page, could be read, in small print, the final lines of the erratic story of Thomas Williams, the young Sydney carpenter who had found his way to Melbourne by way of California in the 1850s. After winning and losing small fortunes in the liquor trade, Williams became an auctioneer. Old patrons of the Golden Fleece Hotel must have been surprised to hear his voice extolling the merits of a horse or an armchair but soon the loud voice was going, going, gone. Moving to the gold diggings at Mount Blackwood he built a hotel, which also failed. He was the kind of man who kept on climbing even when the ladder was falling.

He trudged to that mecca of the unconquerable, the newer gold rushes; and for five years he sank shafts. At Chinaman's Flat, near Maryborough, with money either won from gold or borrowed, he made the unpredictable decision to build a theatre. The one-time carpenter could easily build a theatre but running it must have been riskier. He 'did well for a time', we learn. Chinaman's Flat today not only has no theatre but also has no audience; and the initial decline of the population probably closed his theatre.

Williams moved from place to place like a readdressed letter. After five years in the solid gold town of Ararat he ran the Bulls Head Hotel among the vineyards and diggings of the nearby town called Great Western. Finally, in 1875, he went beyond the end of the railway line, and in the tiny wheat town of Rupanyup 'he built the hotel which he now conducts, and in which he is doing a good business'. That was the report of his affairs after thirteen years in the town. He had never been so long in one place. Whether in all his wanderings a wife or partner was with him – or whether she was left behind – he offers no clue.

We leave brickmaker Usher and his sturdy sons at his wheat farm near Jeparit. We leave carpenter Williams presiding over the bar and the dining room of his hotel in the same Wimmera district. Their struggle to be independent, and the manner in which they bounced back after reverses, was repeated in tens of thousands of lives. One such life was that of James Menzies, a skilled tradesman-painter who in 1893 came from Ballarat to run a general store selling groceries and clothes in the town nearest to Usher's wheat farm. His son Robert Gordon Menzies, born one year later in the house behind the store, was to become prime minister.

3

The governments provided few social services. There were no pensions for the old, for widows, for crippled breadwinners or the unemployed. The official view was that charity was not needed in the land of plenty. In most colonies, in the forty years after 1850, poverty was less common – though not less humiliating – than in any country in Europe.

Those few social services that did exist were mainly in institutions: lunatic asylums, hospitals, benevolent asylums for the very old, orphan schools, and homes for the deaf and dumb and the temporarily destitute. Most institutions relied almost as much on voluntary donations as on government support. Most issued a long list of commands that dictated their residents' hour of rising, when they could eat, when they could smoke, when they could visit their dormitory, and what work they had to perform – if capable of work. People tried to keep away from these places. Today, in discussing the disadvantages of Aborigines of that past period, the tendency is to ignore completely the disadvantages suffered by other Australians living near the bottom of the ladder.

The Destitute Asylum in Adelaide, perhaps the oldest of these institutions, stood no nonsense, no malingering. Its residents wore a uniform – if they left the asylum without permission they could easily be identified. They could leave the grounds only on one afternoon of the week. They could receive visitors only on a Wednesday and then only for three hours. If parents were inmates they could see their children once a month. Those who were fit had to do regular work, the women at cooking and sewing, the men at gardening. In 1872 most of the 247 residents were males and were too sick or too old to work. Those who did not wish to enter the asylum could receive outdoor rations if they passed the tests for 'destitution'.

Most parts of the world, Western or Eastern, believed in harsh punishments on those who defied the discipline imposed on them. The schoolroom was disciplined sternly, with physical punishment for those who were troublesome. Behaviour in the street was often disciplined: drunkenness in a public place could lead to a heavy fine or a few days in prison. The emphasis was on personal responsibility. A century later, social rules were to leap to the other extreme, and to enthrone rights rather than responsibilities.

Old people and invalids suffered unduly in Australia. Most possessed no relatives in the whole continent, and therefore during severe sickness or in old age they were thrown onto public charity. Tasmania was first to face this question because it had an unusually high proportion of old people by the last third of the nineteenth century. It simply placed the old and the infirm in 'invalid depots'.

The prevailing creed was that people should be encouraged, through their own hard work and thrift, to save for the rainy day. If the government cared too generously for the old, it would be fostering extravagance in those who were young. When it was alleged that the bedding at the Brickfields Invalid Depot in Tasmania was miserable, a royal commission of 1871 retorted that an attractive poorhouse or invalid asylum would punish those who had been thrifty. It would compel 'the honest self-denying workman', who shunned the public house, to pay an additional tax in order to support those old folk who had once revelled in the public house. This generation was convinced that most of the poor people had only themselves to blame. 'What is the cause of all this pauperism?' enquired a visitor who observed 800 old and destitute women and men at the asylum in New Town. The reply of the superintendent was emphatic: 'Drink, unhesitatingly, drink.'

Since 1890 the prevailing explanations of poverty have tended to swing from the extreme position of placing virtually all blame on the poor and unemployed to the other extreme of placing all blame on society as a whole. A century ago such a swing of considered opinion was inconceivable. Society then could not yet afford to undermine the incentives to hard work and thrift because the standard of living relied on those incentives. Poverty was on no account to be encouraged: otherwise, the poor might multiply. Thus the Hobart Benevolent Society set up a wood yard, and the unemployed young men who sought help were simply handed an axe and paid a few pence hourly to chop firewood. In 1871 the Tasmanian government seriously considered compiling a list of all those who were receiving public charity, and even posting it on the walls of police stations. The aim was partly to humiliate them.

Private generosity was vital, and often impressive. If all the public and private gifts and good works bestowed on the orphans, the poor, insane, sick and old could be added together, they possibly would exceed the government's contributions. Christian churches were the leaders in most of these activities. In every town the clergy also carried out many roles – the listening, the reassuring and visiting – that professional social workers and doctors now fulfil, and were the fundraisers, the volunteers who gave their time.

Occasionally big gifts of private money went overseas: in 1846 a large sum was collected in New South Wales towards the relief of the famine in Ireland and Scotland; and in the early 1860s another large sum was collected to relieve distress in Lancashire when the American Civil War disrupted cotton supplies and closed the textile mills. The severe famine in India in the late 1870s led to relief funds in all the colonies and the contribution of at least £65 000 by February 1878: the sum seems small today but it equalled the weekly wage for about 30 000 Australian workingmen.

In hundreds of workplaces the custom was to send round the hat and collect money for neighbours in trouble. At the back of Bourke about 1890 a lanky shearer named the Giraffe would sometimes take around his wide cabbage-tree hat collecting banknotes and silver coins for the latest casualty or cause: the woman whose husband was drowned in the Bogan flood, a bullocky who was so drunk that he was run over by his own wagon, or the sick jackaroo who had no money to take home to his wife and children waiting in Sydney. Henry Lawson wrote a story about the warm-hearted Giraffe, and it was included in one of his bestselling volumes of short stories, *Send Round the Hat*.

While the hat was being passed from man to man, the women had their own version of sending around the hat: plates of sandwiches, bowls of hot soup, and bundles of second-hand clothes for the poor; the nursing of the sick; and the caring for a neighbour's children when a new child was born. In the farmlands, neighbours might club together to bring in the harvest for a widow whose husband had suddenly died. In many towns at least one storekeeper gave struggling customers an amount of credit, which was far beyond the call of duty; and this helps to explain why grocers were usually high on the list of bankrupt occupations.

By the end of the century a social philosophy applauding mateship and kindness was widely held in the outback, the mining fields, and in thousands of city houses. One verse by Adam Lindsay Gordon, the poet who committed suicide in 1870, appeared again and again in autograph books and keepsakes:

> *Life is mostly froth and bubble,*
> *Two things stand like stone,*
> *Kindness in another's trouble,*
> *Courage in your own.*

4

In the southern half of the continent for several generations most of the stations gave food to swagmen, sundowners and 'travellers' who called there during the course of their journey. In the Riverina in the 1870s most stations gave a large piece of fresh meat and a pannikin of flour to all callers, irrespective of whether they were searching for work or dodging work. Free sugar and tea were often given out. At isolated sheep stations at certain times of the year as many as thirty or fifty men might arrive, usually at about sundown, to receive free rations.

In the outback camaraderie, the mateship was occasionally extended to Chinese, Kanakas and African-Americans in the bush. Many of those men who in life were sometimes treated as outcasts were given a respectable burial. William Lockhart Moreton, a pastoralist, riding near Wilcannia on the Darling River in 1870, chanced to call at a lonely grog shanty just after the Creole cook had died. The cook was a Catholic and, in his last hours, had requested that he be buried on a chosen hill and that he should lie facing the sunrise. The four men at the shanty placed him in a coffin made of thin planks of white pine and carried him to the hill and buried him.

In districts where Chinese had long been settlers, individuals were usually treated sympathetically when they were in distress. Wealthy Chinese, who were known for their own acts of charity, were respected or even venerated by large sections of the public. At their funeral, crowds lined the pavements to see the horse-drawn hearse pass.

The Aborigines received many kindnesses as well as many acts of meanness. Their need for help and a little understanding had never been stronger. Almost everywhere their population was diminishing and it was widely predicted that the race would be extinct within a lifetime. In Tasmania the last local full-blood Aborigine died in May 1876. Named Trucanini she had lived in comfort in Hobart in her last years, smoking her pipe and drinking at bedtime her hot spiced ale. Several other full-blood Tasmanian women still lived far away, on Kangaroo Island, but by 1890 they too were dead. There remained many Tasmanians who were partly Aboriginal, and some proclaimed their pride in that fact.

In nearly every region of the northern half of Australia, the old Aboriginal life was virtually unchanged except perhaps for the arrival of a strange infectious disease, a blunt iron tomahawk or those fragments of glass that served as knife blades. There most Aboriginal adults had not even seen a European and not heard the sound of a gun or seen the wheel marks of a dray. They lived their traditional life with its ingenious way of hunting and gathering food and its old rituals. It was as if there were two distinct and separate Australian worlds – an Aboriginal and a European. It was in about the year 1880 that the traditional world and its way of life no longer prevailed on as much as half of the physical surface of Australia.

The 'in-between' Aboriginal people became the more typical – camping on sheep and cattle stations and sometimes receiving rations from the owners, or clustered in government camps, or sleeping in flimsy shelters on the edges of outback towns, the children rarely attending school and few of the parents regularly working for wages. They were a people lost in their own land but in another sense they were surrounded by relatives and friends, and still sustained – and sometimes divided – by intense family and tribal loyalties not often witnessed in white families.

The governments treated Aborigines with a mixture of neglect and concern. In Victoria where they were few by the 1880s, they usually received more help than did the poorest white people.

5

A little-known episode in South Australia hints at the vast variety of contacts between Aborigines and the newcomers. Pinba, better known as Logic, was a small child in the Cooper Creek region in 1861 when the explorers Burke and Wills died there. As a young man he was convicted of murdering a white stockman in self-defence and spent nearly five years in Yatala Prison in Adelaide, a model prisoner, before he tried to escape. He was fired at by the guards but no bullet hit him. So he began on foot the long journey towards his arid homeland.

Travelling by night he covered long distances. He kept to the side roads or the unfenced bushland, knowing that police and black trackers were already searching for him. On his long journey north he was helped by people on the farms through which he passed. At different places he was given a blanket for his bedding, boots for his bare feet, and a butcher's knife and tomahawk with which to cut food. Drinking water, tea and food were handed to him, and gifts of such luxuries as tobacco and even a second-hand brown tweed suit were gladly accepted. So that he could carry water he skinned a possum and made a waterbag from the skin. To inhale smoke from his clay pipe might have attracted attention in the night, so he chewed rather than smoked tobacco. Day and night, he had to be alert.

He did not always disguise his whereabouts. At farmhouses he sometimes told people that his name was Logic, even before he asked for 'tucker'. Presumably a few farmers later told the police that the wanted man, with brown suit and bare feet, was in their area. Others preserved his secret. By all accounts he remained positive and cheerful during his eight weeks of walking and hiding.

In the Flinders Ranges, he was recaptured and taken in the train to Adelaide and the prison. But such was the public clamour that he should be treated with justice and mercy that the premier, John W. Downer, successfully recommended that he be released; and at Christmas 1885 the hardy Aborigine began his return journey by train and foot to his homeland. Such sympathy and compassion were more likely to be shown in South Australia.

We cannot understand this period of history until we put aside our modern concern for human rights and for privacy. In this period no excuses were accepted in many sections of society. Personal responsibility was an axiom, and applied in ways that would now be seen as unfair and even outrageous. Here in 1869 is a newspaper reporting how a prisoner, accepting his sentence of death, offered no excuses. Aged twenty-five and born in England, James Ritson had been a costermonger selling vegetables on the streets of Melbourne until he committed his first murder. Readers were told that at seven on the morning of his execution he had to be awakened from a sound sleep, how he washed for the last time, how his irons were knocked from his legs, how he requested and received more than the standard prisoner's breakfast, and how he acknowledged – to the clergymen who consoled him – that his sentence was just. When he was led to the gallows and the cap was pulled over his eyes and the official hangman shook his hand, the prisoner had a last request. He wished the cap to be removed so that he could have one last look at the world. His wish was granted. Such reports usually added details of the pain accompanying the dying seconds of the hanged man or woman.

6

As the welfare state did not exist, people had to save money with which to meet emergencies. The purchase of a house was one form of security practised more widely in Australian cities than in England. In 1891 four of every ten Melbourne householders and three of every ten Sydney householders owned or were buying their house. Likewise in the cities the lodges and friendly societies provided funeral benefits and a pension for a widow, or a small income when a breadwinner was sick. After the creation in 1848 of the famous Australian Mutual Provident Society in Sydney, a cooperative company owned by Australians, life-assurance policies soared.

Other mutual societies entered the field, and in the 1870s the National Mutual pioneered new forms of insurance that gave the policyholder a protection such as no society in any other land provided. New clients no longer had to forfeit policies when, through sickness or poverty, they were unable to continue their quarterly payments. Presbyterians set up the Australian Widows' Fund and the Rechabites set up the T & G Society to favour, with cheaper rates, those customers who abstained from alcohol. The big Australian companies with their branches in every colony and New Zealand outbid the old British companies for new members; and in 1886 the Colonial Mutual Life Assurance Society, a Melbourne newcomer, even began to sell policies vigorously in London, in competition with the AMP.

Travelling salesmen and lecturers spread the message that insurance was the way to prepare for old age. American companies, hearing about this country where a higher proportion of the people took out insurance policies than in the United States or Canada or Great Britain, arrived in the 1880s. The Equitable Life spent £363 000 on a block of land, perhaps the most expensive block so far purchased in Australia. At the corner of Collins and Elizabeth streets in Melbourne arose its granite and marble palace dedicated to thrift and forethought. At that time perhaps one-quarter of the country's population was covered by life insurance.

For people in trouble the government was the helper of last resort; until its taxation system was transformed it could do little to ease social and economic distress. And the taxation system was not likely to be reformed quickly because most people believed that high taxes discouraged savings and self-reliance.

We are so accustomed to the idea that the rich should pay much higher taxes than the poor that we forget that the idea was a late-comer to Australia. Whereas the United Kingdom imposed an income tax on the wealthier citizens and also estate duties on the landed gentry, Australia in 1860 collected nearly all its taxes indirectly. The main taxes were the import duties on opium, tobacco, alcoholic spirits and other luxuries, the excise duties collected from Australian distilleries, and the tax that was collected from those who exported or dug for gold. Few of these taxes weighed more heavily on the rich than on the humble labourer.

The largest single source of government revenue was the windfall income, which each colony gained from the sale of its public lands. That income could not last forever. Indeed, the decline in revenue from land sales was often the spur to collecting new taxes. Victoria, Tasmania and South Australia were the first to see their revenue from land sales dwindling dangerously, and significantly they were quick to impose new taxes on the assets and income of the wealthy and, before long, the not-so-wealthy.

Tasmania has long been singled out by historians as an unusually conservative colony but it initiated the income tax. In 1880, faced by a heavy deficit, it imposed a tax of ninepence in the pound – or roughly 3.5 per cent – on that part of a person's income earned from such pieces of property as shares and houses. South Australia in 1884 went a step further and imposed the first Australian tax on income earned through personal exertion. From this tax the big majority of people were exempt because somebody earning less than £300 a year paid no tax.

The new income tax aroused indignation. One politician in New South Wales denounced it as the work of Satan. 'If,' he said, 'the Devil had sent a representative here to institute a means of destroying the morality of the people, he could have found no better instrument than an Income Tax.' He was simply suggesting in his exaggerated way that thrifty and diligent people provided jobs and created wealth, and that an income tax was an act of theft.

The citizens of the two most populous colonies, Victoria and New South Wales, were entirely spared the income tax until 1895, a year of depression. Even then their average wage-earner paid no income tax. The direct taxes on wealth kept on growing. Negligible in 1860, they yielded perhaps one-fifth of the government's tax revenue by 1901 and were to supply more than half by 1941, a wartime year. The welfare state – understandably, hungry for taxes – had found a special home in Australia, and large numbers of families rejoiced.

7

In the forty years since the discovery of gold the economic progress – progress was an incantation more than a word – had been swift. The population was now three million, having been multiplied by seven. Parliaments, juries and free institutions had taken root in a land that back in 1850 still bowed, on most major issues, to decisions made in London. The new machinery and the gadgetry of ease could be seen everywhere – in the railways that stretched far inland, the tall blocks of offices in larger cities, the ships and cranes at the wharves, the gasworks, the refrigeration chambers, and the hydraulic power that propelled the passenger lifts to the upper floors of the new hotels. The standard of living had so improved that a housewife in the larger cities, with such household amenities as gas and running water and a sewing machine, probably had more comfort than the typical housewife in almost every other city in the world. The thousands of schools and churches, the high circulation of daily and weekly newspapers, the abundance of leisure in the towns, the relative sense of social security, the ease of travel in steamships and trains, the larger and more weatherproof houses – these were advances that, added together, were to dwarf the slow material gains of the following half-century.

An unusual blend of circumstances had created this age of prosperity. Perhaps the strongest piston of prosperity was the abundance of new natural resources. Australia's pace of development owed much to the wide grasslands, the virgin soil ready to grow cereals, the untapped deposits of gold and copper, coal and tin and silver-lead, and to the forests that yielded building materials and firewood. Here was a bonanza, and most of its choicest parts were used for the first time between 1840 and 1890. These natural resources had been little used in the Aboriginal epoch but in the half-century to 1890 they were exploited, often with energy and ingenuity. Rarely in history had people explored, occupied and used such a vast terrain so quickly.

The strenuous application of new techniques was possibly the second piston of the long era of prosperity. Much of the prosperity came from fatter cattle and heavier fleeces and more appropriate breeds of wheat. It came from hundreds of labour-saving devices, from the post-and-rail fences that replaced the shepherds, from the wire fences that replaced post-and-rail fences, from the corrugated-iron spouting and water tanks, from the artesian bores and the creaking windmills that supplied underground water on the plains, and the new irrigation schemes of the 1880s. Fewer hands produced more wheat because of new ploughs, mechanical harvesters and the travelling steam threshing machines. At harvest time, in the kitchens of the larger farms, the dining table seated perhaps only ten men where once there were thirty, and those ten men with the aid of horsepower and steam power did more work each day than the vanished team of thirty.

A former miner who revisited a large goldmine in 1890 would hardly have recognised the mode of work. Thirty years earlier he had climbed down ladders to reach his working place but now he was whisked down the shaft in a safety cage that travelled more rapidly than a lift in the latest city building. Powerful pumps dewatered the workings; dynamite and other powerful explosives had superseded the old blasting powder; and in the latest mines mechanical rock drills were beginning to replace hand-hammers in the drilling of holes. That the new rock drill was filling the still underground air with particles of sharp dust and ruining the lungs of many miners was not yet recognised.

Almost everywhere steam was doing work that was once performed by the sheer physical strength of teams of workers. Visitors to the mills and factories saw the steam or smoke from a distance, heard the throb of the pistons and crushers and mills, and once inside they saw a crisscross of overhead belting that conveyed the energy from the working engine to the scattered machines. Those who did not visit factories knew, from the advertisements in newspapers and the painted signs on delivery carts, that this foodstuff or that commodity was now miraculously made by labour-saving machines driven by steam. Eat our steam biscuits. Take your suit to our steam laundry. Most steam was produced by firewood in the interior or coal on the coast, and by the 1880s nearly a thousand ships a year carried the coal away from Newcastle. There on the crowded wharves the handling of the coal was increasingly mechanised, as readers of *A New Geography for Australian Pupils* learned in 1885: 'The noise is stunning, for yonder come trucks of coal running down to the edge of the water. Great cranes seize them, whirl them into the air, swing them over the hold of the vessel, turn them upside down, and so empty coal into the ships below.'

By 1890 the fast steamship dominated the passenger routes to Europe, and the long and often stormy voyage past Cape Horn had given way to the calmer passage across the Indian Ocean to the Suez Canal and the Mediterranean. The international tele-graph was now the fastest way of sending important news. Within the larger cities the trams, trains and cabs provided cheap and regular transport in streets where, in the late 1840s, nearly every-body walked and only the wealthy could call on riding horses or a horse and carriage. And in capital cities the first telephones were installed in the decade 1878 to 1887, though calls outside the city were still impossible.

Mechanised transport now saved human labour on a huge scale. In a continent possessing few navigable rivers and no inland canals, the railway was the miracle. When the railway between Melbourne and Sydney was completed in 1883, and a banquet of food was set out in the locomotive shed at Albury under the new Edison elec-tric light, the New South Wales premier, Alexander Stuart, publicly recalled the early ways of inland travel. Thirty-one years ago he had ridden horses day and night in order to complete the overland jour-ney from Sydney to Melbourne in six and a half days. To return by sea, he recalled, was longer. A clipper ship, becalmed day after day, only reached Sydney after sixteen days. His audience laughed. Now the iron horse made the journey in one day and night.

A railway so cheapened the cost of transport that it created industries where previously there were none. It gave birth to dis-tant wheatlands and new dairying districts, and opened forests to the timber-miller. It enabled low-grade or remote mining fields to treat ores that, without a railway, were unpayable. It saved pastoral districts in time of drought and sent their wool quickly to market. Between 1875 and 1891 the railways expanded from 2500 kilometres to more than 16 000.

Old modes of transport were also used more effectively. Draught horses of improved breeds replaced bullocks, and farmers used large teams to pull the plough, thus reducing the labour costs for each hectare. In the dry outback the camel was introduced at first by explorers and then by carriers. Sir Thomas Elder, a rich pastoralist, imported 124 camels and thirty-one 'Afghan' camel men in 1865 from the port of Karachi in the present Pakistan, and the pack camels increasingly became carriers of wool, station supplies, mining equipment, and food and alcohol in the dry outback. At one time half of the continent and its sparse, struggling population relied on pack camels.

In 1850 the central streets of only one city, Sydney, were illuminated by gas lamps, but by 1890 most towns of a few thousand people were so lit. In smaller towns household lamps burning kerosene – a word coined in 1854 – supplanted the old tallow candles in the sitting room. A whole range of night meetings and activities had become more convenient, night work had become safer, and in most houses people could read or sew at night without undue strain to their eyes; gaslight and kerosene lamps were thus the allies of compulsory education. By the early 1880s the electric light was the latest fashion, and audiences in the theatres rejoiced that it was cooler than gas in summer and caused fewer headaches. The heyday of electric power still lay far ahead.

Machines entered offices. The first effective typewriter – the vigorous competitor of handwriting – was the product of Remington, a New York firm that made breach-loading rifles for the soldiers in the American Civil War and then, the war ending, had to look for new tasks for its engineering equipment. Only a few of these heavy, clattering machines were employed in Australian offices by 1880, for women were slow to be entrusted with the machine that became their speciality. Banks and life-insurance offices were reluctant to employ women, and expected them to retire permanently when they married.

Australia had its own inventors, mostly men of little schooling who fastened their mind on new problems and would not let
go. In the farmlands, hundreds of part-time inventors devised new
or improved old machines. South Australians between the 1840s
and 1870s invented a range of simple machines that prepared, tilled
and harvested the wheatlands with more speed and less labour.
They invented the stripper, which, drawn by horses through the tall
wheat crop, combed the wheat from the stalk and partly threshed
it. They invented the heavy iron-roller, which toppled and crushed
the Mallee scrub. They invented the stump-jump plough, which
neatly jumped over buried roots still left in the roughly cleared
ground, and they made iron ploughs and drills that were more
suited to hard dry soils. Victorians in the 1880s led in developing
the combine harvester, a machine that now harvests much of the
world's wheat.

In Geelong the newspaper editor James Harrison was a brilliant pioneer of mechanical refrigeration but was almost too far
ahead of his time. His important cargo of hard-frozen meat was
shipped to London in 1873 in the sailing ship *Norfolk,* which possessed no refrigerating plant and so could not adequately preserve
the meat. In the 1870s a young Melbourne watchmaker, Louis
Brennan, invented a retrievable torpedo, which he eventually sold
to the War Office in London for the huge sum of £110 000. In
Sydney in 1893 Lawrence Hargrave, son of a Sydney judge, made
a vital step in aeronautical engineering when he invented the box
kite, thus advancing knowledge of the vital question of how a
flying machine could be made stable while in flight. And a decade later the young Melbourne engineer A. G. M. Michell was
working on his revolutionary device, the thrust bearing, without
which the huge ocean liners, oil tankers and battleships would be
impracticable.

8

A willingness to use and experiment with machinery was thus one of the causes of the high standard of living. A mountain of commodities produced by few hands: that was the secret of colonial Australia's prosperity. In turn the willingness to import or invent machines was spurred by the frequent shortage of labour and the abundance of capital. British capital financed much of the mechanisation, including the railways, with long-term loans raised in London at 3, 4 or 5 per cent. Part of our prosperity rested on borrowed money.

Other factors promoted prosperity. The years 1850 to 1890 were unusually peaceful; Britain fought in only one major war, the Crimean War lasting from 1853 to 1856, and it was short and victorious. All the dislocations of a major war were thus avoided. Moreover in this long period most of the cost of defending Australian ports and sea lanes was still paid by the British taxpayer. After Britain withdrew its garrisons in 1870 the Australian colonies had to supply their own little armies, which mainly consisted of part-time volunteers.

One spur to the high prosperity was not appreciated at the time. From the late 1840s to 1890, the main rural districts experienced favourable weather, if measured against the following half-century. We are only now beginning to realise how favourable was the climate in the south-eastern corner of Australia for those grazing and cropping industries that were so important then to economic life.

Some of these advantages promoting material progress were squandered. There was a zest for taking risks that leaped beyond the bounds of common sense. Thousands of useless mining shafts were sunk on the basis of airy hypotheses and blind rather than reasoned speculations, and steam engines were installed at mines that possessed no ore to crush. Thousands of new farms were large enough for England but too small for Australia and much of the work on those farms was wasted. In good years in the far outback, pastoralists were tempted into country so poor that in the end they had to retreat. Railways were built to districts that did not have enough traffic – and never would have enough – to pay for the trains. Breakwaters and stone harbour works and long piers were built for ports that then faded away. Permanent towns were built on goldfields and then the gold ran out, leaving fine churches, schools, banking chambers, shops and even town halls to serve only a fraction of the people for whom they were built. Risks were inevitable in the process of opening new natural resources but many of the risks taken were extravagant.

In the cities mistakes were also made, perhaps even on a larger scale. A normal city can cover up its 'ghost towns' and abandoned factories but in Melbourne the ghost suburbs were too widespread to be concealed when the gargantuan building boom of the 1880s came to a halt.

The standard of material life would have grown even more quickly but for a changing rhythm of work. The hours of work in city jobs and in mines and in railway camps were tending to decline. Many people reached the stage where they preferred more leisure to more money. The warm summer climate placed a premium on leisure. So too did the high proportion of single men who, having no family to care for, could live comfortably on their wages – so long as they retained their job. The preference for leisure often raised the enjoyment of life and here the spectator sports had a popularity that was virtually unparalleled. In 1886, by the lake in South Melbourne, a crowd of 34000 attended an Australian Rules football match when Geelong was the visiting team. Probably no such crowd hitherto had attended a football match in England, the home of soccer; at the FA Cup Final a larger crowd was not reported until the 1890s. Noticeable in Australia were the women who thronged to sporting events, even football matches.

Already a crowd of 100 000 is said to have seen the running of the annual Melbourne Cup, and eighty-four special trains carried spectators to the racecourse in 1888. Such an enormous crowd was possible because spectators could see the field of racehorses from the distant Scotchman's Hill as well as from the grandstands at Flemington below. In Sydney the long sloping shorelands of the harbour and Parramatta River held even larger crowds who – mostly without the expense of an admission fee – could watch the professional scullers whenever world championships came to Australia. The two largest funerals in the nineteenth century were those of a professional sculler (Henry Searle) in Sydney and a jockey (Tommy Corrigan) in Melbourne.

Inevitably the attitude to leisure permeated the attitude to work. This is a fact to be observed rather than deplored. Why should Australians continue to work their heart out simply because in the British Isles that had been the only way in which an honest man could feed and clothe his family?

The declining tempo of work was most visible in the cities. The grinding, exhausting labour belonged more to rural occupations, to people who were still their own bosses, and to many housewives caring for large families. In 1890 most rural people worked a least sixty hours a week, and others even worked eighty. A typical farm labourer worked long hours for low wages and had to live in a shed or hut on the farm. He belonged to no trade union. He had few leisure hours except perhaps Sunday afternoon. On the dairy farms, which multiplied late in the nineteenth century, the children were also hard toilers once they reached the age of eight or nine. On a weekday they might milk cows for two or more hours in the early morning, walk to school, and after leaving the schoolroom at 4 p.m.

they returned home and milked cows again until perhaps 7 p.m. At the weekend they continued to milk the cows, rejoicing that they did not have to attend school. The mechanical milking machine lay far in the future.

Many men and a few women were professional cargo carriers who carried on their backs the heavy bags of flour and sugar to the hill farms. In pioneering districts with a high rainfall the mud was thick on all the new roads in winter. Occasionally a passenger who wished to reach a nearby hotel was physically carried there, and his luggage too. He was carried not by a horse or vehicle but by a strong man.

In the hilly districts not too far from the coast, packhorses carried heavy loads along tracks that were too steep for a horse and dray. At the small ports south of Sydney lines of packhorses arrived with a keg of homemade butter balanced on each side of the horse. Further south, bullocks did not haul a cart but were fitted with packs that could carry iron pots and other heavy items up steep hills. The man who drove these pack animals had to be strong. On the expanding wheatfields machines harvested the wheat, but the wheat was stored in heavy bags that had to be lifted onto men's shoulders and carried to the wagon. The forklift truck had not been invented; the light crane was too expensive except for busy wharves. People who were human workhorses did not have to watch their calories. Photographs of people hard at work in 1890 usually show lean faces.

In the cities a waning pressure of work was recorded. Sir Richard Tangye, owner of a large engineering works in Birmingham, made his fourth visit to Australia in 1886; and in his diary he expressed unease at the casual approach to work in what he called 'the land for my lord the workingman'. He claimed that in the city the workman did a small amount of work each day. The word that fell from his frothing lips was 'scandalous'. It was a time of mild economic slump in Sydney and he was vexed to hear the unemployed, in calling on the government for work, demanding the standard wage of eight shillings a day. He said that they should be willing to work for less. When the government arranged for a free train to convey the unemployed to the country to grub out tree stumps, more than half of the train was empty. Where, he enquired, were the remainder of 'these scoundrels'? Tangye thought that he knew where they could be found: 'lying on the grass in the public parks, and smoking short pipes'. He noted in his diary that the unemployed here preferred to pick and choose rather than to pick and shovel. In contrast, he heard with pleasure of an eighteen-year-old Essex migrant who was rising each morning at five o'clock to groom four horses, driving a cart to market to collect greengroceries, eating no breakfast until he returned to his master's shop, and finishing his day at eight in the evening.

Visitors who saw the working habits of many Australians were peeping into the future and not liking it. Admittedly, Tangye had the bias of an old man and a factory-owner. He was also more likely to see idleness when he was overseas than in England where workers, knowing whom he was, worked busily in his presence and then slowed down after he had been escorted from the factory floor. And yet he could not be dismissed as an unsympathetic observer of workingmen. After all, he had been one of the first owners in Birmingham to give his employees a holiday on Saturday afternoons.

9

The forty years had been blessed by an unusual assortment of advantages. We had virgin soil, rich mineral deposits and many untouched natural resources to reward the first comers. We did not have to depend on one dominating export, and so we did not stumble if the price of that export fell. We were quick to adopt or adapt the new ideas of a great era of invention in the North Atlantic. We were at peace with the outside world, and in the more populous parts of the country the weather was relatively favourable. Throughout the forty years the world's richest moneylender, Great Britain, sent out capital, enabling us to enjoy a high standard of living at the very time when we were spending heavily on railways and reservoirs, on opening up the land, on the building of towns and a variety of debt-incurring works.

Through hard striving by people in every section of society and through an unusual combination of conditions the country had achieved much. But now the striving in boardrooms and in offices as well as on work floors was easing a little, at the very time when the other advantages were falling away. And the pride in the forty years of achievement was itself a hazard, because serious setbacks were virtually unimaginable and therefore would be more damaging when eventually they arrived.

CHAPTER EIGHT

Sugar, pearls and 'the coming of the light'

In the nineteenth century vital decisions that shaped the politics of today were made quickly by politicians and civil servants on the banks of the River Thames. They largely drew the political map of Australia. They determined how many colonies should exist and where their boundaries should run.

In the generation between 1825 and 1859, English politicians were not afraid of drawing boundaries and proclaiming new capital cities in what they called Australasia. They created seven separate colonies and abolished one, the now-forgotten colony of Northern Australia.*

Even more colonies were likely. During the remainder of the century Australia's population increased from one to three million, but no more colonies were created. Whereas the westward

---

* The new colonies were Tasmania (1825), Western Australia (1829), South Australia (1834, but first settled in 1836), New Zealand (1841), Northern Australia (1847), Victoria (1851) and Queensland (1859).

movement of people across the United States of America was accompanied by the creation of a jigsaw of new states, in Australia the movement of people into new territory between 1860 and 1900 created no new colonies.

2

The British government had long envisaged a string of separate colonies around the coast of Australia. It saw no reason why eventually tropical Australia should not also have a string of colonies as its population multiplied. It was even willing to create the first colony in tropical Australia before that vast region held even 300 white people. In London in 1846 William Ewart Gladstone, the young secretary of state for the colonies, decided that a new penal colony should be centred on the coast of central Queensland. George Barney, a military engineer who in Sydney had begun the building of the present Victoria Barracks, was sent north to found the colony.

Colonel Barney was proud to be lieutenant-governor of a colony larger than Western Australia. His rule formally covered all of the present Queensland except the far south. The sandy beaches of Fraser Island were within his command but Gympie and the Sunshine Coast were just outside. His domain extended as far west as Uluru, and as far north as Torres Strait. If it had remained – instead of the present Queensland – a strong northern colony, it would have exerted profound effects. It would have served tropical economic interests. It would probably have become a stronghold of indentured coloured labour even into the twentieth century.

As the capital city of northern Australia, Barney selected what is now the aluminium port of Gladstone, in a southern corner of his colony. There on 30 January 1847, in front of his wife and daughters and a cluster of perspiring officials and a swarm of mosquitoes, he proclaimed the birth of a new colony. It was elaborately planned; pardoned or well-behaved convicts were to come as the labour force; the members of its legislative council were formally named; and even the first government gazette was issued, in clear hand-writing. In equally clear handwriting, in a sealed envelope in a locked despatch box aboard an Australia-bound ship, was another letter that – unknown to Barney – announced that the colony was to be abandoned. In London, Gladstone had been replaced by Lord Grey. It was almost as simple as that.

Lord Grey himself liked the idea of forming new Australian colonies; the only question was when and where. In May 1849 in London a committee of the Privy Council reported that the 'most cursory inspection' of the maps and charts of Australia indicated that, as the population spread out, new colonies should be created, mainly by separating them from existing colonies. The commit-tee could think of few stronger social evils than the tendency for remote settlers to have no vote and no influence if they lived far from the capital city. In calling for the creation of a new south-ern colony ('on which we would humbly advise that your Majesty should be graciously pleased to confer the name of Victoria') they noted that Sydney and Melbourne not only had different climates and natural resources but lay at 'a great distance from each other'. On such arguments Victoria was created in 1851.

As even Melbourne and Sydney seemed to be far apart, that was a clear argument for creating more colonies. In December 1859 the colony of Queensland was born. It held 23 500 white people, and a much larger number of Aborigines.

The first parliament in Brisbane governed a colony that was smaller by about one-sixth than the present Queensland. A long rectangle of territory in the far west of the present Queensland was still nominally part of New South Wales. The site of the Gulf port of Normanton lay just inside Queensland, by only a few kilometres. But the present mining city of Mount Isa and also the inland Birdsville and coastal Burketown were part of that elongated rectangle that in theory was still governed from Sydney rather than from Brisbane. No white settlers lived permanently in that Carpentaria rectangle. Curiously, when the explorers Burke and Wills made their final dash to the Gulf of Carpentaria, they travelled through this remote rectangular outpost of New South Wales. They reached the marshy shores of the Gulf in February 1861, one month before they were transferred to Brisbane's realm by virtue of a document signed in London. Thus with a stroke of the pen Queensland was enlarged by about one-sixth.

Another vast expanse of the tropics awaited a ruler. The Northern Territory – not yet known by that name – belonged to no colony until July 1863 when South Australia took it over. In the following year it appointed Boyle Finniss, a former premier, as the inaugural ruler. His first settlement at Adam Bay was abandoned in 1867, to be replaced two years later by Port Darwin.

Of Darwin's many defects the first was simple: it was too far away. There was no overland road from Darwin to Adelaide. There was not even a railway until 2001; and so for long the main contact was by sea. And yet Darwin, by sea, was further from Adelaide than from any other capital city.

3

An east–west line drawn between Carnarvon in Western Australia and Bundaberg in Queensland divides Australia in half, but all the capital cities lie south of the line. The south still rules the north.

This might not have mattered if the northern half possessed its own advantages. But the northern half was hotter and less attractive for European immigration. Its problems and obstacles were unusual and required their own solutions. Alas, the entire northern half of Australia, by 1863, was governed by three remote cities – Perth and Adelaide and Brisbane – that were likely to prescribe southern solutions for northern problems. This was the equivalent of warm Athens governing cold Oslo, or warm Cairo governing snowy Moscow.

For the first time, a sustained effort was made to settle the more promising parts of tropical Australia. Goldfields, pearling ports, sugar plantations and pastoral districts were opened in scattered parts of the vast north. The question of whether separate colonies should be created there now rested with Australian governments in the south as well as with the government in London. Naturally the Australian governments were reluctant to support secession movements that deprived them of status and potential wealth. Likewise the British government was not likely to offer support if it thereby antagonised public opinion in the temperate zone of Australia. For London to encourage a 'home rule' movement in, say, north Queensland might, by implication, ignite that more explosive issue: should Ireland also be granted 'home rule'?

In the Northern Territory, the few white settlers were even more remote from a seat of government. In 1886 its lonely port of Darwin held about 200 Europeans, 700 Chinese and numerous Aborigines but sent no parliamentarian to Adelaide – a sea journey lasting almost one month.

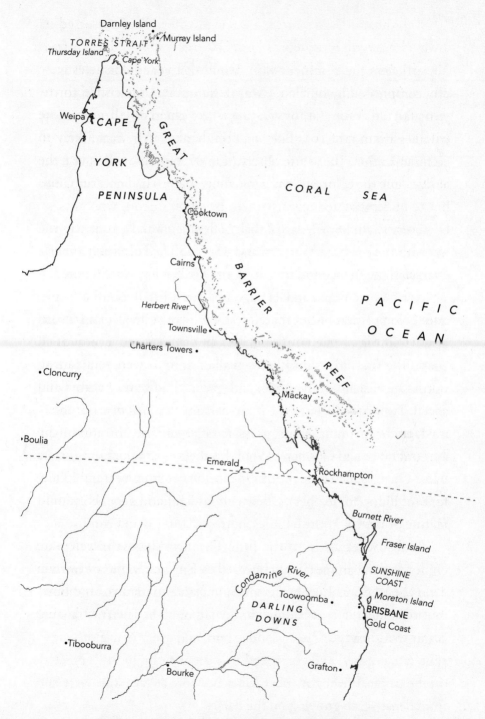

Queensland, from Torres Strait to Darling Downs

4

Nevertheless the continent was shrinking. Every colony was quietly compressed by quicker, cheaper transport. In less than thirty
years the old argument for creating a long chain of self-governing
colonies around the coastline had been weakened by faster lines of
communication. The astute observation of 1849 was no longer true;
at that time the colonists living in remote regions had no alternative
but to be represented in parliament by city residents 'who possess
but a very slight knowledge of their constituents and a faint sympathy with their peculiar pursuits and wants'. So had occurred a sharp
change in the theory and folk wisdom of remote representation.

North Queensland and its huge area surely had to become a separate colony. It was one of the success stories of British colonisation,
despite all the obstacles of climate and distance and a reef-lined
coast. The first flocks and herds walked into or were shipped to
north Queensland in about 1861 and spread almost everywhere with
speed. Twenty years later the huge pastoral stations or runs occupied, at cheap annual rents, grasslands larger than the combined
area of France and Germany. Wool was their most valuable product.
Most Queensland cattle produced income not from beef but in the
form of hides (for leather), tallow (for fat) and horns for the manufacture of British knife-handles, buttons, lanterns and combs.

In 1880 beef came to the fore. The first successful cargo of
chilled Australian meat was conveyed to England in the steamship
Strathleven. Soon Europe became a massive market for the beef,
mutton and lamb that had previously fed only the few Australians.
Sugar was already a Queensland export, and every year more sugar
cane was crushed and converted to a sugar syrup in mills erected
on the tropical river flats near Mackay. More sugar farms were cut
from dense scrub growing on the flats.

A string of sugar and gold ports arose along the northern coast. Mackay was a sugar town; Townsville was the site of a boiling-down works and then the port for the pastoral country and the deep goldfield of Charters Towers, which, discovered in 1872, became Queensland's second-largest town for some years. Further north in the 1870s Cairns was founded by a publican as the port for the Hodgkinson goldfield, and Cooktown became the river-port of the Palmer goldfield with sixty-two grog shops for the European diggers and a host of shops and opium dens for those Chinese who crowded into some of the more northerly goldfields.

When the sugar cane was tall and ripe, it was cut by labourers imported under contract from the Pacific Islands. Most came from the New Hebrides (now Vanuatu), the Solomons and other nearby Pacific Islands and were called Kanakas. They arrived – some had been kidnapped – worked hard, and went home when their contract expired. It is sometimes called slavery, but by most definitions it was not. In the early years the death rate was high, but replacements came from the same islands. They enabled Queensland to outstrip New South Wales as the heart of the sugar industry.

For much of the nineteenth century, the climate of north Queensland was believed to harmful, especially for people of European descent. Accordingly the white people living and working there had to pay a high annual fee for life assurance. This was in keeping with the practice of British life-insurance companies, most of which charged a high annual sum to any overseas member or client living in or near the tropics. Likewise the biggest local company, AMP, initially charged those living within 25 degrees of the equator a high fee. At first the policyholders living at Bundaberg in Queensland and Carnarvon in Western Australia paid that excessive fee, as did those living in Cooktown, Darwin and other towns nearer the equator.

The medical belief persisted that white people doing hard manual labour under the tropical sun thereby shortened their life. All around the globe, cotton and cane sugar were produced by coloured labourers, not only because they accepted lower pay but because their bodies were said to be acclimatised. Most Australian sugar-growers, if they were to compete in the world market, had to adopt the same policy. In the canefields on the tropical coast of Queensland – but not further south – only dark-skinned people were employed. Other parts of Queensland saw these South Seas or Kanaka workers as a potential danger to living standards. One major political party – led by Samuel Griffith, a brilliant Brisbane lawyer – threatened to ban the import of more Kanakas. With such a ban, however, the sugar industry in the tropical north faced decline, even ruin. One solution was for north Queensland to break away, and so cease to be governed by the parliament in Brisbane.

The secessionists became vocal in north Queensland, especially in the port of Townsville where in 1882 they formed a Separation League. Mainly people of the sugar towns, they were alarmed when in 1885 the parliament in Brisbane gave notice that the importing of Kanaka labour would eventually cease. Promptly a petition of protest with 10 006 signatures was sent from north Queensland to Queen Victoria, pleading that she permit them to form a separate colony.

The British government was not impressed. It rejected arguments that, a few decades earlier, it would have found persuasive. Its final reply was that a region should not be permitted to secede unless the parliament of that colony gave its consent. In terms of such a reply neither Victoria nor Queensland would have gained self-government a few decades earlier.

5

One of north Queensland's dynamic politicians was the pale-faced, intense Irishman named John Murtagh Macrossan who, arriving to dig for gold, became a businessman, newspaper owner and cabinet minister. Willing to compromise, he tended to prefer coloured labour on the coastal sugar lands and white labour on the inland goldfields of north Queensland. In 1890 in Brisbane he lost his motion for secession by the narrow margin of thirty-two votes to twenty-six. Two years later, the legislative assembly voted in favour of separate lower houses for north and south Queensland with a common upper house to which each would send representatives. This idea, however, was defeated in the legislative council.

A year later came the bank crashes and a depression that fatally weakened the secessionists and strengthened those who believed in One Queensland. Soon the political mood in Australia itself – and Queensland too – was swinging. The federating of the Australian colonies, not the creation of new ones, was the goal.

6

The Torres Strait Islands – crucial to the proposed colony of North Queensland – lay between the northern tip of Queensland and the nearer coast of New Guinea. Stepping stones to Australia, mostly sandy but a few volcanic, about twenty were inhabited permanently. Their people, Melanesians, had lived there for perhaps 3000 years. Compared to Aborigines on the nearby mainland they were mere newcomers.

The Islanders practised a humbler version of the revolution resulting from the domestication of plants and animals. They lived in permanent houses surrounded by bamboo palisades, and wherever the volcanic soil was rich they grew coconuts and bananas, yams, taro, sweet potatoes, sugar cane, plantains and other produce in neat gardens. Unlike the people of New Guinea they did not keep pigs but were skilled in harvesting shellfish and netting or spearing fish, turtles and the massive dugong. These heavy grey mammals lived in shallow tropical waters, suckled their offspring with their own fresh milk, and gave birth – under the sea – to a single calf at intervals as long apart as five years.

Bold boatmen, the Torres Strait Islanders built large outrigger canoes that were superior to the sturdiest Aboriginal vessels. When the English naval explorer Matthew Flinders was near Murray Island (known in the local language as Mer) in about 1803, three decorative outrigger canoes crewed by some forty or fifty men approached his ship, giving Flinders time to admire their sailing skills: 'how these long canoes keep the wind, and make such good way as they do, without any sail, I am at a loss to know'. On the following day another seven long canoes, including one or two from nearby Darnley Island (Erub), came into sight, their sailors eager for nails and anything else made of iron.

For centuries, the Torres Strait Islanders had traded with the nearer Papuan and Australian coasts. Later they joined Sydney traders in collecting the local trepang or sea cucumber that in distant China was prized as a delicacy, and in 1869 the discovery of pearls opened a glittering era in which Islanders were paid to dive for the pearl shells. The islands were firmly on the commercial map.

Then came the preachers. Representing the London Missionary Society, their Protestant evangelical empire already spread from Tahiti to Sydney. Their practice was to recruit native preachers, Bible-readers and translators, and their wives too, from various Pacific Islands and equip them as pathfinders to distant shores. The

Torres Strait Islands were to form the beachhead from which they set out to win converts in nearby New Guinea.

On the evening of Saturday 1 July 1871, Reverend Samuel Macfarlane and six Polynesian helpers – originally from the French-governed Loyalty Islands near New Caledonia – duly reached Erub. As an intruder Macfarlane could well have been killed, but he was welcomed by Dabad, an elder renowned for his fighting prowess. More missionaries arrived from Rarotonga. Soon most of the Islanders became Christians.

In Aboriginal regions there had never been such a swift chain of conversions, nor had schools been established so successfully. Whereas today the word 'invasion' is often employed in mainland Australia, the day of Macfarlane's arrival at Erub is known as the Coming of the Light, and 1 July is still celebrated as a national holiday in Torres Strait.

These islands belonged to no European power until 1872 when, on behalf of Queensland, most were formally annexed by Britain. Seven years later the more easterly islands such as Erub and Mer were annexed. Though Islanders were often treated arbitrarily, they received stronger political rights than did most Aborigines on the mainland. During the crisis of World War Two they manned their own strong regiment and several of their skilled navigators operated armed patrol boats on the long north Australian coastline.

It was observed that the Islanders were willing to do jobs that called for sustained physical work, week after week. That was to be expected of a gardening people, for the domestication of plants is really the domesticating and disciplining of the people who have to tend the plants. The British understood more readily the Islanders' way of life and their form of land tenure and mostly respected it. In 1992 the famous plea by Eddie Mabo for land rights was less that he and his four colleagues were unable to occupy their traditional land on Mer but rather that they did not possess clear legal title to it. Today the Torres Strait Islanders are more dedicated Christians than are mainstream Australians of European ancestry. In the referendum of 1999 – should Australia become a republic? – their voting preferences were more conservative than those of most Aborigines. In the words of George Mye, one of their oldest and strongest leaders, the Queen was still 'central to the religious, cultural and civic traditions of the people of the Torres Strait'.

The history of the Torres Strait Islanders seems to offer support for the proposition, set out in Volume 1 of this work, that peoples who had experienced the gardening revolution – whether in Scotland or New Guinea, Finland or New Zealand – were more likely to see eye to eye and partly understand each other. In contrast the Aborigines often paid – and still pay, in part – a high penalty for their remarkably long period of nomadic isolation.

7

The narrow part of Torres Strait forms one of the more perplexing shipping routes in the world. There two seas meet – the Arafura Sea from the west and the Coral Sea or Pacific Ocean from the east. Often the level of one sea is much higher than the other. In certain phases of the moon the high tide prevails in the western end while it is low tide at the eastern end. As a result a fast flow of seawater – in essence the equalising current – repairs the contrasting levels of the two oceans near their meeting point. The Torres Strait Islanders, observing this daily event for several thousand years, call the westerly current the kuliss and the easterly current the gutat.

For decades the official guidebook to sea pilots pointed out that even in a favourite shipping route, the Prince of Wales Channel, the 'tidal streams are rapid and uncertain'. More important, a sea-captain new to the strait and selecting his own channel – with the help of the latest charts – was advised to anchor before sending a small boat ahead to survey the 'sunken dangers at the west entrances'. He was also warned not to enter the channel 'with the sun ahead'. Even today, large ships cannot pass through the strait without engaging a special pilot who knows intimately its waters and moods.

As the strait was a vital short cut to Queensland from many ports in Asia, it attracted more and more ships. In the 1880s, British migrants came in subsidised liners through the Suez Canal to the Indian Ocean and Singapore, where they transferred to a British India Steam Navigation ship that conveyed them to a chain of tropical Queensland ports extending all the way from Thursday Island and the gold port of Cooktown along to Mackay, Rockhampton and so to Brisbane. Between 1884 and 1891 at least seven ships were wrecked in or near Torres Strait, the most notable being the handsome steamship *Quetta*, which, on a moonlit night, sank near Thursday Island with the loss of 133 lives.

Thursday Island flourished as the commercial pivot of Torres Strait. Small and hilly, it lay only 40 kilometres north of Cape York – the most northerly point of the continent. By 1900 it was probably Australia's most cosmopolitan town, with groups of Japanese, Melanesians, Chinese, Filipinos, and the Malay-speakers who often served as divers in the large pearling fleet. Here extended a long jetty for passenger and cargo ships, a quarantine station in which infected passengers were confined, a customs house, a hilltop fort, a pilot station, a hospital, banks and many shops and hotels, while on a hill with a sea view stood the airy, wooden Anglican cathedral, named the Quetta All Souls in memory of the passengers who had drowned.

In the forward defences of Australia, Thursday Island was more important than Darwin until the 1920s. Lying close to the narrow

stretch of Torres Strait, and close to New Guinea, Thursday Island
was strategic. If another European nation – say, Germany – acquired
the adjacent New Guinea coast, it could – in time of war – patrol
the strait and endanger Australian shipping. Already a segment
of Queensland's northern border extended to islands lying within
swimming distance of that part of New Guinea called Papua. Why
not extend Queensland's border to Papua and even across the
heights of the Owen Stanley Range (far higher than any Australian
mountains)? As an additional bonus Papua might yield rich gold as
well as cheap labour for Queensland's large sugar estates.

Sir Thomas McIlwraith, the ambitious premier of Queensland,
resolved to annex that strategic corner of New Guinea that was
closest to Queensland. Early in 1883 he instructed Henry M.
Chester, the police magistrate on Thursday Island, to sail the 540
kilometres across the sea to New Guinea and hoist the Union Jack
on the shore of the deep harbour of Port Moresby.

London did not approve of Queensland's flagpole annexation.
Why should it approve of this young Australian colony initiating
Britain's own foreign policy? The government in London did not
yet fully realise that Germany, a mere infant as a coloniser, held
determined designs on an adjacent part of New Guinea and on
the islands already named New Britain and New Ireland. In 1884
a German squadron annexed them. McIlwraith's foresight and
fear seemed to be justified. In reply, Britain belatedly endorsed
his plan, and set up a protectorate based on Port Moresby. In 1888,
Queensland, Victoria and New South Wales each agreed to share
most of the cost of administering the huge mountainous territory.
Formally it was annexed as British New Guinea.

Adventurers were already visiting this land that was feared
for its malaria. For more than a decade Port Moresby had been a
new home for the London Missionary Society and its South Seas

preachers and its celebrated Scottish missionary James Chalmers. Already Australian prospectors were digging for gold along the coast. Even Australian journalists were ashore, and both the Melbourne *Age* and the *Sydney Morning Herald* landed separate expeditions in 1883 to explore the rugged terrain lying towards the towering Owen Stanley mountains. Sixty years later these mountains were to be part of the defence lines of Australia.

CHAPTER NINE

The banks
crash

It seemed impossible that the prosperity of Australia would fade. But the Promised Land failed to fulfil its promise. Not until the decades after the Second World War did it regain a place among the world's most prosperous nations.

2

The depression of the 1890s arrived in three stages – a moderate slump, followed by bank crashes, and then by drought – and each stage deepened the depression. The first stage was visible in many towns in 1891, being marked by unemployment, lower export prices, and a fall in investment and new building projects. Such slumps had come occasionally in the previous thirty years – usually when export prices were falling and a boom in the property and share markets had gone too far. In the late 1880s the boom had been excessive, and the intoxicating optimism gave way to a mood of sobriety and hesitation.

The slump also owed much to the increasing wariness of those British investors who had created so many jobs by subscribing to the loans of the six Australian governments, by placing deposits in the London and Scottish offices of Australian banks, and by buying shares in Australian mining, pastoral and finance houses. In some years of the 1880s one-fifth of Britain's new overseas investments came to Australia. Here was the great financier of the world pouring money into a continent holding fewer than three million people.

Australia could not hope to absorb sensibly so much capital so quickly. Between 1885 and 1890 Australia's borrowing from overseas was heavy, but by 1891 it was light. The fall was sufficient to throw tens of thousands of people out of work.

The next stage of the depression was a shock: the banks were suddenly besieged. No private institutions were so respectable, so monumental and so powerful as the finance houses. Banks had more prestige here than they had in England, the United States, France and probably almost any country in the advanced world. In most Australian cities the noblest buildings were the churches and the big banks. Indeed, the head offices of most banks were built like temples with vast chambers decorated with Italian marble, fine-grained woods, chandeliers, and even stained glass in Gothic windows. From the internal balconies the head banker could look down on a scene of splendour and extravagance, financed by the thrift of customers in Australia and the British Isles.

The big banks were public companies whose shares were prized. Their dividends were regular and generous. They promoted much of the economic development of the continent and their branches could be found in every town: usually two-storeyed buildings with ornate facades that would have pleased any English provincial city. Four of the biggest Australian banks held, between them, more than 600 branches, a statistic that must have flabbergasted English and American bankers. On the boards of the main banks sat not only rich men but also many of the leading politicians.

The colourful banknotes that circulated everywhere were issued not by the government but by the private banks. As bankers did not believe that their activities should be closely regulated by governments, and as they had been remarkably free from disasters, the banks were regulated less than those of almost every country. This more than anything was to deepen the banking debacle. The bankers and politicians could not foresee a serious banking crisis, and were unprepared when crisis came.

The lifeblood of an Australian bank – when the gold standard dominated finance – was gold coin and bullion. Every bank had to keep sufficient gold in its safes and vaults to pay, without prior notice, any customer who wished to withdraw a deposit or to cash a banknote. A bank that happened, on one busy day, to be short of gold coins could not compel a customer to accept paper money. Banknotes were not legal tender, and every note carried in flowing script a guarantee signed by the bank's own manager: 'I promise to pay the bearer on demand one pound sterling'. In law £1 sterling was a gold sovereign.

During economic uncertainty the banks had to keep a higher proportion of gold in their vaults, but they could only build up their stock of gold sovereigns at the expense of the money they lent to the public. The temptation to skimp on the hoard of gold and to lend out as much money as possible was always present. And yet if the month came when a bank, through miscalculation, was seriously short of gold, then it had to close its doors, reconstruct its business, and thereafter incur odium. Indeed, it might never reopen its doors. In Europe in the nineteenth century many banks failed not because they were unable to meet their obligations but because they failed to meet those obligations instantly.

Depositors in Australia occasionally panicked and rushed the banks and demanded their money in gold. These runs or rushes on banks were usually met with ease. Once the customers found that the bank calmly paid out as much gold as was required, they themselves became calm. In the following weeks they quietly and shamefacedly returned their money to the safety of the bank. If the news became public that a bank had made unsound loans to businessmen, then customers naturally feared for the safety of their own deposits in the bank and withdrew them permanently. Curiously, in 1885 there were fears that the Russians might invade Australia, and the branches of some banks were almost emptied of gold by nervous depositors. Presumably they buried their sovereigns in the garden or behind the bricks in a fireplace or a wall. Obviously gold could be hidden and hoarded with more safety than paper money because gold did not catch fire, could not be destroyed by damp and could not be nibbled by mice or washed away by floods. To hoard gold at home was therefore common. The danger of the hoarding habit was that it could jeopardise the safety of banks and indeed the economic prosperity of everyone.

3

In 1891 a shiver ran through every Australian banker. For the first time since the 1840s a large bank was rushed by panicking depositors and was bled to death. The Bank of Van Diemen's Land had been founded in 1823 when the name of Tasmania was little used, and its business was sound until the late 1880s when it lent heavily to Tasmanians who gambled in silver shares. In August 1891 it closed its doors and attempted to meet its debts by offering all its banking premises as prizes in a lottery at £1 a ticket.

In April 1892 the Bank of South Australia was assailed by rumours of mismanagement, which were partly true. Founded in London, it had been the first bank in South Australia and had commenced business in a tent on the beach at Glenelg and had financed many of the great families and many of the main enterprises in the colony. Two months after it had closed, the New Oriental Bank, a London house that was once strong on the Victorian goldfields, closed without creating severe hardship. Then came a pause in which only the small Federal Bank went into liquidation. So far the only banks to fall had not been among the top twelve. If the eliminating of the smaller banks had gone no further, only good would have resulted.

In the autumn of 1893, however, one of the most vigorous banks fell under public suspicion. The Commercial Bank of Australia had been founded in Melbourne in 1866, and in an era of racial and sectarian loyalties it was especially strong among Methodists and popular with the Chinese for whom it printed special banknotes. It eventually ran a remarkable network of branches spreading from Collingwood to Darwin and – the price of growing so fast – also held many risky accounts older banks had eschewed. To finance its multiplying customers it busily gathered deposits in Scotland and England.

Just before the Easter of 1893, the head office of the bank in Collins Street seemed unusually busy. Customers were entering and leaving in surprisingly large numbers. Knowing that their own savings would be endangered if the bank ran out of gold, they were withdrawing their savings and demanding that they be paid in gold sovereigns. By demanding gold rather than banknotes they did not realise that they hastened the event they feared – the closing of the bank. In many of the banks that closed, less than one-tenth of the total deposits had been withdrawn in the panic; but that was enough.

During April 1893 five banks closed. The streets and hotels and clubs and vestries were full of rumours. The new telephone wires that now linked the larger business houses within a city were abuzz with gloomy gossip, predictions, and rumours of dishonesty in the boardrooms of smaller banks.

A bank could fall with astonishing speed. The National Bank of Australasia was first assailed by panicking depositors at its relatively unimportant Perth office on Monday 17 April 1893. The panic was heightened by a rumour that there was a run on the head office of the bank in Melbourne. In fact there was no such run, but now rumours were racing across the continent. In the last fortnight of April the National Bank at its many branches paid out nearly 45 per cent of its gold. On Monday 1 May the crisis was acute. The bank did not open its doors, and they remained closed for weeks.

In Brisbane it was unthinkable that the colony's largest financial institution, the Queensland National Bank, could fall, and in Sydney the idea of the old Commercial Banking Company of Sydney failing to meet a request for gold seemed sacrilegious; but these banking houses were about to fall.

4

An alert government probably could have halted this chain of events at an early stage. Unfortunately, in Victoria – the centre of banking – a new government had won office in January 1893, just when the collapse of the Federal Bank signalled the start of the panic. The new premier was James Patterson, a gold-rush migrant who had become a slaughterman and butcher on the goldfields and then an auctioneer in the Melbourne suburbs. His treasurer, G. D. Carter, a gold-rush migrant now in his early sixties, had been a wine-merchant but knew something of banking because he sat on the board of the Bank of Victoria. Patterson and Carter had no rational notion of what to do when Melbourne was gripped by hysteria. In a last twitching gesture they went in a special ministerial train to the bayside town of Frankston on Sunday evening 30 April and, at a hasty meeting of the executive council in the holiday house of the acting governor, instructed him to sign a proclamation that closed all the banks in Victoria for a week. The proclamation advertised to the world that Victoria was in a state of crisis: it did nothing to ease the crisis.

In Sydney many politicians were tempted to see the crisis in banking as largely a Victorian event, a punishment for reckless optimism. But panic was already visible in Sydney where the powerful Australian Joint Stock Bank had closed. Fortunately for Sydney its premier, George Dibbs, had been longer in office than the Victorian premier, and also knew more about the ways of banks.

In 1866 Dibbs was living in the Chilean port of Valparaiso, buying wheat for shipment to Australia, when he heard of the failure of the major London bank known as Agra and Masterman's; and for the next eight years he was virtually bankrupt. Raising himself up again, he won the West Sydney seat in parliament in 1874, and was twice premier for short periods before beginning in 1891 a full term of office. As his older brother Thomas was general manager of the respected Commercial Banking Company of Sydney, Dibbs was not unaware of banking policies and dangers, and he also probably realised that almost every nation in Europe and North America possessed what no Australian colony possessed – a simple law that permitted banks to smother a panic with paper money when a state of emergency was declared.

Sir George Dibbs – his own financial affairs in chaos – held resolute views on how to be a leader. When, on 10 February 1892, depositors clamoured for their money at the Savings Bank of New South Wales in Barrack Street, this burly politician went to the bank, stood at its doorway, and urged the customers to go home. The bank, he said, was safe. With his own hand he wrote out, and pinned to the door, a notice affirming that his government would guarantee the safety of the people's deposits. Fifteen months later, when far larger banks were besieged in Sydney, he acted just as decisively. On 3 May 1893 his government passed a Bank Notes Act, and on 15 May it declared that for the following six months the act would be in force. In effect the act permitted certain banks approved in New South Wales to pay out their own printed banknotes instead of gold. The banknotes were now legal tender, and anybody in New South Wales could pay for food, land or any goods or services simply with banknotes. Only at the main office of each bank in Sydney could people convert banknotes into sovereigns, but the need to convert notes into sovereigns was less urgent because notes were now accepted everywhere. This sensible act instantly eliminated the scarcity of gold coin, a scarcity that had so devastated the savings and property and livelihood of people.

Unfortunately the new law was first enforced only after the huge Commercial Banking Company of Sydney closed its doors. While it therefore failed to save the bank that was managed by Dibbs' brother, it probably prevented the panic from engulfing Sydney. Moreover it released stocks of gold that, no longer required in New South Wales, could reinforce endangered banks in other colonies.

Throughout Australia only three important banks remained open. The oldest in the land, the Bank of New South Wales, was still doing business; so too were the London creations of the 1830s, the Union Bank and the Bank of Australasia, which later were to come together to form the present ANZ Banking Group. These three banks had, on the whole, been managed soundly during the boom. Fortunately they also owned a string of branches in New Zealand, which in 1893 was relatively prosperous and so could release gold for the banks' needs in Australia. Although it is now believed that these banks survived solely because they were sound, no bank anywhere could hope to survive a crisis of such intensity unless governments intervened.

People were numbed by the rush of events. On 4 May 1893 the Anglican Bishop of Melbourne, Dr Goe, called for all people to prepare to observe a Day of Humiliation and Prayer, but by the time the actual day of prayer commenced on 17 May another seven banks had fallen. Thousands of Australians, laypeople and clergy, agreed with Goe that the depression was a divine punishment for their eagerness to be rich.

At the start of the year, Australia had twenty-two note-issuing banks. By the end of autumn, thirteen of those banks were closed and were receiving legal and financial repairs. In Victoria and in Queensland two-thirds of all deposits were locked up in those closed banks. In New South Wales more than half of all deposits were locked inside those banks that had closed. In Australia as a whole every second customer was debarred from a bank. The distress was deepened because most of the building societies and lesser financial institutions were virtually insolvent.

Nothing in the history of English banking could match our disaster of 1893. My own research can find nothing in Germany, France or Holland to compare with this collapse. Even in the United States, where one-branch banks were almost as plentiful as tobacconists' shops, I doubt whether a disaster of such magnitude had occurred. In 1893 the United States also experienced a dangerous panic of depositors, but the proportion of the nation's savings that was locked up was small compared to the proportion in Australia.

A throbbing nervousness hung over the country in June 1893. Nobody knew when another run on the surviving banks might suddenly begin. Debts that fell due in the normal course of business could not be paid. The market in shares and real estate was dislocated, and a buyer with ready cash could buy shares and land at bargain prices. But, all values being chaotic, what was a bargain price?

5

Nearly all the banking companies that in 1893 had closed their doors prepared to reopen them. Each bank had to reconstruct its business, compelling its shareholders to subscribe more capital in order to strengthen the balance sheet. Each had to meet its depositors in Australia and Britain and persuade them to agree to withdraw their money in slow stages and sometimes on less favourable terms. Each finally had to submit its scheme of reconstruction to the highest courts for approval. During this delay, commercial chaos was not far away. The first bank reopened five weeks after it had closed and the last bank nineteen weeks after it had closed.

The crisis had shattered the confidence of most overseas investors. At the very time when Australia needed investment for public works and private projects, money was being withdrawn. The ebb of funds was acute, and in the worst year a staggering sum equal to 40 per cent of Australia's export income was eaten up simply in paying interest on those overseas debts that had been incurred in the balmy years. The depression of the 1890s would remain the deep scar in the country's history in that long period between the convict era and the massive casualties of the First World War.

PART TWO

The
Restless
Era

CHAPTER TEN

Retreat
from paradise

In Melbourne, suburban streets were lined with new houses but nobody wished to rent them and no nightwatchman came to guard them. In rows of houses gaslight fittings, water pipes and floorboards were systematically pilfered until only the brick shell remained. Thousands of families were destitute. In South Melbourne in 1894 one charity organisation alone was supplying bread, meat and vegetables to 800 people, most of whom were the wives and children of men who had gone up-country to seek work. No old-age pensions and no sickness or unemployment benefits were available for those in need.

The heart of Melbourne at weekends seemed almost as quiet as a cemetery. New skyscrapers stood like tall stucco headstones, and many headstones were blank. Some of the tall offices became boarding houses, and the new lodgers walked along the uncarpeted corridors, their footsteps echoing, to rooms that were lit dimly.

The glut of skyscrapers was less painful than the glut of brick-layers, slaters, tuck-pointers, stonemasons, carpenters, cabinet-makers, architects and surveyors. Melbourne remained the biggest city in Australia but it was only a question of time before it was surpassed by Sydney.

Victoria had gained heavily through net immigration in the long run of prosperous years, but that gain was exceeded by the net emigration in the depressed years. In essence, between 1891 and 1905 Victoria lost, through emigration, a greater total of people than it had gained through immigration in the previous thirty years. The long shipping lane across the Great Australian Bight to Albany and Fremantle became one of the busiest, as tens of thousands of unemployed Victorians went to Western Australia. Another outflow went to the booming gold city of Johannesburg, where Australian Rules football was regularly played at the turn of the century.

As the young men led the exodus from Victoria, the marriage rate and then the birthrate declined. As the old people stayed behind, the death rate ultimately increased. For sixty years after the bank crashes Victoria persistently had the nation's lowest rate of natural increase – the excess of births over deaths. While Victoria was the worst affected, nearly every colony except Western Australia suffered from the slump.

Governments at first had made hurried plans to entice the city unemployed into the country. Frightened of political violence if hungry people remained in the cities, most governments provided free land and money for rural cooperatives and peasant settlements. Victoria set up at least seventy-eight settlements, each with a managing committee. In 1894 these settlements extended from the southern Tasmanian village of Southport, which was founded by the ladies of Hobart, to the radical Queensland communities at

Roma. In South Australia a chain of 'village settlements' sprang up near the Murray River. In most of these villages the people worked their own little paddocks but on a few they shared the land and the ploughs and working horses.

The Leongatha Labour Colony, Victoria's largest, was a block of forest where unemployed men from the city could clear the timber. The men chosen in Melbourne had to be able-bodied, of good character, and destitute. As wives and children were not allowed to live at the labour colony, married men tended to come only if they could find no work elsewhere. The main consolation at the colony was the short working day, the long dinner break, and the cheerful smoke-ohs where the men could yarn. The hard work of clearing the scrub, tending the bonfires of the cleared timber, and grubbing out the green stumps of giant eucalypts was not done with the breathless tempo of the private farmers in the neighbourhood. And yet in the first six years a total of 3500 men worked at the labour colony, staying on average about three months; and many regained the 'spirit of self-dependence' that was a goal of those who had founded the colony at a public meeting in the Melbourne Town Hall.

2

William Lane was a perpetual migrant and in 1893 he was preparing to move again. Born in Bristol, the son of a landscape gardener, he had first migrated to North America before returning to England, from which he set out as a migrant to Australia. Here he became an editor of radical newspapers, and in 1890 he founded the Queensland *Worker* with the motto of 'Socialism in Our Time'.

Lane had visions of ultimately founding a communal utopia, and many bush workers were attracted by his vision. His socialism was more like the intense communion of a small religious sect than the socialism set up by a government. Preferring rural life, he hoped that the outback would supply him with the ideal recruits – strong and straight people who possessed 'the manliness which town life destroys'. In his utopia, property would be held in common. Men and women were to be equal. Members were to remain teetotallers until the colony had been founded and the hazardous first stage of settlement was over. 'Coloured people' could not join. Nor could people of bad repute, couples who lived together but remained unmarried, or traitors to the labour movement.

Lane thought South America might provide the area he was seeking. It was far away, like every utopia. It might also offer a sharper climate than the sweaty Brisbane where Lane worked at his journalism and where the summer lethargy made commentators and visitors doubt whether the Australian race would ever become very energetic. This was an era when many intellectuals attributed much of Britain's greatness to a bracing climate, and Lane doubted whether any great society could arise out of a sea of perspiration. High country in South America was his first choice, and three of his colleagues eventually found 200 000 hectares of free land in the inland republic of Paraguay. If he could succeed in building his socialist colony there, he hoped that 'a world-wide revolution would speedily be brought about'.

In Sydney in 1893 the promoters of paradise bought a sailing ship of 598 tonnes. Built of blue gum and bloodwood her only flaw was her name: *Royal Tar* was not the most appropriate name for a republican barque. And now the passengers began to arrive from many parts of eastern Australia, though not from Victoria. Many were outback men who had not sniffed a salt wind for years. Some were city families who had not lived for long in Australia. When the ship was about to sail, the passengers numbered 120 adults and 100 teenagers and children; a few others had been sent ashore at Balmain with measles.

Many more people wished they could join the ship. On a winter Sunday an outdoor rally of 10 000 people assembled on the Sydney Domain and wished them well. The chairman of the rally was John Christian Watson, who was to become, eleven years later, the first Labor prime minister of Australia.

The little ship sailed away on 16 July 1893. After passing icebergs near Cape Horn it eventually reached the port of Montevideo and transferred passengers and cargo to a river steamer. The barque then sailed back to Adelaide where she was to take on more settlers. Meanwhile Lane and the pioneers slowly travelled 1200 kilometres up the wide river to the city of Asunción where the president of Paraguay waited on the wharf to welcome them. By steam train and then bullock carts they went east to a deserted orange grove in a grassy clearing, and in that corner of their vast estate they built and thatched their huts, made bricks, dug gardens, and put up fences and stockyards. They also quarrelled. The disputes centred on those who drank too much or worked too little, on the leadership of the generous but tetchy Lane, and the question of how communal their utopia should be. More than one-third of the settlers abandoned their New Australia before the second contingent arrived from Adelaide.

The rift was so deep that Lane and his more ardent followers decided to found their own commune at Cosme, about 100 kilometres away from New Australia. Among the later recruits was Mary Gilmore, the sparkling essayist and poet whose face now looks out ever so seriously from Australia's blue $10 note.

For several years Cosme was a hardworking, frugal team amid the cane fields. The teamship, however, was not extended far, and

Lane's men refused to play New Australia in cricket. The idealism in the competing colonies slowly sagged. In 1899, when Lane returned to Australia, it was clear South America's soil was no more fertile than Australia's for achieving radical and democratic reforms.

3

Most people who found a utopia in the 1890s found it on a mining field. The industry was revitalised by a new era of discovery in the 1880s and early 1890s. A string of mining camps sprang up, all the way from western Tasmania to the Kimberley in north-western Australia, Croydon near the Gulf of Carpentaria and Chillagoe in the hills beyond Cairns. The spearheads of mining had moved into the ancient rocks of the Precambrian zone that dominated the western half of the continent. There many of the gold lodes were massive and the rewards for large companies were high. So too were the obstacles.

Western Australia was the new magnet of mining. A chain of gold rushes, beginning in the far north-west in 1886 and reaching Kalgoorlie just one month after the bank crashes in 1893, provided work for tens of thousands. Indeed the timing and the magnitude of the main gold rushes in the Coolgardie, Kalgoorlie and Leonora districts were influenced by the depression in the eastern colonies. Labour and capital, previously idle, poured into Western Australia to search for gold and to develop promising lodes. The more indications of gold they found, the more people and money poured in to intensify the search. Gold towns of hessian and calico and canvas arose on dry plains where not a horse travelled a decade earlier. Between 1894 and 1897 the population of Western Australia doubled.

A water engineer was the hero of the main goldfields. Born in Ireland and experienced in building harbours and railways in New

Zealand, C. Y. O'Connor was enticed to the vast colony of Western
Australia. In 1895, when the gold towns around Coolgardie were in
a state of excitement, O'Connor was instructed by his premier, John
Forrest, to fetch water. In response he proposed to build a reservoir
in the hills near Perth, lay a steel pipeline across nearly 600 kilometres of country to Coolgardie, and supply it with a permanent
flow of fresh water. Nowhere in the world had water been piped so
far. Moreover another obstacle stood in O'Connor's way: the land
sloped gently uphill on the long route, so that the pipeline would
require a chain of eight pumping stations to deliver the fresh water
to distant gold towns. The scheme was imaginative and bold. One of
the most expensive public works so far planned in Australia – and
initiated by the colony with the fewest taxpayers – it was approved
by the Forrest Government in 1896.

Meanwhile the gold towns and the mines scavenged the water
they needed. Rainwater that fell on the roofs of huts, houses and
shops was collected in iron tanks, but it was only a fraction of the
water needed by the mines and their boiler houses, stamp mills,
compressors and other steam-driven machines. And it was only a
fraction of the water needed by the working horses, by the laundries, and by the private kitchens and bathrooms – only hotels and
large houses had the luxury of a proper bathroom. Fortunately
most districts had a source of very salty water lying in white shallow lakes. Such water, however, was costly because it first had to be
heated by local firewood and converted into steam, which in turn
was condensed into fresh water.

Water-selling became a busy occupation. People who sold
pies in the streets could earn more money by selling water. Bush
mechanics owning a cart to carry their iron tank and other equipment erected their water condensers and stacked their firewood
on the shores of salt lakes – close to the tracks along which the

incoming gold-seekers travelled. Randolph Bedford, a mining journalist who had been to many rushes, marvelled at the strange sight of these primitive waterworks when he camped at night on the dusty road to early Coolgardie: 'After the long day the condenser-fires glare on the salt like blood on ice, and the camp fires burn the spinifex with the odour of Ribbon of Bruges.'

Another source of water appeared when the goldmining shafts went deeper. Night and day the mines' pumps brought this heavily salted water to the surface. After being treated it was consumed on a large scale by towns and mining companies. Horse-drawn carts delivered it to nearly every house and hut at a high price.

Eagerly awaited was the long pipeline that, in 1902, finally reached Coolgardie – the original destination for the water. The handsome town – significant enough to have a new federal electorate in its name – was now declining; and the pipeline was extended to Kalgoorlie and its celebrated Golden Mile. A city of some 30 000 people, and the second-largest in the entire western half of Australia, Kalgoorlie held grand banquets when the pipeline delivered fresh water, pumped all the way from a reservoir near Perth.

Victoria lost its title as Australia's largest gold producer and did not regain it. The big mines in the west dwarfed Victoria's richest. By 1907 three mines on the Golden Mile had each paid more than £2 million in dividends to shareholders – not one mine in Victoria had reached half that sum. A century later the west was still the nation's premier producer of gold.

The gold rushes had transformed the west. It quickly passed Tasmania in population, and by 1901 it held two of the nation's ten main cities – Perth and Kalgoorlie. By 1930 it no longer relied so heavily on gold. A host of its miners had become farmers on the dry wheat belt lying closer to the coast, and wheat at times challenged gold as the main export.

4

Across the nation in the 1890s, thousands of people moved back to the land. Their small farms clung to steep hills or occupied small clearings in forest and scrub. They divided many of the inland plains with a chessboard of tiny paddocks. With the aid of the new cream separator the output of butter soared, and for the first time Australia became a steady exporter of butter to Britain. At the same time, so much frozen mutton and beef was sent away in the refrigerated chambers of steamships that during the 1890s frozen meat temporarily exceeded wheat and flour as an export.

In the long-distance movements to new mining fields and farmlands, Victoria and South Australia were the main losers of people and Western Australia and Queensland were the main gainers. As these latter two colonies held more than half of the continent, their natural resources seemed infinite in the minds of promoters and pamphlet-writers. In 1860 they had less than 4 per cent of Australia's population but at the end of the century they held 18 per cent, and would continue to grow in wealth and national influence.

CHAPTER ELEVEN

A fearful drought

The new settlers had explored the land: the climate they had barely begun to comprehend. After all, most Australians lived in regions where reliable knowledge of the weather did not go back more than eighty years. That was not long enough to discern any clear pattern of rainfall.

2

Thousands of farmers who had sowed grain on the remote plains before 1890 were buoyed by the faith that in most years the rainfall was reliable. In the leading wheat colony, South Australia, many had come to believe that their own iron ploughs, by breaking up the soil, were indirectly changing the climate. They argued that the ploughed ground was more capable of absorbing and conserving the rain, and moreover that moisture in the ground could induce more regular rains. In the mid-1870s the minister for agriculture officially blessed the theory that rain followed the plough. Here was one of the rare instances in Western civilisation where the drays and wagons of the pioneers carried not only Bibles, axes, seeds, blankets and the paraphernalia of the kitchen but also what was believed to be a new climate.

A few influential scientists proposed another theory that was equally optimistic. They believed that forests, not the horse-drawn plough, would change the local climate. Plant trees, they argued, and the rain will follow the trees. In Victoria a board reported to Parliament in 1867 that the systematic planting of forests and the conserving of existing bushland would lead to 'a more continuous rainfall in districts that are now subject to long and excessive droughts'. In 1878 the young Scottish forester who had come to Adelaide as the official conservator of forests made the astonishing announcement that a scarcity of trees had made inland Australia an arid place. Few farmers, at first, took notice of these theories. They carried their axe wherever they went, chopping or ringbarking the larger trees. They were determined to sow grain on every inch of soil they could clear. In some ways they were surprisingly successful. In few other parts of the world were crops being grown with such a low average rainfall.

After three dry seasons hit the farmers beyond Port Pirie and Port Augusta early in the 1880s, the South Australian government at last applied the theory. They set out to plant trees to bring the rain. The trees planted beyond the dusty town of Quorn had not grown high before wheat farmers in the vicinity were retreating, defeated by the arid climate. In many Australian regions the pastoralists could survive with a lower rainfall. They remained cheerful, built mansions and long shearing sheds, and allowed their sheep or cattle to multiply. And all along they kept careful rainfall records.

The longer they lived, the more they tended to think that the weather came in cycles with long periods of ample rains followed by long dry periods. This was probably true in the south-eastern quarter of Australia, the source of most of the rural produce. Indeed, as early as 1877 the talented young Sydney meteorologist Henry C. Russell devised a theory of nineteen-year cycles – after perusing the records of rainfall, ransacking the diaries of old colonists and collecting the weather stories told by the Aborigines.

Lake George, near the rural village of Canberra, was one of Russell's weather gauges of the past. Aboriginal stories suggested that this largest inland lake in New South Wales was dry in the 1790s or perhaps earlier. The lake certainly was again dry in the 1840s, and heavy wool drays crossed it and stockmen's huts were even built in places normally covered by deep water. Then for several decades the rains came with more regularity.

Russell was doubted by a few of the extreme optimists. Henry Hayter, a leading statistician in a land where the official yearbooks were the Bibles of material progress, could foresee no serious drought in the future. In 1890 he reassured a science congress that he could see no limit to the sheep and cattle which 'this great continent' – to use his own phrase – would ultimately support. In short, the animals could multiply and multiply. He did not live to see the grass dry up: he died on the eve of the great drought. We now know what the farmers and sheep-owners of south-eastern Australia could not know. In their region they were experiencing the final phase of a climatic paradise in which droughts had been shorter and less frequent.

3

The drought that began in about 1895 shocked nearly all schools of thought. Tens of thousands of small farmers suffered. In Victoria for three years the wheat belt produced virtually no wheat for export; and many bakehouses and confectioners were selling bread and cakes baked from Californian flour. Farmers slid deeply into debt. Blacksmiths and farriers, storekeepers and cordial makers in the small towns totted up with slate and pencil the increasing sums owed them, and they in turn owed increasing sums to banks, traders and agents in the city.

In the interior the price of fodder soared. If a traveller decided in 1900 to drive his buggy 800 kilometres across the plains on any track between Hughenden in north Queensland and the New Mallee in South Australia, he would have paid a small fortune along the way for chaff and hay for his horses. In 1901 the protector of Aborigines in west Queensland travelled 1600 kilometres and found even the wildlife had largely vanished. He counted only seven bustards, five kangaroos and one emu in all that long journey. In such dry conditions, countless Aborigines would probably have died but for the rations they were given by the government and by scattered friends.

Many old pastoralists, household names in their district, were fighting to survive. In the tropical ranges near Hughenden, Robert Christison watched the blue sky each day for a sign of a rain cloud. As the grass disappeared, men were sent to cut the mulga scrub so that the leaves could be eaten by sheep and cattle; and Christison noticed how, at the sudden sound of an axe, the skinny sheep would break into a run in the hope that green leaves were awaiting them. In the whirlwinds of dust that brushed across the bare ground, the cattle sometimes became invisible from only five steps away.

Robert D. Barton, living out towards the Barwon River in New South Wales, experienced drought from 1897 to 1902. He had a brief sense of relief when heavy rain fell on April Fools' Day 1899.

In the long heat the ground cracked open, and several cracks were so deep that the horse wagon carrying the sheepskins sank to the axles. When only 5000 of his sheep remained, he drove them east to the uplands of New England where rains were more regular. There he put up a tent, lived on bread and salt beef, and, with his dog for company, waited for news that the rains had fallen at home.

In many districts even the widest roadways were congested with travelling stock. In 1899 drovers set out with 14 000 sheep on a short journey from Evesham station to Rockhampton, and 11 000 sheep died on the way. In the same year, 2500 fat sheep were driven only 70 kilometres in the Gilgandra district in New South Wales, and on the road 800 died of thirst. Parched sheep often were unable to drink when they reached a dam, and pannikins of water had to be poured down their throats.

The older pastoralists had spent a lifetime on the land, and perhaps more than any other group of new Australians they had come to terms with it, but even they did not know the full range of its moods. In the 1880s they had spent huge sums in boring for water and in scooping out dams in the dry rim of the pastoral country. Their own experience suggested that they should prepare more for scarcity of water than for scarcity of grass. In this drought, however, millions of sheep died from starvation rather than thirst.

Overstocking was another sign of unfamiliarity with the new land. Too many cattle and sheep grazed in the years of expansion, and they imposed strain on the vegetation and topsoil. The grass and scrub eaten annually by sheep, cattle, horses, rabbits and other herbaceous animals on the eve of the drought must have been many times the amount consumed by the native animals a century earlier. The country therefore would be slower in recovering from a drought. The drenching rains, when they came, would be less fruitful than if the land had been stocked cautiously.

In a large country no drought is universal. In every year between 1895 and 1903 a few districts had lush or passable seasons. There were even regions that, normally vulnerable to drought, escaped lightly. Between 1895 and 1903 the Gulf Country of Queensland experienced only one miserable year. The western side of Australia did not suffer as severely as the eastern.

It is surprising to discover that some of these years were marked by a few freakishly cold months and by warmer Decembers. On 7 August 1899 the snow fell heavily in Melbourne, and at lunch-time schoolboys were throwing snowballs in the Fitzroy Gardens. In the first week of July 1900 many railway lines in New South Wales were blocked by falls of snow heavier than any previously recorded. A white blanket spread westwards from the Upper Hunter to Condobolin, and in the town of Bathurst many verandas and roofs collapsed under the weight of snow. A year later a heavy fall whitened virtually the length of a straight line drawn between Melbourne and Brisbane.

Dust storms mingled with snowstorms. In south-eastern Australia the total area ploughed for wheat in 1900 was almost six times as large as that ploughed in 1866, and a vast extent of that tilled soil was no longer compacted by moisture and so it crumbled into powder and was blown away by the winds. Many fences were submerged by the drifting soil and stretches of railway were buried too. On the afternoon of 12 November 1902 so much soil was blown from the interior that in Melbourne and many inland towns the sun was almost hidden by the dust in the air. Dust blown from Australia reached the mountains of New Zealand and sprinkled the snow like pepper on sugar.

In one decade the number of sheep estimated to live in Australia had been almost halved, falling from 106 million in 1891 to 54 million in 1902. Fortunately the output of wool did not fall so drastically. The number of cattle too had almost halved since 1894, declining from twelve to seven million. Shiploads of wheat had to be imported by flour mills and bakers in 1902. The cities and towns, being so dependent on the rural industries, suffered more from this so-called Federation Drought than from the terrible drought that arrived about 100 years later.

The devastating year was 1902; in the next year the rainfall was mostly favourable, but the drought returned to some large regions of the continent. Significantly, in the twentieth century the two driest years in the continent as a whole were 1902 and 1905, a fact indicating that the drought extended for longer than is normally believed. Several big cities and their hinterland continued to suffer. From 1901 to 1910 Sydney did not once exceed its average annual rainfall. For an even longer period Brisbane exceeded its average only twice. After the drought officially was over, the seasons for four decades were relatively dry in the south-eastern quarter of the continent.

The losses of a long drought are not all measured in statistics. Much of the loss is worry, disillusionment and humiliation. Even when a drought is almost over, graziers have no sure way of knowing whether it has finally ended. A drought can die slowly, its dying watched almost disbelievingly by tens of thousands of families who are close to insolvency.

On the northern plains of Victoria – now replacing South Australia as the main wheatfields – Farmer Coote kept a diary. His neat ink entries show that in each district the end of a long drought can be identified only in retrospect. On 5 March 1903 he noted that the overnight rain had been so heavy that his dam overflowed and sheets of water covered his paddocks, but a week later he was surprised to see – at eight in the morning – a fierce dust storm. Towards the end of that month he recorded another two dust storms driven from the outer lands by the northerly winds, and blackening the sky with dust. In the first half of April, sporadic dust storms stung his face and half-blinded him. Later in the month heavy rains fell, the big horse Bess was bogged while pulling the plough, and soon the new grass was sprouting everywhere.

That was not his diary's last reference to red dust. On 1 July, with a high wind blowing, he rode a horse into the town of Quambatook. 'Dust flying for the greater part of the day,' he wrote. But in his region his drought was over.

4

The drought, which ran until the early 1900s, vividly marked a new phase in the climate of the south-eastern quarter of Australia. A climatic map of that vast block of land embracing Birdsville, Longreach, Rockhampton, Sydney, Melbourne and Adelaide shows the arid zone moving slowly towards the coast long after that drought was over. The arid zone encroached on the semi-arid zone, and the semi-arid zone invaded the more favoured zone. From the late 1880s or the early 1890s through to the end of the Second World War this most productive rural area of Australia was to experience, on average, relatively dry seasons. The evidence suggests that the fluctuations in climate in the south-east quarter of the continent were one of the vital causes of the long prosperity of the forty years to 1890 and of the leaner half-century that followed. It was then that the country that had often floated in the blue sky of fantasy came down to earth.

The drought marked a step in the slow discovery of our climate and resources, but another kind of discovery was even slower. The continent had to be discovered emotionally. It had to become a homeland and feel like home. The sense of overpowering space, the isolation, the warmth of summer, the garish light, the shiny-leafed trees, the birds and insects, the smell of air filled with dust, the strange silences, and the landscapes in all their oddness had to become familiar. Nearly every immigrant arrived with strong north European preferences in landscape, sunlight, colour, temperatures and vegetation – preferences that Australia could rarely meet, except perhaps in Tasmania and on the opposite coast. These preferences lived on through the songs and hymns the migrants carried here, the poems and paintings, the school lessons and sermons, and in the names they placed on the map. Waves of new immigrants came to bolster the European influences. The physical mastering of Australia was swift and often dramatic, but the emotional conquest was slow.

Nature, in the eyes of most Australians, remained an enemy. W. M. Elliott bought hilly land in South Gippsland in 1879 and like tens of thousands of pioneers he fought the forest. A third of a century later, old and almost blind, he recalled his life as a pioneer and wrote down his wishes for the future that, he knew, he would not live to see. Viewed from his hilltop home, with its Irish name, 'the whole district lies stretched out before me in one grand panorama'. To his delight it was as grassy and green as Ireland: 'Not a vestige remains of the vast forest that once so stubbornly resisted our labours.'

Not a vestige! Thousands of pioneers still hoped to recreate the landscape of the British Isles, their hedges and fruit trees and green and pleasant fields, to the exclusion of almost everything Australian.

5

A few artists built bold bridgeheads in an alien land. In the late 1880s, a school of young painters discovered the summer and gloried in the hot north winds, the white dry grass, the distant blue ranges and the strong light; but the summers they prized were those in the coolest corner of the continent and they set up their painting colonies on the rural outskirts of Melbourne. Henry Lawson, rising young author of short stories and poetry, described vividly the dry plains near 'the Back of Bourke' but he warmed to the people more than to the terrain, heat and dust. In 1904, in another region of New South Wales, young Dorothea Mackellar wrote 'I love a sunburnt country' – a revolutionary statement – but her wide brown plains and her ragged mountain ranges were in the fertile valley of the Hunter River, not far from Newcastle.

Most Australians did not love a sunburnt country. Farmers preferred a reliable rainfall; bank managers and city merchants preferred to deal with customers living in towns where the economy did not suffer from drought. The governors, who came from the British Isles, still retreated in summer to the cool hill towns – to Sutton Forest and Mount Macedon and the Mount Lofty Ranges and other colonial Simlas. On hot days most people did not sunbake on the beaches: they stayed beneath the verandas, shade trees and parasols. The Australian tropics were seen widely as a white man's grave, and medical opinion doubted whether white children born in Brisbane would have the stamina and physique and energy of those born in Melbourne. The night sky was probably more attractive than the summer sky at midday to most Australians; and in the competition to design an Australian flag in 1901, more than half of the flood of ideas and sketches contained the stars of the Southern Cross.

Most people were still strangers in a new land. The land was only half won.

6

Australia exulted in collecting statistics because they were the neon signs of progress, but by 1900 most statistics were gloomy. Population statistics were the gloomiest of all. The birthrate was falling, partly because the depression was postponing marriages and partly because contraceptives were increasingly used. Migrants too became a rarity. In the fifteen years to the end of 1890 Australia's net gain through migration had been more than half a million people. In the following fifteen years the gain was a mere 8000, and in some years more people sailed away than arrived. Drought, coming soon after the bank crashes, deprived Australia of any remaining appeal.

By 1905 at least half of Australia's best-known painters temporarily lived in Europe. Drawn there by the excitement of the new painting ideas and practices in Paris and London, they were also pushed there by the sick economy and the scarcity of rich patrons in Australia. Perhaps the two most famous painters, Tom Roberts and Arthur Streeton, spent the best part of a quarter-century away from home, whereas Fred McCubbin stayed in Europe for only a few months.

Margaret Preston, 'a red-headed little firebrand of a woman', left Adelaide and studied in Munich and Paris in the years 1904–07. Hans Heysen, a rarity among these young Australian artists because he was not British, was sent overseas through the generosity of four South Australian businessmen, and he painted the River Marne or the bleak view from his upstairs Paris studio instead of the gaunt eucalypt trees that later were to make his name. In his long exile George Lambert occasionally burned a gum leaf, the aroma reminding him of home. Hugh Ramsay after two years in Paris suffered from the cold and returned with tuberculosis, dying when not yet thirty.

From the exodus of Australians, many countries gained. When at last in 1935 New Zealand elected its first left-wing government, most of the ministers – and the prime minister, Michael Savage – were Australians who had left their homeland in the depressed years. South Africa was another gainer, and Johannesburg acquired a colony of Victorians who played their own native code of football. Vancouver attracted Australian migrants, including the Kingsford Smiths; they eventually returned with their young son, who two decades later became the celebrated trans-Pacific aviator. Even San Francisco, after its earthquake in April 1906, received an influx of Australian tradespeople. But by then the tide was turning in Australia's favour.

CHAPTER TWELVE

The rocky road
to Federation

The citizens of the six Australian colonies often viewed each other as foreigners. Each colony had its own defence force. There was a Victorian navy and a Tasmanian army. Men in spectacular uniforms, the Tasmanian soldiers were volunteers from the rifle clubs, with a permanent force of two dozen artillerymen who manned the forts near the two main ports. South Australia in the 1880s possessed two torpedo boats and an old wooden corvette that was manned only on public holidays. These toy navies and armies were independent of one another, and proud of their independence.

Each colony issued its own postage stamps in bright colours. A portrait of the Queen usually graced each stamp, but in 1899 Tasmania disgraced itself, in the eyes of many loyalists, by printing large scenic stamps showing waterfalls and mountains and bays rather than the face of Queen Victoria. The colonies imposed duties on goods imported from their neighbours; and at crossing places on the intercolonial borders, and occasionally in little border towns in a semi-desert, arose customs houses. The Townsville hotelkeeper who wished to serve Sydney beer as well as local beer had to pay an import duty of twopence on each Sydney bottle that was allowed through the customs house. The colonies built their railways into the interior with different designs and gauges. After the New South Wales and Victorian railways first met in 1883, it was possible then to travel by train from Melbourne to Sydney, but all passengers and cargoes had to change trains at the border station of Albury. The travellers' clocks and watches also had to be turned forward or backward at Albury.

Each colony kept its own time. When the clocks in Queensland showed it was midday, the clocks in New South Wales indicated it was 11.52 a.m. plus 43.1 seconds. At the same moment a Victorian clock showed the time as 11.27 a.m., with an additional 47.7 seconds. Adelaide was about twenty-five and a half minutes behind Melbourne time. Perth was about one hour and fifty-seven minutes behind Melbourne time. The essence of the present system – with three separate time zones – was created in 1895 after the leaders of the six colonies reached an amicable agreement.

2

On so many matters each colony pursued its own policy. Their schools and textbooks usually differed. Their electoral laws, their shopping hours at weekends, the opening hours of hotels, and the laws regulating or helping Aborigines were not always the same. The money in each Australian purse and pocket was not the same. Thus a family entering another colony soon learned that most of the banknotes in circulation there were strange, though the gold, silver and copper coins were familiar. In winter sports the separate colonies had their own preferences, and in 1900 two colonies mainly played rugby and four played Australian Rules. A few colonies even attempted to shape their own foreign policy, independent of Britain.

Anthony Trollope, the bestselling English novelist who arrived in the early 1870s to see his sons, was perturbed at the lack of Australian unity. After all, he wrote, the colonies were just like many English counties side by side. They spoke the same language, and were attached to the same mother country.

By the 1880s new forces were breaking down mental if not political barriers. Australian nationalism was strong and sometimes aggressive. Australia was no longer peopled largely by men, women and children who were born in the British Isles and who thought of them as home. By 1891 two of every three Australians were natives of their own country. The growth of an Australian spirit could be seen in every colony and every class of society. In 1873, when the Victorian team of eighteen players trounced W. G. Grace's 'All-England Eleven', the *Australasian* weekly newspaper reported that many spectators still applauded the English team. By the 1890s many Australian spectators were hissing and hooting at the visiting English cricketers.

This aggressive nationalism was expressed each week by the popular weekly *The Bulletin*, with the motto 'Australia for the Australians'. Pride in Australia was becoming a unifying strand in national thought.

Faster transport enabled leaders of the colonies to confer more easily. By 1890, Adelaide, Melbourne, Sydney and Brisbane were linked by railway, and that stimulated commerce, both of goods and people. National conferences of merchants, trade unionists and politicians from the capital cities became more frequent. The barriers between the colonies were breaking down. The last twenty years of the century witnessed large movements of people. Thus, several hundred thousand Victorians went to New Zealand, to new Queensland gold towns, to Sydney, the Riverina, the mining fields in Western Australia and the forests of western Tasmania. In the 1870s and 1880s perhaps 40 000 South Australians emigrated to the wheatlands of western Victoria, the silver mines of Broken Hill, and the capital cities of the east. My estimate is that in 1900 about one in six of Australia's population had moved to another colony in the preceding twenty years.

Defence was to be the main issue on which Australians agreed. All the colonies wished to be secure against foreign naval attack or an invasion. So long as Britain ruled the seas, Australians did not need to think systematically about defence. The fact that in the century after the defeat of Napoleon Britain engaged in no major war – except the short Crimean War in the 1850s – did more than any combination of factors to make federation, in most years, a minor topic. But Britain's command of the world's seas was now under challenge.

Self defence was not simply a question of buying armaments. In the eyes of most Australians, Chinese immigration was viewed then as a defence topic. It was slowly recognised that there must be a uniform law restricting – not banning – the arrival of Chinese into Australia and New Zealand. Why should this uniform policy be pursued? The argument, pointing towards the Chinese, was based on 'a rational view of the dangers to those British communities which might in the course of time flow from a people numbering more than 400 million, whose language, laws, religion, and habits of life are alien to those of Her Majesty's subjects in Australasia, and whose geographical position makes the danger more imminent'.

Fear of a foreign naval power sometimes drew the colonies together. In 1885 many Australians had the jitters after they heard the rumour of a Russian invasion. Later the accidental cutting of the telegraph cable between Darwin and Java created more fears of a foreign invasion. The premiers of the colonies agreed on strengthening their defences and resolved to subsidise the British naval squadron that, based partly in Sydney Harbour, guarded Australian and adjacent seas. A British soldier, Major-General J. B. Edwards – veteran of the Crimean War and the Indian Mutiny – reported on Australia's land defences in 1889 and deplored the medley of armaments, the divided command, and a railway system that would jeopardise any quick movement of Australian troops made in order to thwart an enemy attack on a major port. The general somewhat neglected to emphasise that navies were far more important than armies for Australia's defence. Furthermore, those defences were closely tied to Britain's, which seemed at that time to be in no danger of losing their supremacy. In fact the danger was just over the horizon, for Germany was acquiring colonies in the South Pacific and developing a strong navy capable of patrolling the sea lanes.

The defence forces – land and sea – of the seven colonies of Australasia numbered 30 000 men in the year of Edwards' visit, but not many more than 1000 were full-time paid servicemen. Here was one oddity of the peaceful nineteenth century – this large cluster of colonies employed nearly as many politicians as permanent soldiers and sailors.

If there was ever to be a federation of the colonies, the politicians somehow had to be cajoled, inspired or logically persuaded that they themselves must be federated. They had to come together. They themselves personified the divisions that made Australia not one land but six. Edwards' report was the occasion for one of the most individualistic politicians to call for federation. Sir Henry Parkes, almost the patriarch of colonial politics, had for long been running hot and cold towards the idea, but he now ran hot. He is often called the Father of Federation, but such a title he deserved only briefly. The birth of a nation called for many fathers, none of whom could be pre-eminent, and when Parkes died the federation was only a balloon floating beckoningly in the air.

3

Portraits of Parkes display a very broad nose, a mouth-obscuring beard and long white hair breaking over his ears: an imposing face that resembled a lion's. The son of a failed farmer and handyman in England, Parkes became an apprentice to a bone-and-ivory turner, and he practised that craft briefly in Birmingham before he and his wife sailed to Sydney in 1839 as subsidised migrants. His first surviving son was born on the second-last day of the voyage, and his last surviving son died almost a century and a half later – in August 1978 – so that this one generation of Parkes' children covered three-quarters of the European history of Australia up to that time.

Parkes worked for wages in his first years in Sydney, mostly as a minor customs official on the waterfront. In 1845, he opened a shop in Hunter Street, and made bone-and-ivory articles for the few who could afford them; with saw and lathe he converted the tusks of elephants into the handles of knives and forks and luxury articles ranging from combs to false teeth. Restless, he was always starting again in this Land of Start-again. His next venture, in 1850, was the radical *Empire*, a newspaper that launched him into politics. Eight years later he became insolvent.

After a visit to England as a highly paid recruiting agent for immigrants, he set up again in Sydney as an importer of Birmingham fancy goods but by 1870 he was again insolvent. That did not prevent him from enjoying a period of political success, and a salary when he was premier of New South Wales. Again an importer of English ivory goods in the mid-1880s, he became insolvent for a third time and premier for a fourth time. His presence, as a mature statesman, was commanding and almost unworldly.

The rising Melbourne politician Alfred Deakin observed that Parkes often wore a 'far-away expression of the eyes, intended to convey his remoteness from the earthly sphere'. Parkes displayed one of his far-away looks in October 1889. At a banquet at the New South Wales border town of Tenterfield, he proposed a federation of the six colonies, perhaps of the seven, for New Zealand might join in too. He expressed the idea with such emotion that few who heard him were not inspired. He informed the assembled citizens of that remote rural district that they had come to a crossroads in their history. Australia was now an infant United States, standing on the threshold of unity. He explained that the infant United States held only three and a half million people when it rebelled against England, and today Australia held that many people. Surely, he said, 'what the Americans had done by war, the Australians could bring about in peace'. Four months later, at a banquet in the new hall of Parliament House in Melbourne – the very hall where the first federal parliament was much later to assemble – he spoke the memorable line: 'The crimson thread of kinship runs through us all.'

4

After experiencing years of coolness and years of warmth towards the idea of an Australian federation, the New South Wales government became almost an enthusiast. Accordingly it invited the leading politicians of the colonies to a grand conference or convention in Sydney, where in 1891 delegates from the six Australian colonies and New Zealand came together to draw up a constitution for a new nation. Their discussions were surprisingly successful. Even a name for the nation was agreed upon. It was

Parkes who suggested the 'Commonwealth of Australia', though Queen Victoria privately disliked the word 'commonwealth', for it stemmed from that short, rebellious period of English history in which King Charles I was put to death.

The enthusiasm for creating a new nation did not last. Soon the depression – not the federation of the colonies – leaped to the front of politicians' minds. But after the first shock had passed, the federation was seen as a pep pill that might restore prosperity. Just as England in the 1970s was to hope that its entry to the European common market might yield an economic miracle, so various groups in Australia clutched at the idea of their own common market. It helped to keep alive the federal movement in those years from about 1892 to 1896, when politicians' minds were turned elsewhere.

The depression created an even sharper stimulus to federation by toppling Victoria and thereby increasing the prospect that New South Wales might gladly join a federation. No longer was a federated Australia likely to be dominated by Victoria: indeed it might well be dominated by New South Wales. Victorian politicians in the 1890s still remained the more eager advocates of federation, but they were joined by a growing group from New South Wales. So the tallest barrier to federation – the barrier of rivalry separating Sydney and Melbourne – began to subside.

Private societies preached the virtues of a federation for Australia. Prominent was the Australian Natives' Association, a friendly society and nationalist lobby that caught the imagination of young Victorians. Many of these societies met in July 1893 at the river-port of Corowa, on the border of New South Wales and Victoria, and actually designed the path that led to the creation of the Commonwealth. Corowa itself suffered from the Victorian– New South Wales rivalries. The flour from its mills had to pay an import duty in order to enter Victoria, just across the river. This grievance, tolerable in a prosperous year, was deplored in 1893 when towns were feeling the pinch.

At Corowa the enthusiast who devised the vital formula for federation was not even a politician. John Quick had emigrated from Cornwall to the Bendigo goldfields as a two-year-old, had left school at ten, and worked in a noisy stamp mill, foundry and printing shop. Reading and studying at night, becoming a lawyer and that colonial rarity, a doctor of laws, he sat in the Victorian parliament for nine years until, still a young man, he lost his seat.

At the conference in Corowa Quick argued that the people themselves should control the movement towards federation. He proposed that the electors in each colony should elect delegates who would meet and devise a federal constitution that, in turn, would be voted upon 'by some process of referendum' in each colony. If approved by the people, the constitution then would be submitted to the British parliament for final approval. It was not at first sight a very practicable concept. After all, no nation in the world had been created in such a way. But eventually the Australian premiers agreed that Quick and his colleagues at Corowa had found a simple, ingenious formula.

Another political trend helped Quick's formula. The governments in the colonies were becoming more stable. Politics had long been a game of musical chairs, and a long-lasting ministry was rare. In Australia's six parliaments between 1856 and 1910 only a few men held the office of premier for a term of five or more consecutive years. To be exact there were thirteen such men, and significantly seven of them reigned in the 1890s. Therefore the decisive movement to federate coincided with the first period of political stability in the six colonies. Vital negotiations were less likely to be broken – as in 1891 – simply because a premier who negotiated them was defeated at the polls soon after. Federation might not have been

achieved if Reid (New South Wales), Turner (Victoria), Kingston
(South Australia), Nelson (Queensland), Braddon (Tasmania) and
Forrest (Western Australia) had not each been enjoying in the
1890s a long period of office.

In March 1897 the federal convention assembled in Adelaide
to debate the merits of the constitution that had been quickly
drawn up in Sydney in 1891. Ten delegates came from each colony –
except Queensland, which sent none. The New Zealanders who
had joined in the debates in 1891 were also absent: their colony was
relatively prosperous and had less economic incentive to federate.
Some of the giants of the 1891 convention were not to be seen in
Adelaide – Henry Parkes was dead and several others had faded out
of politics. Of the fifty delegates who now assembled in Parliament
House in Adelaide, two were octogenarians but most were under
the age of fifty. Half of the delegates had been born in Australia.
Only three of the delegates were Catholics, and only one was a
trade unionist and none a woman.

The members of the convention reassembled in Sydney, and
then in the fiery heat of January and February 1898 they met in
Melbourne. Thorny questions, one by one, were solved. The constitution was ready to be taken to the people for their verdict. On 3 and
4 June 1898 the men of Victoria and Tasmania and South Australia
went to the polling booths – in South Australia the women went
too – and voted strongly in favour of federation. In many towns the
voting was close; but in the farmlands of north-west Tasmania and
the city of Ballarat the voting favoured federation by a majority of
more than twenty to one.

In the late nineteenth century Australia, for some purposes,
can be divided into two spheres of influence: the one based on
Melbourne and the other on Sydney. The Sydney sphere of influence
was more wary of federation. Embracing New South Wales and

Queensland, this sphere sometimes saw federation as a Melbourne ploy or plot. Moreover, New South Wales and Queensland were crippled less by the recent depression and still possessed deep reservoirs of natural resources that – irrespective of whether federation was achieved – were likely to promote prosperity. They therefore had less need for the common market that federation would create.

On Friday 3 June 1898 the men of New South Wales voted on federation, Queensland still abstaining. The verdict was awaited with anxiety in Melbourne. The fear that New South Wales might vote no was increased by its government's insistence that unless at least 80 000 voters favoured federation, the poll would be regarded as a rejection of federation. As only 77 600 people voted yes, the result was regarded as a rejection. In Sydney most electorates actually opposed federation. Here was a shattering blow to the patriots in other colonies.

Concessions were made to entice the voters of New South Wales. They included the promise that the permanent federal capital would be in their territory. In 1899 the revised constitution was taken before the people. Again Victoria, Tasmania and South Australia voted more strongly for federation than in the previous year. Not one electorate came close to voting no. In New South Wales, on 20 June, the voters went to the polls. Though clusters of electorates still voted strongly against federation, the yes vote triumphed. And yet if less than 13 000 voters had changed their mind, the federalists would have lost.

In Queensland three months later its voters went to the polls. Again the victory was not decisive. Queensland would not have joined the federation but for the massive yes vote from those people living in the tropical north. If 4000 voters – a mere four or five trainloads of voters – had changed sides, Queensland would have voted against the federation. In the following year Western Australia voted yes, largely on the votes of the people living on the goldfields.

If the two latecomers – Queensland and Western Australia – had not possessed an enthusiastic band of federalists in several remote regions where goldmining was strong, the new Commonwealth of Australia – confined to only four states – would have occupied less than half of the continent.

In the light of the conflicting interests and opinions, the arrival of federation was almost a miracle. Moreover it was achieved without strong support from the new Labor parties. They remained hostile or lukewarm towards federation. They saw it as a diversion from crucial social and economic grievances and from the fight of labour versus capital. On several vital occasions in the following century Labor expressed a preference for one central government rather than a federal system.

5

The new constitution of the Commonwealth of Australia consisted of 128 clauses, most of which were no longer than one sentence. The printed document could be read with ease by almost anybody who devoted half an hour to the task; but few bothered to read it in full. The document emphasised that the Commonwealth had power to impose taxes and the sole power to impose import and excise duties. As import duties were the main source of government income, the Commonwealth in its first decade was compelled under section 87 of the constitution to return to the states three-quarters of the net revenue that it raised from import and excise duties. The constitution said that henceforth commerce between the states would be free; and the old customs houses on the colonial borders ceased to function, except in Western Australia, which was permitted – until 1906 – to protect its local industries by taxing imported goods. The new Commonwealth was given power over the combined army and combined navy. The new Commonwealth could make the laws on immigration and emigration, on posts, telegraphs, telephones and similar services, currency and coinage, and banking and insurance except where carried on by the state governments. The new government was to control such services as census and statistics, meteorology, coastal navigation, and weights and measures.

There were also wide areas in potential dispute. Thus the Commonwealth had no direct power in the vital field of industrial relations except for the authority to settle industrial disputes that extended beyond one state. Likewise the Commonwealth had the power to grant old-age and invalid pensions, but unemployment and medical benefits were not formally added to its constitutional powers until 1946. The states remained powerful. Their laws had more effect on the daily life of everyone. Their combined budgets far exceeded the early federal budgets. The employees of each of the larger state governments outnumbered the employees of the federal government, because the states retained control of the railways, police and prisons, government schools and many other public activities. The creation of the Commonwealth was essentially a series of compromises, of shotgun marriages and threatened divorces; and in the opinion of Alfred Deakin it was achieved by 'a series of miracles'. Without those untidy compromises, no federation could have been achieved.

A wealthy Scottish nobleman was invited to be governor-general of Australia. More than a decade earlier he had become governor of Victoria when he was only twenty-nine years of age, and the small Victorian wheat town of Hopetoun still carries his name. Lord Hopetoun returned in 1895 to the British Isles with a reputation as a popular sporting governor; and in the following years he continued to keep his beagles and those small harrier hounds used in hunting the hare, and became well known for riding 'vigorously but unluckily to hounds'.

Coming again to Australia late in 1900, his first duty as the incoming governor-general was to select a prime minister to preside over the new Commonwealth until the first elections could be arranged. In his hunt for a prime minister, Hopetoun again 'rode vigorously but unluckily', choosing the premier of New South Wales, Sir William Lyne. The choice was unwise, for Lyne lacked national prestige and had not displayed the federal sympathies necessary to muster a ministry of talented men from all the states. On Christmas Eve 1900, Hopetoun acknowledged his own error by inviting Edmund Barton to form a ministry. Though Barton had not risen higher than the acting premiership of New South Wales he had led the federal crusade in that colony where, above all others, a tactful leader was essential.

Born in Sydney fifty-one years previously, the son of a businessman and pioneer stockbroker, Barton did not believe that the heart of Australia lay on the beautiful shores of Sydney Harbour. His imagination spanned the continent, and indeed he had coined the memorable sentence: 'For the first time in the world's history, there will be a nation for a continent, and a continent for a nation.' Barton was said by some to be no more than a gifted layabout, a gregarious man who devoted to dinners and conversations at his Athenaeum Club a volume of time that, if spent on his law books, could increase his renown as a barrister. But it was precisely those qualities of charm and patience – qualities more likely in a man of leisure – that made him such a successful seeker of those compromises that alone made a federation possible.

Barton quickly selected his cabinet. His seven ministers included three premiers of the colonies. Indeed there would have been a fourth but for the fact that the South Australian premier had left Adelaide on a short Christmas holiday and could not be contacted.

CHAPTER THIRTEEN

The frail small ship

On the first day of 1901, at Centennial Park in Sydney, Lord Hopetoun proclaimed the inauguration of the Commonwealth of Australia. That day, the six customs departments and their staff formally joined the Commonwealth, but the postal and defence departments and their post offices and ships and artillery were not transferred until two months later. Edmund Barton – duly sworn in as first prime minister – may have thought on that first day of 1901 of the strange brew of motives and events that created a united Australia. There was the hope of financial gain for thousands of merchants, farmers, factory owners and labourers. There was the idealism and pride and all the complex emotions of nationalism and Empire. To a smaller degree there was the recurring fear of a foreign invader who could only be repelled by a united Australia.

The first months of a new nation are usually all-absorbing, but external events seized the headlines. Three weeks exactly after the inauguration of the Commonwealth, Queen Victoria died. Perhaps no other death in the twentieth century so captured the people's imagination. She was the most famous woman in the world (no film star or pop star existed then) in the eyes of most people of 1901. The most celebrated monarch in history, she presided over the largest empire the world had seen.

Though she had not travelled much further from home than the Swiss lakes, her name was sprinkled liberally across the world's atlas. Two of the six colonies – Victoria and Queensland – were named after her. Hundreds of Australian streets and other geographical features ranging from lakes and rivers to deserts were called Victoria, and her face – the best known in the world – appeared on nearly all Australian postage stamps. After her death in her palace in the Isle of Wight, the news sent by telegraphic message in relays across Asia and so to Australia set in motion nearly every church bell, banner, flag, pipe organ, brass band and piece of artillery.

Australia was only one minute old but thousands of its soldiers and sailors were already at war, for the Empire. Soldiers from every colony were fighting the Boers in South Africa. They first fought under the British or colonial flags, but the Australian flag with its Southern Cross was promptly designed. That year three Australians won the Victoria Cross for valour, and in one battle, fought at Wilmansrust, eighteen Victorians were killed. Meanwhile naval contingents had sailed from several Australian colonies to fight the Boxer Rebellion in China.

2

Plans were made quickly for the first federal elections, because Barton's cabinet was simply the caretaker. At the end of March, across the country, from the sleepy yellow-stone towns of central

Tasmania to wooden-stilt towns in north Queensland, thousands of polling booths were ready for the voters to elect their thirty-six senators and their seventy-five members of the House of Representatives. That first federal election had little in common with today's elections. The political leaders each managed to speak in no more than three states, for the campaign was quick, the inter-state journeys were long, and there were no national organisations to arrange the itinerary of leaders. Women, except in South and Western Australia, were not permitted to vote.

Curiously, although the election was spread over two days, the results were finalised earlier than they are today, for no pref-erences had to be counted. The election was virtually a deadlock. The Protectionists, of whom Barton was the informal leader, won most seats in the lower house and the Free Traders won most seats in the upper house; but the small Labor Party held the balance of power in both houses. To aggravate the confusion, most members saw themselves, on most topics, as representing their own corner of Australia rather than a political creed.

In May 1901 the newly elected members came in train and ship for the opening of Parliament in the temporary capital, Melbourne, a city that some had never seen. They came not always knowing what side they would take on some of the important debates, and some did not know which party they would join.

Many of the new parliamentarians, far from home, had no pros-pect of seeing their wife and children for many months. Members from north Queensland and Western Australia usually had to travel for at least one week by coastal steamship just to reach their elector-ate. The idea that an elected member should spend the maximum time in his own electorate was not yet the rule, and some members brought their family to Melbourne and settled there for the dura-tion of the parliament.

Several of the new politicians tried to keep their origins a secret. William Henry Groom, as observed in Volume I, had reached Sydney in an English convict ship in 1849, and after serving his sentence – and an additional one – he moved to Toowoomba in southern Queensland where his new wife helped him along the road to commercial success. The proudest day of his life was in May 1901. As the oldest member of the House of Representatives he was given the honour of making the first full-length speech, which he proceeded to deliver with 'dignity and gravity of manner', according to one report. 'Now, sir, we are commencing yet another page of our history,' Groom gravely said to the speaker of the house. It was astonishing that an old convict should proudly turn that page.

He was the first federal parliamentarian to vacate his seat. In the early hours of 8 August 1901 he succumbed to pneumonia; and at 2.45 that afternoon the prime minister, Edmund Barton, moved that the house of representatives do now adjourn: 'I may inform honourable members that the body of our deceased fellow member will be conveyed to the railway station, to be taken thence to Queensland by the express, at a quarter past five this afternoon.' Groom's funeral train rushing through the night is a haunting echo of the convict era. His talented son won the by-election for the vacant seat. So was created the first of many political dynasties in federal history.

3 .

Federal loyalties and functions grew slowly. Most of the vital Commonwealth institutions did not suddenly materialise in 1901. The High Court of Australia did not sit until late in 1903, and a large minority of politicians even opposed it as an extravagant addition to a mature system of courts. The three justices of the court – Sir Samuel Griffith who had been chief justice of Queensland, Sir Edmund Barton who had just resigned as prime minister, and Senator R. E. O'Connor – were fathers of federation, knew the dangers of the conflict between the Commonwealth and states, and usually restrained the growth of federal powers when legal controversies arose. The Commonwealth takeover of Papua from the British was also hesitant, and the first Australian governor did not reach Port Moresby until Easter Sunday 1907. The Northern Territory of South Australia, which during the federal negotiations of the 1890s was expected soon to be transferred to the Commonwealth, was not transferred until New Year's Day 1911.

A long railway crossing arid country to link Port Augusta (South Australia) and Kalgoorlie and thus providing a land route to Perth was crucial to a united nation, for Western Australia was remote. Meanwhile it was approachable only by sea – except for a few overlanders who cycled across more than half the continent on the roughest of tracks. Barton genuinely promised a railway to the west in his policy speech of January 1901 but it was not completed until 1917. Meanwhile, Western Australians were entitled to feel disappointed and even deceived.

Many of the vital services that seemed tailor-made for central control remained with the six state governments for many years. The Commonwealth was even slow in taking up activities assigned to it by the federal constitution. It did not take over the weather bureau and the regular forecasts until 1907 or control of the lighthouses around the coastline until 1911, and was even later in issuing its own postage stamps and banknotes. The first Australian ambassador was not sent abroad until 1910 when Sir George Reid, the witty rotund free-trader who had been briefly prime minister, went to London with the title of high commissioner. The Commonwealth did not raise its first foreign loan until 1912 when it borrowed half

a million pounds, a portion of which was to be spent on building
Australia House in the Strand in London. It was the First World
War that breathed vigour into the Commonwealth and magnified
its influence.

4

When the twenty-two Labor members and senators assembled in
an unglamorous basement in Parliament House in Melbourne on
8 May 1901 they probably did not share strong hopes that they
would be more than the number-three party. And yet Labor's rise
as a political power was swift. In the first fifteen years of federal
politics it held office more than any other party. In the next sixty-
six years, however, it became the regular party of opposition, only
beginning in 1983 its longest period of power under Hawke and
then Keating.

In the state parliaments Labor had many victories, and its share
of the seats was more than doubled between 1900 and 1909. The
mining boom at the turn of the century gave rise to new electorates
and they favoured Labor. The great drought threw more seats into
Labor's hands, for many of the small farmers at first thought Labor
was their natural ally. Labor was also the most cohesive and disciplined party, whereas the other two parties suffered because at least
half of the political leaders from the six colonies had crowded into
the federal capital where they jostled each other for power.

The funds and organising skills of the rising trade unions
helped the Labor Party, and the party in turn fostered the unions.
Thus the federal Conciliation and Arbitration Act of 1904 gave
preference to unionists, thereby drawing into the unions thousands
of workers who had previously hesitated to join. Another federal
law in 1909 further protected trade unions by decreeing that their

members could not be victimised for taking part in union activities. The dice, which for long had been loaded against unionists, was more and more loaded in their favour. Between 1901 and 1914 the trade unionists increased from about 100 000 to half a million, and their votes usually backed Labor. The party that, being newer and smaller, had done least to create the Commonwealth was at first its main beneficiary.

When Labor won office in April 1904 it was one of the first leftist governments in the history of democracy. Its first cabinet was inexperienced – how could it be otherwise? The prime minister, John Christian Watson, was aged thirty-seven, a broad-shouldered man of middling height who saw the world through eyes of sapphire-blue. By trade he was a compositor and printer with the stumpy fingertips once common in those who each year had to pick up, hundreds of thousands of times, the small metallic letters of the alphabet. He was neither a notable orator nor a shaper of grand policies, but he had tolerance, goodwill and common sense. He was to leave parliament when still young, moving first to a gold-dredging venture in South Africa.

That first Labor cabinet included two British emigrants who were to rule the country for twelve of the next twenty years: William Morris Hughes will dominate part of the following two chapters, while the minister for trade was Andrew Fisher, once a Gympie goldminer and engine driver, who later served as prime minister in the year of Gallipoli.

Senator Gregor McGregor was the veteran of the first Labor ministry, being fifty-five years old. Once a wrestler, he still resembled one, with his squat physique. He had emigrated from Scottish shipyards to South Australia where he worked as an agricultural labourer and then as a union organiser. A teetotaller, he often quoted the Bible, but was one of the minority of senators who had opposed the ritual of opening each day's proceedings with the Lord's Prayer. He was half blind, the result of an accident while he was felling a tree. Before delivering a speech, he would sit down and listen carefully to a helper who read aloud the relevant facts and statistics. A retentive memory was valued much more in 1901 than it is today.

Of the remaining ministers, E. L. Batchelor had been a railway engineer in South Australia and Hugh Mahon a printer and journalist on the Western Australian goldfields. Mahon was the only Roman Catholic minister in a party in which Catholics were to become very influential. He was to be expelled from the federal parliament in 1920, on the motion of his former colleague Hughes, after making a 'seditious speech' that attacked the British Crown and supported Irish liberation.

The Labor ministry of 1904 is sometimes seen as a landmark in Australian nationalism, because Labor was later to pride itself on its nationalism. It is therefore a surprise to find that most of Labor's early ministers – unlike their rivals – were relative newcomers to Australia. Half had arrived in the flood of migrants of the years 1883 to 1886 when Australia was booming, and their political ideas reflected more the experience of their homeland than their new land. Arriving with a sense of the injustice of the old world they soon found that in Australia the injustices were fewer, though here the injustices disturbed them the more because they were less to be expected.

The Free Trade Party, one of the three main parties, was a disappointment to its champions. It was almost the largest party after the first federal election, but in all held office for only a few months, and in 1909 merged with the Liberal Party. Its stronghold was New South Wales, its members included a few intellectuals, and its leader, Sir George Reid, was one of the wittiest and most eloquent members in the first half-century of the Commonwealth. Almost a conservative party, in its brief life it was the one strong voice against the regulationism that became the main Australian ideology for three-quarters of a century.

Between 1901 and 1909 the most victorious party in the federal parliament was the middle-road Liberal Party. Labor and Liberal both were reformist parties without being militant; and for almost a decade each party was willing to support the other in parliament though in elections they were usually strong rivals. The Liberals were led for the first two years by Edmund Barton, a native of Sydney, a convivial and eloquent barrister who was widely trusted. Its next leader was Alfred Deakin, a Melbourne barrister who in his three terms as prime minister proved to be one of the most creative politicians in Australian history. The son of an accountant in the gold-rush coaching firm of Cobb & Co., Deakin read widely, wrote lucidly, delved into exotic religions, and displayed that oratorical ability that was a wonderful asset in the days when politicians often spoke in a crowded hall or from the flare-lit balcony of a country hotel. On his few visits to England his 'silver-tongued' speeches were admired by connoisseurs of oratory. A practical politician, when young he had toured India and California before legislating for Victoria's first big irrigation scheme, and when prime minister he often rode his bicycle in Melbourne, once receiving a summons for riding on the footpath. His political career was to be cut short by a cruel blow – loss of memory.

Deakin's Liberals or Liberal Protectionists – for they strongly supported a tariff against foreign imports – were more a Victorian party, though they held rural seats in New South Wales and southern Queensland, and a scatter of seats in other states. Of the ten Liberals who held portfolios in the Deakin ministries of 1905–08, four were lawyers by profession. The early Liberal ministries were more rural than the early Labor ministries, and included two farmers and pastoralists and two land surveyors. The only minister who had not been born in Australia was Senator Thomas Playford, and he had lived here for half a century. The Liberal Party attracted the fathers of federation; and even in 1905 – when some of the fathers had died or become judges – Deakin's cabinet of eight included three men who had been premiers in the 1890s – John Forrest of Western Australia, Playford of South Australia and Sir William Lyne of New South Wales. Understandably Deakin's party showed a slightly proprietorial attitude to the Commonwealth – it was largely their child. The largest party after the first federal election, the Liberals were the smallest by 1906. Three years later they fused with the Free Traders under the name of the Fusion Party.

Perhaps it was inevitable that the Deakin Liberals should have been squeezed out, just as another middle party, the English Liberals, was to be squashed by pressure from both right and left in the 1920s. And yet the political history of the half-century after the death of the Deakin Liberals suggests that perhaps the country lost by their death. Increasingly the main liberal-conservative party became absorbed in increasing the country's wealth, and concerned itself rather less about the question whether that output was distributed in the nation's best interests. In contrast the Labor Party became absorbed in ways of redistributing wealth and was concerned less with practical ways of producing wealth.

5

The new parliament promptly set up the White Australia policy. As Edmund Barton the prime minister made clear, it was intended to be a permanent and emphatic policy: 'These races are, in comparison with the white races – I think no one wants convincing of this fact – unequal and inferior. The doctrine of the equality of men was never intended to apply to the equality of the Englishman and the Chinaman . . . Nothing in this world can put these two races upon an equality.'

White Australia was the favoured term until about 1940. An unfortunate name, especially in retrospect, it might haunt Australia for decades to come. Today Asian people are entitled to take some offence at it, though they fail to observe that their own nations' immigration policies are, by most criteria, more restrictive today than Australia's was or is. The label White Australia was not an accurate description of the policy. The Indigenous Australians were not white and they remained part of the land. Likewise the large minority of Asians still living in Australia were entitled to remain here, and their children and grandchildren too.

Under the Immigration Restriction Act of 1901 it was difficult for an Asian or African to enter the country. A few were granted permission: in the first year of the law four Assyrians, six Indians and eight Japanese legally entered. Not one Chinese was admitted as a migrant, but some newcomers were allowed to stay for long periods as businesspeople and students. No restriction was placed, so far as is known, on the entry of people of darker skin arriving from Mediterranean Europe. As a seemingly civilised form of control, a dictation test – a demand that the prospective immigrants communicate in a specified foreign language – was imposed on migrants thought to be undesirable. Between 1908 and 1915 hundreds of foreigners were so excluded. A total of 158, mostly Chinese, were actually stowaways. Another 131 were excluded primarily for reasons of ill health, and nearly all were British, though one was Japanese.

The main fear embedded in this restrictive policy was that immigration from Japan and China would be too large and disrupting. In contrast many Australians of that era felt sympathy towards individual Chinese whom they knew. The unusual career of Thomas

Bakhap would have faltered without that sympathy.

A Ballarat orphan born to a very young Irish mother, Bakhap was adopted in about 1868 by a Chinese storekeeper, Gee Bak Hap, and became fluent in the Cantonese language. Moving to the tin-fields in north-east Tasmania where Chinese were numerous, Bakhap became a tin miner and also an interpreter and lobbyist for the local Chinese. Despite his fair complexion and handlebar moustache he encouraged the belief that he himself was half-Chinese, but it is doubtful if that camouflage cost him any votes. From 1909 he was successively a Liberal member of Tasmania's lower house and Australia's Senate, and a firm upholder of both the White Australia policy and of Chinese culture – a rare blend of doctrines to be housed in the one mind. Nationalism also spurred him. His belief was that Australia, being so close to Asia, had to learn how to defend itself.

After the Chinese question had been rehandled, the Pacific Islanders or Kanakas awaited their verdict. For decades their hard work had been vital for the sugarcane plantations on the fertile coastal soils of the Pacific's tropical coast. In effect they were guest workers, not unlike the Asians working in the oil-rich lands of the Middle East today, and it was resolved that they should be sent home to their islands. Who would work in the cane fields once they were gone? White labour would become the norm, and a federal subsidy would be paid to sugar producers so that they could afford the higher wages. In the summer of 1906–07 the Islanders were ready to sail away to the Solomons, New Hebrides and other groups of islands. Parliament agreed that more than 1000 should be allowed to stay – mainly those who had lived continuously in Australia for twenty years or owned freehold land.

Under the new laws, the highly protected sugar industry continued to flourish, especially in the tropics. The men, women and children of Australia soon learned that the sugar that they spooned into their tea or consumed in their lollies and biscuits was dearer than it would otherwise have been. The protective tariff was applied to a wide range of imports, and in 1908 the import duties became decidedly higher. But Australia was not yet as protectionist as the United States and certain European nations.

In remote Australian places, groups of Chinese, Japanese and Afghans flourished. Old men went home, but sometimes the younger Chinese visited their Asian homeland and then quietly returned. The existence of some ghettos was barely known to most well-informed Australians living in the big cities. At Thursday Island and several other tropical ports those suburbs typically called Jap Town caused scant concern until Japan's armed forces threatened Australia in 1941.

6

British New Guinea was formally taken over by Australia in 1902 and renamed Papua. According to one count, Port Moresby the capital then had thirty-six male and eleven female Europeans and just a few houses and offices. The north Queensland firm of Burns, Philp & Co. was the main trader, with its own jetty and big store. It also owned a plantation in Papua with 20 000 Arabian coffee bushes and high grasslands on which grazed Lincoln and crossbred sheep.

In the whole territory of Papua lived only 500 Europeans – missionaries, goldminers, planters, and the magistrates and other government officials. How many Papuans was not known: it was thought that there could be half a million but there was no effective way of counting people who lived in mountains and plateaus that had not even been explored by outsiders.

The Australian government now was solely in charge of Papua, partly because Britain already owned enough colonies. For some years Australia postponed the question of what to do with this land of steep mountains, high rainfall, dense vegetation and tropical diseases.

Many members of the Labor Party disapproved of Australia acquiring such a colony. Alfred Deakin as prime minister felt sympathy with this view but he saw the strategic value of a land that lay opposite tropical Australia and, potentially, flanked one of the world's vital sea lanes. In a crucial debate in 1906 he insisted that Australia had to govern Papua largely in the interest of its own people. Usually, he said, their wellbeing came first, 'even before that of men of our own colour'. Deakin's hope – and that of the incoming governor, Sir Hubert Murray – was that new varieties of agriculture would raise the standard of living of the people. With only a little financial help, Papua was to be conducted into the modern era and not merely be, as an early British official wished, just 'a sort of glorified curiosity-shop and extensive and very expensive ethnological museum'. Australia began to govern Papua, confident that there it would not meet the same trouble in devising policies for Indigenous people as it had faced at home.

Murray arrived there as the head of the colony – his British predecessor had committed suicide. An Australian, Murray was an impressive scholar of the classical languages, briefly the amateur boxing champion of England, and eager to do his best in all his assignments. As governor or 'administrator', he knew there was little money to spend. He spent it carefully.

7

The apportioning of the south-west Pacific among the European powers was like the partitioning of Africa, which was now almost

complete. The Antarctic was the only continent that was not yet
divided into colonial claims. Australia in its own name wondered
whether to make a claim.

Douglas Mawson of the University of Adelaide, an experienced young explorer, led the Australian expedition. He hoped, as a
geologist, to discover minerals, and later he did dredge evidence of
brown coal from the ocean floor. A wide range of scientific investi-
gation – extending from climate to biology – dominated his plans.
He wished ultimately to 'hoist the Australian flag in land which
geographically should belong to Australia'.

Mawson knew that this was a momentous time in the exploration of the Antarctic. He could not know that four days after
he set out on his voyage, the Norwegian Amundsen reached the
South Pole, and four months later his rival, Scott, would win the
rival attempt. Compared to such mighty names Mawson could not
expect international glamour, but it came to him.

The *Aurora*, a tiny steamship of 600 tons, its decks crammed
with stores and equipment and 266 tons of coal, prepared to sail
from Hobart on the long journey to the Antarctic. On the afternoon
of Saturday 2 December 1911, a crowd stood on the pier and nearby
waterfront; the governor and his wife arrived to farewell Mawson;
and Captain J. K. Davis pointed his ship downstream while a military band played 'God Be With You Till We Meet Again'. After
steaming slowly down the harbour, the ship waited for a fishing
boat to arrive from the shore nearby with a pack of Greenland
sledge dogs and their supervisor, Belgrave Ninnis. Neither he nor
the dogs would see 'home' again.

Another ship carrying more members of the expedition,
a flock of fifty-eight sheep and a second load of coal, steamed from
Hobart. The two ships met far to the south-west at Macquarie
Island where scientists and technicians set up a camp and began

to study the climate, for it was rightly believed that daily weather reports from the far south would enable more accurate forecasts of Australian weather. Known then as wireless telegraphy, radio was sufficiently advanced to persuade Mawson that for the first time regular messages could be transmitted across the wide ocean from Antarctica to Australia. As the distance was long, Macquarie Island might serve as a relay station for daily weather reports sent by radio. Meteorology, more than any other science, spurred this expedition.

Captain Davis, like Mawson, was in his late twenties but already one of the best icefield mariners in the world. The success of the expedition depended as much on his judgement as on Mawson's. He had to guide his ship through seas littered with ice, unload his cargo where no harbour existed, and leave for home before the sea again clogged with ice. On approaching his destination at Commonwealth Bay he found to his dismay that the ice was 80 sea miles north of its previously recorded position at that time of the year. Safely landed, Mawson and his party watched the *Aurora* steam away and then settled down to spend their first working winter on their isolated base.

Late in 1912, the days becoming warmer, Mawson and two companions commenced a long journey with their dogs pulling two sledges across the snow-covered landscape. Food provided the main cargo for the sledges, along with six big tins of kerosene as fuel for their Primus stove. On 14 December 1912, 500 kilometres from their base, they faced disaster. Ninnis and his sledge – carrying most of the food and one of the two precious tents – fell into a crevasse and disappeared from sight. For a short time the dogs were heard moaning far below, but no sound came from Ninnis. When silence fell and all hope had gone, Mawson read aloud the Anglican burial service from the prayer book.

Forced to retreat with only one sledge, Mawson made headway.

Then his Swiss-born companion, Xavier Mertz, fell ill and, becoming weak and then delirious, died along the way. It is now believed that Mertz died from malnutrition or from the toxic effects of eating a surfeit of dog's liver. Again Mawson read the burial service, painfully holding open the page, for his fingers, like his feet, were frostbitten.

Alone, with no dogs to help, Mawson pulled his sledge forward in raging winds. Once he fell down a crevasse and, dangling on a rope, clawed himself up. Growing weaker, he was still weeks away from his coastal base where, he hoped, the *Aurora* would await his arrival. Once departed it would not return for almost another year. Mawson, at last nearing the coast, saw the smoke rising from the funnel as the ship disappeared towards Australia.

He had left behind six men at the base camp, and day after day they kept a constant lookout for him. They felt excitement and anxiety when they saw, in poor visibility, a heavily clothed man and his sledge coming towards them. Rushing forward to assist the man they saw it was Mawson. He explained that his colleagues would not return. At the base camp he and his team lived through another terrible winter.

Mawson's expedition was remarkable. On numerous topics, whether magnetism or bacteriology, biology or meteorology, his scientists added more than any previous explorers to scientific knowledge of this land of ice and wind. They recorded, at more than 320 kilometres an hour, the strongest wind so far measured in the world. They were also the first, after serious setbacks, to employ radio in that continent. Though the wind toppled the wireless aerial occasionally, and a roaring and rushing noise muffled many incoming messages, the team's acute sense of isolation was ended. After his perilous journey Mawson was able to send away a radio message announcing that he was safe. In Melbourne his long-standing fiancée, Paquita Delprat, was overjoyed, though months would pass before Captain Davis could again reach the Antarctic base and bring home Mawson and his team.

Mawson was to return to the Antarctic in 1929, his costly expedition largely financed by the Melbourne confectionery maker Macpherson Robertson. The stern, unshakeable Davis was again the captain of the expedition's ship. An outcome of this latest adventure was that Australia was viewed globally as a vital pioneer of the Antarctic. In 1936, after formally taking over most of the icy territory already claimed by Britain, Australia was the nominal possessor of four-tenths of Antarctica. That the region, both the land and ocean, was to be a vital laboratory for the study of the world's climate was not yet realised.

8

In the decade before the First World War, the distant places in Australia's sphere of influence exerted an unusual influence. Broken Hill in practical terms was remote; and a premier of New South Wales who wished to visit this third-largest city in his own state had to travel by train from Sydney to Melbourne and so to Adelaide and then through rural South Australia to Broken Hill, a succession of rail journeys covering more than 2000 kilometres. Broken Hill was a stronghold of trade unions, one of the world's important producers of silver, lead and zinc, and the operating base of big mining companies including the Zinc Corporation (now known as Rio Tinto) and the Broken Hill Proprietary Company (now known as BHP Billiton).

BHP in 1910 had clearly passed its richest years on the Broken Hill field. When metal prices were low it temporarily closed parts of its big mine. But in that same region it also owned the largest deposit of iron ore known in the nation at that time, and each year a small tonnage of that iron ore was a valuable flux or ingredient of the silver-lead smelting process at nearby Port Pirie. The idea was obvious: why not build a steelworks and convert the iron ore into iron and steel? Clearly BHP's future was more in steel than in silver. A consultant, David Baker, coming from Philadelphia to assess the prospects, was impressed. He recommended that the iron ore be shipped from South Australia to Newcastle, the coal port not far from Sydney, and that there a big steelworks be built.

The foundations of the steelworks at Newcastle were on mangrove swamps, close to the port. It was a sign of the industrial enthusiasm of the times that land reserved for a botanical garden was willingly surrendered to enlarge the site. After all, the annual output of steel was a barometer of a modern nation's strength. On the other hand, a few critics feared that such a large steelworks would puff black and white smoke over the city, day and night, perhaps impairing the health of invalids. The critics were informed that steelworks 'make hardly any smoke', a strange reply that was cheerfully accepted at first.

The steelworks were officially opened on a sunny weekday in June 1915, a wartime year. Among the invited guests were the Hoskins family, whose smaller iron and steel works stood at Lithgow on the other side of the Blue Mountains. They did not realise that twenty years later they would be gobbled up by the efficient BHP. Another seventy years passed by, and BHP was the biggest mining company in the world.

CHAPTER FOURTEEN

Gallipoli

Britain was in decline. Ruler of the widest empire the world had seen and the largest navy to sail the seas, it was slowly waning. In 1900 its far-flung empire and mighty navy diverted attention from the industrial decline of what once was called the workshop of the world. For several decades, few Australians glimpsed this decline.

While Britain was lagging, optimistic Germany resembled an economic miracle, so fast was its growth in various spheres. In some ways it outshone the China that boomed in the early 2000s. Germany was the hub of science and new technology. Its army was the most successful in Europe, and its swift victory over France in the war of 1870 and 1871 was partly the result of railways organised to carry a mass of soldiers and munitions speedily to the front line. Its armies could easily expand, for Germany's population was the fifth largest in the world. Germany's steelworks expanded so swiftly that soon their output exceeded the combined tally of the three main nations that were to oppose it in the coming war: Britain, France and Russia.

Nothing did more to reveal German ambitions than the completion in 1895, on German soil, of the deep Kiel Canal. Even today it is surprising to stand on the deck of an ocean-going ship and see dairy cows grazing to left and right. This canal enabled the expanding German navy to steam safely between the Baltic Sea and the North Sea.

2

Germany also acquired its first overseas colonies. By the year 1900, German East Africa, South-West Africa (now Namibia) and the West African territories of Cameroon and Togo flew the German flag. In the west Pacific, German possessions stretched from a harbour in north China to New Guinea and Samoa. In New Guinea, on opposite sides of the Owen Stanley Range, Germany and Australia became colonial neighbours. In the main Australian ports the flag seen most often, after Britain's flag, was the German. It was a broad fear of Germany, and a fear that Britain's naval dominance was declining, that persuaded Australia to build its own new navy and place an order in 1909 with British shipyards for one large cruiser and two destroyers. Australia also resolved to introduce compulsory military training for the older boys and young men. Left-wing as well as right-wing politicians strongly supported this emphasis on an armed Australia.

The First World War, widely expected, began in August 1914. Within one week Germany had invaded France and Belgium; Austria was fighting Serbia; and Austria and Germany were fighting Russia in the east. Turkey had not yet decided how to respond, but finally it entered the war on Germany's side in October 1914.

Italy was expected to join as another ally but in the new year it became, instead, the enemy of Germany and Austria. The war quickly spread to Africa and the Pacific.

Britain expected it to be a short and victorious war. Perhaps it would end before the first Australian soldiers – now rushing to enlist – could reach Europe, but first the enemy had to be defeated in the southern hemisphere too. German warships were already steaming somewhere in the vast Pacific, and so a surprise attack on an Australian port was possible. As Germany possessed the north-eastern corner of the island of New Guinea and adjacent strategic islands such as New Britain, New Ireland and Bougainville, its bases were dangerously close to Queensland. German naval vessels using Rabaul as a coaling base could prey on Australian merchant ships. The port of Rabaul and its wireless station had to be captured, and six Australians were killed in the fighting.

Early in October 1914, Tasmanians reported that they saw strange objects in the sky. Perhaps they were German aeroplanes that had been launched from a German raider that was lying in a remote western Tasmanian harbour and awaiting the opportunity to attack a convoy carrying New Zealand troops and horses to the war zone in the northern hemisphere.

Military officials in Hobart, knowing that the deserted south-western harbour of Port Davey could conceal a large German warship, sent three men to investigate. They left Hobart in the Derwent Valley train, led their packhorses on the next stage of the long journey, and finally walked with their own supplies and two boxes of carrier pigeons. Stretches of the old foot-track were overgrown and the men used axes to clear the way. They came in sight of Port Davey after six days. Finding no ship in the lonely harbour, they released two homing pigeons that carried to Hobart two copies of their reassuring scribbled message. The overland expedition reflected the sense of vulnerability that many Australian officials felt in the opening months of the war.

On 1 November 1914, in the safe harbour of Albany in Western Australia, a convoy packed with some 30 000 Australian and New Zealand troops was ready to steam west into the Indian Ocean, towards an unnamed destination. The largest fleet hitherto seen in Australian seas, it carried 8000 horses. More and more horses would cross this wide ocean, and in the end 121 000 made the voyage, from which only one returned. The presence of so many horses confirmed the old precept that nearly every new war is expected, at first, to be a replica of the previous one. Horses had been vital in the Boer War, and a cavalry charge sometimes sent disciplined troops into panic and retreat; but the crowded Western Front in France in 1914 offered almost no role for the cavalry horse.

Most Australian soldiers believed that they were on their way to fight the Germans on the battlefields in France. Turkey, however, had just entered the war as one of Germany's allies; and in London there arose the fear that the Turks might attempt to capture the Suez Canal. Promptly the canal and Egypt became the destination of the Australian convoy. In December the Australian and New Zealand Army Corps – the Anzac force – disembarked at Alexandria and for several months they camped in sight of the ancient pyramids of Egypt.

In Europe itself stood two main battlefronts. On the Eastern Front, extending almost from the Baltic Sea to the Black Sea, the Russians confronted the German and the Austro-Hungarian armies. There, armies advanced and retreated, month after month. In contrast the Western Front – there the Germans fought the French and British – extended from the English Channel and the North Sea all the way to neutral Switzerland, and was soon to become the scene of deadlocked warfare.

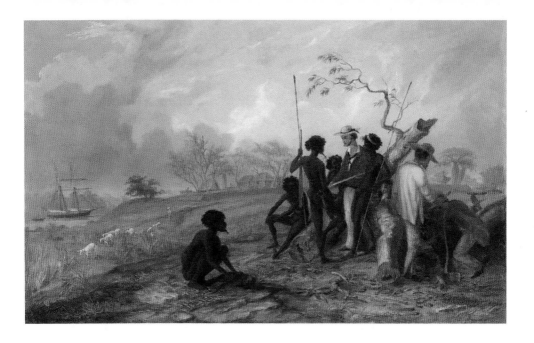

Aborigines at the Victoria River in the Northern Territory, as seen by English artist Thomas Baines in 1855. He travelled with the explorer A. C. Gregory.

Thomas Baines with Aborigines Near the Mouth of the Victoria River (detail), *N.T.*, by Thomas Baines, 1857 (National Library of Australia, nla.obj-134296782)

The homestead of Dunlop sheep station fronted the flooded Darling River (far left) in 1886. Aborigines gather in the foreground, followed by white employees – and more than 100 000 sheep are scattered out of sight.

Homestead, Dunlop Station, Darling River (detail), by Charles Bayliss, 1886 (National Gallery of Victoria, Melbourne)

Nannultera the batsman poses at the Anglican mission at Poonindie, near Port Lincoln in South Australia in 1854. In 1868 Aboriginal cricketers from Victoria form the first Australian sporting team to tour England.

Portrait of Nannultera, a Young Poonindie Cricketer (detail), by J. M. Crossland, 1854 (The National Gallery of Australia, Canberra and the National Library of Australia, Canberra)

Diggers in Victoria in 1858. Standing by a creek, they inspect a prospecting pan in which alluvial gold is shining. They had to stand perfectly still so that the photograph would not be blurred.

Group of Diggers, by Richard Daintree & Antoine Fauchery, ca.1858 (State Library of Victoria)

Melbourne in 1885–86. The city was about to boom, and cable trams would replace the horse-drawn cabs standing in the middle of Bourke Street.

Allegro con brio, Bourke Street West (detail), by Tom Roberts, 1885–86 (National Gallery of Australia, Canberra and the National Library of Australia, Canberra)

In January 1857 New South Wales plays Victoria at cricket in the Sydney Domain, before 'a vast concourse of spectators'. One year later leading Victorian cricketers, to keep fit, devise a winter game: Australian Rules football was the result.

The First Cricket Match Between NSW and Victoria, Played in Sydney Domain (detail),
by Samuel Thomas Gill, 1857 (National Library of Australia, nla.obj-134361456)

When the first federal parliament was formally opened in Melbourne in May 1901, rising artist Tom Roberts was commissioned to paint the scene. Exactly 100 years later, parliament met again in the same building for one afternoon.

The Big Picture, by Tom Roberts, circa 1903 (Royal Collection Trust/© Her Majesty Queen Elizabeth II 2016)

Australia was the first country in the world to give women the dual rights to vote and to stand for the national parliament. Here the graffiti women conduct their crusade with white chalk.

Three Women Writing Pro-Suffragette Graffiti on a Wall in Chalk, 1900–1910, from the Papers of Bessie Rischbieth (National Library of Australia, nla.obj-250831564)

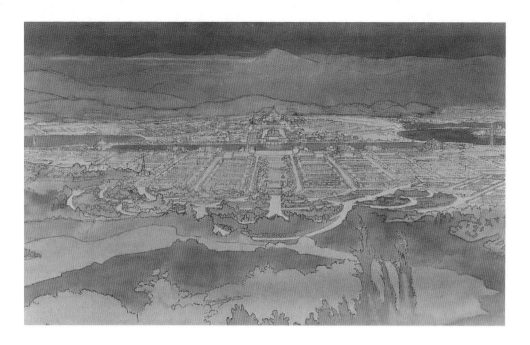

Marion Mahony Griffin was a young American architect. In 1912 her handsome drawings, envisaging the Canberra-to-be, helped her husband Walter win the competition for a design of the nation's capital.

View from Summit of Mount Ainslie, by Marion Mahony Griffin, 1911 (National Archives of Australia, A710,49)

These Australian Soldiers of the First World War are being towed to Anzac Cove, and are among those to give birth to the Gallipoli legend.

(Australian War Memorial, ID A02781)

Wool was king. Weighing a fleece shorn from a stud merino at Wanganella in the Riverina in 1921, captured by George Lambert. Beatrice Falkiner, fashionable wife of the owner, lolls against a bale of wool.

Weighing the Fleece (detail), by George Lambert, 1921 (National Gallery of Australia, Canberra)

A young Jewish immigrant, Yosl Bergner, painted *The Pie Eaters* in 1940.
The gloomy sauce bottle and empty plate point to a time of austerity.
The Pie Eaters, by Yosl Bergner, 1940 (Yosl Bergner/DAN Gallery, Tel Aviv)

Wartime men of power. From left to right: General Douglas MacArthur,
John Curtin (prime minister 1941–45), Arthur Fadden (1941), and Ben Chifley
(1945–49). All were members of the Advisory War Council.
General MacArthur at a Meeting of the Advisory War Council, 1942 (Australian War Memorial,
ID 042925)

In the Second World War meat was rationed and could be bought only with official ration coupons as well as money. A sole man can be seen in the queue, probably in Sydney.

Meat Queue (detail), by Max Dupain, 1946 (National Gallery of Australia, Canberra)

In 1953 Russell Drysdale painted Aborigines visiting a once-prosperous tropical town. The war memorial stands in the central square.

Shopping Day (detail), by Russell Drysdale, 1953 (Art Gallery of New South Wales)

Tobacco Road in Victoria's Ovens Valley. As the 1950s was the wettest decade
in many farming regions since the 19th century, car-pushing on a muddy, skiddy
road was a common sight.

Tobacco Road, Ovens Valley (detail), by Jeff Carter, 1956 (National Library of Australia, nla.obj-147206695)

In the 1950s Albert Namatjira became the first Aboriginal artist to achieve
fame. In painting his own homeland near Alice Springs he often fixed on
sites of spiritual importance, but the dramatic landscape itself appealed
to city art-buyers. *Portrait of Albert Namatjira*, by Frank Henry Johnston, 1958,
(National Library of Australia, nla.obj-141828409)

The stern human faces of Collins Street, as seen by John Brack in 1956
when this Melbourne street was the financial capital of the nation.
Collins St, 5 p.m. (detail), by John Brack, 1956 (© Helen Brack)

Migrants lining the deck as their ship is about to tie up in Sydney after the long
voyage from Europe. It is 1966, and ships are being challenged by aircraft as the
main carrier of migrants.
Migrants Arriving in Sydney, by David Moore, 1966 (David Moore Photography)

A polling booth in a sheep district near Canberra at the 1969 federal election. The nation was peppered with makeshift polling stations on 'election Saturdays', especially after voting became compulsory in the 1920s.

Country Polling Booth, ACT, 1969 (National Archives of Australia: A1500, K21454)

Vincent Lingiari of the Northern Territory led the strike by cattle workers that eventually resulted in the Wave Hill station returning to Aboriginal hands. In 1975 the prime minister, E.G. Whitlam, ceremonially pours soil into Lingiari's open hands. *Prime Minister Gough Whitlam Pours Sand into the Hands of Traditional Landowner Vincent Lingiari*, by Mervyn Bishop, 1975 (Reproduced with permission from the Commonwealth of Australia through the Department of the Prime Minister and Cabinet)

After an Australian yacht won the America's Cup in 1983, the speech-making and champagne-pouring crisscrossed the country. John Bertrand, the skipper, is third from the left in the front row, and next to him sits Alan Bond, the owner.

Final Press Conference, Australia II *Victory,* by Daniel Forster, 1983 (© Daniel Forster)

Australia Day – honouring the raising of the British flag in Sydney on 26 January 1788 – is celebrated more widely than ever before. To many Aborigines it is 'invasion day'; but new migrants often embrace the celebrations.

Australia Day Crowd, 2001 (*The New Daily*)

The Gold Coast, and its small holiday resorts of the 1940s, eventually became one of Australia's ten largest cities and a magnet for tourists. In 2015 its population passed 550 000.

Gold Coast, Burleigh Heads Beach, by Kerrie Brailford, 2014 (© Kerrie Brailford)

In summer, huge white cruise ships anchor in Sydney Harbour alongside other vessels of all shapes and sizes. And yet for most of the long Aboriginal history the site was dry land, reminding us that the great shaping event in our peoples' history was the massive rising of the seas.

A Woman Paddleboards with Her Dog, by Brendon Thorne, 2015 (Brendon Thorne/Stringer/ Getty Images)

Soon it was impossible for either army to advance more than a few hundred metres. New firearms made the battleground so dangerous. The latest machine guns could fire hundreds of rounds a minute. The artillery – the big guns that lobbed shells from afar on the enemy troops and trenches – was immensely powerful compared to the guns of the Napoleonic Wars. Moreover new barbed-wire fortifications halted the advance of those soldiers who had survived the deluge of bullets and shrapnel. The armies sought shelter by quickly digging long and deep trenches. The trench was a little fortress and a temporary home, but the home became permanent.

On the Western Front in 1914 the war was deadlocked before Christmas. There was no thought of negotiating a peace treaty, because both sides still hoped for a definite victory. But perhaps the civilians at home – especially the mothers and fathers of the fighting soldiers – would suddenly demand peace. No, they demanded victory.

From this military deadlock arose the plan for a thrust against Turkey in 1915. Turkey and its Ottoman Empire – the new ally of Germany – was seen as 'the sick man of Europe'. Having recently lost short wars in Asia Minor and Libya, this weakling seemed incapable of defending successfully the Dardanelles – that narrow seaway linking the Mediterranean and Black seas. Therefore, if the Allies, fortified by the strength of the British navy, landed near the mouth of the Dardanelles, they would capture the Turkish forts. Then they would fight their way the short distance to Constantinople, the capital of the Ottoman Empire. In the final stage the Russian fleet, waiting in the Black Sea, would bombard Turkey and land its own troops.

The defeat of Turkey could end the stalemate. Invasion could tip the scales in favour of Russia and therefore in favour of its allies,

Britain and France. Thereby would be opened for the first time a sea route along which the Allies could send munitions to Russia. That nation operated the biggest army in the world, but its soldiers were short of almost all supplies, even boots. With the aid of the new supply line through the Dardanelles, a re-equipped and revitalised Russian army might win major victories on the Eastern Front. In turn that would compel Germany to divert troops from the Western Front, thus increasing there the prospect of Anglo-French advances. So the Germans, it was hoped, would be squeezed and hemmed in from both east and west.

Winston Churchill, the English politician then serving as first lord of the admiralty, did more than anybody to promote this secret plan. His scheme, however, had at least one grave defect: it ceased to be secret. British and French ships tried to destroy Turkish forts at the mouth of the Dardanelles, and failed. The Turks thus were emphatically warned. Later, in April, the slow build-up of British and French naval, supply and troop ships in the Greek islands near the Dardanelles gave further warning. The Turkish defences were strengthened. The Allies, too confident of success, were not prepared for the disaster that began at dawn on the first day.

At three o'clock on the morning of Sunday 25 April 1915 the moon sank and the darkness was complete. As the roofless boats loaded with Australian soldiers were slowly towed by small steamboats towards the Turkish shore, the silhouette of low hills and steep cliffs appeared in the faint light. The boats grated into the shingle of the beach, and soldiers with heavy packs and rifles waded ashore. From the higher ground came the fire of Turkish rifles and machine guns.

Throughout the day the invaders went ashore in waves, and casualties were heavy. The British commander thought of retreating, even of evacuating, such was the chaos. But a footing had been won by the end of the day. It was more a toehold, for the front line was no more than 3 kilometres in width, and rarely extended more than 700 metres from the beaches. Of the hundreds of Anzac soldiers who died that day, one was the grandson of Peter Lalor, who had led the rebellion at Eureka on another Sunday sixty-one years earlier.

As in France the firepower was so deadly that the opposing armies soon dug trenches. The deadlock repeated itself. The lines of trenches were so close together that the eyes and mouth of the enemy soldier could sometimes be seen. The rugged country provided places in which snipers could hide and aim their rifle if an opposing head suddenly appeared above the trenches. A celebrated Australian sharpshooter was Billy 'Sniper' Sing, a Queensland kangaroo shooter who was partly of Chinese ancestry. He killed about 200 Turks with his calm and accurate shooting.

The Australians who served at Gallipoli in the course of the campaign have now been analysed and assessed by several generations of dedicated historians. About nine out of every ten of the soldiers were single men. At least three of every ten were immigrants, born in Britain. Most were very young but four of every ten soldiers were aged twenty-six and older.

Later an English historian, an admirer of the Australians, discovered in the 1960s that the official British histories of Gallipoli did not reveal the full truth. At the request of the British government of the day there was deleted the accusation that 'not all Australian units and individuals behaved heroically on April 25th, 1915'. In the course of the campaign, however, the great majority of individuals deserved praise, for they faced dangers and privations that they could not have imagined when they enlisted in Australia.

The following labels appear on the map:

ODESSA Russia's greatest export city with huge wheat warehouses, a harbour that was ice-free for almost 12 months annually and a railway to Moscow, 1136 km north.

Odessa

N

0   100   200 km

Sevastopol
Russian naval base

RUSSIA

BLACK SEA

BULGARIA

Constantinople (Istanbul)

Gallipoli Peninsula
Anzac Cove
Dardanelles

OTTOMAN EMPIRE

ARMENIA

The Gallipoli campaign, 1915

3

Soldiers lived in little dugouts and in holes cut in the cliffs and on the gentler slopes of Gallipoli. They learned to sleep through the deafening noise of the shells exploding nearby. At night the dead were buried, a chaplain reading the service and marking the place where each man lay. The wounded were evacuated to hospital ships whose lights at night could be seen, close to the shore. Heroes, named and unnamed, emerged. At Gallipoli, nine Australians were awarded the Victoria Cross, the first being conferred on Albert Jacka from Victoria and the last on another country boy, Hugo Throssell from the Western Australian wheatfields.

The mail from Australia arrived irregularly in large mailbags, and was devoured. Cigarettes and tobacco were not plentiful, and alcohol was often scarce. At night, when a large crowd could safely gather out of reach of a Turkish bombardment, the reading-aloud

of Australian poetry and the singing of popular hymns were enter-
tainments. The hymns would sometimes be sung softly so that the
Turks would not suspect that here was an easy target for a well-
aimed shell. A few chaplains later recalled that these were among
the most memorable days of their lives.

Summer came, and heat and thirst. Flies swarmed over the
unburied corpses and the faces of the living. The trenches were 'alive
with lice and it is impossible to keep free from them'. Dysentery
and diarrhoea disabled one-quarter of the men in a regiment at the
same time. Scurvy later set in – the same deficiency of vitamin C
that had crippled seamen and convicts during the long voyage to
Australia one century earlier. For those who remained healthy, one
pleasure was to walk to the beach and bathe naked.

In August 1915, with the aid of reinforcements, attempts were
made by British, French, Australian and New Zealand soldiers to
drive back the Turks. Bold attacks were launched to capture prominent hills fortified by the enemy. The casualties in these battles were
massive, though the scene of the intense fighting could be smaller
than a car park in one of today's big supermarkets.

August 1915 was crucial. The head of the German navy, Admiral
Alfred von Tirpitz, analysing the Gallipoli campaign from afar,
confided to his diary that the Turks might well be defeated by their
British, French and Anzac invaders during that month, and that
in consequence the war could well be 'decided against us'. On 8
August the New Zealanders, as if half-confirming Tirpitz's prediction, captured the strategic summit of Chunuk Bair, within sight
of the crucial straits leading towards Constantinople. Perhaps the
opportunity for a major breakthrough had arrived. Like many other
opportunities, it was lost.

In little more than seven months the attacking armies at
Gallipoli lost about 46 000 men. Of those who were killed in action

or died of wounds or disease, 2700 were New Zealanders and 8700 were Australians. The French lost 9900, the British more than twice as many. On the other hand Turkey and the Ottoman Empire lost at least 87 000. Braver and hardier than expected, the Turks won the respect of many of their enemies at Gallipoli.

The British commander, Sir Ian Hamilton, believed that the Dardanelles was still the vital gateway to an early Allied victory in the war. Give him more troops and munitions, he pleaded in October, 'and in one month from to-day, our warships will have Constantinople under their guns'. Losing his argument, Hamilton was recalled to London.

Even to equip the Allied troops for the coming winter was a forbidding task. To warm the troops at night, and to protect them from frostbite, 10 000 oil stoves would be needed, and the oil too. Cargo ships must carry from Britain a small mountain of equipment, which would then be loaded into tiny vessels and ferried ashore. To build winter shelters called for 5000 tonnes of corrugated iron. As these military and transport obstacles were overwhelming, Gallipoli had to be abandoned.

Could the large Allied armies retreat without heavy loss of life? Storms at sea might interrupt the evacuation and leave tens of thousands of soldiers stranded on the shore as prisoners. A disaster was possible – as many as 70 000 troops might be killed or wounded if the evacuation was mishandled.

In mid-December they prepared to leave Gallipoli quietly. Calm seas, dull skies, fog and mist all came to the aid of General Brudenell White who organised the Australians' departure. It was to be one of the most skilled evacuations ever conducted. The Turkish leaders were deceived into assuming that the Australians were still there, huddled in the cold shelters and trenches. They did not yet know that on successive nights an army had crept to the shore where the small boats carried them silently away.

A succession of politicians, poets and historians affirmed that Australia came of age on Anzac Day, 25 April 1915, and that a new nation was revealed to the world. It was true that the Australian soldiers had fought a determined enemy on its home ground, that they had played for the first time in a 'match of the day' in a world league, and moreover had drawn the match. But such a coming of age has its roots in earlier events and Australian attitudes.

Gallipoli, seemingly pointless and even a blunder in the eyes of certain modern historians, did pay a final dividend. The mistakes of 1915 were remembered when the invasion of Nazi-occupied Europe was being planned by Churchill and American leaders during the Second World War. Churchill, above all, understood from his own shattering experience with Gallipoli how difficult it was to mount a sea invasion against a well-fortified foreign shore. So Gallipoli helped to shape D-day in June 1944, when the massed forces from the United States, Britain, Canada and other allies began to invade France. The largest seaborne invasion in the history of the world, it was based on the principle that surprise was all-important. Such was one lesson painfully and humiliatingly learned in 1915.

CHAPTER FIFTEEN

The scythes
of war

Australian soldiers, rested and reinforced after their ordeal in Gallipoli, reached the muddy trenches in France in 1916. Allotted a section of the extensive front line, they fought alongside French, British, Canadians and others. Facing the Germans with their trenches, their concrete fortifications, their entanglements of barbed wire, heavy artillery, howitzers and machine guns, they knew that neither army had effectively broken through the rival defences. The casualties were massive in number. Even the unarmed were vulnerable. In 1916, near Pozières, Albert Coates noted how the stretcher-bearers and a wounded man lying on the stretcher were all 'blown to pieces' by a German shell.

The technology of warfare had reached such a peak that, for several years, victory for either side seemed impossible. The modern history of Australia had been essentially the heartening story of new technology conquering nature. The latest mechanical innovation

had nearly always been welcomed as a friend; but now on the battlefields of France and Belgium the latest in military technology
slaughtered friends and enemies alike.

2

The prime minister, Andrew Fisher, in poor health, resigned on
27 October 1915, towards the end of the Gallipoli campaign.
William Morris Hughes, called 'The Little Digger', was to lead the
nation for the following seven years. Born in the London suburb of
Pimlico, an only child, he was moved to a small Welsh farm after his
mother died. Teaching in London, and seeing no future, he sailed
at the age of twenty-two to Brisbane as an assisted migrant. He
worked in the outback and cooked on a coastal ship before moving
to Sydney where he became a jack-of-all-trades. He could mend
an umbrella, lend a hand in his wife's tiny shop, organise a waterfront dispute, and carry a soapbox to a street corner and stand on it
and attract a crowd with his breathtaking oratory. When in Sydney
in 1894 he won a seat on behalf of the infant Labor Party, his supporters bought him a new suit. Seven years later, when winning a
seat in the first federal parliament in Melbourne, his mental agility
impressed many who met him for the first time. Photographs show
a small and slight man with a thin elfin face and big ears that were
to become increasingly deaf, but no early recordings exist to display
his wit and powers of persuasion.

Hughes believed that his nation could have been victorious at
Gallipoli if, on several crucial days, it had possessed a larger army
and ready reinforcements. In his 'Call to Arms' leaflet, which eligible men received in the letterbox just before Christmas in 1915, he
argued that if the recruiting had been more vigorous 'the Australian
armies would long ago have been camping in Constantinople, and

the world war would have been practically over'. He was adamant that Australia should send more reinforcements to its existing volunteer army in France. The sure way now was to conscript young men, train them as soldiers, and compulsorily send them abroad. With unemployment often above 7 per cent, it should have been easy to conscript idle men, but the Labor Party insisted that Australia's army – unlike most of the other wartime armies – should consist solely of volunteers. This was more than a plea for civil liberties. Many ardent trade unionists who backed the Labor Party were not convinced that it was the people's war. They condemned it as a war between capitalists striving for commercial supremacy.

So long as the war was expected to be short and victorious, the public mood was patient or enthusiastic. But the daily lists of casualties in the newspapers grew long. Moreover the financial cost of the war now imposed penalties on the average wage-earning family. Prices of food, clothing and fuel rose more rapidly than wages. Industrial unrest was the result.

Railways and coalmines, wharves and coastal cargo ships were the main places of discontent. The government railways in New South Wales were probably the largest industrial organisation in the nation, employing more than 42 000 people, and one of their strikes in 1917 was to dislocate the economy as much any strike hitherto recorded in Australia. In that year, seven times as many working days were lost through strikes as in the last peacetime year of 1913. Many wage-earners now saw no valid purpose in the war.

Voluntary enlistments were no longer sufficient to fill the gaps left by those Australians wounded or killed in France. Recruits in 1916 were fewer than in the year of Gallipoli. After touring battlefields in France, Hughes regretted that his country allowed large numbers of fit young men, whether employed or unemployed, to take no part in the war. Statistics compiled at the end of the war were to confirm that Australia equipped, clothed, armed and sent overseas a lower proportion of its fit men than did Britain or New Zealand.

The Commonwealth possessed the power to draft soldiers and to send them overseas, but Hughes was not certain whether voters would support such a drastic step. Clearly the idea of conscripting soldiers was strongly opposed by a phalanx of Labor voters, while many Irish-Australians asked why should they fight for England when it refused to allow Ireland to govern itself. After the Sinn Fein rebellion broke out in Dublin in Easter 1916, and its leaders were secretly tried and executed by the British government – partly on the orders of Sir John Maxwell who had been prominent in the Gallipoli campaign – thousands of Irish-Australians were incensed. An even larger number, and most Catholic bishops too, continued to support Australia's role in the war. Conscious of the emotional turmoil, Hughes decided in 1916 to hold a referendum.

Dr Daniel Mannix, who next year was to become archbishop of Melbourne, entered the debate in September 1916 and widened it. A recent arrival from Ireland, Mannix was in his early fifties, an excellent scholar, and a witty orator who soon learned how to project his voice and reach huge crowds at open-air meetings. He surpassed the late Rev. John Dunmore Lang as the most charismatic and con-troversial churchman ever to appear in a public place in Australia; and he appeared often. He soon learned to be, outwardly, a patriot. 'Australia', he sometimes argued, 'has done her full share – I am inclined to say more than her full share – in this war.' He predicted that an enlarged Australian army would suffer more deaths, which in turn would lead to heavier taxation in order to care for so many limbless soldiers, war widows and orphans after the war.

As the debate about conscription became fiercer, adjacent topics became involved. The debate sponsored pairs of bitter opponents:

Liberal versus Labor, English versus Irish, Australian nationalist versus Empire loyalist, Protestant versus Catholic, and even Labor versus Labor. Male and female entered this cauldron of factors, for noticeably more women than men favoured conscription.

The referendum was fixed for October 1916, and for the first time voting was compulsory for all adults who lived within 5 miles of a polling booth. The question placed before them was slightly complicated: 'Are you in favour of the Government having, in this grave emergency, the same compulsory powers over citizens in regard to requiring their military service, for the term of this War, outside the Commonwealth, as it now has in regard to military service within the Commonwealth?' To this question, 51.6 per cent of the voters said no, their voices being loudest in South Australia and New South Wales. In contrast, the powerful votes in favour of conscription came from Western Australia and Tasmania. Support also came from Europe, where Australian soldiers sometimes expressed disdain for the fit young 'cowards' in their own hometown who had refused to enlist.

Labor, the most successful party in federal politics in the previous ten years, was hopelessly split by the emotional debates. Three weeks after the referendum, Hughes walked out of the federal Labor caucus – his expulsion was imminent – and took with him one-third of the Labor politicians. Joining forces with the Liberal opposition he was able to remain as prime minister. So a new party, the Nationalist Party, was formed to embrace the victors of this deepest split so far experienced in Australian political life. In May 1917 Hughes and his 'Win the War' Nationalist Party won the federal election with a massive majority.

Hughes was tempted again to seek approval from the people for his aim of conscription. Mannix, taunted and provoked, intensified the debate, insisting that it was becoming the Protestants' war. So many of their clergymen were speaking from the recruiting platforms that, in his view, those platforms should be 'purified and disinfected'. As the second referendum came near, many of Mannix's public meetings ended with his audience singing 'God Save Ireland'. In December 1917 the voters, this time with a larger majority, disapproved of conscripting men – essentially single men – to join the army.

The debate was over; the bitterness remained. The Russian revolutions of late 1917, and the withdrawal of Russia from the war, inspired many Labor supporters. They insisted that Australia should begin to withdraw from 'the imperialist and capitalist war'. When the federal conference of the Labor Party met at the Savoy Hotel in Perth in June 1918, at a time when a British victory was not certain, the delegates from New South Wales called for a ban on any further Australian soldiers sailing to Europe. Their proposal was narrowly defeated – by fifteen votes to thirteen. Thousands of women and men whose sons, brothers or fathers were fighting at the French front or lay buried in Gallipoli now tended to view Labor as the party of disloyalty. Federally but not in the states, the party marched from failure to failure, losing all but one election in the next twenty-three years.

3

Germans formed the largest European group in Australia in 1914. Their stronghold was South Australia, but German names were also common in the wheatlands of western Victoria, in rural pockets to the north of Albury, and in south-east Queensland. They built Lutheran churches and often listened to German-speaking pastors, and many read German-language newspapers. Numerous children attended small day schools that taught the German language. As the war stirred deeper emotions, Germans were penalised. Many whose loyalty was suspect were interned – the final total was 2879 – along with captured German seamen. Lutheran pastors were denounced, including several whose sons were away at the war and did not return. In 1917 in South Australia the fifty-two German schools were either closed or provided with a government teacher who spoke no German. The German names of various villages and local landmarks were replaced by the surnames of British military heroes; and on the main road between Sydney and Melbourne the township of Germanton was renamed Holbrook in honour of a British submarine hero who had never seen the town. After the war 700 Germans were expelled from Australia and more than 4000 others chose to leave voluntarily. For seven years after the war no German, Austrian and Hungarian immigrants were admitted to Australia.

In the course of the war, national life was changed in many ways. The hotels were closed at six o'clock in the evening, and in Victoria and South Australia the early closing of hotels remained the law for half a century. Income tax was first imposed by the Commonwealth in 1915: the state income taxes already existed. The Commonwealth debt soared, and the care for the wounded, the war widows and dependants became a huge item on the federal budget in the 1920s. The gold sovereign and half-sovereign almost disappeared from the banks and cash registers, and did not reappear after the war ended on 11 November 1918.

Some say that the war was ended by events on the battle-field, especially on the Western Front, and that Sir John Monash did more than any other general to deliver victory to the Allies. A Jew of German descent, an eager citizen-soldier as well as a versatile civil engineer before the war, he was in his late forties when he served at Gallipoli. Promoted to lieutenant-general while

serving on the Western Front, he quickly discovered how to coor-
dinate the role of the advancing soldiers, the heavy armoured tank,
the big guns at the rear and the infant aircraft above, in such a way
that the enemy in his small sector of the Western Front was pushed
back mile after mile. In the summer of 1918 he led Australian and
American soldiers in the Battle of Hamel – 'all over in ninety-three
minutes' – and won three other victories.

In the last two months of the war the advancing Canadians and
Frenchmen and the British soldiers in other sectors of the front line
bore the brunt of the fighting, but Monash as much as any Allied
general had ended the four years of military deadlock in France. The
forces that defeated Germany and her allies, Austria-Hungary and
Turkey, consisted not just of soldiers. Germany was also defeated
by the long British naval blockade that deprived it of imported
raw materials, munitions and food, and by the fear that the United
States, though slow to harness its industrial might, would soon tip
the scales against Germany's army.

After the war Monash returned to civilian life in Melbourne,
an engineer again. To the men he had led and to the Australian
people everywhere he was not quite a folk hero: he was simply
respected and admired. That a Jewish citizen rose so high in military circles throws into doubt the frequent allegations made today
that Australians were exceptionally racist as a people. On the day
of his funeral in 1931 at least 250 000 people stood in Melbourne's
streets to pay their respect to his passing coffin, though the day was
overcast and cool.

Australians had fought in most of the important theatres of war.
In towns and suburbs the names that were to be written on the
larger war memorials – Flanders, Ypres, the Somme, North Sea,
Salonika, Palestine, Gallipoli – embraced only a fraction of the
places where they had fought. Australian nurses too had cared for

thousands of wounded in hospitals, and in those hospital ships that lay near Gallipoli, safely at anchor, their white lights ablaze at night.

Australians had flown many of the primitive aircraft that observed enemy movements on the Western Front or dropped bombs or fought rival German aircraft. They had staffed camel corps and wireless squadrons in the Middle East. They had taken part in the daring raid on the German defences in the Belgian port of Zeebrugge. They had been present in the capture of Jerusalem from the Turks in December 1917, and had climbed the walls of Old Jerusalem and visited the grotto of the Nativity that Christmas. How strange that the liberators of Jerusalem, the city that Christendom for hundreds of years had longed to liberate, should have included the light horsemen recruited from Western Australia.

Other Australians were to fight in 1919 with a British force in northern Russia, where a South Australian bank clerk, Arthur Sullivan, won the Victoria Cross; and others were to sail past the southern Russian port of Rostov-on-Don in 1919 and make contact with the Cossack breakaway republic before it fell into Soviet hands. But for most Australians in arms the war ended in November 1918. And now this great adventure, these four years of hardship, this nightmare of death, pain, fear, mud, din and stench, and also times of fun and friendship, were over.

During the four years of war 417 000 Australians enlisted, and 318 000 sailed overseas to fight. In the history of the world no army so large had travelled so far to fight in a war. Of those who went overseas, 59 258 were killed in action or died of wounds or were missing and presumed dead. Australia thus lost more men and women than the United States lost in the war.

Almost six times as many Australians died on the Western Front as died in Gallipoli. In France and Flanders a total of 44 000 Australians were killed in action or died of wounds. Another 300 died from the effects of poison gas. In all 114 000 were wounded, of whom 700 inflicted their own wounds. In addition, 1942 Australians died from diseases and other causes.

A malady called 'shell shock' was increasingly experienced, especially after the Battle of Pozières in 1916, but most of the medical officers on the battlefields were not trained to detect mental illnesses. When soldiers were rattled by the noise, the sight of friends killed, or their own deep fear, they might express openly their distress, but as a result they could be condemned as shirkers or cowards by their own officers. To respond or pander to them was viewed as lowering morale at a time when morale was vital. It was not realised that the time to tackle trauma was immediately. When shell-shocked soldiers did enter mental hospitals, most doctors did not know how to treat them. Sleep, a healthy diet and maybe a week in bed were often prescribed. This proved to be a feeble recipe for mental health.

The mental casualties ran into thousands and eventually tens of thousands. It is now estimated that perhaps one in every ten Australian soldiers who were at the Western Front suffered severely from war neurosis. When finally they returned home the quality of their lives, and often those of their wives and children, was impaired.

For Australia's people the war's main effect was to cut down a generation. If, on the eve of the war, a fortune teller had pointed to all the Australian men between the ages of twenty and thirty, and had predicted that a number equal to 60 per cent of that age group would be killed or permanently disabled in the coming war, she would have been ridiculed but she would have been correct. The scythe of war cut mainly through the babies of the late 1880s and the 1890s. 'Nearly all the best of our young men went to the war,' wrote one soldier who returned with his Military Cross, 'and it was inevitably the best who took the greatest chance of death.' He was not an apologist for war; he was the country's most gifted statistician. Many of those who in the normal run of time would have become the country's ablest politicians, scientists, priests, poets, trade-union leaders, judges, teachers, surgeons, farmers, clergymen, entrepreneurs and artists were blown to pieces in France or buried at sea or in Turkish soil.

4

The war aims of most Australians had been simple: to protect Australia and the might of the British Empire against what was called 'the military despotism' of Germany. The aims had been partly fulfilled. Germany had been defeated, even humiliated. Its homeland had been reduced in area, its navy had been destroyed, the huge army and brave air force disbanded, and the economy weakened for a decade by the fines or reparations imposed by the victors.

Australians generally did not realise that Britain too was a casualty of the war. In the economic sense it was one of the defeated nations. Its economy did not recover its prewar strength, lost many of the valuable overseas investments, and its merchant fleet during the submarine warfare in the Atlantic Ocean was broken. Moreover Britain's long naval supremacy had been weakened by the rapid rise of the navies of the United States and Japan. Sea power itself was about to be challenged by aircraft – no other machine had been so advanced by the war.

The signs of British decline were shielded from the eyes of most Australians. The propaganda had rather magnified Britain's outstanding contribution to the world: its vitality, its creativity, its courage, its refusal to admit defeat. Pride in success became an unnoticed problem after the war. The peoples of the British Empire did not yet see the red light that had been flashing on the scoreboard of industrial nations since the end of the nineteenth century. Likewise in the new technologies Britain was no longer the automatic leader. The land that had led the world in successful innovation in the age of steam and that had dominated – even in 1850 – every facet of transport from the railway locomotive and electric telegraph to the iron steamship, was still an impressive performer but not a record-breaker. After 1860 most of the important industrial innovations did not come from the British Isles. The telephone, radio, the electric power station, the motor car and aeroplane, the steel-frame skyscraper, dynamite and a long line of other devices reflected the increasing power of the United States and continental Europe.

5

It seemed that Australia would retreat from the entanglements of the world once it had brought home all the soldiers and sailors, nurses, stretcher-bearers, aviators, doctors, prisoners of war and others who were in Europe and at sea. And yet Australia promptly jumped, as never before, onto the world stage. Early in 1919 Prime Minister Hughes prepared to join the peace negotiations in Paris not only as a leading member of the British Empire's delegation but loudly representing Australia in its own right. Of all the leaders' voices his was one of the loudest in demanding that Germany pay the entire cost of the war.

In Paris the Big Four stood dominant – Wilson of the USA, Lloyd George of Britain, Clemenceau of France and Orlando of Italy. And below them were numerous nations who, reciting their own nation's war casualties, could outbid Hughes when he said

proudly that he spoke on behalf of 60 000 Australians who were
now lying in foreign soil. And yet there were times when Hughes, by
persistence, wit and audacity, became a major player who knocked
President Wilson of the United States 'completely off his balance'.
Perhaps no Australian politician, to this day, has made such a mark
for so long on the global stage as Hughes achieved in the first half
of 1919. For his country he won a mandate to govern German New
Guinea, and a 42 per cent stake in the small island of Nauru, which
owned phosphate deposits of high value as fertilisers for wheatlands in Australia.

Hughes also gained victory – some would call it a defeat – in
the debate about one moral and political principle. The Japanese
delegation at the conference wished to insert in the covenant of
the new League of Nations (the precursor of the present United
Nations) a statement affirming the principle of racial equality. Japan's desire was understandable. Hughes himself was not
unsympathetic – so long as the covenant carried the distinct pro-
viso that every government should be permitted to control its own
immigration policy. Public opinion in the United States quietly
favoured Hughes's stand. Ironically Japan itself, in its immigration
and citizenship policies, eventually became a quiet but dedicated
supporter of the Hughes dictum.

In Australia today an influential group is embarrassed by
Hughes's refusal to affirm unconditional support for the principle
of racial equality. In fairness to Hughes he was more liberal than
they realise. After meeting the Japanese leaders who negotiated
in Paris, he positively affirmed that 'in intellect, culture, keenness
and general capacity they need not fear comparison with the representative statesmen of any nation'. As for Japan, 'she has earned for
herself a place among the great nations and sits amongst them on a
footing of equality'.

Billy Hughes proved himself shrewder and more realistic than Woodrow Wilson who, on returning to America, failed to sell the peace treaty to his own nation. In contrast Hughes sailed home to Australia, left the ship at Fremantle, made his way on the new transcontinental train across the Nullarbor Plain, and – after an absence of more than a year – sold the treaty to the Australian people and parliament.

He was to remain a politician, the only sitting survivor of that first national parliament, until his death in Sydney in 1952. Stooped and deaf but mentally vigorous, he had just reached the age of ninety; but, still full of surprises, he announced that he was a mere eighty-eight.

CHAPTER SIXTEEN

Sky and earth: the 1920s

In 1921, Australia was invited to send a delegate to attend, at short notice, a meeting of the new League of Nations. It was too late to despatch a prominent statesman by the earliest mail steamer, but a federal politician, S. M. Bruce, was known to be already visiting Europe on private business. A hurried search for him was organised, and his whereabouts were discovered in France by a former Australian soldier who, having married a war bride, was managing a garage in the port of Dieppe. Among the French cars that day stood the unusual vehicle Mr and Mrs Bruce and their personal chauffeur had brought with them to Europe. An expensive Sunbeam, its body had been built in Melbourne, and a plate inside the car announced its homeland.

Located at the golf course, Bruce promptly agreed to be the Australian delegate, and he proved to be one of the few ex-servicemen in a league of some forty nations dedicated to preventing another war. 'I had little idea what the League of Nations was,' he confessed. A few days later he was in Geneva where, recalling his experiences of war at Gallipoli, he gave to the seated delegates one of their most memorable speeches.

Though young, Bruce was soon to be the next prime minister. He thereby joined that generation of world leaders who had to face a revolution in transport and diplomacy, for young wartime aviators were transforming travel and would soon shape warfare.

2

The long Indonesian archipelago – with the rise of aviation – again played a crucial role in Australia's history. This string of islands, forming stepping stones extending all the way from Asia, was the route along which the first settlers reached Australia more than 50 000 years ago. Along these stepping stones came the Asiatic ancestors of the Polynesians, who discovered so much of the South Pacific and eventually New Zealand. The islands also carried the latest Western technology. Almost one century after the Sydney district was settled by the British, the Indonesian islands and sea straits provided a route along which the overland telegraph line and underwater cable brought the latest news from Europe to Darwin in 1872, and so to Alice Springs and Adelaide.

In 1919, one year after the First World War ended, the same route enabled a primitive aircraft to reach Australian soil in a series of short hops. Without it the British aircraft piloted by the South Australians Ross and Keith Smith could not have flown from England to Darwin. Bert Hinkler, the Queenslander, also used this route in 1928 to make the first solo flight from England to Australia. His flight was as impressive as that of the more famous Charles Lindbergh who in the previous year flew nonstop from the United States to Paris in his single-engine plane.

To pilot a plane from England to Australia was brave. To attempt to fly from the United States to Australia was doubly brave because the journey crossed the world's largest ocean, and the distances separating each landing field were vast. At first, experts believed that only a flying boat could conquer the South Pacific because, in a crisis, it might be able to land on the sea if its engines ran out of fuel. But the Australian aviators Charles Kingsford Smith and C. T. P. Ulm resolved to attempt the journey in a powerful Fokker aircraft that could not land on water. Equipped with three engines and sufficient tanks to carry the large volume of petrol needed on the longest part of the route, their *Southern Cross* also employed two of the latest radio transmitters so that at certain stages of the flight they could communicate with nearby ships at sea or distant airports. Much of their equipment was simple – old nautical charts, magnetic compasses and a marine sextant – while the seats were light wicker chairs not even fastened to the cabin floor.

So heavy was the loaded aircraft that the longest runway in the world, at Oakland near San Francisco, was selected for its take-off on 31 May 1928. The first leg was to Honolulu, so far away that aviators had died in their attempts to reach it. More hazardous was the second leg to Suva in Fiji. There, by good fortune and skilled navigation, Kingsford Smith landed on the cramped Albert Park after dodging tall palm trees on the boundary; thankfully long branches of the trees had been lopped before he arrived. That leg – probably the longest nonstop flight so far made in the world – had taken thirty-four and a half hours.

The noise in the aircraft was deafening, even when the flyers used earplugs. As the cabin could not be heated, the cold at high altitudes was intense. The four flyers had little room in which to move, let alone to sleep, and of course there was no space – let alone a sufficient supply of water – for a lavatory. Hot tea or coffee was poured from a thermos flask that ceased to be hot as the hours passed. A persisting fear was that winds or storms would so retard their aircraft that the supply of fuel would not last.

On the tenth day of their journey they reached the New South Wales coast at Ballina, having been blown off course by unexpected winds. Then they headed north to Eagle Farm in Brisbane and a crowd of spectators and motor cars that, long before sunrise, awaited them. The conquest of distance – reported in headlines across the world – was wonderful news for all Australians. They did not yet realise that aircraft would be so repeatedly improved that, in the space of fourteen years, the Japanese would fly long distances at speed in order to drop bombs on Australian and American soil.

New Zealand hitherto had been considered too far away to be reached by aircraft, but Kingsford Smith and Ulm flew to Christchurch in that same year. Their problem was to return safely to Sydney, for normally an aircraft must face a headwind on the westwards flight. Day after day they waited for a favourable weather forecast at Blenheim – a corner of the South Island now dotted with grapevines – before they could attempt the return flight to Sydney. They set out, knowing that they might have to turn back when halfway across the Tasman Sea, if the weather forecast proved to be astray.

In the infant era of aviation Kingsford Smith was ultimately viewed as the champion Australian flyer, but he might not have succeeded without the help of Ulm, a meticulous organiser and later an able pilot. Like nearly all the adventurous aviators in Australia, both were young veterans of the First World War. Dying in separate accidents while flying across distant seas, their bodies were not found. That was the fate of other aviators of the day.

3

The Reverend John Flynn was not the first to think that aircraft could bring medical aid to the outback; but he acted with quiet determination to provide it. An itinerant Presbyterian minister, he had begun, just before the First World War, to preach in cattle stations, goldmining camps and roadside hotels in a lonely area embracing half the continent. Working under the banner of his Australian Inland Mission he enlisted other travelling padres who held services where three or four adults and a child or two might be gathered together. Some of his padres rode camels but later a sturdy motor vehicle was used.

Flynn also recruited nurses, and they set up makeshift hospitals, mostly in places too small to be on the typical map of Australia. If patients required urgent surgery they were initially sent over rough roads to the nearest major hospital, which might be 500 kilometres away. But perhaps the surgeon could be flown to the patient or even learn to be his own pilot. The idea, so simple, was costly to implement. More important, how could the outback nurse or cattle station first send a message to the doctor?

Electricity was almost unknown in the outback, and a radio transmitter was rare. A cheap solution was found by an Adelaide engineer, Alfred Traeger, who, borrowing an idea from a German trench on the Western Front, built a cheap pedal radio transceiver. Thus, nurses in the outback or people at an isolated cattle station could supply power with their feet and transmit by radio an urgent message. At first in morse code or in print, and much later by phone, the message could almost instantly reach a remote doctor or a larger hospital. The last part of the formula called for a small aircraft. One was hired in 1928 from the little outback airline now called Qantas, the acronym for Queensland and Northern Territory

Aerial Services. The cramped interior of the aircraft was modified so that a stretcher holding a patient could be squeezed inside. The first passenger, an underground miner injured in the new silver-lead mine at Mount Isa, was flown across the rugged ranges to the hospital in Cloncurry.

Aborigines on Mornington Island, in the Gulf of Carpentaria, were among the first to benefit. Previously, sick patients had to be conveyed from the island by boat and then by motor vehicle along rough roads to Cloncurry. Now, in response to a radio message, the flying doctor landed on the island and if necessary flew a danger-ously ill patient all the way to hospital. The nurses and flying doctors recruited for the flying-doctor service risked their life. In 1932 at the tiny west Queensland township of Birdsville, Sister Gilbert felt the pain of appendicitis. Her colleague tried to pedal power into their wireless but it was silent. As a last hope she was driven along dusty corrugated roads to faraway Cloncurry, where she died on the oper-ating table.

Radio, commonly known as 'the wireless', was a sensation, and challenged the telegraph system as a deliverer of messages. In 1927 the first telegrams were transmitted by beam wireless between Australia and England. On 30 April 1930 for the first time the prime minister in the new capital city, Canberra, spoke on a tel-ephone to the British prime minister in London, from which city were 'beamed' the clear and genial words: 'What an age, my dear Mr Scullin, we are living in.' At that time an international phone call of a mere three minutes cost about one week's take-home pay for most workmen. Moreover the 'interference' on the line, espe-cially in daytime, often prevented a distant voice from being heard with clarity.

Western Australians could not yet make an interstate land-line call. The first line of wires to Perth, stretched on poles erected alongside the new transcontinental railway, was opened in December 1930. Tasmanians had to wait another five years before a seabed cable was laid from Apollo Bay in Victoria to their own town of Stanley.

All day long, and for a few hours in the evening, the new radio stations broadcast messages, talks and music to an increasing circle of listeners. When Dame Nellie Melba sang in *La Bohème* in Melbourne on 13 October 1924, her voice was broadcast, with the aid of a tall wireless mast in the outer suburb of Braybrook, to an audience of some 160 000 people. That was not counting the children who lay in bed and listened to her through the static of the 'crystal set' that they themselves might well have made. In 1925, Sydney and Melbourne opened their first commercial stations, and in 1928 the Australian Broadcasting Company (later called 'Commission' and then 'Corporation') was formed by the federal government. Within a decade its stations were the patrons of serious music in Australia, and employed more than 300 full-time musicians but few news reporters. The Second World War was to turn the ABC into a news hunter.

4

In the interwar years the farmers were more numerous than before or after. They multiplied with the help of fresh British migrants and also Australian soldier-settlers who, returning from the battlefields, were given small farms and lent money with which to buy livestock, fencing materials, ploughs and simple harvesting machines. Growing numerous foods – from sugar in the tropics to hops and apples in southern Tasmania – they were especially strong in the wheat industry, which now employed more than 200 000 people in one way or other during the busiest months.

This was the last time in Australia's history when the dream of owning one's own farm remained widespread in the cities. The welfare state in its infancy gave little help to most people, whereas a farm – so long as it was not deeply in debt – offered social security. To be a farmer was the ambition of many immigrants; and the absence of a 'boss' and the sense of independence could not be measured in money. But the farming life was hard and tiring both for women and men as well as children who took part in the daily tasks. On dairy farms – more numerous than before – the cows had to be hand-milked every day of the week, morning and afternoon. The milking machine was not yet common.

The country and the city enjoyed a multitude of family ties, and a typical holiday for a city child was to visit rural relatives. Country and city laughed at each other, usually with a sense of fun. City people, suspected of being sharpsters and tricksters, were called 'city slickers'. As if in retaliation, farmers were called 'country bumpkins', while the 'Sunday-best' hat and dress worn by their wives aroused an affectionate or slightly scornful whisper when they visited the city. Comic strips in the daily newspapers centred on country folk such as Ben Bowyang of Gunn's Gully, born in the Melbourne evening *Herald* in 1933. Three years later came the crowd-pleasing radio serial called *Dad and Dave*, which dwelt on hillbilly-like behaviour at the little settlement of Snake Gully. For more than 2000 episodes its theme music was Jack O'Hagan's song 'Along the Road to Gundagai'. Lying halfway along the narrow main road between Sydney and Melbourne, the riverside town of Gundagai and its roadside statue of a dog on a tuckerbox fascinated that generation of radio listeners. To a radio audience each evening a little township could offer human variety, for the farmers mixed with such miscellaneous battlers as woodcutters, rabbit trappers, fencers, bee-keepers, blacksmiths, bush nurses, visiting priests and parsons, and seasonal workers such as potato diggers and shearers and haymakers and fruit pickers.

Though the cities were slowly dispensing with the horse and its delivery cart, the farms employed big draught horses more than in any previous decade. The nation's horse population reached its peak during the First World War, but many farmers continued to prefer horses to tractors; and the big teams of Clydesdales, Suffolks and Shires pulling wagons, ploughs or harvesting machines were an impressive and common sight. In the 1920s many farmers bought a car, the favourite being the sturdy T-Model Ford with its thin tyres, its running board crammed with luggage, and a full waterbag hanging on a hook in case the water in its radiator reached boiling point.

5

At their best, Australian farms remained more innovative than the factories spreading across the suburbs. The story of a new-found 'weed' illustrated a willingness to experiment. Subterranean clover originated around the Mediterranean shores where it grew on the roadsides as a weed, and must have arrived here, though not noticed, in bales of hay or as a hideaway in pot plants, an illegal immigrant that relished the acidic soils and slowly spread.

'Sub clover' was capable of drawing vast amounts of nitrogen from the atmosphere. Its leaves are horizontal whereas the typical grass blade is vertical, and so it absorbed solar energy with ease. Thriving quietly in farms, here and there, for maybe half a century, it was finally noticed and admired in 1889 by Amos Howard, a dairy farmer at Mount Barker in the Adelaide Hills. On this memorable day his neighbour was away, and Amos took the opportunity as a 'rural stickybeak' to walk over to the adjacent farm where he observed patches of this prolific plant. Collecting seed he let it grow on his farm, but nearly twenty years passed before he sold seed to an Adelaide nurseryman who resold parcels of it to farmers. The secret was out.

Innovation is usually not a gigantic step but a series of small jumps involving various enterprising people whose names are soon forgotten. Near Perth the Guildford Grammar School, importing Howard's seed from the Adelaide Hills and cultivating it in the agronomy plots, found that it suited the state's sandy soils. Other farmers and agricultural scientists decided which varieties of clover suited this soil or that, and which clovers should be sown early or late in the season. Clovers so improved the fertility of the soil for graziers and crop growers that by the 1950s they were declared to be one of the giants of rural history. Howard died long before his achievement was widely appreciated.

6

Farmers actually suffered from many of the events that were viewed as achievements for the average city family. Thus the Harvester judgement of 1907, by increasing the income of factory employees, actually forced wheat farmers to pay more for their most important item of equipment – the horse-drawn machine that harvested their wheat. The superior wages won by railway workers were another triumph, but the farmers, in paying for trains to carry their wheat to port, indirectly subsidised the workers' pay packets.

The largest Australian group to speak with a weak voice in the parliaments, the farmers learned a lesson from New Zealand. There, the rural people helped to create the Reform Party under the leadership of William Massey, known as Farmer Bill. Winning office in 1912 and holding it for sixteen years, his success as a rural leader spurred the forming of farmers' leagues or parties that won a few seats in various Australian parliaments. In the federal election in December 1922 the new Country Party won the balance of power. With Dr Earle Page as their leader, these rural politicians showed their muscle. They refused to serve under the prime minister, Billy Hughes, and with a growl or two he stepped down in favour of Stanley Bruce. Page and his colleagues, though far outnumbered by their allies, secured five of the eleven seats in the new coalition cabinet. Here was a landmark in Australian politics.

Bruce and Page were alike, for both were returned soldiers and also relative newcomers to parliament. Their two parties, however, were far apart. The given names of the leaders were revealing, for Bruce's second name was Melbourne, being the city of his birth, while his colleague's third name was Grafton, that New South Wales river town being his birthplace. Page's party was largely rural and Bruce's was largely urban. While Bruce's Liberals were protectionists and the ally of manufacturers, Page's Country Party politicians were more sympathetic to free trade. One-third of a century later the lessons learned from the Bruce–Page Government were clear. Despite occasional splits and near-divorces, the two parties were to form one of the longest and most influential coalitions in the history of a modern democracy.

As the new federal treasurer in 1923, Page tried to reward farmers. Often the sums of money were small but the symbolism was vital. As the nation's farms multiplied, new fences were a priority, and so rolls of barbed wire were sold to farmers at a subsidised price. There was rejoicing in the Goulburn Valley in Victoria where the new fruit canneries – the buyers of local apricots, peaches and pears – were subsidised so that the prices paid to orchardists were higher. The Derwent Valley in Tasmania cheered when the Bruce–Page Government subsidised the growers of the hops that were a vital ingredient of beer. In the vineyards of the

Murray Valley the producers of dried fruits and fortified wines were helped. In milking sheds strung across a vast strip of coastal Australia there was delight when the price of butter was boosted. The cattle farmers welcomed the subsidies for their exports of meat and even live cattle. The wheatlands, which formed the largest realm of the Country Party, had to wait longer for substantial help. The woolgrowers waited in vain: as the nation's main exporters they were too numerous and competitive to be subsidised. On the other hand the sugar farms and mills on the Pacific coast had been safeguarded against cheap foreign sugar since the first years of Federation.

Nearly every industry was receiving some form of protection or bonus from Canberra. But who actually paid directly or indirectly for the costs of the protection? Everybody paid, often without knowing the exact price. Australia really was a merry-go-round on which most employers and employees cheerfully rode, deluded by the myth that they travelled free. In boarding the merry-go-round in 1923 the Country Party had gained, but in the following half-century it was a rare year when they gained as much as Liberal and Labor gained for their supporters.

Bruce and Page shared views they were willing to fight for. Their ardent opinion was that the nation's trade unions – now among the world's most powerful – were too disruptive. Certainly the early postwar years were shaken by strikes and lockouts and violence. On 24 March 1919 in the streets of Brisbane an anti-Bolshevik demonstration led to fights in which many people were wounded. In May the waterfront at Fremantle witnessed a struggle between unionists and non-unionists, and police and soldiers intervened. One person was killed, more than thirty were injured, and the premier was almost hit by rocks thrown at him in what was called the Battle of the Barricades or Bloody Sunday. In the same month a general strike began at Broken Hill, one of the most militant workplaces. Lasting for eighteen months it gave the silver-lead-zinc miners the shortest working week of any industry in Australia. On 29 June 1919 in an industrial dispute at the meatworks at Townsville, shots were fired, and nine people wounded. Western Australia in 1920 experienced a long strike by schoolteachers and other public servants. It was orderly, however, compared to the disruptions in the public sector in Victoria where police went on strike in November 1923. As looting was widespread, special constables had to be recruited.

In the crucial industry of coalmining the industrial peace was endangered by underground accidents in the period 1921–23. In two disasters – at Mount Mulligan in north Queensland and at Cessnock in New South Wales – ninety-six men were killed. The postwar economic slump increased tensions: the BHP steelworks at Newcastle were closed for months, causing wide unemployment. Any closure in basic industries disrupted the whole nation, and the Bruce Government in 1926 initiated a referendum that, if passed, would give the Commonwealth the power to intervene when essential services were disrupted. The people voted no.

Bruce and Page declared war on the Australian seamen, who had already declared war on the government. Coastal shipping was more important to economic life than it is today, and the New South Wales black coal, crucial to the economy, was always carried in ships to Melbourne and Adelaide. Though Western Australia rejoiced in 1917 in its new transcontinental railway, the trains carried mainly passengers, leaving the bulk of the cargoes to interstate ships. Likewise the string of towns along the Queensland coast – the longest line of active ports in the nation – depended far more on coastal shipping than on the interstate railway that ran along the coast.

Understandably the Australian Seamen's Union, fired by the success of the 1917 revolution in Russia, exploited its bargaining position. Defying the arbitration tribunals, and breaking agreements, its members disrupted coastal shipping in 1925. The departure of ships was suddenly delayed: maybe a crewman was missing or a rope was unsafe. After Bruce retaliated, seamen went out on strike. With the aid of a new law Bruce tried to deport two leaders of the ever-fighting union: Jacob Johnson, a Swede, and Tom Walsh, an Irishman. Both were deemed to 'be injurious to the peace, order, and good government of the Commonwealth', but the High Court saved them from deportation, and the disruptions in coastal ships, wharves and coalmines continued. The Bruce–Page Government's repeated attempts to thwart and subdue the more militant unions largely led to its own defeat at the federal election of 1929.

7

Australia no longer stood near the bottom of the world's population ladder. In reaching a total of five million it had passed a cluster of other nations, ranging from Switzerland to Greece, Bulgaria and Chile. To boost that population rapidly became a new national priority. While migrants from Britain remained the dominant group in the 1920s, for the first time southern Europeans arrived in numbers. The census of 1911 had counted 6700 people of Italian birth, a group no larger than those born in British India, but by 1933 the southern Europeans – especially Italians, Greeks and Maltese – had so multiplied that they were more numerous than those migrants who had come from the rest of continental Europe. Significantly, Italians were among the few non-British peoples who could enter Australia without possessing a valid passport.

In several districts riots were directed against Italians and the fact that their culture was different. When self-employed they worked longer hours. In the Kalgoorlie underground mines when they took up contracts they were seen as unfair competitors. Their poor knowledge of English – most came from Italian villages where illiteracy was high – could endanger the safety of other miners deep below the earth when messages warning of danger had to be passed on clearly by word of mouth. There is no doubt some were inexperienced and endangered lives by their use of explosives. There was also a layer of prejudice and puzzlement on both sides. In January 1934, after a leading footballer was accidentally killed by a Northern Italian barman in Kalgoorlie, riots broke out, shops were looted, and more than sixty Mediterranean cafes, clubs and houses were burned to the ground.

Of the flood of people emigrating from Eastern Europe to the Americas, only a trickle was diverted to Australia. One Russian immigrant was Sidney Myer, and he hawked articles in a horse and cart around the old goldfields near Bendigo before setting up a shop there in 1900. After opening a department store in busy Bourke Street in Melbourne in 1911 he staged more bargain sales, monster sales and one-and-only sales than the city had previously seen. His Myer Emporium became, reportedly, the fifth-largest shop in the world.

In a country that prided itself on its Britishness, four of its most celebrated citizens in the 1920s were Jewish. Sidney Myer was the dynamic shopkeeper and philanthropist, Sir John Monash was the most famous soldier, and Sir Isaac Isaacs was to be the first Australian to hold the office of governor-general of the Commonwealth. The fourth, Professor Samuel Alexander OM, was becoming the most praised British philosopher, but his talent was first detected when he was a schoolboy in St Kilda.

Not all the Jewish immigrants succeeded. The Watens had sailed from Odessa to Palestine in 1911, and three years later they moved with their little son and daughter to Western Australia, then a haven for migrants. The father, notable for his stiff red moustache and halting English sentences, hoped that by opening a drapery shop he would be rewarded for living in a strange land. Mrs Waten felt no such hope. Her feelings were to be described by her son Judah: 'Ever since we had come to this country she had lived with her bags packed. This was no country for us.'

8

The Commonwealth possessed no permanent capital city, and Melbourne was merely the temporary home. New South Wales had been promised the federal capital as an inducement to enter the federation, but where exactly that capital should be was a vexatious question. After the federal parliament met in Melbourne in 1901, the New South Wales members favoured sites that were near Sydney. In contrast Victorian members preferred a site that was as close as possible to their own border. The dispute was a sign that the emotional forces against federation were still powerful.

Not until the end of the third year of the new federal parliament did members even agree to vote, for the first time, on where they should build the new capital city. On 8 October 1903 a majority in the House of Representatives selected Tumut as the site. Nestling in a valley at the western foot of the Snowy Mountains it possessed some of the alpine glamour without the intense cold. Tumut was about two hours away from Gundagai railway station, which in turn was a tortuous journey from the nearest station on the Melbourne–Sydney railway. Significantly every Victorian member of the lower house, irrespective of his party, voted for Tumut because it was closer to Victoria. This choice did not persuade the members of the Senate, whose vote was equally important. They voted for Bombala, in the high country. After more debate the support switched to Dalgety, on the banks of the Snowy River and also near the Victoria–New South Wales border. Far from the main railways, Dalgety's bracing climate, mild summer and remoteness from Sydney were seen as its main virtues. In 1904 it was chosen as the federal capital, by act of parliament. Today, alas, it holds just over 200 residents.

The search and the debate went on. By the year 1908 the charming countryside around Yass and Canberra appeared more attractive to federal politicians. Nearly all the New South Wales members of the lower house now supported this site, being much closer to Sydney, but most members from South and Western Australia and from Victoria still preferred the freezing heights of Dalgety. In October 1908, the House of Representatives indulged in nine successive ballots before Yass–Canberra won narrowly by thirty-nine votes to thirty-three. It was the Senate's turn to vote. Every senator from New South Wales voted for Yass–Canberra, but only one Victorian senator gave his support. Now if one senator could be persuaded to change his mind the long dispute might be over. Senator J. H. McColl of Bendigo was persuaded. On the second ballot he supported Yass–Canberra. The inland city of Bendigo had thus provided the men who quietly solved the two deadlocks in the federal movement: Quick who devised the democratic solution by which the electors took over the federal movement in the 1890s and McColl who finally resolved the site of a federal capital.

Sydney celebrated. The city that once had been the most reluctant to vote in favour of federation had been rewarded with the capital city, tucked away in its own hinterland. Similarly the rural

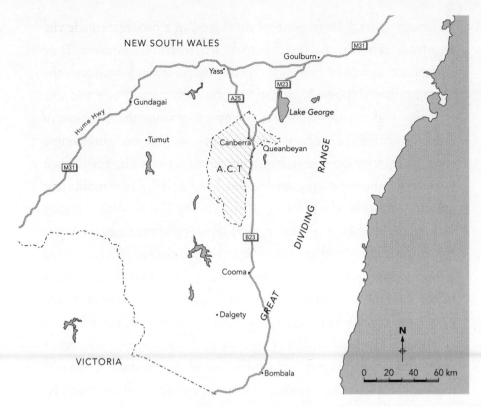

In search of a capital city, 1900–08

district that had actually voted against federation in the late 1890s was now to be the federal capital. In Melbourne *The Age*, masticating the indigestible news, concluded that the decision to select Canberra, 'so woefully inaccessible', was a folly. The governor-general disagreed, arguing that a new city was needed because Melbourne and Sydney were already overcrowded.

Canberra was the first capital city to possess an Aboriginal name. Just a village, its post office received a small bag of mail from the Queanbeyan railway station each weekday. On Sundays in a dry summer the puffs of dust could be seen converging slowly on the handsome St John's Church as the farmers and pastoralists came in gigs, jinkers and miscellaneous carts along the gravel and dirt roads.

In January 1911, a large zone of rural land in this selected district was transferred from New South Wales to the Commonwealth, along with a block of land at Jervis Bay where it was hoped that the Commonwealth's own busy port would arise.

Here was perhaps the first opportunity since the creation of Adelaide, three-quarters of a century ago, to plan imaginatively a city. An international search was made for a plan. The third prize went to a Frenchman, the second to a Finn and the first to a young architect from the Great Plains of the United States. Walter Burley Griffin, the winner, was born in rural Illinois and practised architecture in Chicago where he spent five years in the office of Frank Lloyd Wright, who was then rising slowly to fame. In 1911 Griffin married a talented fellow architect, Marion Mahony, and she contributed that sense of detail that her unpunctual husband sometimes lacked.

Walter Burley Griffin's prize-winning concept of Canberra embraced and cuddled those beautiful wooded mountains and park-like pastures that then, perhaps even more than today, represented Australian ideas of natural beauty. It was almost as if the Heidelberg school of painters had moved camp to Canberra and chosen the site for him. In the centre of that narrow valley he designed wide circles and avenues as if he were laying out corridors for formal dances. In contrast most Australians preferred the familiar rectangle.

Griffin supervised the slow construction of the federal capital from 1913 to 1920 but he also designed elsewhere. He made plans for the irrigation towns of Leeton and Griffith in the Murrumbidgee Valley, for the streets of the outer suburb of Eaglemont in Melbourne, and with his wife in the 1920s he created the model suburb of Castlecrag on a bushland promontory overlooking Middle Harbour in Sydney.

Meanwhile his Canberra was thought to be taking shape. Tents housed the first construction gangs. A couple of office blocks arose like sentry posts. The small emerging suburbs were still separated by paddocks from the distant railway station, and the population did not reach 4000 until about 1925. Two years later, the federal parliament, still sitting in Melbourne, resolved to meet in the new white parliament house in Canberra for the first time on 9 May 1927. A large crowd, drawn from every corner of Australia, was expected but did not arrive.

The Duke of York, who nine years later became King George VI, was to open the new parliament. Now in his early thirties, he could be embarrassingly nervous in public and irascible too, without warning. As he often stammered, a public speech could be painful for him and his audience. Fortunately a year previously he had begun to take lessons from Lionel Logue, an Adelaide speech therapist who had migrated to Perth and finally to London where he became a healer of the speech impediments of shell-shocked soldiers. A Christian Scientist, Logue imparted a kind of spiritual assurance as well as skills in breathing and enunciating. On the momentous day in Canberra, thanks to Logue, the duke reached a level of calmness and confidence almost new to him.

In creating a distinctive city, Griffin did not have his own way, but he made his imprint. Today, Canberra and its amphitheatre of blue hills, its wide tree-shaded avenues and long lake, radiate a low-key charm and a certain majesty. The simple white-painted parliament house still stands, but its successor, opened during Australia's 200th birthday in 1988, seems a visual intruder rather than the palace of one of the world's more vigorous democracies.

CHAPTER SEVENTEEN

The world Depression

The world depression did not spring from a clear blue sky. In the 1920s, Australia experienced unemployment that averaged 9 per cent annually. The factories, which were now employing more people than all the rural industries, were not very competitive. The flow of capital from overseas – mainly borrowed by the seven Australian governments for public works – had created jobs but also heavy debts. Much of the borrowing had been spent on the dream that almost everybody – returned soldiers or suburban British migrants – could become a farmer. For only a few years did the prices of wool, wheat, butter, base metals and other exports sustain that dream.

Since the war New York had overtaken London as the globe's financial citadel. In September 1929 the share prices in New York reached new heights but one month later they crashed. The price of American shares fell by about 40 per cent in two months. The tidal wave from Wall Street reached the shores of every country. Australia – saturated with debt – was vulnerable. In the space of a year the inflow of foreign capital was halted, and the price of Australia's main exports, already falling, plummeted.

The world depression was like a contagious disease. The disease was an inability or a reluctance to spend. Without that spending, the jobs of tens of millions of people ceased to exist. In Australia unemployment approached 20 per cent and still increased. As the whole Western world was engulfed in the Depression, the feeling of bewilderment was intense. The nineteenth century, which gave birth to the word 'unemployment', had experienced nothing like it. The passive way in which most people accepted their fate was to arouse incredulity when recalled half a century later.

The political situation did not help Australia. An election for the national parliament was held on 12 October 1929, exactly twelve days before the crash of Wall Street. The retiring conservative government was trounced; and the swing was so strong that the prime minister, Stanley Melbourne Bruce, lost what seemed to be one of the safest of seats. After the new parliament had been sworn in, many Labor members adjourned to the Hotel Kurrajong in Canberra and jubilantly sang the left-wing anthem 'The Red Flag'. While Labor's leader, James Scullin, held a handsome majority in the House of Representatives, he was weak in the Senate, where only seven of the thirty-six members were his supporters. His hands therefore were tied.

2

Canberra, a town-planners' town and now the capital city, possessed no main street, displayed no advertising hoardings and sold no alcohol. In feel, spirit and geography it seemed remote from the rest of Australia. Its government departments did not yet preside over economic life. The state governments, far more powerful than they are today, collected their own income taxes, made most of the welfare payments and ran big business enterprises, including the railways. If a national policy was to be formed for fighting the Depression, the state governments had to agree to it. Not all were willing to agree. Several of the state Labor governments even clashed with the Labor government in Canberra. The new premier of New South Wales was J. T. Lang, a suburban auctioneer and real estate agent, a magnetic speaker and left-wing populist. He resented the large interest payments that the Australian governments owed to England. He was willing in certain circumstances to repudiate his state's debts. In the end the federal government stepped in and punished him.

The country was manacled by past policies. Its wages were so high that many industries could not compete with overseas competitors. It was importing more than it could pay for. Its currency was seriously overvalued. During this crisis in the balance of payments, the Bank of New South Wales initially stepped out as leader. In January 1931 it devalued the Australian pound – traditionally at par with the English pound – by 30 per cent. Melbourne banks opposed – even Canberra opposed – this bold decision by the big Sydney bank. They soon had no alternative but to agree.

It was a sign of the dispersal of economic authority that the private banks were sometimes more influential in shaping policy than was the Commonwealth Bank, which was supposedly the central bank. Even the federal treasury was said to be 'little more than the government's department of accounting'. Some eighty years later the complaints became frequent that its forecasting even on its home ground often missed the mark.

Unemployment spread. In the steel and coal city of Newcastle, the Broken Hill Proprietary Company received so few orders for steel rails, wire netting for farms, corrugated iron for the roofs of new factories and shops that it had to dismiss half of its employees. For three years it paid no dividend. In the main streets of Australian cities the sight of the steel frame of a new office block stretching upwards became rare. The census of June 1933 reported that only 253 new dwellings were in the process of being built in Sydney, only five in Canberra, and only one in the whole Northern Territory – the dwellings of full-blood Aborigines, being humble, were excluded from this count.

For those who held jobs, the practice of working only three or four days a week – or only three weeks in every four – became widespread. In many workshops nearly all the jobs disappeared. In Collingwood in 1929 stood a millinery factory whose forty-five employees – mostly women – could not imagine that two years later only one employee would remain: in hard times the latest fashion in female hats was a luxury and could be dispensed with. On the other hand Coles and Woolworths, relatively young chain stores that sold at bargain prices, increased their profits in every Depression year except 1931. Coles' enticing motto, 'Nothing over two and six' (meaning nothing over two shillings and sixpence), signified that it was the cheapest shop imaginable. Most of the small bakeries and grocers and butchers allowed trusted customers to buy goods on credit. Some lost heavily when customers became penniless or suddenly left town without paying their debts.

People who had money were frightened to spend it for fear that the Depression would become more severe; yet by refusing to spend their money they deprived others of work. In essence their frugality increased the distress around them. One reassuring fact, however, was that relatively few people starved in the Depression.

In many businesses the volume of work was trifling. Taxi drivers had flourished in the 1920s, but when the Depression deepened, most people decided that taxis were a luxury. On the evening before a race meeting, taxis would take their place in a cab rank outside the racecourse, and the drivers would sleep in their cabs in readiness for the early afternoon when the first racegoers left the course. A successful gambler was likely to hire a cab. He might even tip the driver.

Most farmers worked for small rewards. For four years the average bag of wheat was grown at a loss. Many farmers simply had to borrow money in order to live. Their fear was that they might sink so far into debt that their farms would be confiscated. This happened to few; but the fear remained. Fortunately most state governments passed moratorium laws that reduced the ability of banks and other lenders to foreclose on those farms for which payments had fallen behind.

In Western Australia we read about out-of-work people in the coalmining town of Collie relying on the local 'soup kitchen', which served 100 meals a day. Near Perth we see men jumping on a freight train and, without a ticket, travelling outback in search of work; rarely were they prosecuted for paying no fare. Here is a doctor whose backyard is lined with bags of wheat, delivered to him by farming families who had no cash with which to pay their bill. We glimpse women setting up house and making furniture out of wooden packing cases, and erecting walls out of flimsy hessian.

Across the nation could be heard the incessant knocking on back doors and front doors, the rap-rap of itinerant people asking for just one day's work or a sandwich and hot mug of tea. How many letters, seeking work, must have been written to personal friends, to members of parliament and to former employers.

Country towns were the temporary goal of people on the move. On the banks of a creek or river, they set up a tent or shanty while they looked for work. They came on foot with a sugar bag of possessions slung over their shoulder, or rode a bicycle that was overloaded. Occasionally a tumbledown car carried a whole family. A few arrived with dogs and musical instruments, and at night the mouth organs and the barking could be heard. Many of these camps showed generosity and a sense of solidarity. In rain or heavy frosts, those who had no tent might be offered shelter by utter strangers.

Makeshift ways of helping the unemployed were devised by governments. Food rations were handed out. Free clothing, footwear, firewood and schoolbooks were issued to the needy. In assigning relief work – always at low wages – an unemployed married man was given first preference. He might be given work one week in three, a single man only one week in six. Each state had different rules and varying levels of generosity, but New South Wales was the leader. Those who were unemployed knew that it was better to be out of work there. The New South Wales government was paying sustenance – or 'susso' – to three times as many people as the Victorian government was supporting in the middle of 1932. Enterprisingly Western Australia arranged for as many as 1750 city boys to find low-paid work on farms, but could not afford to provide them with railway tickets or suitable clothes.

3

Would the banks hold firm, or would some totter and crash, as in 1893? Fortunately the nation now had few young banks, and a young bank is often shaky because it has attracted the more precarious business that older banks have shunned. Likewise the main currency in people's pockets was Commonwealth notes and coins, and they were trusted more than the private banknotes, though not the gold sovereigns, that had circulated in the early 1890s. The country now had a mechanism whereby the central bank could, if it so wished, save a trading or savings bank that was bleeding to death with the slow withdrawal of deposits.

Early in 1931 one of the biggest banks was endangered. The Government Savings Bank of New South Wales, old and trusted, was said to be the second largest in the British Empire. When Lang was conducting his successful campaign at the state election in September 1930 his critics suggested that the bank might no longer be safe if electors voted for his 'reckless' policies. After he was elected his policies seemed to confirm these predictions. More and more customers crowded into the bank's palatial head office in Martin Place. They took out their savings partly because they were in need but more because they were in doubt. In one day, 22 April 1931, they withdrew the grand total of £1 678 000. The bank closed its doors, and for weeks a vital part of the savings of a notable proportion of the ordinary people of New South Wales was locked up.

Like most of the big banks that had closed their doors in 1893 the Government Savings Bank lacked ready cash to meet the sudden demands placed on it by customers. It bled to death through lack of a bandage. Its failure locked up more money – and certainly more money of the needy – than had any of the fallen banks in 1893. But its failure was not contagious and few other banks, all of them small, closed later that year. Thus Australians were spared the plague of banking disasters that hurt the United States in the 1930s.

The low point in national morale was probably reached in January 1931. During that year, a national policy for fighting the Depression was agreed upon. Known as the Premiers' Plan – the state premiers were more important collectively than the prime minister in shaping the economy – it cut wages and pensions and reduced the interest paid to Australians on government bonds; in short it reduced the income of those who were mostly better off than the unemployed. The plan encouraged governments to balance their budgets by 1934. Already the duties on imported goods had soared – the biggest increase in the tariff in Australian history. It is doubtful, however, whether these plans hastened recovery from the Depression.

Under the Premiers' Plan those full-time workers who received wages or salary from a government were relatively safe. They continued to work full time in schools, police stations, railway offices and taxation departments. For several years their real standard of living actually improved, because they received the same wages as in the past but their cost of living fell. For a generation to come many parents guided their children into government jobs, knowing that in another depression they would possess economic security.

Migrants no longer wished to come to a country where the chance of finding a job was small. For five years more people emigrated than arrived. The armed services felt the pinch, and the spending on defence was cut. The annual income of hospitals and mental asylums fell, but illness did not diminish. Fewer students stayed for the last years of secondary school. Holiday resorts waited in vain for an overflow of summer visitors. One statistic of the Depression was the decline in phone calls, after years of dramatic increases.

The economic chaos must have astonished those pioneers of the Labor Party who had seen paradise within their reach and those generations of Liberals who had thought parliaments would ease the loads of everybody who was heavy-laden. Australia for a time had been the nation that would show Europe how to plant a Garden of Eden. It was true that most Australian breadwinners in the year 1931 possessed the minimum wage, regulated conditions of work, a 44-hour week, a method of arbitrating industrial disputes, and often a payment for overtime. There was just one piece missing from that jigsaw of social benefits: to those who had no job, most of the benefits meant nothing.

For the Labor Party the Depression was a disaster. In Canberra the federal cabinet fell apart, one part falling to the right and the other to the left. Joseph Aloysius Lyons, a talented teacher who had become premier of Tasmania and then the acting treasurer in the Scullin ministry, resigned from the Labor Party in March 1931. He and five of his Labor colleagues were soon persuaded by Melbourne business leaders to join a new party known as the United Australia Party, which replaced the right-wing Nationalist Party. In May, Lyons became the leader of the new party and therefore the leader of the opposition. Six months later the Scullin Government, increasingly attacked, was forced to call for a new election. The economic problems had proved so far to be insoluble.

Scullin had won forty-six of the seventy-five seats in the lower house at the previous election, and now in December 1931 he won a mere thirteen. Many of his ministers – and two future prime ministers, Curtin and Chifley – lost their seats. In January 1932, Lyons began his seven years as prime minister.

4

It is tempting to paint the Depression years entirely in dark colours but there were triumphs, especially in engineering. Sydney had long suffered because it was divided in two by the harbour. Most residents lived on the south shore; but if new suburbs were to grow, the vast areas of bushland and rocky cliffs on the opposite shore had to be unlocked. Sydney needed a large bridge rather than a fleet of ferries to carry the daily procession of trains, cars and trucks from shore to shore.

For the bridge an energetic Australian engineer, J. J. C. Bradfield, supplied planning and technical skills, and an English engineer, Ralph Freeman, designed the steel arch that – 503 metres long – was a monster by world standards. To Sydney spectators a sure sign that the bridge was taking shape was the regular arrival of three small cargo ships carrying blocks of granite from an inland quarry near Moruya, 200 kilometres to the south. In Sydney tall granite-cloaked pylons, standing on opposite shores, were in place long before the steel arch dominated the skyline. Cosmetic more than structural, the pylons were created at heavy expense mainly to convey the visual impression that the Harbour Bridge was not only bold but secure. Robin Boyd, distinguished architect, thought that 'the stonework was welcome as a necessary addition', because it diverted the eyes away from the 'ugly' steel of the mighty arch.

On 19 March 1932 the Harbour Bridge was formally opened. No other peacetime event in Australia had spurred such pride. Here was a young nation completing one of the world's engineering marvels. The widest and almost the longest bridge span so far, it was described by one Sydney newspaper as like 'the Pillar of Hercules bestriding the tide'. It carried a roadway and railway that dwarfed ships passing below. That it used English as well as Australian steel dulled the achievement in the eyes of some Australian nationalists.

Melbourne's own building marvel, a war memorial larger perhaps than any in England, was also completed during the Depression. Known as the Shrine, it resembled a temple of the ancient world.

5

In these years the young cricketer Don Bradman was widely admired as the number-one Australian. A country boy at a time when Australia was more rural, he had taught himself how to hit and guide a cricket ball, for coaching clinics for young sportsmen were rare. In his chosen sport he was methodical, calm and efficient, with physical courage and presence of mind. His footwork and sense of balance, his eye for the likely course and pace and spin of each ball bowled to him, were extraordinary.

Bradman was not a playboy. In a decade when a cigarette was dangling on many players' lips after the day's game was over, he abstained. He did not celebrate far into the night; he went to bed early. 'I always obtained best results by seeking quietness,' he said of his mental approach. On the cricket grounds of England and Australia he did not outwardly seem to show pleasure at his own success. That was the spirit of the game and the era. To boast, to celebrate one's success in public, was almost taboo.

Bradman's fame came partly from the infant state of international sport. There was no sign yet of today's flood of international contests in a variety of sports. Horseracing was confined to local and New Zealand horses; world surfing contests were unknown; and the America's Cup meant nothing to a Hobart sailor. The Olympic Games were not yet a world-halting event and, moreover, Australians competing in them gained only a fraction of the sporting successes they were to enjoy later. Four different codes of football were widely played in Australia, and so no nationwide football hero could emerge in what was the most popular and crowd-pleasing sport.

As a vehicle for nationalism, cricket was more important then than now. This helps to explain why Bradman as a celebrity towered above any Australian footballer, swimmer, runner, cricketer, sailor or tennis player of today. Perhaps never again will there be a single sport so central as cricket – nor a sportsperson as crucial as Bradman – to Australia's self-esteem. And yet Bradman arose in an era when money, professionalism and specialist coaches and trainers did not dominate big-time sport. A homemade player, he was a product of his parents' backyard and a cricket club in a country town. A leading historian of sport, Gideon Haigh, reminds us that even today's sporting stars stand on the shoulders of hosts of amateur players who founded or played for thousands of earlier sporting clubs scattered across the nation and, after their playing days were over, mowed the grass and sat on the committee and attended the annual working bee as unpaid volunteers.

6

Among the legends that arose from the Depression was a mysterious gold prospector named Lewis Lasseter. A small, persuasive, possum-faced man, he knew the outback, though how well he knew it became the topic of some controversy. He spoke, it was said, of a heroic expedition that he had once made all alone from Queensland to Alice Springs, and then west to the quiet port of Carnarvon. He confidentially retold his story in Sydney in 1930, when the Depression was deepening, and he added the golden garnish that on his journey of long ago he had found a huge reef out in the dry wilderness. If only he could lead an expedition back to the remote site he would unveil a new Kalgoorlie that would revive the nation's economy. Lasseter's new expedition – financed by a syndicate in which leaders of the Australian Workers' Union were prominent – left Alice Springs in the crisp winter days of 1930 with a six-wheeled Thornycroft truck, an oxy-welding plant, a two-way wireless, a ton of provisions, a boring machine and a plant for converting salt water into fresh. A light aircraft was to follow. Rarely had such a well-equipped expedition set out in search of gold in Australia. But it found nothing, and even lost Lasseter – almost certainly he was deluded.

After the death of Lasseter the legend of his gold reef grew. Vast numbers of Australians continued to believe that the gold was there, waiting for a discoverer. Gold, in fact, was the only major industry that boomed during the Depression. Goldfields that were dying in the 1920s came to life again, and new goldfields were found at places as far apart as Tennant Creek (Northern Territory) and Cracow (Queensland). Big companies were formed to apply new techniques and the economies of large-scale production to fields that had previously been unprofitable. By 1933 the Western Australian gold towns such as Kalgoorlie, Norseman, Wiluna and Coolgardie were more prosperous than any capital city or industrial town.

In Western Australia the Depression and the promise of gold stirred up a popular movement for the creation of an independent nation. The last of the six colonies to decide to join the Commonwealth, it was the first to decide to leave. The crusade for secession embraced a majority of voters from each of the three major political parties, and even a few federal politicians. The wheat farmers were especially sympathetic, seeing the Commonwealth as essentially run by the cities of the east. Western Australians were constantly reminded that their rural and mining industries had to subsidise indirectly the factories 3000 kilometres away. In Perth the government resolved to place the question of secession before the people, and the referendum was held on the day of the state election, 8 April 1933.

The opinion in favour of secession was emphatic. In the state as a whole the people voted two to one in favour of seceding. Of the fifty electorates only six voted strongly against secession, and all but one were in areas where goldmining was strong, and where the Depression was less severe.

The powerful vote for secession was still only a gesture. Under the federal constitution both federal houses had to approve of a state seceding, and they gave the seceders no encouragement. At last, in September 1934, leaders of the secession movement sailed for England to plead, in effect, that Westminster should override the Australian constitution. They carried with them a huge petition of signatures in a polished jarrah case. It proved to be a coffin for the secessionists. By the time it had been opened in England, and the case formally rejected on legal grounds, the Depression was slowly receding, and so Western Australia's main grievance was receding too.

7

Across Australia the unemployment was most distressing in the autumn of 1932 when, according to official estimates, 30 per cent of the workforce was unemployed. In June 1933 the nation conducted a census – the first for twelve years – and learned that 22 per cent of workers had no work, and another 8 per cent could not work full time. But already the factories were hiring more men and women. New houses were rising, sales of new cars were slowly increasing, and recovery was under way. It was a speedier recovery than that which ended the 1890s depression.

For five successive years more people had left Australia than arrived; in the sixth year, 1935, the incoming people were in the majority. The renewed inflow in the following four years came less from Britain than from Italy, Greece, Yugoslavia and other lands of south-eastern Europe. Many Jewish refugees fleeing from Hitler arrived in 1938. But the revival of immigration was not spectacular, and economists predicted that Australia might be entering a long era of a declining population.

Old Australians in the late 1930s could not help comparing the two depressions through which they had lived. The one in the 1930s was shorter. It was also, mentally, less shattering, for it came at the end of an unsettled decade; in contrast the slump of the 1890s had come at the end of perhaps forty fat years. And yet one fact was beyond dispute: the Depression of the 1930s was the more intense. It spared no state or region, and hurt a far higher proportion of Australians. Looking at the longer span of time, one conclusion emerges. The half-century 1890–1940 was, materially, a disappointment.

CHAPTER EIGHTEEN

Skeletons in the nation's cupboard

Jimmy Governor was twenty-five when he died. Of mixed Aboriginal and Irish ancestry, he was handsome in an unusual way, his reddish hair capping his darkish face. His father was a bullock driver, and one or both of his parents must have encouraged him to read. After studying at a mission school in the gold town of Gulgong in New South Wales he could read and write and during his last weeks he spent much time reading the Bible.

Learning many bush trades, including fencing and woodcutting, he was also skilled as a 'black tracker' – a form of detective work at which Aborigines excelled. Employed to search for escaped prisoners or lost children, the trackers used their powers of observation to see almost-invisible footprints, twigs or tiny branches unintentionally broken by humans, blades of grass bruised by a human heel, and a dozen signs that other searchers would have missed.

In 1898 Jimmy married a pregnant sixteen-year-old white girl,

Ethel Mary Jane Page. The presence of three given names suggests that at least one of her parents was socially ambitious. Working as a domestic servant for the Mawbeys, who were farmers near Gilgandra, Ethel was taunted by Mrs Mawbey and a female school-teacher for marrying an Aborigine or, to use one of their phrases, 'black rubbish'. Relations between the Mawbeys and the Governors may have been strained further after Aboriginal relatives, arriving to live with Jimmy and Ethel, increased the demands on the Mawbeys for food rations, because Jimmy and Ethel were paid in rations as well as cash. Whatever the causes, Jimmy's anger against the Mawbeys smouldered, and on the evening of 20 July 1900 he acted. In company with Jacky Underwood, a one-eyed Aborigine from Queensland, he used native weapons to kill five members of the Mawbey household; all but one were female.

Underwood was arrested, but Jimmy Governor had no intention of surrendering. He and his brother Joe killed another four white settlers, including a baby. Soon the brothers were being hunted by mounted police and armed civilians. So far as is known the brothers, unlike the Kelly Gang in Victoria some twenty years earlier, were not often given food and useful information by local residents. Self-disciplined, they rarely touched alcohol. Sometimes they left behind handwritten notes that taunted their pursuers and pointed to their incompetence.

The brothers, while being pursued, knowingly ran risks. As the inland can be sharply cold on winter nights, they lit fires in order to keep warm. So carefully were the fireplaces selected in the hilly terrain, and so frugally was the wood added and arranged, that hardly anybody saw or sniffed the rising smoke. When walking or riding they covered their tracks. When near a railway line, the brothers would walk along the steel rails, knowing that they would leave behind no footprints.

Country people who lived near the brothers' escape routes were frightened. Wives and children – even husbands – fled from farmhouses or huts. A reporter from the *Mudgee Guardian* called at thirty-five homesteads and found that only four were inhabited – such was the rate of desertion. For fourteen weeks newspaper readers who followed the hunt wondered how the two brothers could escape capture. The main answer was simple: they were practising the arts of the Indigenous bushman.

In the end they were declared to be outlaws. They could legally be shot on sight. By the time they were captured they had travelled more than 3000 kilometres, often in rugged terrain.

Convicted for murder, Jimmy was hanged in a Sydney gaol in 1901. Ethel married again, gave birth to nine children, and in Sydney she lived long enough to see the end of the Second World War. Another quarter-century passed, and Jimmy Governor became a minor folk hero, thanks to a novel written by Thomas Keneally.

2

In 1900 other Aborigines were fighting a rearguard action. In the Kimberley, they fought the incoming cattle. After all, they retained the right, under Western Australian law, to hunt kangaroos and other native animals on their old lands, and so they viewed the cattle as consumers of scarce grass and water. When possible they speared cattle and fed on them. Understandably the cattle killers were pursued as thieves and arrested.

The problem was how to escort the killers on the long route to the nearest courthouse and prison. Police needed incentives – their task was arduous compared to the capture of a town thief. The practice grew of giving police an incentive payment based on the number of days they spent in escorting cattle thieves. For every prisoner in his charge, guilty or not, a policeman received a 'cost of living allowance' of eighteen to twenty-nine pence a person a day. From this sum he easily made a handsome profit by feeding them less with costly flour and sugar than with lizard, kangaroo and other native foods procured at no expense along the way. Cattle thieving – for the police of the north-west – became the favoured crime, accounting for nine of every ten arrests.

It became almost a habit to arrest not only the spear-carrying 'cattle stealer' but also a wife or two if present and a child if capable of walking a long distance each day. In that way the 'cost of living' allowance paid to a policeman for a fifteen-day journey was attractive, for it almost doubled his income.

To convey the captives a long distance to a courthouse or prison the police turned them into a walking chain gang, reminiscent of the forgotten convict system. How else could numerous prisoners be escorted securely through familiar territory where they had every incentive to escape? Unfortunately the light metal chains often were fixed to the neck rather than the wrists – a painful practice – and the chain of the foremost prisoner was linked to the saddle of a mounted police officer. The chains usually were not removed to lower the risk of drowning when the police and Aborigines had to cross a river. Larger expeditions succeeded only with the cooperation of native constables who sometimes were armed with Winchester repeating rifles.

In the Kimberley the three local gaols were soon packed with 'cattle thieves' – innocent and guilty. Prison sentences were usually short (sometimes shorter than those for European thieves) but the released prisoners then had to find their way home, carrying bags of flour as food for the journey. A royal commission in 1905 investigated these iniquities, and the neck chains became rare. Eventually several cattle stations were set up by the Western

Australian government for the sole benefit of Aborigines – a symbolic step that long preceded the campaign for land rights.

Within the closely settled districts many Aborigines did hard rural tasks week after week, though others saw no point in regular work. In the late nineteenth century they did not work often for the pearling industry, and they shunned the expanding sugarcane farms in Queensland that especially needed them as outdoor workers. To ride horses, however, was a pleasure, and often their skills were vital on remote cattle stations. While their money-wage was small, payment usually included flour, sugar, and fresh beef and mutton given to the Aborigines' relatives who camped more or less permanently near the homestead. Many teenage girls and adult women were employed as household servants and some as mistresses. A few, on horseback, worked on the large cattle stations in the north, and were doubly valued because they could quickly gather additional food for the evening meals eaten far from the homestead.

In seasonal tasks such as shearing and fruit picking, Aborigines were more willing to participate than they are now. In the Mount Gambier district of South Australia they had once been described, in the words of an experienced pastoralist, as 'fairly civilised, smart, sharp as needles' and relied on to do a good day's work. That was high praise. Numerous white workers would not have been described as 'sharp as needles', even by loyal friends.

Simple misunderstandings arose even when blacks and whites hoped to coexist in peace. One episode occurred on the fringe of the north-western desert in about 1914. The owner of a new sheep station lived in a simple house, and his late-evening habit was to take outside a shovel of hot embers collected from the kitchen stove. On one such night, to his surprise, a tall naked Aborigine was standing at the door, a long spear in his hand. The nomad had rarely knocked on a door – his traditional dwellings did not possess such a thing – and he simply assumed that the owner would eventually appear. Suddenly the door opened and the two utter strangers were face to face. The owner's instantaneous reaction was to toss the hot ashes at the waiting Aborigine, who instantly dropped his spear and ran as fast as he could, crashing into a wire fence in the darkness. The incident could have – but did not – led to violent retaliation.

Near the coast of the Northern Territory, on the East Alligator River, Paddy Cahill and his wife, Maria, had frequent contact with tribal Aborigines, who would call for bread, sugar and tobacco, and then vanish. Sometimes they brought gifts of food. During a few weeks of 1917, after flocks of magpie geese nested in the surrounding swamp, Aborigines brought to Cahill's homestead a total of 21597 eggs.

The Cahills, if so requested, acted as rough dentists and doctors. They would pull out teeth and attend to burns, which were a frequent happening at those Aboriginal camps dotted with little open fires. The local people already knew something about the outside world, especially the battles of the First World War, and at times they clamoured to see battlefield photographs in the illustrated newspapers that had slowly come all the way from London. In the far outback the next generation of Aborigines would adapt more readily to the Western world or increasingly comprehend it.

3

The main churches felt a duty to help Aborigines. Their aim was to turn them into fellow Christians, meanwhile feeding, clothing and caring for them. John B. Gribble and his wife were invited to open an Anglican mission and school near the sandy bed of the Gascoyne River at Carnarvon in Western Australia. There Gribble did not make himself popular by noting the cruel treatment of Aboriginal women by both black and white men. He himself employed the 'leftovers', his first helpers being an Aborigine with one foot and another Aborigine with blindness in one eye. Returning to eastern Australia he founded other Aboriginal missions, the last being near Cairns where malaria wore him down. His tombstone praises him as 'The Blackfellows' Friend'.

In the northern half of the continent the number of Anglican, Catholic, Presbyterian, Methodist and Lutheran missions was to increase notably after 1875. While these missions are now derided by a more secular society – and they certainly had their defects – their very existence reflected goodwill towards Aborigines. Missionaries were the main voices against injustices. The complaint of pastoralists was that the missions 'spoiled' the Aborigines, while the complaint of anthropologists – and they were few – was that the missions destroyed the traditional culture. On the other hand the more learned missionaries set out to record Aboriginal cultures.

Carl Strehlow, a 23-year-old German, arrived at the Finke River in Central Australia in 1894, and made the Hermannsburg Lutheran mission a little oasis for the study of Aboriginal religion and culture. Besides translating chapters of the Bible into the Arrernte and Luritja languages, he gained insights into what local Aborigines thought, and by 1920 seven volumes of his writings had been published in Frankfurt. On totemism – the belief that each Aborigine had a spiritual relationship with a certain plant or animal – Strehlow was seen by many European scholars as the authority.

This landmark Lutheran mission pleased and surprised newcomers. On their arrival – it was 1927 – they were encircled by people, and black hands were outstretched by small boys with curly hair and glistening eyes, and then the old grey-haired men offered handshakes too. Despite the drought many of the mission's cattle were alive, the irrigated tomato plants were so tall their tips could not be touched, and enough kangaroos and other native animals survived to feed hunters' families at festival time. On the first Sunday the church was packed, children sitting in the aisles, the congregation loudly singing German tunes and words learned by heart, and that dignified local evangelist Moses Tjalkabota, wearing his white suit, about to preach in the Arrernte tongue. And yet Christians in Australia still focused more on converting and educating people overseas – in New Guinea, the New Hebrides (Vanuatu), Fiji, Tonga, India, China and Sudan.

4

Aborigines' skills were widely imitated in bush life and their words were adopted by new settlers who, after a time, did not realise their alien origin. The largest single source of these borrowed words was the Dharug nation in the country near Sydney. British colonists were soon borrowing such Dharug words as dingo and warrigal, boomerang, corroboree and nulla-nulla, and by the year 1800 adopting their names for such animals as koala, wallaby and wombat. These words, slowly finding their way across Australia, joined the daily language of both whites and blacks.

The pronunciation of Aboriginal words was altered in the course of their slow migration from one language to another. Billabong, now a keyword in Australian nationalism and song, was first learned in the 1830s from the Wiradjuri people in the southwest of New South Wales. Major Mitchell the explorer, who was perhaps the first to express the word on paper, pronounced it as 'billibang'. For decades other English-speakers said billybong or billibong. When six decades later 'Banjo' Paterson wrote his famous song about the swagman 'camped by the billabong', the old pronunciation was in decline.

One of the best-known Aboriginal words of today was little known as late as 1900: this was the long wooden musical instrument from the Yolngu people in Arnhem Land, the didgeridoo or didjeridu. That word was a rarity even in its home region where it was mostly called the yidaki. Most Aborigines alive in 1914 had never heard the music of the didgeridoo, let alone the word.

In the states where Aborigines were numerous, a few special reserves were set aside for them by government officials. Here they were given simple food, clothes, blankets, but they lost part or all of their liberty. Often an air and mood of listlessness prevailed. Moore River Settlement, on the sandy plain north of Perth, was selected by the protector of Aborigines in the 1930s as a refuge for the 'aged and indigent who had nowhere else to go'. There they shared simple shelters with 'problem Aborigines' who drank too much, prisoners discharged from gaol but now far from their traditional home, and orphans and neglected children. Ambitious Aboriginal families did everything possible to keep away from such reserves.

It is claimed that most Aborigines by the 1930s were 'imprisoned' within this widespread patchwork of reserves, but the evidence disputes such a view. In June 1934 the supervised camps held only 18 000 of the 78 000 Aborigines who had been counted in a special nationwide census. In contrast another 35 000 – perhaps an inflated statistic – were reported to be nomadic, while about 13 000 were in paid employment.

5

During the first three generations of contact with the British, most Aborigines who had the choice did not embrace the new way of life. At first they had no wish to live in houses with wooden instead of earthen floors, with iron cooking stoves instead of open fires, and a dinner table to sit at, though they did appreciate a permanent supply of fresh water from wells recently sunk. European dogs they acquired eagerly. Dogs would sleep beside their owners, and a very cold night came to be called a two-dog night, as if dogs were blankets. Aborigines quickly relished European goods such as flour and sugar, a pot of tea, a pipe of tobacco and strong alcohol in the form of spirits. In their craving for Western foods and intoxicants, some Aboriginal groups abandoned their homeland and migrated long distances to towns. The anthropologist W. E. H. Stanner thought that in the Northern Territory some of these migrations were so long-lasting that he doubted the assertion that all Aborigines had a deep, persisting affinity with their 'clan country'.

The official stream of thought insisted that hard and regular work, a willingness to save money, and the acquiring of a house and other possessions were desirable virtues. Understandably, they were not high virtues for most Aborigines. In the course of thousands of years they had successfully fashioned their traditional way of life with an alternative set of values. They valued leisure; they valued family ties, and accepted an obligation to share wealth and possessions with relatives. Given this set of values, they could not necessarily contribute to national wealth in the same ratio as did mainstream Australian employees. But their intelligence was widely praised by many who lived with them.

Margaret Bain served as a Presbyterian missionary in the outback before agreeing in 1968 to become a resident adviser to people living at Aputula near the Finke River. She spoke their language and earned their trust. An 'original thinker', in the opinion of one anthropologist, she increasingly noticed not only the close mental similarities between black and white Australians but also several profound differences. Even when they spoke the same language they could misunderstand. For example, the two peoples did not think alike about quantities and numbers – a hallmark of Western civilisation.

Aborigines initially misunderstood discussions about the future or about hypothetical or contingent events. The crucial word *if* meant very little to them. Thus, senior men from Aputula, making the long journey to meet government officials in Alice Springs, were asked what they would like if the government formulated new plans for their welfare. They replied that they wanted land for themselves and also a permanent supply of fresh water for their little town. Returning home, they announced confidently that these assets 'would soon be available'. The months passed and nothing happened. 'White people are liars,' they finally concluded. In a variety of other ways the governments also misunderstood Aborigines and their way of thinking and speaking.

While the treatment of Aborigines was often punitive, the governments had for long been punitive towards mainstream Australians who had to live on public charity. If the very poor and the old were fortunate enough to find a place in a city benevolent asylum in 1890, they were permitted to go outside its doors for only a few hours a week. They had to work for token wages or none. Their visitors were restricted. In 1900 the new old-age pensions were available in only two colonies, and were paid only to people who had contributed to the workforce of that colony for a long period. In contrast most Aborigines receiving government help did not have to work and could live with their relatives.

The understandable tendency is to conclude that most Aborigines lived in gloom, and yet they could remain amused for days after experiencing something funny: 'Aboriginals laugh far more than white people,' wrote one sympathetic outback observer.

The typical Aboriginal groups did not yet seek to be represented in a parliament, and did not demand the vote. They did not yet feel a sense of unity. As late as 1900 the leaders in the far south had no political links with those in the far north. In contrast the New Zealand Maori – with the advantage of a small area – formed distinct alliances, some for and some against the British. Politically astute and well organised, they received as early as 1867 the permanent gift of four Maori seats in the parliament. Admittedly Aborigines had already been granted the opportunity – rarely used – to vote in Victoria, New South Wales and South Australia though they lost that right if they received welfare.

The start of the twentieth century was an opportunity to bring Aborigines into mainstream life. The six colonies were federating, and the new national parliament had to decide who was entitled to vote. In 1902 it resolved that Maori could vote if they were resident in Australia, but Aborigines could not vote unless they were already on the voters' roll of their state. Most Aborigines had no interest in voting but the few who did were intensely disappointed by the new law. On the other hand the electoral laws in several states did not exclude Aborigines from voting.

6

Arnhem Land – named after a Dutch ship that touched the northern coast in 1623 – was not typical of tropical Australia. It had strong summer rains, dense vegetation in places, and impressive sources of food on its coast. Not suited to sheep, and possessing no rich gold deposits, it was late in attracting European settlers. Indeed most of it was converted into an Aboriginal reserve in 1931, and missionaries and government officials were the only outsiders allowed entry.

In the following year Japanese fishermen were murdered by Aborigines at Caledon Bay, in north-east Arnhem Land, and many of their possessions were looted. From Darwin mounted constables went out to investigate, and one was fatally speared. A suspect named Dhakiyarr Wirrpanda or Tuckiar was arrested, tried in distant Darwin and sentenced to death. It then became widely known that he could speak no English, that no official interpreter was present, and that Judge T. A. Wells who instructed the all-white jury said more than a judge should say. Even the legal knowledge of the barrister who earnestly defended the prisoner was open to criticism. In November 1934 the High Court was unanimous in overthrowing the verdict, and Dhakiyarr was released.

On the other side of the continent, Aboriginal leaders were emerging. It was not easy to be a leader, as was discovered in 1925 by Fred Maynard who in the Sydney suburb of Surry Hills organised a short-lived association in the face of official hostility. Another leader was William Cooper, a member of the Australian Workers' Union who came from the Yorta Yorta territory near the junction of the Murray and Goulburn rivers. In January 1938, as the first Aborigine to lead a deputation to a prime minister, he wished to know from Joseph Lyons why Native Americans and Maori retained large areas of land by treaty with their new rulers, whereas the Aborigines received only a few small areas. This thorny question, discussed in Volume 1, did have an explanation, but Cooper understandably wanted land rather than explanations. He also requested permanent Aboriginal seats in federal parliament.

Aboriginal leaders, assembling in the Australian Hall in Elizabeth Street, Sydney in 1938, on the 150th birthday of British Australia, declared it 'a day of mourning'. Some of these protesters, imitating a British tradition, are said to have worn black armbands. In an unusual display of unity they passed a resolution deploring 'the Whiteman's seizure of our country'. One of their eloquent supporters was the black Victorian footballer Doug Nicholls, who some forty years later was to become the governor of South Australia.

In the crowded hall he proclaimed that 'Aboriginal people are the skeleton in the cupboard of Australia's national life'. These protests were not endorsed by David Unaipon, the best-known Aboriginal leader who, remaining in Adelaide, continued to be an independent spirit.

Somehow a new deal for Aborigines had to be created. A united approach was essential. As the states were in charge of Aboriginal affairs everywhere except in the Northern Territory, it was vital that the state ministers should meet the relevant federal minister for the first time. In Canberra in 1937 they met and all agreed that the part-Aborigines should have the same rights to education and employment as other Australians. Two years later the anthropologist Stanner challenged the rising optimism: 'Unfortunately, the problem of the bewildered, undernourished, neglected, badly "protected" blackfellow is not so simple.' It was not one problem, he added, but 'a series of extraordinarily intricate and difficult problems'. Months later the problems and puzzles were shelved again by the Second World War.

PART THREE

The Ascent of Another Australia

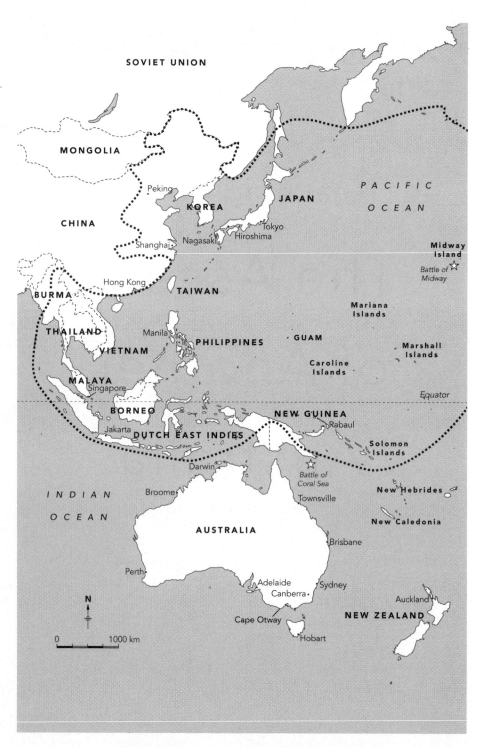

Japan's southwards thrust, February 1942

CHAPTER NINETEEN

'That reddish veil': the Pacific war

The news from Europe was grim. In March 1939, Hitler's troops occupied Prague, the capital of Czechoslovakia. On 7 April, Good Friday, Italian troops invaded Albania. That same day, Australia's prime minister, Joseph Lyons, died in Sydney, and it was rumoured that the tense news from Europe precipitated his heart attack. The young Robert G. Menzies succeeded Lyons as prime minister and was blooded into office by months of ominous news. On 3 September, after learning that Hitler had invaded Poland, he announced that Australia along with Britain and France was now at war with Germany.

2

Whether the war would be worldwide or confined to Europe was not certain. For the preceding one-third of a century, many

Australians had expected that Japan would become their main enemy. Ever since Japan's victory over Russia in the war of 1904–05, many politicians thought that one day Japan would attack Australia or sever its sea routes to the outside world. The notable general Sir John Monash feared Japan in the 1920s. One reason why the White Australia policy was maintained so strongly was the belief that it prevented Japanese migrants from pouring in and, if war broke out, cooperating with a Japanese force landing on Australian soil.

On the other hand British naval and military leaders did not view Japan as a major threat. They trusted that the new Singapore naval base – slowly being fortified – would help the British navy to defeat a Japanese attack. Moreover in the late 1930s the British had reached a vital agreement with their French allies: if together they were fighting a war against Germany, and if Japan thereupon snatched the opportunity to attack the British and French colonies in South-East Asia, the French navy would guard the Mediterranean and the Atlantic, thus allowing Britain to despatch warships and aircraft carriers to oppose Japan's navy. As for Italy, a British ally in the previous war, a common view was that it was not likely to be an enemy. These assumptions proved to be wrong.

Australia relied too heavily on Britain for its defences. Australian voters had to be persuaded that they should spend more on their own armed forces, but a large wing of the Labor Party favoured neutrality and isolationism. The First World War, in its final stage, had split the party, thus exerting long-term effects on Australia's security. In 1918 Labor's federal executive called for a new-style Australian army while the whiff of the Russian revolutions was in the air. Australia's officers were to be elected. To proclaim where real power lay, the practice of saluting was challenged. Fortunately Labor was in opposition, federally, and the plans were shelved.

Eventually more moderate voices won control of Labor. J. H. Scullin, who led the party back to power in 1929, was referring to Japan when he said: 'if ever a certain power sought to invade the fair land of Australia'. How far he would then rearm his nation was not certain, for he believed generally in disarmament. Meanwhile money had to be saved. During one Depression year, the peacetime army, mostly militia, fell from 47 000 to 27 000. In 1931 no new students were admitted to the army's and navy's training colleges.

The Liberals, under the name of the United Australia Party, regained office under Joseph Lyons in January 1932 and slowly increased spending on defence. John Curtin, who became Labor's leader in 1935, slowly turned his isolationist party around so that it faced the outside world. He himself thought that Japan, rearming itself month by month, was a serious threat, and that Australia needed a strong air force and more airfields and aviation fuel depots. Nonetheless during the 1937 federal election Curtin implied that Australia should not engage in an overseas war, especially in Europe, until a referendum of the people had been held. In advocating that policy he was walking the narrow plank. A nation in peril cannot conduct a referendum, fritter away valuable weeks and expect an enemy to abide by the result.

Australians were deeply divided on the question whether, if a second World War did occur, they should take part. Many who remembered the horrors of war in the trenches preferred not to think about it. Others were absorbed in the daily struggle to live, for unemployment was serious. The non-Labor government, led by Lyons, made Australians prepare for war but was reluctant to impose very high taxes to finance adequate rearmament. Generally a democracy is less eager than a dictator to prepare for war, but often more determined in fighting it once the war is under way.

Command of the air was to prove as important as command of the sea. Australia had always bought its main warships from Britain, and it also expected to buy its military aircraft from Britain when the need arose. Suddenly Britain needed its own aircraft for its own defence. On the eve of the war its confidential advice was that when London was bombed by the Germans, it would probably suffer 160 000 deaths in the first twenty-four hours. The prediction proved to be wrong, but it explains why, when war was imminent, Britain was reluctant to sell modern aircraft to Australia.

Australian National Airways, or ANA, a private company created by the Holyman family of Tasmania, was Australia's largest commercial airline in 1939. It possessed the nation's only four aircraft suitable for patrolling the long coastline. In the first week of the war those four aircraft were refitted, camouflaged and provided with Vickers machine guns. The vital sea convoys carrying the first Australian troops to the Middle East in 1940 were escorted part of the way by ANA planes – until the superior Lockheed Hudsons were imported from the United States.

Australia was already making is own fighting aircraft. Essington Lewis, the chief executive of Broken Hill Proprietary Company, while visiting Japanese steelworks and other industries in 1934, had gained the compelling impression that Japan was secretly preparing for war. Back in Australia he and his chairman, Harold Darling, persuaded other companies to join a BHP syndicate formed to make military aircraft. The first model, based on a Californian training plane, was called the Wirraway, an Aboriginal word for 'challenge'. It flew successfully in March 1939. Faster than many of the older aircraft in Britain's air force, it was still not fast enough for modern war.

3

In September 1939 Hitler swiftly conquered Poland, and the Soviet Union shared in the spoils. Then the war almost hibernated until May 1940 when Hitler's highly mechanised army, aided by command of the skies, invaded Norway and Denmark, Holland and Belgium. Those small nations quickly surrendered. That powerful nation, France, unexpectedly was conquered with ease. Masses of French people were led away as prisoners of war. A puppet government under the aged military hero Marshal Pétain was permitted to govern the far south of France. The French overseas colonies, with no motherland to defend them, were open to conquest by Japan. Above all, the collapse of France scuttled the careful Anglo-French stratagic plan for defending Singapore. France's navy, one of the strongest in the world, was powerless to help.

After Hitler's conquest of France, Italy entered the war on his side. Suddenly the Mediterranean, intended to be a peaceful lake controlled by British and French battleships, became a playground for German submarines and Italian warships. Egypt's western desert was invaded by Italian and German troops, and the Suez Canal – a vital sea route for Australia – was in danger of falling into Hitler's hands. Australian and New Zealand troops were shipped to Egypt, as in 1914, to fight alongside the British. Eventually the Suez Canal was saved.

Britain, led by Winston Churchill, was fighting for its existence. Its main allies were Canada, Australia and New Zealand, though their contribution to the war effort, measured by population, fell short of Britain's. Meanwhile the sea lanes on which Britain depended for much of its food, metals and munitions, and all its oil, were disrupted by German submarines, now using the occupied ports of western France as bases. In November 1940 Menzies in a frank moment told his Advisory War Council that in the long run 'the United Kingdom might be defeated in the war'.

Hitler's quick conquest of most of Europe blew on fear like a giant bellows. The defeat of two major colonial powers, France and Holland, meant that their colonies were vulnerable. French Indochina and the Dutch East Indies – so rich in oil – were vulnerable to a Japanese invasion in 1941. Britain too was overextended, and unable to defend effectively South-East Asia – if Singapore, Malaya, Java, Burma and Hong Kong were attacked.

Menzies, as Australia's prime minister, continued to urge Churchill to send more warships and aircraft to Singapore. The complacent reply was that the Japanese were not air-minded and that their aircraft were not 'even comparable with those of the Italians'. General Thomas Blamey, head of the Australian army, was also mistaken. He agreed that the Japanese military threat was exaggerated. One month before the Japanese were to attack Pearl Harbor and Malaya, he recommended that more Australian soldiers should be sent not to East Asia but instead to the Middle East where they could help the British evict the strong German army from North Africa.

Meanwhile Canberra in 1941 experienced months of political turmoil. Menzies resigned as prime minister, and eventually two independents crossed the floor of the house and voted in the Labor Party led by John Curtin. Labor was to rule for eight years.

Curtin was the son of a police constable in the Victorian gold town of Creswick – by coincidence the hometown of Menzies' mother. A clerk, union organiser and journalist before moving to Perth, Curtin was by background more a pacifist than a wartime leader. He possessed, however, the gift of converting enemies into friends or sympathisers. He united the Labor Party, which had been split by the Depression – two rival Labor parties sat separately in the federal parliament until 1940. He had the ability to see what was essential. He made himself the effective and sometimes the inspiring leader of a nation at war.

4

Japan resolved to attack the main United States naval base in the Pacific. Aircraft carriers and all the accompanying ships sailed towards Honolulu by a long, roundabout route in order to surprise a crucial part of the American navy. They succeeded. On the morning of 8 December 1941 (Australian time) their aircraft flew away from the deck of the massive carriers and attacked the American fleet, trapped in the harbour. They inflicted enormous damage.

On the same day, thousands of sea miles to the west, Japanese planes prepared to attack the main American base near Manila in the Philippines. Flying over the South China Sea they surprised the American planes, waiting in neat rows on the ground at Clark Field. America's airpower in the west Pacific was torn away in the space of a few days.

The Japanese army promptly invaded the Philippines, winning victory after victory against the American forces led by the senior general Douglas MacArthur. There was no point in the United States sending reinforcements on the long sea route to Manila, for the Japanese now commanded the surrounding sea and air. A convoy already on its way with aircraft and other military supplies to the Philippines was diverted to Brisbane, which it reached safely.

We like to think that the United States' help came after our prime minister, Curtin, publicly pleaded for it. But the first help arrived before his eloquent appeal for American aid appeared in the afternoon Melbourne *Herald*. Emphasising the crisis facing his nation, he began his article with a verse by his poet friend Bernard O'Dowd:

> *That reddish veil which o'er the face*
> *Of night-hag East is drawn . . . Flames new disaster for the*
> *race?*
> *Or can it be the dawn?*

Perhaps the British navy would reach Singapore, grasp the command of the encircling seas, and so prevent the Japanese from reaching Australia. Deep was the sense of relief, not long before the Japanese entered the war, when two mighty British battleships, *Prince of Wales* and *Repulse*, passed South Africa, entered the Indian Ocean and finally reached the spacious harbour of Singapore. Unfortunately a crucial British ship was absent from this fleet. An aircraft carrier, it had run aground in the West Indies.

Soon after the Pacific War began, the two battleships sailed from Singapore into the open sea. About 240 kilometres away, hunted by Japanese aircraft, they were detected. Desperately needing fighter planes to protect them, they were alone and vulnerable when a striking force of eighty-five Japanese torpedo bombers approached. At 11.45 a.m. a torpedo fired from a low-flying Japanese plane crippled, and soon sank, the *Prince of Wales*. At 12.30 p.m. torpedoes sank the *Repulse*. Of the combined British crew of nearly 3000 sailors and officers, almost half were killed. Meanwhile the surviving Japanese planes – only three were lost in the fight – flew back to Saigon, 400 sea miles to the north, carrying their astonishing news. Here was the first decisive victory of an air force over big battleships in the open ocean. No less important, Japan after the first day had won undisputed command of the air over land as well as sea.

Decisive victories were won by the Japanese, and won with ease. They invaded British Burma, a vital source of oil and rice. They advanced into British Malaya, a source of rubber and tin, and the independent monarchy of Thailand. They invaded the Dutch East Indies, an even richer source of oil. Already the occupier of a large part of China, the Japanese attacked Hong Kong, which surrendered on Christmas Day 1941.

At home, Australians listening on the radio to the chilling news did not yet realise the magnitude of the Japanese victories, partly because the news was either censored or unbelievable. Worse news was to come. Vivian Bowden, who was Australia's main diplomat in Singapore, confidentially warned Canberra that the naval base was likely to fall because the British and Australian weakness in the air 'is assuming landslide proportions'.

The Japanese continued to sweep down the Malay Peninsula like an army carrying out a textbook display: what was not in the textbooks was their skilled use of aircraft and bicycles. The Australian, British and Indian soldiers defending the peninsula were often in retreat, though superior in numbers. Within six weeks of the invasion, the Japanese soldiers were advancing close to Singapore. It surrendered meekly on 15 February 1942.

Lessons can be learned by comparing the landing at Gallipoli in the First World War with the collapse of Singapore in the Second World War. Whereas at Gallipoli the Australians and their allies held the superior equipment and also secure lines of supply, for they commanded the sea and were able to evacuate everyone, they had no such advantages in South-East Asia. They could not organise a calm and orderly retreat of their soldiers from Singapore and Java. Nearly all Australians, even the nurses and civilians, were captured and sent as prisoners to camps where the death toll was to be high.

Suddenly most Australian leaders realised their nation's peril. Their military and naval alliance with the British – the core of their history for 150 years – was shaken and almost snapped. The pending disaster was glimpsed by the Australian Broadcasting Company, which, increasingly the source of radio news, changed its theme music. Its news bulletins hitherto had been introduced by the stirring brass-band version of 'The British Grenadiers', but now it was replaced by the tune of the nationalist song 'Advance Australia Fair'.

5

The advance of the Japanese forces was so speedy that Australia's northern coast was in their reach. On 19 February, four days after the fall of Singapore, Darwin was attacked by 240 planes launched from Japanese aircraft carriers far out to sea or from nearer Indonesian islands, recently captured. The first bombs fell on Darwin at 9.58 a.m., creating some panic. A second raid came just after midday. Surprisingly, more bombs were dropped on Darwin that day than on Pearl Harbor during its devastating raid ten weeks previously.

Darwin Harbour was sheltering more big ships than at any time in its history, and eight were sunk including the United States destroyer *Peary*. The air defences were shattered too, and four of the five American Kittyhawks that had tried to counter the Japanese Zero fighters were shot down. At least 243 people, including the civilian staff of the post office, were killed in that raid.

Canberra concealed the extent of the deaths and damage for fear that panic or defeatism might undermine the spirit of a nation that was now in peril. For days the public was led to believe that only about a score of Australians, mostly postal officials, had died. These early attacks, the first of many, were feared to be a prelude to an actual invasion of Darwin or other northern ports.

The pearling port of Broome, in Western Australia, was another Japanese target. Now the haven for Dutch flying boats arriving with women and children being evacuated from Java, it was raided on 3 March by Zero planes using a red-earth runway made by the Japanese who had just captured Kupang in Dutch Timor. On the day of the raid sixteen flying boats were in Broome harbour and six aircraft at the local airport. All were damaged. On the following day, from the same airport in Dutch Timor, the Japanese again bombed Darwin. Across the nation the fear of air raids was contagious. To protect civilians and especially children, many kilometres of air-raid trenches were dug in parklands and school grounds, and in backyards of Australian cities far to the south.

Vital knowledge of the shipping in Australian ports was collected by a large Japanese submarine. On 18 February – three days after the fall of Singapore – the submarine surfaced about 160 kilometres south-east of Sydney, and on that moonless night the crew assembled their portable seaplane and squeezed two airmen into its cabin. Exploiting the beam from the Macquarie Lighthouse as a beacon the plane flew over Sydney at a low height, observing twenty-three ocean-going vessels in the harbour, and then flying past North Head at a speed of 90 knots before returning to the waiting submarine.

With similar bravery the seaplane pilot flew near the Point Lonsdale Lighthouse and over Melbourne's Laverton airfield and Williamstown docks in the early-morning light. As no senior Australian pilot could imagine a Japanese plane emerging so far south, there was no ready-made scheme to pursue such an intruder. The Japanese plane flew past Frankston and Cape Schanck and then to the waiting submarine. The ports of Hobart and distant Wellington and Auckland and Suva were inspected by the submarine and seaplane in the same systematic way. Here was a quest for strategic information such as Australia and its allies could not match.

For two weeks the Allies hoped – a nervous hope – that they might save the Dutch East Indies and its oilfields from Japanese occupation. HMAS *Perth*, a light cruiser, and almost the last Australian fighting ship in the region, was in the company of Dutch warships and the American cruiser USS *Houston* near the strategic Sunda Strait, at the western end of Java. The Allied vessels, however, were hopelessly outgunned. Hit by Japanese torpedoes, the *Perth* was abandoned in the first minutes of Sunday 1 March 1942. In all, 353 of the crew were killed aboard the ship or when she sank; mourned too was the ship's grey-and-white cat named Redhead. The surviving sailors became prisoners of war, and more than a hundred did not see home again.

March 1941 was another disastrous month for Australia's leaders and those civilians who closely followed the censored news. The Dutch East Indies slipped into the hands of Japan. Rangoon, the capital of Burma, was captured. It was only a matter of weeks before the Philippines fell. The island of Timor, bravely defended by a small Australian force, was doomed. Rabaul had long been captured and was now a Japanese naval base, and even Lae and Salamaua – on the northern coast of New Guinea's mainland – were captured by the Japanese. Isolated ports such as Townsville and Port Hedland were bombed, instilling the fear that these air raids were the heralds of a Japanese invasion somewhere along an endless coast that was largely unguarded. The fears were to be heightened when midget Japanese submarines crept into Sydney Harbour, evading the defensive line built to keep them out.

General MacArthur, leaving the Philippines just in time, safely reached Australia where he was ordered by Washington to direct the Allied war effort in the entire south-west Pacific. With his wife and young child he came south from Alice Springs in the slow steam train called the Ghan. On the little railway station at Terowie, in the South Australian wheat belt, he issued his famous statement: 'I came through, and I shall return.' Making his headquarters in Melbourne and then in Brisbane, the supreme commander was seen by few citizens walking along the streets. His voice was rarely heard on radio. And yet during his three years in Australia, MacArthur was, by shaping world history, far more influential than John Curtin, the prime minister.

6

The stark fact was that the sky was often more important than sea and land, but Australia was weakest in the air. Thus in December 1941 it was mainly defended by two classes of aircraft, both of them inadequate. The Brewster Buffalo had many defects, including American engines that tended to overheat in the tropics. The local Wirraways in their hundreds were the main defender of Australia and New Guinea, and though faster, their maximum speed was less than 200 miles an hour. In contrast, Japan's Mitsubishi Zero achieved a maximum speed of 330 miles an hour and carried stronger armaments. There was no comparison.

Everywhere the Brewsters and the Wirraways were downed. The sole decisive victory of a Wirraway was on Boxing Day 1942, when it shot down a Zero near Gona in New Guinea. Even the superior Hurricane aircraft that Britain sent to Singapore when that city was about to surrender could not match the Japanese planes. One Hurricane pilot, lucky to survive when his plane crashed, was John Gorton who became prime minister of Australia a quarter-century later.

As a faster combat aircraft was urgently needed, it was designed at the Commonwealth Aircraft Corporation in Melbourne by Friedrich David, a Jewish refugee who had worked on aircraft in Germany. It was called the Boomerang. Armed with machine guns and cannons, its Pratt & Whitney engine could produce double the horsepower of the Wirraway, and was capable of 305 miles an hour. In mid-February 1942 the government approved its manufacture, and on 29 May the first test flight was made. Though not as brilliant as the British Spitfire, it excelled in low-flying attacks on Japanese posts. Some observers even argue that with more determination Australia could have been flying Boomerangs instead of Wirraways by the end of 1941. A sequence of powerful fighters and bombers was made in Australian factories – an impressive achievement for a small nation that did not yet fully manufacture its own trucks and cars.

For the first time in warfare the decisive naval weapon was the aircraft carrier – a combination of ship and plane and airfield, all in one. It was indispensable. As the Pacific was the largest of all the oceans and as it possessed few islands, the big aircraft carrier was the alternative to islands. In the middle of 1942 it was about to display its value, and so determine the ultimate outcome of the Pacific War.

Spurred by success the Japanese leaders made another bold decision. They decided to capture Port Moresby and that coastline of New Guinea that was so close to Australia. Early in May 1942 two Japanese fleets were deployed in secret. One fleet sailed from Rabaul, recently captured from the Australians, and conveyed an army and landing craft towards Port Moresby. The more powerful fleet, making a longer and circuitous voyage from the other side of the equator, captured the island of Tulagi in the Solomon Islands – the small Australian garrison had just abandoned the island – and set up a seaplane base. The fleet then sailed to the Coral

Sea, where it was close to an American fleet that had just been rein-forced by two Australian warships, *Australia* and *Hobart*, newly arrived from Sydney.

Both sides possessed aircraft carriers – the key to victory – and a vast ocean in which to play hide and seek. For several days, the bat-tle was fought by planes that took off from the long decks of the aircraft carriers or sometimes from distant land bases and located the enemy's ships. Heavy damage was inflicted on ships and planes, but neither side could claim the victory.

The Japanese knew that it would be too dangerous to proceed with their invasion of Port Moresby. They made an orderly retreat. Their aircraft carriers sailed away, meeting the Americans again four weeks later near Midway Island, north of the equator. Already the Americans had cracked the Japanese code: their knowledge of the enemy's plans enabled them to trap those Japanese air-craft carriers that had launched the attacks on both Pearl Harbor and Darwin. On 4 and 5 June 1942 the core of the Japanese navy, including four aircraft carriers, was sunk. In the two world wars this battle of Midway Island was more significant than any other naval victory.

The Japanese continued their war with the same determi-nation. Though their forces so close to Australia were far from home and inadequately supplied because of the long sea route, they launched new attacks. In July a small Japanese army set out to cross the high Owen Stanley Range and reach Port Moresby on the opposite coast. As the gap or pass near Kokoda was 2200 metres above sea level – almost as high as the tallest mountain in Australia – the slippery foot track prevented the carrying of ade-quate armaments and food rations. Soon the Japanese snatched the village of Kokoda from a few Australian defenders and pressed ahead. On 13 September they were within 50 kilometres of Port

Moresby, where several correspondents of Australian newspapers had recently been posted. The newsmen, for their own safety, were flown back to Sydney before they could report even a minor victory.

General MacArthur was not impressed with the young and inexperienced Australian soldiers until he learned that newly arrived American soldiers were thwarted even more by bouts of malaria, the steep terrain and the lack of modern transport. Here was an ancient form of warfare where the fastest supply chain consisted of thousands of Papuans carrying in supplies on their backs and carrying out stretchers holding the wounded. In this arduous terrain the Japanese were driven back by Australians and Americans who coordinated their campaign, sometimes brilliantly.

In the war fought in New Guinea, malaria was the persistent enemy of both armies. It began with the shivers, and then fever and intense sweating set in. Many soldiers, becoming thin and anaemic, were as useless as if they had been wounded by ammunition.

Quinine, a medicine made from cinchona bark, was the most effective remedy against the malarial parasites that lived in the red cells of human blood. But Japan had just captured Java, which produced 95 per cent of the world's quinine. Therefore the Allied forces lacked fresh supplies of quinine at the very time when the tropics had become the main fighting zone of the war against Japan. By the end of the year, malaria and dysentery were crippling soldiers fighting in the Kokoda–Buna campaign. Lieutenant Colonel Edward Ford, an expert in tropical medicine, arrived in Port Moresby where in General Blamey's tent he devised simple and overlooked precautions. Thus after sunset, when mosquitoes appeared in swarms, soldiers were ordered to wear long trousers instead of shorts, and to sleep always inside a mosquito net. At the same time, as a preventive of malaria, the traditional daily dose of quinine tablets was replaced by the effective antimalarial drug called mepacrine (known by the trade name Atebrin or Atabrine), a German invention of 1932.

Brigadier Neil Fairley, who had been a young doctor with Australian troops in Palestine and Egypt in the First World War and was now a specialist in tropical medicine, was invited to experiment with the treating of malaria. In June 1943 in the tropical port of Cairns he began to conduct medical tests on 900 healthy volunteers – a massive experiment by world standards. After infecting them with malaria and treating them with different remedies, he found that a higher dose of mepacrine enabled a soldier to live in a malarial jungle for several months without catching the disease. Australian troops soon became less vulnerable than the Japanese to malaria. Lord Mountbatten was to apply Fairley's formula successfully to British soldiers fighting in the tropics, especially during the campaign to recapture Burma from the Japanese.

Dysentery weakened thousands of soldiers in New Guinea in 1942; as a remedy Fairley became an advocate of the anti-infective drug known as sulphaguanidine, and two scientists at Sydney University devised a method of manufacturing it in quantity. At Braybrook in Victoria the second-largest such factory in the world made the drug, initially for Australian soldiers but ultimately for the British armies based in India. Control of tropical diseases was one of the hidden turning points in the Pacific War.

Some day it might well be argued that Australia's lasting contribution to the war was not its brave defence forces but its medical discoveries. In 1940 in England the South Australian Howard Florey discovered the vital antibiotic penicillin, the early doses of which were quickly transported to treat infected wounds in military hospitals in North Africa. In Australia the Commonwealth Serum Laboratories began to manufacture the drug, arranging scores of thousands of pint bottles in which grew the mould. The first batches were rushed to the Australian army in New Guinea in March 1944.

A year after Florey's penicillin was first tested in England, a remarkable discovery was announced at a small medical meeting in wartime Australia. Norman Gregg, who had won the Military Cross on the Western Front in 1918, practised as an eye surgeon in Macquarie Street, Sydney, where he learned much from his own observations and from what a friend called 'that excellent clinical observer – the mother'. On Wednesday 15 October 1941 – seven weeks before Pearl Harbor – Gregg informed a meeting of colleagues in Melbourne that babies born with a congenital heart disease or other birth defects were sometimes the victims of rubella or German measles contracted by their mothers in early pregnancy. His simple but startling discovery – rubella had been viewed as a harmless infection – was reported in the newspaper while he was returning in the train to Sydney. That same morning two mothers separately rang his surgery to explain that each in the course of pregnancy had caught rubella and that their baby had been born deaf. The magnitude of his discovery was soon apparent across the world. Gregg always remained humble and even self-deprecating when discussing the kind of breakthrough that a brilliant team in a modern research institute would give a fortune to have made.

It was in Europe that the crucial battles of the war were being fought, for the defeat of Hitler was the prime aim of Roosevelt, Churchill and Stalin. The air war over Europe engaged most of Australia's experienced pilots and navigators in 1942 and 1943; and in the eyes of Australian schoolboys their nation's heroes were Keith 'Bluey' Truscott, Clive 'Killer' Caldwell, Peter Isaacson and other celebrated pilots rather than the soldiers fighting in the Pacific War. Three of every ten Australians killed in the Second World War were aviators.

7

The federal government now controlled the economy more than ever before – except perhaps in the first convict years. Departments decided where people should work, who could travel and how far, and who should be called up for the armed forces or compelled to remain in their civilian occupation. The price of almost everything was regulated – rent, food, clothing, corrugated iron and shares.

Melbourne – it was still the home of large federal departments – and Canberra tightly controlled what was called manpower, but so many women entered the workforce that the word 'manpower' became outmoded. Between 1939 and 1943 the women in the paid workforce increased by 31 per cent. Soon there were 732 000 uniformed people in the armed forces, and close to 70 per cent of Commonwealth spending went into defence. The making of munitions and wartime equipment became a huge industry, and there was intense pride in some of the innovations. The Owen machine gun, perfected by its Australian inventor in 1942 and manufactured by Lysaght's factory at Port Kembla, was highly valued by troops in New Guinea, for it was accurate and sturdy, and unlike certain rival guns it was not readily jammed while firing. Pride was intense too in the larger cargo ships and the smaller warships built in Australia, especially at Whyalla and Newcastle.

Shipbuilding was vital, for numerous cargo ships were sunk by enemy submarines on the busy sea lane between Newcastle, Sydney and Melbourne. For internal and interstate traffic the sea routes at that time were more important for Australia than for any major industrialised nation in Europe. Ships were also the major transport to and from the battlefront in New Guinea and the adjacent islands, and one tragedy was the sinking of the northbound hospital ship *Centaur* by a Japanese submarine near the Gold Coast in May 1943, with heavy loss of life.

Residents, especially Germans and Japanese, who were thought to be a danger were interned in prison camps, some for the duration of the war. On 5 August 1944 a crowd of Japanese prisoners of war at Cowra, south-west of the Blue Mountains, made a well-planned escape. Four Australian guards were killed, and 234 Japanese. To protect public morale and to prevent vital information becoming known to the enemy, the main newspapers were censored, though not so heavily as in European countries. On 17 April 1944 newspapers in three cities were totally suppressed by the censor. The Communist Party and the religious sect Jehovah's Witnesses had already been declared illegal.

A modern nation has to be entirely reorganised in order to defend itself adequately, and in wartime the rulebook is almost as important as the rifle. Petrol was rationed in 1940 and soon the typical private motorist was entitled only to enough petrol to travel just over 110 kilometres a month. Tea and sugar were rationed in 1942, along with clothing and drapery. Men's clothing was rationed more severely than women's. To save cloth, waistcoats and double-breasted suits could no longer be made for men nor bloomers for women. Later the decision to ration knitting-wool was considered a severe hardship, for at least half the women in the land were capable of knitting socks and jumpers and scarves.

Every Australian received a ration book, and a specified number of paper coupons – cut from the book with scissors – were handed to the shopkeeper along with the cash. From 1943, partly as a result of severe drought, the rationing extended to butter and then to meat and briefly, in 1945, to eggs. One aim of food rationing was to ensure that supplies were available for the big numbers of Australian and American troops in Australia and for export to

Britain where rationing was severe. Shelves in many shops and stores were half-empty, for many imports from overseas ceased, and even Australian-made cigarettes and beer could be scarce. Another layer of wartime regulations decided the maximum size of a new house. The houses of the 1940s were notable for the tiny front porch, the small rooms with low ceilings, and the absence of a veranda and wide eaves.

'The enemy thunders at our very gates,' announced the prime minister, John Curtin. Inside those gates the governments and civil servants finally controlled almost everything. But compared to most peoples in the British Isles and continental Europe, Australians were not called upon to accept notable sacrifices to their standard of living and their nutrition. Here the rationing of most foodstuffs was ended not long after the war, whereas in the United Kingdom it could not be ended.

Britain was a weaker nation, financially, because of the war. Australia was a stronger nation, but it remained an isolated one. No British monarch and no leader of any major nation – and no Pope and no Archbishop of Canterbury – had ever visited Australia. Likewise in the six years of war, not one of the military and political leaders of the main allies – Britain, France, Russia and the United States – visited Australia. General MacArthur came and stayed but, influential as he was, he could not be ranked as one of Washington's four highest military leaders in those years. In September 1943, however, an unprecedented visit was organised.

Perhaps the most important foreigner to step on Australian soil so far, Eleanor Roosevelt was the wife of the president of the United States, who was then – with Joseph Stalin – the world's most powerful person. Travelling in a big Liberator bomber with a fighter plane as escort, she toured Pacific battlefields and hospitals and, with not a word of advance publicity, arrived in Australia in September 1943.

Dressed in her Red Cross uniform she was welcomed by John and Elsie Curtin at a banquet at Parliament House in Canberra. In the following year she was to welcome the Curtins to Washington – it was unusual for Curtin to travel outside Australia.

Curtin lived long enough to hear that Berlin was captured, that Hitler had committed suicide, and that Germany was conquered and disarmed. The Pacific War, however, seemed far from over. In June 1945 Curtin watched anxiously, from afar, the landing of Australian troops in Sarawak, Brunei and other coastal strips of Japanese-held Borneo. He did not know about the atomic bombs dropped on two Japanese cities in August, and the dramatic and unexpected end to the war: he died in Canberra in the previous month. His first major biographer, summing up Curtin's complex personality, called him charismatic, determined, moody and even 'queer', unusually willing to blame himself, vacillating, opportunistic, sentimental, courageous, cold and aloof but also warm and sympathetic. He was designated even by political opponents as a great prime minister.

Curtin, it is said, sometimes lay awake at night, thinking of the Australians in uniform facing peril on sea, on land and in the air. In the six years of war a total of 558 000 men and women served outside Australia – or about 200 000 more than those who served in the First World War. But the death toll of 27 000 was less than half of that in the First World War, and the Australians wounded in the years 1939–45 numbered only one-fifth of those wounded in the previous war. It is sobering to think that more Australians were killed on the Western Front in France and Belgium in three years of war than were killed in all the theatres of war between 1939 and 1945.

CHAPTER TWENTY

Woomera, migrant fleet and spaceship

When the war against Japan came suddenly to an end in August 1945, Joseph Benedict Chifley was the prime minister. Son of a Bathurst blacksmith, he was proud to have worked on the New South Wales railways where he ultimately drove the powerful up-country locomotives. For his role in the general strike of 1917 he was demoted to fireman, but after eight years he was reinstated. He could have remained bitter about that experience, but learned from it.

Aged forty-three when he first entered the federal parlia-ment, 'Ben' Chifley was briefly Labor's minister for defence in the dying months of the Scullin ministry in 1931, but lost his seat in parliament and did not regain it for another nine years. That this outsider became treasurer in the new Curtin Government in 1941 – and four years later the nation's postwar leader – was an unusual tribute.

2

Tallish and good-looking, benign in facial expression and often photographed with his pipe in his hand, Chifley could muster a plain, powerful argument, which he presented in a gravelly voice. Speaking in the open air to large crowds, without the aid of a microphone, had impaired many voices, and Chifley described his own as like 'a lot of rusty old chains knocking together'. He was not only prime minister but also a part-time councillor of a rural shire near Bathurst – a sign that he retained his grassroots loyalties. He continued to hold the two elected posts, and sometimes in the winter darkness he would leave Canberra and his prime ministerial duties and travel across the ranges to attend a meeting of the Abercrombie Shire Council at little Perthville at 9.30 a.m.

He enjoyed several years of high triumph. An upsurge of unemployment had been widely feared by Australian soldiers and nurses returning from service in New Guinea and Borneo, by men coming home from the navy and from air-force bases, and by munitions workers whose wartime factories would soon be closed. But those within the armed services who were released from duty, even before the war ended, easily found work in factories, steelworks, road gangs, railways, farms, shops, government offices and schools. In July 1946 Chifley could announce with pride that 500 000 men and women had been released from 'defence and other government occupations' and nearly every one of them had found work.

His government was busy and often constructive. It displayed dozens of new laws and institutions on its drawing boards. It used the postwar prosperity to widen the welfare state. It gave ex-servicemen and women the opportunity to study full time at university and receive a living allowance too.

Conscious that defeat in war had been narrowly averted, all leaders agreed that the nation must become stronger in order to face future threats. This determination shaped the following quarter-century. There was a massive attempt to make Australia self-sufficient. Eventually factories employed – not always efficiently – close to one-third of the workforce, making Australia a far more significant manufacturing nation than it is today.

The end of the war also spurred a new faith in Australia. 'The new order' was the catchcry of these years. How to make the nation a fit place for returning heroes, and a more secure home for all Australians, was the theme of books and pamphlets. This burst of idealism and plain enthusiasm was visible in politics, religion and the expanding universities. Many Protestant ministers thought that a semi-socialist paradise on earth, not least in Australia, was attainable. Many Catholic priests in contrast preached that godless communism – the mask of Satan – could ruin this land of hope.

Chifley was trapped in the tug-of-war contest within the Labor Party, between a Catholic right wing and a more secularist left wing. Himself a Catholic, he had left-wing views on the profit motive and the private banks – he thought they had behaved harshly in the recent Depression. He announced in 1947 that Labor would nationalise all the private banks. Not even Britain, in the height of its semi-socialist phase, ventured that far. Two years later Chifley had deep trouble in coping with communist-led unions that dominated several essential industries. In July 1949, a time of strikes, he reluctantly sent troops into mines in New South Wales in the hope of producing that coal on which so many of the nation's industries, gasworks, power stations, ships, railways and tramways depended. Several million people relied indirectly on black coal for lighting, heating and cooking in their houses. As their gas and electricity now were severely rationed – even more than in wartime – they felt that they were the prisoners of a few trade unions.

It was the 1940s that gave Australia a clear foretaste of the present system of social welfare. With high tax revenues it was easy to finance welfare, and with full employment and prosperity the demand for welfare payments by citizens was lower. Already a nationwide pension scheme helped many old or sick citizens, though people (except war widows) were not eligible unless they had lived in Australia for twenty years. The total payments by the Commonwealth had remained cautious until 1940, when a small regular payment called child endowment was designed to help larger families; the one-child family was not yet eligible. Two years later pensions – mostly subject to a means test -were introduced for widows, deserted wives, certain divorcees, and wives whose husbands were in prison or a mental hospital. In 1943 a small funeral allowance was available for pensioners, and that was followed by vital payments for the unemployed and for ex-servicemen who wished to study full time.

In the next thirty years, federal and state governments were to introduce a comprehensive free health and hospital system and free secondary and tertiary education for large numbers, and multiply public housing and other amenities. Governments of both the left and right favoured these welfare schemes, and it was a brave politician or commentator who whispered that sustained welfare payments might eventually produce less worthy families and citizens, and lower the level of individual responsibility.

3.

When Ben Chifley was defeated by Bob Menzies in the federal election of December 1949, it marked the end of an age. For eighteen of the past twenty years Catholic-reared prime ministers, all of humble origin, had led Australia. More than forty years would pass before another reached the top again. The 1949 election was also a watershed in federal politics. The eight years of Labor rule, the longest until that time, came to an end, and there began under Menzies an astonishingly long period of rule by him and his Country Party allies. In all, Menzies was the prime minister for nearly nineteen years. Such a long tenure of office is unlikely to be surpassed in this century.

Born in the small Victorian wheatfields town of Jeparit, Robert Gordon Menzies had a strong desire to be a politician – not surprising because his father sat in the Victorian parliament, his uncle had sat in federal and state parliaments, and his father-in-law in both federal houses. That was not all. Menzies' own maternal grandfather, John Sampson, was an underground goldminer who, with W. G. Spence, pioneered what became one of the main arms of the Australian Workers' Union. Sampson, a dogged unionist then in retirement, was proud of his politically precocious grandson. Master Robert Menzies, tall for his age, was 'a sort of infant prodigy' while not yet a teenager.

As Menzies later was to become the leader in conservative politics, he was frequently imagined as coming from a privileged home. It was not true. Most country storekeepers, like his father, were in debt until the annual harvest or wool clip was concluded. Menzies gained his later education only with the aid of scholarships, one after the other. Graduating in law from the University of Melbourne, in almost no time he was a brilliant, talked-about barrister. He also made enemies, and his friend Percy Joske noted that he 'employed his cutting tongue without hesitation'. Though Menzies was widely seen, by critics, as always remote from working people, he actually made his legal reputation when aged twenty-five by appearing in the High Court on behalf of a leading trade union. A busy negotiator behind the scenes, he was Victoria's deputy premier at the age of thirty-seven, and the prime minister at the age of forty-four, after the sudden death of Joe Lyons.

Young people now ask their grandparents: what was he like? He was tall, and well fleshed, and wore a grey felt hat and double-breasted suit long after such clothes were disappearing. In his heyday he moved in a slow and stately way, like an important ship leaving a harbour. In his speeches he was deliberate and eloquent with a deep, mellow and resonant voice. Some thought that his accent was English, some thought it was Australian – in short it was just right for his era. He had an actor-like sense of timing, and mastery of the cutting reply. At a rowdy political meeting in Tasmania he once responded: 'I didn't come here to talk to the sons of convicts but to the decent people of Launceston.' Today, in contrast, many decent people of Launceston are proud to see themselves as the descendants of convicts. As Menzies aged, his pointed remarks became more benevolent, but the wit flickered inside them.

Menzies was the first – and maybe the only – national leader of whom it could be safely said that he was capable of rising to the top of almost any ladder he dared to climb. His first ascent ended in 1941, when he lost the confidence of several of his senior colleagues. To his private secretary he reportedly said on the night of his defeat: 'I'll lie down and bleed awhile.' Politically he was wounded deeply but not mortally.

He eventually recovered by remaking his political party. He formed the Liberal Party of Australia, which replaced the United Australia Party. It was democratic, federal and nationwide and kept big business at arm's length. Especially in Victoria it enlisted women at every stage and – in what now would be called affirmative action – gave them equal say in all the major committees, including those that selected candidates for parliament. The Australian Women's National League, an old and experienced political group led by Elizabeth Couchman, became part of the Liberal Party and the core of many branches. It is probable that no political party in the history of the democratic world had gone so far in allying itself with women.

With Menzies as leader, the new Liberal Party was launched in 1945 at Albury, a symbolic site astride the border of the two most powerful states. Victory did not come easily. In 1946 Menzies lost the first federal election he fought as a Liberal, and three years later he succeeded handsomely. He was installed in the prime minister's office in Canberra for only a few months when he sensed that Australia was again facing an acute military crisis.

4

The Cold War began when the Hot War of 1939–45 was barely over. An Iron Curtain (a phrase popularised by Churchill) was drawn across Europe, forcibly dividing east from west. In 1948 Berlin was blockaded by the Russians. Communism was expanding and, one year later, China became communist, so that now a continuous 'red zone' stretched across Europe and Asia from Albania on the Adriatic Sea to North Korea on the Pacific Ocean. This enormous red world, in area larger than the British Empire, sharpened the fears about communism held by most Australians.

A gallup poll, interviewing 2000 Australians during the Berlin Wall crisis, revealed that most thought that their nation should fight with the Americans against Russia or supply vital aid. Curiously 1 per cent thought that they should fight on Russia's side. A big majority of voters, even Labor supporters, wanted compulsory military training so that their nation would be militarily prepared for another war, a war probably against communist nations.

Most Australians believed that a world war would erupt in the next quarter of a century. The fears increased in 1950 when the Soviet Union announced that it had developed an atomic bomb. In the same year Britain, with the consent of Canberra, triggered an atomic bomb placed in the hull of an empty British frigate, deliberately anchored near the Montebello Islands – 130 kilometres from north-west Australia. In the following year, more nuclear tests were conducted in the Great Victoria Desert. Britain was then granted a permanent testing site at Woomera, about 800 kilometres north-west of Adelaide and close to the transcontinental railway. In 1952 Britain was to become the third nation to develop its own nuclear weapons.

With the armed support of China and the backing of the Soviet Union, communist North Korea was a formidable threat. At the end of June 1950, in a swift invasion, it captured the capital of South Korea. Initially the United Nations' forces seemed incapable of saving South Korea. Australia had already promised help with two naval vessels and a fighter squadron, and on 26 July it promised ground troops, which eventually numbered nearly 5000. They were alarming months, reminding Menzies of the crisis in Europe before war began in 1939. Even Japan, though completely disarmed, was feared while the Korean War was waged close to its shores. One worry was that during this war, Japan might somehow be persuaded to begin secret negotiations with the Soviet bloc in return for its freedom. In December 1950 a Washington document labelled 'Top Secret', and read intently after it reached Canberra, carried the ominous phrase: 'if Japan should again become aggressive'.

In the hope of thwarting China's massive army in Korea, the head of the United Nations forces, General Douglas MacArthur, threatened to use nuclear weapons. That threat sent shivers into kitchens, schoolrooms and parliaments in much of the world. In Washington, President Truman, alarmed at the possibility of a nuclear war, replaced MacArthur.

The turmoil in Korea, finally ending in a stalemate, was a landmark in the military and diplomatic history of Australia. It led to the signing in 1951 of the ANZUS Treaty, with the promise by the United States – a conditional promise – to send armed forces across the Pacific Ocean to defend Australia, New Zealand and even Papua New Guinea in the event of an enemy attack. The Korean War also spurred an ambitious manufacturing project in Australia. Forty-eight jet bombers were built between 1953 and 1958, and some fought in the Vietnam War.

In its military alliances Australia moved trustingly towards the United States, with two steps forward and one step back. Britain in the eyes of the public remained the preferred ally in almost every facet of national life except military strength. Britain's wartime courage was vividly remembered and honoured. The national day, Anzac Day, honoured Britain as well as Australia. In law and language and literature and religions the British Isles were the model, and Oxford and Cambridge were viewed as the noblest universities of the world. British technology was still admired. The few leading Britons who visited Australia were circled, soon after their ship was tied up at the wharf, by eager reporters from radio stations and newspapers. The visit of Queen Elizabeth II for more than a month in 1954 – the first Australian tour by a reigning monarch – was a stirring, tingling success that was not equalled thereafter. In this decade the rivalry with Britain was also strong. Rising Australian nationalism was always ready to denigrate as well as praise Britain.

After the Korean War, Menzies courted Japan as a trading partner. While he is associated in the public mind with deep loyalty to Britain, and the favoured photograph shows him tenderly escorting the Queen in Canberra, he was the leader who guided his country towards Asia. His allies in the Country Party were especially convinced that Australia's trading future, in wool and wheat, did not lie with Britain. Japan, already the chief wool buyer, offered a huge market for rural Australian commodities. Australia in turn offered Japan a valuable market for cars and other manufactures. In 1957 Menzies – to Labor's dismay – signed a special trade deal with Japan. By the time he retired, Japan was on the verge of becoming our main trading partner.

In the struggle for supremacy between the United States and the Soviet Union, outer space became vital. On 4 October 1957, Moscow created excitement and dismay by launching the first earth satellite, named Sputnik. From thousands of Australian verandas and hilltops, people waited at the predicted times for a glimpse of Sputnik's light moving across the night sky. On 12 April 1961, the Russian Yuri Gagarin became the first flyer to orbit the earth, his journey taking a mere one hour and forty-eight minutes. The sobering sight of the Russians leading in this most scientific of military activities shocked the United States and its allies. The shock was intensified in October 1962 when the missiles of the two mighty nuclear powers, Soviet Union and United States, confronted each other in Cuba and the west Atlantic. The brief Cuban missile crisis was probably the closest to a nuclear catastrophe that the world so far has experienced.

In the 1950s Menzies spent less money on defence in order to finance national development and large-scale immigration. His defence budget, notably small for a nation that envisaged peril ahead, forced him to woo powerful allies. He continued to court the United States, though it had undermined Britain, France and Australia during the Suez crisis. For Washington he wrapped a gift in tinsel in 1962: his government allowed its remote and unpopulated North West Cape, on the Western Australian coast of the Indian Ocean, to be the home of a new American naval-communications base. It would gather information and perhaps guide US submarines and other naval vessels in nearby and distant seas. The base spread unease among Labor supporters who feared that it might drag Australia reluctantly into another Pacific war.

5

How could Australia become stronger? The Second World War had inspired a popular demand to increase population so that if the nation was again imperilled, it could resist an invader. A vigorous immigration policy, launched in 1945 by Chifley's Labor government and enlarged and diversified by the Liberals under Menzies, turned first to Britain. The fares of most migrants were paid in full or subsidised, and jobs awaited them on arrival.

Refugee camps in Europe were searched for potential migrants. The minister for immigration, Arthur Calwell, on visiting Europe, greeted Jews who had survived the death camps at Buchenwald and Auschwitz or had somehow evaded the ruthless round-up in Nazi-occupied countries extending from France to Hungary. In Australia he encouraged Jewish Australians to fill out the paperwork so that their relatives could be located in Europe, inspected medically, and, if fit, brought out at the government's expense. In years to come critics were to maintain that Australians were innately anti-Semitic. The criticism, true in some places and at some times, was exaggerated, for in the twentieth century few nations – in proportion to their own population – had surpassed Australia in welcoming Jews; most came from Poland and Hungary. Indeed Melbourne late in the twentieth century was said to hold more survivors of the Holocaust than any single city in Europe.

There was briefly a plan to plant a Jewish colony in Western Australia. A Jewish league had tried to acquire three big pastoral stations in the East Kimberley district where Jews could set up their homeland for maybe 59 000 refugees from Europe. In Perth the government and various trade unions and churches were sympathetic to the Jewish emissary, Dr Nachman Steinberg, but war intervened. After the war the plan was revived, but Canberra was less enthusiastic. It would be almost impossible to prevent many Jewish settlers, in times of difficulty, from leaving their new Kimberley homeland and moving to Australian cities where economic prospects were attractive. Moreover Australia would lose control of its own borders. The idea was also unpalatable to Calwell, who thought it was unfair to 'take this land from homeless Aborigines and give it away to homeless Jews'. The British Isles at first were the main source of new migrants. Of the 1 800 000 people living in Australia in 1963 but born elsewhere, four out of every ten had come from the United Kingdom and the Republic of Ireland. Another 228 000 migrants were born in Italy, half having arrived during the past seven years, and another 109 000 had come from Germany. Thus for several years the largest inflow of non-British migrants came from two lands – Germany and Italy – against which Australia had recently been fighting. These 'enemy' migrants and their children became enthusiastic or supportive Australians much earlier than many doubters had anticipated, though popular memory forgets how many families returned home in the 1950s and 1960s.

Of the foreign-born people living in Australia in 1963, another 102 000 were from Holland, 77 000 from Greece and 60 000 from Poland. The Greek inflow was quickening, and was noticeable for the huge numbers coming from certain islands and mainland districts. Nearly half of the Greek immigrants at one time came from three small islands: Ithaca, Kythera and Kastellorizo.

Across the nation could be found thriving groups of Baltic peoples and Hungarians and Ukrainians – nearly all fleeing from Russian occupation. The strong inflow from Yugoslavia and Turkey came later. By 1973, the successful migration program was fading, along with the slogan 'populate or perish'.

Since the end of the war, the population had leaped from seven to thirteen million. Almost six-tenths of that increase in population had come from new migrants and their children. Nearly all of those migrants had come from distant Europe, but recently an increasing minority had arrived from nearer Asia. Here was a glimpse of a turning point in Australian history.

6

Arthur Calwell, as the first federal immigration minister, had upheld the White Australia policy in public while quietly allowing various Asian people to enter or stay. He had a gift for witty and pithy phrases, and his memory is haunted by a quip that he made during a debate in the federal parliament in 1947. Defending his decision to expel a Chinese resident named Wong, and referring to the allegation that the wrong Mr Wong was being deported, Calwell went on to add: 'There are many Wongs in the Chinese community, but I have to say – and I am sure that the honourable member for Balaclava will not mind me doing so – that two Wongs do not make a White.' White was actually the name of the Liberal member for Balaclava, then sitting opposite Calwell in the chamber. The allusion to the 'two Wongs' evoked the well-known saying that 'Two wrongs do not make a right'. Nowadays that witty retort is rarely quoted without being lifted from context. Moreover, the vital capital letters were mischievously altered to read 'two wongs do not make a white'. Of course the play of words, and the use of nicknames, and the role of public laughter, were more valued in daily life then than now. In retrospect, however, Calwell would have been wiser if he had been less witty. Perhaps much of today's commentary against him is unfair, for he was a compassionate spokesman on behalf of Aborigines, a friend of many old Chinese-Australians, the instigator of a move in 1958 to grant Australian citizenship to Chinese residents of Papua New Guinea, and a supporter of the Indonesians in their struggles for independence against Holland. As minister for immigration he was normally carrying out a policy supported by the great majority of Australians and expected of him by the law.

In the 1950s, under the Menzies Government, the migration rules were eased further. If applicants from Asia were mainly of European ancestry and relatively educated, they could gain permission to immigrate. The Asian wives of Australian citizens – most were Filipinas – were admitted. Asian children who arrived to attend Australian schools, spoke English and had relatives here were usually allowed to stay and eventually become citizens. Victor Chang, a Chinese-born lad who was to become a celebrated heart surgeon in Sydney, arrived in this way in the 1950s.

Younger Australian diplomats privately urged Canberra to overturn its policy. They were appealing less to equity and morality than to pragmatism. The typical Asian migrants had altered: they no longer wore wide coolie hats, and were no longer uneducated. Therefore it was an insult to treat 'the most educated and advanced Asian individual' as if he or she were the same as a coolie who could not be assimilated in Australia. The Colombo Plan, whereby Australian universities in the 1950s began to educate selected Asian students, displayed a new empathy.

In 1964 the entry of Asians was made easier. Two years later, they were eligible to settle permanently if they possessed special trade or business skills, or talents in science or the arts. We now know that between 1966 and 1975 the new residents of non-European descent increased by about 63 000. Two-thirds of these people were Anglo-Indians, Burghers from Sri Lanka, and other people of mixed descent. Many succeeded here in the professions and commerce, and their children too. The White Australia policy was dying, the major political parties slayed it, and its death was quick. Within a few years each was claiming that it was the first to open wide the doors. Al Grassby, a colourful Labor minister, is often credited with finally ending the White Australia policy in 1973, but the main and more difficult steps had been taken by the quiet Liberal minister Hubert Opperman six or seven years earlier, and other steps had been taken in the 1950s. There was little public opposition to the wide opening of the doors.

The idea is still widespread that Australians were among the world's most persistent racists until the White Australia policy was abolished. But in 1900, and long after, almost every part of the Western world was wary of large-scale immigration from poorer, low-wage countries whose reigning culture was different. Asians at times were wary of outsiders. Between 1860 and 1914 it was safer to be a Chinese gold-digger living in Australia than to be an Australian, especially a female missionary, living in China.

Until the 1950s, or later, all European nations preferred to be populated almost entirely by people of their own culture and ethnic background. When France began to admit French-speaking colonists from North Africa, and Britain began to admit West Indians who spoke English – and were Christians and played cricket – the radical policies were not imitated at the immigration checkpoints of most of their European neighbours nor those in Asia as a whole. Even the United States made only halting steps to end its policy of exclusion. In 1943, partly in order to appease its wartime ally Nationalist China, the Congress voted to permit a total of 105 Chinese, surely a token number, to enter as migrants each year. In mid-century an immigration wall was normal and kept in repair in most parts of the world, but in the following half-century most of those walls were lowered or razed – with strong exceptions in Africa and Asia.

Keith Hancock, as a young historian in Adelaide in 1930, tried to give a sophisticated survey of the merits and weaknesses of the White Australia policy in an Asian world that was then very different to today's. He insisted that it was a practical, not a noble policy. In his opinion, experience in various parts of the world emphasised 'that labourers of different colours are seldom sufficiently meek to live side by side in human brotherhood'. Australia's standard of living, political independence and its culture would be imperilled by massive inflows of Asian labourers who did not 'agree upon essentials'. A nation – he argued – could commit suicide if it gave 'a share of political power to aliens unable or unwilling to accept and defend what most it values'.

When finally Australia did admit numerous migrants from Asia, Hancock – now Sir Keith and twice as old – rejoiced in the changed attitude to Asia. His view was that the newcomers were no longer illiterate labourers but educated people who came from a region that was now dynamic.

CHAPTER TWENTY-ONE

Across the sea
rolls thunder

In the 1960s this part of the world was threatened by major and minor wars. The port of Darwin was much closer to Asian points of tension than it was to any other Australian capital city, and from Darwin several of the danger zones could be reached after two hours in a military aircraft.

Indonesia was the most powerful of the very near neighbours. Its president, Sukarno, wished to expand the borders of his young nation, and by 1960 he was emphatically laying claim to the Dutch or western half of New Guinea. Known as Irian Jaya, this rugged equatorial region displayed one mountain so high that it was capped by ice and snow. As its southern coastline was only 250 kilometres from the tip of Cape York and only 400 kilometres from Arnhem Land, it was of vital interest to Australia. Furthermore Dutch New Guinea also bordered Papua New Guinea, a colonial possession that Australians knew would some day be liberated. For all these reasons the future of Dutch New Guinea – in the opinion of all Australian political parties – was as vital to Australia as it was to Indonesia. No solution would possibly please both nations.

In 1960 the United Nations General Assembly called for Australia to take 'immediate steps' to grant independence to the people of Papua New Guinea, even if politically and educationally they might not yet ready to govern themselves effectively. The Soviet Union and India – to the disgust of Menzies – strongly supported this call. It became increasingly clear that the United States, desiring Indonesia's friendship, would not back Australia in this important dispute.

On the first day of May 1963, by agreement, Indonesia raised its own flag as official caretaker of Irian Jaya. Six years later it was confirmed as owner by a so-called referendum among local leaders. So effectively did Indonesia organise the flow of Javanese to the new province that today they form about half of the population.

On the western boundaries of Indonesia arose another point of tension. Sukarno in September 1963 took offence at the creation of the new nation of Malaysia. Consisting of the former British colonies in the Malay Peninsula, as well as Singapore (which withdrew two years later) and North Borneo and Sarawak, suddenly the infant Malaysia felt Sukarno's sting. In Jakarta a mob attacked the Malaysian embassy and burned down the British embassy. As Indonesia now had the third-largest communist party in the world, the fear in Canberra was that it would gain China's support. What if Indonesia's government became communist and formed an alliance with China, which itself was likely to become a nuclear power within three years? Menzies as prime minister was confidentially advised that President Sukarno was veering to the left and that he might fall firmly under the influence of Beijing.

The Confrontation or Konfrontasi between Malaysia and Indonesia simmered and occasionally boiled, especially in Borneo. In defence of Malaysia, Australia sent soldiers, paratroopers, commandos, helicopters and two minesweepers, one of which exchanged shots with an Indonesian vessel. For a time Menzies feared that Australia and Indonesia would go to war. He even granted permission for Britain to use Darwin as an airfield from which to bomb Indonesia, if tensions grew.

To prepare Australia for deepening trouble with Indonesia, the Menzies Government resolved to conscript young men for military service, beginning in January 1965. Only those whose birthday fell on certain days – the days being officially chosen by lottery or ballot – had to join the armed services. Even they could seek an exemption on the grounds of family hardship, strong religious beliefs, the desire to complete a university or trade course, or a willingness to serve as a volunteer for the next six years in the Citizen Military Forces. Conscription was popularly but not accurately condemned by critics as a ticket for death, though only a fraction of the young Australian conscripts were to die in armed combat in South-East Asia.

Unexpectedly the tensions with Indonesia waned. President Sukarno was deposed by his own army, and Chinese residents who were expected to be his cheer squad were slaughtered in their tens of thousands. By then Vietnam, recently a French colony, had become the hotspot, though many Australians continued to fear Indonesia because it was nearer and more populous.

2

After the French had retreated from Indochina, communists ruled North Vietnam and a weak dictator ruled the south. If communists won their military campaign in South Vietnam, they might – with the help of China or Russia – conquer or infiltrate Indochina, the new nation of Malaysia, and perhaps Indonesia too. By 1965 these fears were so widespread that Lyndon B. Johnson, the American president who had succeeded the assassinated John F. Kennedy, resolved to intervene. He poured marines into South Vietnam and deployed aircraft to bomb North Vietnam. On 29 April 1965 Menzies announced that Australia would join in the war. Four weeks later the first battalion of Australian troops sailed away in the aircraft carrier HMAS *Sydney*, reaching South Vietnam a fortnight later. For several years the *Sydney* became a big passenger ferry regularly plying the tropical seas between Sydney and South Vietnam, and the Australian soldiers – eventually numbering 8000 – were assigned their own province to defend and control. By then America's army in South Vietnam was huge.

In Canberra the high defence chiefs had expected victory. Surely the United States, the mightiest military power in the world, would conquer the simply armed Vietnamese communists, even without such help as Australia could offer. But perhaps South Vietnam was beyond help. It was dismissed by one influential Australian journalist, Denis Warner, as an 'uncountry'. He thought it was beyond help, an opinion soon shared by Arthur Calwell, the leader of the Labor Party, though not yet by his successor, E. G. Whitlam, and other senior colleagues.

While the daily newspapers – then far more influential than television stations – supported the war, a notable exception was Rupert Murdoch's infant daily *The Australian*. Another absent supporter was Britain. Here was the first war in our history in which Britain was not an ally.

It is now realised that one of Washington's grave mistakes was to fight in Vietnam without first enlisting a circle of powerful allies whose presence would help to persuade world opinion that the anti-communist war was just and fair. In the end its only willing allies were Australia and South Korea, both of which were lesser powers. Another mistake was the belief that air power and the latest American weapons would quickly defeat a simple, poorly armed enemy that had only the advantage of fighting on its home ground.

3

Harold Holt, a charming career politician, succeeded Menzies as prime minister on Australia Day 1966. He viewed China, which sent no troops to Vietnam, as the hidden enemy: 'While the Chinese communist philosophy of world domination persists, the whole free world is threatened.' Lyndon B. Johnson soon exulted that he had found in Holt an intuitive friend and his loyalest overseas ally.

It was on a visit to the White House on 30 June 1966 that Holt, in the presence of the television cameras and President Johnson, made a simple off-the-cuff remark that he 'would go all the way with LBJ'. To see the incident replayed on television is to see Holt displaying his own spontaneity and charm. The remark, however, began to haunt him, especially after eighteen Australians died in the Battle of Long Tan two months later.

Holt's war in Vietnam retained the public's approval. In a federal election late in 1966 he and his Liberal Party trounced Labor. Even Menzies in his long career had not won such a sweeping electoral victory. In the following year Holt promised even more aid for South Vietnam on land and in the air. At home in his brief term of office he also set in place two symbolic events. He made it much easier for Asians to migrate to Australia, and he staged a referendum that eventually improved the standing and dignity of all Aborigines.

Holt loved the sea and on Sunday 17 December 1967 he went swimming near Melbourne. Now in his sixtieth year, he was often photographed wearing a wetsuit – then a newsworthy garment – in the company of pretty women, and he was with several such women on this bright morning. Unfortunately he chose to swim at a secluded beach at Port Phillip Heads, where the surf was strong and the unpredictable currents were treacherous. Swimming on his own some distance out to sea he drowned. His body was not found. A memorial service in Melbourne drew a crowd of foreign dignitaries such as had not before assembled at an Australian ceremony. In the Anglican cathedral the president of the United States sat near the prime minister of Britain, Harold Wilson, and the heir to the British throne, the young Prince Charles, while foremost in the procession of Asian leaders were the presidents of the Philippines, South Korea and South Vietnam and the young prime minister Lee Kuan Yew of Singapore.

The shifting tides of opinion were already turning against Holt's foreign policy. In South Vietnam early in 1968 the Vietcong conducted its successful Tet Offensive. Heavy raids by American bombers did not weaken morale in the communist regions of Vietnam. Peace talks with North Vietnam were initiated in Paris by the Americans, but the truce simply enabled North Vietnam to import more weapons from the Soviet Union and China, at the same time repairing its own facilities and supply lines. General Sir John Wilton, in charge of Australia's war effort, privately reported in October 1968 that, because of the politics in Washington, the Americans in Vietnam now were fighting 'with one hand tied behind their back'. In the United States and Australia, the war was increasingly seen as unwinnable or futile by well-informed people who watched television – it was a televised war – as well as many of those who conducted the strategy.

By June 1969 President Nixon had withdrawn a contingent of American troops from the combat zone. Similarly, most Australians thought that their own troops should be withdrawn. Anti-war rallies and marches in Australian cities drew enormous crowds. In November 1970 Australia began to withdraw troops, and nearly all were home by 1972, though the war slowly proceeded towards its almost certain outcome. Saigon – the capital of South Vietnam – did not surrender until 1975.

About 50 000 Australians had served a period of duty in Vietnam, and one-third were national servicemen chosen by lottery. The wounded Australians exceeded 3000, and another 501 died, but they were few compared to the 5000 dead from South Korea, 58 000 from the USA, and perhaps 1 000 000 from North Vietnam.

In the end the Vietnam War divided the nation, though less decisively than did the final two years of the First World War. Countless people, especially the more articulate young, were openly against a war in which their own soldiers, sailors and airmen were engaged. Organising the long marches of protest in city streets, the peace movement was a mixture of many overlapping groups. One was against the United States, another was against capitalism and materialism and the Western way of life, and yet another against Australia's long-reigning Liberal government. What marked it out from any previous protest was its support from people under the age of twenty-five. At times it was almost a crusade by a young generation against an older one, and also 'the wellspring of an age of dissent'.

An angry message of the anti-Vietnam protests was that the capitalist, industrial West was mainly to blame for the world's current ills. The protests inspired crusades to protect the environment, to advance the developing world, to foster the power of women and the young, to improve the status of Aborigines and other colonised peoples, and to warn the whole world of the danger of overpopulation and the risk of a nuclear war. They fostered a rebellious mood called the counterculture, at the very time when a new taste in music was being spread among the young by the Beatles, the Rolling Stones and the Beach Boys, who were joined in the 1970s by such local rock musicians as Gerry and the Joy Band, and Billy Thorpe and the Aztecs. Ironically, Sydney's scintillating Opera House was opened on a headland of its harbour in 1973, just when the music of symphony orchestras and the classical opera were often drowned out by the latest sounds and colloquial words.

4

Towards the end of the war in Vietnam occurred one of the major changes in the modern history of Australia. China, no longer in hiding, swam strongly into view. It was one of the most influential events of the past half-century.

For years Australian leaders had been sympathetic towards Communist China – more sympathetic than is now realised. As early as 1955, Menzies and his foreign minister, R. G. Casey, privately believed that Australia should officially recognise the communist government in Beijing. Menzies, however, refused to act because the step would endanger the American alliance that was so important for Australia's defences. At that time Washington and its policies caused him – he privately confessed – 'more sleepless nights than anything else'.

Washington was determined not to recognise Communist China. Posting no diplomat and refusing to allow its citizens to visit China, it also banned commerce. Canberra, more pragmatic than Washington, sold dozens of shiploads of grain to China in the early 1960s, when several of populous Chinese provinces were gripped by famines. Both nations continued to share a fear of China's military ambitions. The Chinese military aid to the North Vietnamese intensified that fear.

In 1971, with the end of the Vietnam War in sight, President Nixon of the United States made a surprise visit to China. He tentatively sought friendship. As the United States and China both were the opponents of the Soviet Union, why should the two opponents not start amicable discussions? At almost the same time Gough Whitlam, soon to win office for Labor in Australia, enjoyed cordial discussions in Beijing. In the following year he won the federal election, and his first days in office displayed his intense interest in China. On Wednesday 6 December 1972, on his instructions, the Australian ambassador to Taiwan was recalled, while in Paris the Australian ambassador discussed with the Chinese embassy in that city Whitlam's plan to grant diplomatic recognition to China as soon as possible. On the following Monday Whitlam announced that the few remaining Australian troops in Vietnam would be withdrawn, thus removing one obstacle to opening cordial relations with China. Three days before Christmas, formal diplomatic relations were established with Beijing – almost six years before the United States achieved that goal.

When Whitlam was defeated at the election late in 1975, it was thought that the new prime minister, Malcolm Fraser, with his pronounced hostility towards communism in the Soviet Union, might weaken the bonds with China. He actually strengthened them, as did his successor, Bob Hawke. Canberra's efforts to forge practical links with Chinese science, commerce, cinema, sport, mining and agriculture were widely applauded.

By the early 1980s China, looking outwards, showed signs of an economic awakening. Its effects on Australia in the following third of a century were to be momentous.

5

No major commodity was more Australian than wool. At one time the wealthiest Australians were woolgrowers, and their grand mansions in the country and their second homes – other mansions in a coastal city – were havens of social life. Along the waterfront the large warehouses and stores smelt of greasy wool. Wealthy British families, wondering what to do with their surplus sons, shipped them to New South Wales where sons of Charles Dickens and Anthony Trollope, the celebrated English novelists, owned sheep stations in the 1870s. At that time in the north of England some cities made much of their livelihood by treating, spinning and weaving Australian wool; and botanists who walked along the river paths near the older mills noticed Australian weeds – the results of seeds imported in the wool fleeces – flourishing in English soil. For long periods this nation grew one-quarter or one-third of the world's wool. In Australia the last golden age for wool was in the early 1950s. The Korean War in 1950–51 elevated the real price of wool to a peak unknown before or after. There began a rural boom such as most districts in the southern half of the continent had not previously experienced. Large-scale farmers or pastoralists whose property had been mortgaged for thirty or forty years turned up at their bank, paid off the mortgage with just one wool cheque, and sailed away in P & O and Orient liners to a holiday in London and the continent. In the 1950s country towns, enriched by wool or wheat, raided the top football clubs in Melbourne and Sydney and poached their champion players. This golden age was assisted by the climate, which became favourable again. From 1945 to, say, 1975 most of the fertile rural districts of eastern Australia received above-average rain. Moreover the rural areas were well served in politics. As late as the period 1975 to 1983, the two most powerful politicians in Australia, Malcolm Fraser and Doug Anthony, represented rural electorates. In the following third of a century the city was to be the home of seven successive prime ministers.

The price of wool – after its peak in 1951 – tumbled in fits and starts. Annual output of wool was still high but revenue was not. Australia began to suffer from the inventiveness of British scientists who challenged wool by creating polyester fibres and synthetic textiles. Wool lost customers in winter, partly because heated offices and houses dispensed with the need for woollen clothing. Above all, synthetic fibres, of which oil was the main ingredient, became much cheaper than wool. Today, many of Australia's once-envied wool estates earn more from selling fat lambs than from fine wool.

For a total of 115 years wool was Australia's main export but in the 1970s its reign ceased. Today wool as an export is far surpassed not only by many minerals but also by beef, with the Aberdeen Angus leading the trade in cattle.

In order to survive, the best Australian farmers had to be experimenters. Thus, in the 1950s they cultivated semi-desert country by sprinkling tiny amounts of copper, molybdenum or other vital minerals. In the 1970s they bred the type of cereal that did not grow large leaves, thus saving precious water. By the 1990s – with the help of computer models – they tilled soil in new ways, and harvested crops with giant machines that, unlike the draught horses, could work day and night. The result was that a farming district might have fifty households where once were 400. Large towns shrank, small towns vanished. To a first-time visitor much of the countryside seemed half-deserted, and yet it was producing – through science and technology – more meat, wool, grains, dairy products, wine, fruit and vegetables than ever before. Except in a few years of extreme drought, Australia was becoming one of the main food exporters in the world.

The population decline in the rural areas was startling. In 1901 the countryside and small townships held half of the population. By 1981 only 14 per cent lived there. The education profession alone employed far more people than did the entire rural sector. At one time there had been family quarrels about which son should take over the working of the farm, but now few sons and daughters volunteered.

6

In contrast mining was buoyant – unexpectedly so. In 1950 the palmy era of mining had seemed to be over. Gold, once the most important metal, was harder to find; and when it was found was less profitable than previously. Of the fifty most productive gold towns in the nation's history most were in decline and many were asleep or almost dead. Australia imported nearly all the oil it consumed, and the prospect of finding a local oilfield did not seem high. The steel industry, and its strongholds at the harbours of Newcastle and Port Kembla and Whyalla, did not possess adequate reserves of iron ore to keep the furnaces busy for a long period. The new aluminium industry at Bell Bay in northern Tasmania had initially to import its raw material, bauxite, from Malaya. The only important base-metal field found in the past thirty years was Mount Isa in tropical Queensland, but its struggle to survive was impeded by its isolation, the nearest port being nearly 1000 kilometres away.

Some of the discoveries in the years 1950–75 seemed easy and simple, but even simple discoveries have to wait for a discoverer who thinks differently, has sharp eyes, and carries elementary knowledge that few citizens possess. Harry Evans, a New Zealander working for what is now Rio Tinto, was searching for oil-bearing structures when in 1955 he saw large quantities of red bauxite near the

sea in north Queensland. Procuring a small fibreglass dinghy and
an Aboriginal guide named Matthew, he surveyed a strip of coastline. When the throttle broke he used a spear to create a makeshift
throttle. The extent of the red mineral-rich cliffs astonished him:
'I kept thinking that if all this is bauxite, there must be something
the matter with it.' The exploration parties arrived, and within ten
years the cliffs near Weipa were found to contain about one-quarter
of the known bauxite in the world.

In the late 1950s, on the opposite side of the continent, another
vast area of bauxite was found in the ranges near Perth by Don
Campbell, who was a gold geologist with Western Mining
Corporation. Further east at Kambalda his colleague Roy Woodall
helped to identify the first big nickel field in the continent, close to
an abandoned gold-rush township. Western Australia, with its vast
area of ancient Precambrian rocks, again became the latest mining
frontier. In the 1960s in the Pilbara one of the world's largest areas
of high-grade iron ore was developed with long railways and new
ports, the first strong signs of the ore having been found by Lang
Hancock, a local pastoralist flying his little aircraft. The promise of huge sums of foreign capital and the assurance of mammoth
long-term sales to Japan's steel industry and the building of huge
deep-sea ships underwrote the Pilbara's iron. It was not yet foreseen
that half a century later this sparsely populated region would be for
one decade almost the lifeblood of the nation's economy. Another
bonus for this region was the extraction, from the 1970s, of oil and
natural gas beneath the shallow seas of the North West Shelf.

On the far side of the continent, beneath the sea near Bass
Strait, Victoria's rich fields of oil and natural gas were found in the
years 1964–66. On the eve of the first severe oil crisis in the Western
world, the nation became almost self-sufficient in oil, and the local
motorists were filling their petrol tanks at a price that Europeans

could only envy. The nation that in 1960 had been a heavy importer of fuels and energy was becoming one of the prized exporters, especially with the opening of large, shallow deposits of black coal close to Queensland ports that – in the opinion of some ecologists – were almost too close to the Great Barrier Reef. From some of the mines came steaming coal and from others metallurgical coal, the one for the powerhouses and the other for the steelworks of East Asia. This was the coast that had first been charted by Captain Cook in his tiny converted coal ship *Endeavour* in 1770, and now its nearby mines were probably the greatest exporters of coal, by sea, in the history of the world.

By 1990 the nation was in the world's top five producers of at least ten different minerals of importance, and the world's leader in lead, bauxite, alumina, industrial diamonds and several lesser minerals. The sheer variety of postwar discoveries was an eye-opener: one of the world's largest deposits of industrial diamonds in the north-west; a big manganese mine at Groote Eylandt in the Gulf of Carpentaria; uranium mines that held a high proportion of the world's richest ore; deposits of mineral sands that on beaches and inland plains yielded rare minerals; and in 1975 at Olympic Dam in arid South Australia the first signs of deep deposits that contained in copper, uranium and gold more wealth than even Kalgoorlie and Broken Hill have yielded in their long history. The main surprise was gold, which, after reaching peaks in 1856 and again in 1903, broke all previous records in 1987 and several later years. Australia today is the second-largest producer of gold in the world.

The dramatic revival of mining owed much to the adoption of new technology: offshore drilling for oil, the gargantuan trucks that worked underground or in open cuts, a revolution in ships, the creation of the nation's longest and most computerised trains, and new metallurgical techniques. Industrial relations improved compared to the prewar era. Political stability, superior in Australia to Africa and most other mineral lands, attracted the immense sums of foreign capital that each project needed. The mechanisation of mining required few employees and in turn they could receive high wages.

Federal politicians were among the boosters of mining by imposing lower tariffs on imported machinery, while Premier Sir Charles Court effected a formula enticing British, American, Australian and other investors to his home state of Western Australia – now the heart of the industry. Oddly, the title of Donald Horne's exciting book, *The Lucky Country*, attached itself to mining fields after the 1960s; he did not realise that they were the products more of ingenuity and efficiency than luck. By 1990 the names of the Australian mineral giants – BHP, Rio Tinto, Mount Isa Mines, Western Mining, Woodside – had become almost household names in financial and mining circles from London to Johannesburg, Shanghai to Rio. The biggest mines, being far from the capital cities, are a mystery to most city-bound Australians who mistakenly dismiss them as just deep holes in the ground. Australia's worst political crisis was spurred in Canberra in 1975 partly by the Whitlam Government's desire to finance and control rich and remote mineral fields.

7

The first wave of postwar immigration lasted until the early 1970s. People came overwhelmingly from Europe, at first from the British Isles and then from continental Europe, with Asians forming a minor inflow at the end. After a lull in migration a second phase gathered speed under Malcolm Fraser (1975–83) and Bob Hawke (1983–91). Whereas Melbourne was the first cosmopolitan city, Sydney had usurped that role by the end of the century.

The fall of Saigon to the communists in 1975 reshaped the

migration. In the following five years, 2000 refugees came by small boats, usually anchoring in Darwin Harbour. But tens of thousands more, having been selected by Australian officials, were granted residency and welfare in Sydney and Melbourne where most were housed and given welfare benefits.

As the factories were declining in importance, and the level of unemployment in 1983 and 1984 was higher than at almost any time in the past half-century, most Vietnamese set foot in an economy that was less able to provide work for the unskilled. An axiom of postwar migration was that an ethnic group should not form a ghetto but should disperse widely. For the Italians, Poles and earlier European migrants such dispersal was easy, because in the 1950s and 1960s new jobs in the bush were plentiful. Understandably the later migrants had neither a wish nor an opportunity to disperse; by 1999 the astonishing tally of 97 per cent of the Vietnamese-born residents were living in an Australian capital city. No other migrant group had ever been so absent from the countryside and provincial cities.

Australia's population acquired a diversity not seen since the gold rushes of the 1850s, when the Chinese on the goldfields of eastern Australia formed more than one in six of the population. Between 1981 and 2000, the Asian population of Australia was multiplied by four. For the first time Europe and especially the British Isles ceased to be the main source of migrants. What had seemed unimaginable at the end of the Second World War swiftly came to pass.

CHAPTER TWENTY-TWO

Cars, coffee shops and black box

At the outbreak of peace in 1945, the nation had held seven million people. Canberra was a small country town that drew down its blinds before dark. Of every 100 Australians, maybe ninety-nine had not yet flown in an aeroplane. Most families owned a bicycle but no car and no telephone.

Even in the cities perhaps half of the houses lacked a supply of running hot water; and when people desired a bath – it was usually a Saturday-night event – they struck a match to light what was called 'the bath heater'. Its main fuel in a city was gas. In tens of thousands of farms and in small towns the water for the bath was warmed in a large copper vessel – it was simply called a copper – by a wood fire burning below. The woodheap or the small woodshed in the backyard was still a centre of activity, though less vital than it had been in 1900.

In the summer of 1945, air conditioning even in a rich family's house was rare. Central heating was uncommon in winter. City houses might possess a small electric radiator or gas fire, but it provided little warmth unless a person almost crouched over it. In winter most people wore woollen jumpers, and so helped the local woollen mills that were then important. Nearly half of the city houses, and nearly all the rural houses, used a wood-fire stove to cook the meals in the kitchen and a wood fire to heat the lounge or living room in winter. Most washing was done with the aid of water heated by a wood fire, and the wet washing was hung on a clothesline suspended from two poles stuck in the ground. Most families did not dream of owning a washing machine, and clothes dryers – and even drip-dry garments – were virtually unknown. At the end of each meal, the plates, cups, dishes and cutlery were washed in a bowl of hot soapy water and then dried by hand, using an oblong piece of cotton cloth called a tea towel. A slow task, it often called for the help of children if the family was large.

A refrigerator was a luxury. In Sydney more than half of the 600 000 households possessed no effective way of keeping cool the meat, butter, milk, soft drinks and beer. Only 40 000 families owned an electric refrigerator – it was too expensive for many. Instead a family ice chest was often seen in houses in the larger towns where existed a works that manufactured ice. The favourite was a Coolgardie safe, which cost nothing to run, and which kept the butter and milk and meat passably cool except on a very hot day. The safe usually stood in a cool spot near the shaded back door or veranda.

2

A housewife performed a wide variety of vital tasks. If the census had set up a category called 'unpaid housewife' it would have been the largest in the whole workforce. She carried out many of the activities later performed for her granddaughter by factories, restaurants and coffee shops, drycleaners and laundries. She knitted jumpers, made many of the clothes, and darned or mended socks, shirts, dresses and underclothes. She ironed shirts and blouses and trousers; the drycleaner shop was considered too expensive. She made jams, pickles, sauces, stewed fruits and soft drinks, and stood them in bottles and jars in her pantry. She made cakes, biscuits and sandwiches; she catered for the birthday parties, entertained friends and relatives to dinner and prepared or cooked everything on the table. She performed fifty other tasks that might today be carried out for her by one of the service industries. The husband and wife grew many of their own vegetables and most of their flowers and some of their fruit, and often kept hens in a small wire-netted outhouse in the backyard.

A big stove was the heart of perhaps half of all households in 1945. Dorothy Hewett, the actress and author, evoked her family's large kitchen in Western Australia: 'a black stove with two huge boiling kettles' that gave out a hissing noise, homemade bread rising in the pans on the hob, and nearby the long table made of pine and covered with lino. In summer the blowflies could be heard 'buzzing angrily' outside the flywire door, while the few already inside the house were prevented by a muslin cover from landing on a sheep's head afloat in a white dish. On a winter evening the kitchen was the only warm room in their house, and there sat 'our father' listening with the aid of earphones to the Test cricket scores relayed from England on his crystal-set wireless.

Numerous new amenities were inside the average suburban house by 1970, the arrival of each an exciting event. An automatic washing machine cleaned the clothes. A vacuum cleaner sucked dust from the carpets or the varnished floorboards. The kitchen depended on electricity and gas for cooking and heating, and a tall refrigerator stood against a wall. The microwave oven – unknown in a private house in 1970 – was to be prized in more than half of Australian households twenty years later. Here, since the end of the Second World War, had occurred a revolution in how people, especially women, spent their time at home.

As late as 1950, maybe half of the household phones were fixed to a wall and people stood while they talked. They looked at their watch, for phone calls made to a distant town or another state were prohibitively dear, and an extra three minutes on the phone might cost a large sum. For these 'trunk line' calls, a person did not yet dial a number and gain quick access, but rang the local switchboard where a telephonist (the word and occupation are now almost extinct) manually connected you to the phone line you were seeking. If she had a spare minute she overheard your conversation. Three out of every four small rural neighbourhoods as late as 1957 had no automatic telephone exchange, and once the local operator ceased work for the evening her customers lost all voice contact with the outside world. The answering machine was unknown.

The local post office was a pivot of communications, its postmen delivering mail twice a day in the cities, and its messenger delivering telegrams at any hour of the working day. Sealed in a smallish envelope and usually typed in capital letters on coloured paper, the telegram contained only a dozen or so words, for each word was expensive. News of deaths was delivered by a telegram to close relatives, and news of a scholarship came the same way, being preceded by a loud knock at the front door. No wedding breakfast was complete until the best man stood up and read aloud the telegrams – some funny, some smutty – which had arrived that day. The deliverer of telegrams was a teenager on a bike.

In the first postwar decades, the factory was far more important as an employer than it is today. Most of the shoes, shirts, boots, cloth and dresses that now come from China were made in the inner suburbs of Australian cities. Most cars were made in Australia. The making of military aircraft was still an important industry, while larger and larger ships were made, culminating in a vessel of more than 70 000 tonnes launched in Whyalla.

Each weekday, between 7 and 8 a.m., a small regiment of people arrived at the big factories, and if business was very brisk they might be replaced at 4 p.m. by another shift of workers. The factory whistle was still heard, announcing the starting time in many industrial suburbs and mining towns. Heavy loads were lifted by physical strength, unaided by machines. On the waterfront, in foundries and railway goods sheds and roadworks, sheer strength was vital. The front-end loader and forklift were novelties. In roadmaking the men with picks and shovels were visible. To die of a heart attack while at work was not uncommon. The decline of hard physical labour, and the advent of new machines and mechanical work tools, was a hallmark of the twentieth century.

It was easy to guess the occupations of people on their way to and from work. They could be judged by their clothes, the bags they carried, and sometimes their hands and face. At work, the butchers, bank typists, tramway employees and many others wore distinctive uniforms. The porter on a railway platform wore a uniform and a peaked cap. The matron of a hospital, the clergyman and the nun, the postman delivering the mail all wore distinctive uniforms and insignia. In a city street most of the white-collar men wore a felt hat, and in church the women's hats were visible. At the weekend people liked to dress up. The crowd at the football was better dressed in 1950 than in 2000, and many men fresh from the factory wore a suit and a wide-brimmed felt hat while they stood on the embankment.

Trade unions, increasingly powerful, demanded more leisure for their members, many of whom, just back from the war, worked fifty or even more hours a week. High was the satisfaction when in 1948 the forty-hour week was granted to employees in the typical industry. Saturday became a full or half holiday for most working people, and shops closed early on Saturday afternoon. In the history of the nation, shopping hours were perhaps at their fewest in the 1960s and 1970s.

Few people worked on Sunday. Shops, theatres and sports grounds in most states were closed, and factories too, but milk bars and corner stores were open in numerous suburbs and country towns. Between the First World War and the 1960s, hotels and bottle shops and licensed grocers were not open on Sunday in more than half of the towns in Australia, and then it was impossible to buy a bottle of alcohol. The exception was a genuine traveller who entered a hotel after coming some distance on that same day.

3

Women were a smaller percentage of the paid workforce. Many left their job when they married, or soon after, and it was normal for them to stay at home until their youngest child had left primary school. Many did not re-enter the workforce. The typical sixteen-year-old girl or boy was in the full-time workforce. Few students stayed on at school until Year 12, and few went to university. Melbourne and Sydney each possessed only one university in the late 1950s, when the Menzies Government awarded thousands of valuable scholarships to students and so promoted a need for new universities. To be an apprentice plumber, electrician or other tradesman was as desirable as to be a university student.

In drapers and grocers, banks and shoe shops the customer was always served by the staff. In a fruit shop the owner resented a customer who, selecting her own fruit and vegetables, served herself.

Railways and tramways had no ticket machines. Motorists were not yet called on to fill their car with petrol, pump the tyres or check the oil and battery. On Saturday, boys did those simple tasks at the local service station; and John Howard who became a long-serving prime minister worked for his father in the Sydney suburb of Earlwood. 'I liked serving petrol,' he once said.

4

Motor vehicles symbolising the era, multiplied faster than the street space and amenities available for them. Traffic lights were few and in peak hours a policeman stood in the centre of busy junctions and guided the flow of traffic. Parking meters were unknown – until Hobart installed them in 1954 – though petrol stations were more plentiful than they are today. The nation had no freeways, few fast roads in the country, and traffic on the Hume Highway went slowly through the main street of nearly every town along the route. The passenger train, selling cheaper tickets than aircraft, and enhanced by the mending at Albury of the broken gauge, still flourished on the main interstate routes. The long-distance bus was not yet a serious competitor, for the state governments did everything within the law or even altered the law to protect their passenger trains from more efficient competitors.

In the wave of prosperity, most people for the first time could afford a new or second-hand car, and the car salesmen were there to help. The Holden was the most popular, and by the 1980s a total of four million of its cars, vans and utilities had been sold. European and American car-makers that used to export vehicles to Australia began to manufacture them here, especially after the Menzies Government in 1956 increased the tax on fully imported models by 30 per cent. At first British cars were favourites – the Austin, the

Morris Minor, Hillman Minx, Vauxhall and Standard, with not a Japanese or German car to be seen. By the late 1950s the beetle-like Volkswagen was more than 50 per cent Australian in content, but German cars were soon ousted by Japanese. Of the North American cars, Ford was for long the favourite, having been made partly in Australia since the 1920s.

New cars became cheaper, and easier to drive. The automatic car replaced the manual gearshift, the steering called for less effort, the windscreen was wider and clearer, and a punctured tyre was less frequent. The household with two cars ceased to be a source of surprise.

A car is now seen often as a menace to urban life, a polluter of the air and a cause of traffic dislocations, but it was originally a liberator for most people. It multiplied the freedom of choice of at least half the population, and especially women. They could decide exactly when and where they travelled at weekends. By driving to work, they gained a wider choice of employment. In 1960 only 15 per cent of people living in Melbourne drove to work but by 1970 the percentage was more than 60. Cars transformed shopping, not always for the benefit of customers. Hitherto the butcher delivered the meat to the back door and the baker delivered the bread, and early each morning a milkman ladled milk into the billy can left at the front gate.

As the early roads built for horse-drawn vehicles could not cope, a network of highways was built. The idea of driving a car right around the continent fired the imagination, and in 1953 the annual Round Australia Trial race was first conducted, sometimes on almost undriveable tracks, of which the 'horror stretch' between Cloncurry and Mount Isa became notorious. Public enthusiasm for motoring was intense, and 50 000 spectators assembled at the Sydney Showground to watch the start of the first race. Damage to the competing cars was heavy, and the driver of the last to complete the route of 10 000 kilometres confessed that he had no difficulty in finding his way: 'I just followed a trail of hubcaps'.

In 1984, with the completion of bitumen roads in north-west Australia, it was feasible to drive in some comfort a car and caravan right around the continent. A couple of years later the last rough section of the Adelaide–Alice Springs–Darwin road was sealed. It became the ambition of many retired couples (known as grey nomads) to buy a caravan, motor van or expensive camping trailer and follow that round-Australia route at leisurely pace, usually in winter.

Too precious to be parked in the street day after day, the car gave rise to the carport and ever-present backyard garage. Cars gave birth to the motor hotel or motel which arrived from the USA to transform holidays and business travel. The mere dozen motels that served Australia in 1954 soon grew into hundreds. With the dominance of cars came the drive-in picture theatre which, like all cinemas, was soon endangered by the television set. Later the drive-in restaurant with a free parking lot changed the eating habits and children's birthdays in most Australian families. The first McDonald's was opened in the western Sydney suburb of Yagoona in 1971 – three years after Sydney tasted its first Kentucky Fried Chicken.

The popularity of the drive-in shopping centre owed much to two young postwar migrants from central Europe: John Saunders was a Hungarian and Frank Lowy a Czech, and in 1959 they built a small drive-in shopping centre at Bankstown in western Sydney. Called Westfield, it provided parking space for fifty cars but some of their later centres catered for upwards of 5000 cars. Inspired by a huge shopping centre opened by Myer in the grounds of an old convent in the Melbourne suburb of Chadstone, they designed a massive one – they coined the name 'shopping town' – at Burwood in Sydney in 1966. Under the Lowy family, Westfield was to design and build huge 'shopping towns' across Australia and in Malaysia, the United States and Britain. In 2012, when London hosted the Olympic Games, one drawcard for foreign visitors was the huge Westfield shopping town near the grand stadium.

Cars carried hosts of children to school in suburbs where they once had walked with a schoolbag on their back. They enabled people to buy a hobby farm and commute long distances each workday. For more than a generation they displaced public transport, making it the resort of the very old, very young and very poor. Motorists eliminated street trams in all the big cities except Melbourne. In the outback the four-wheel-drive vehicle enabled the creation of several hundred Aboriginal outstations or half-townships in remote places. Road deaths reached their peak in 1970, and then declined, thanks to seatbelts, straighter roads, and stricter laws against drink-driving. Victoria led the world in compelling drivers and passengers to wear seatbelts.

5

Tourism employed few people until cars, buses and big aircraft became common. Overseas holidays were unusual, partly because airfares were dear and the sea voyage was slow. The staging of the Olympic Games in Melbourne in 1956 was expected to lure foreign tourists, but apart from athletes and officials, few American or European spectators arrived.

Holiday resorts were small, and in winter the snow resorts were few. Most people who could afford a holiday set their eyes on places not far away. A Sydney family might go to a guesthouse or hotel in the Blue Mountains or stay on the Central Coast, just beyond Gosford, while a Melbourne family might go to Daylesford or Healesville if they preferred the countryside, or visit a nearby seaside town. Surfers Paradise, a tiny resort, gave not a hint that it would become by the end of the century one of the ten largest metropolises in Australia.

The annual period of paid leave was not widespread in 1960. The main holiday time was Christmas and New Year, when maybe one in thirty of the nation's population pitched tents on the beach, in the hills or in a friend's backyard or orchard. Most meals were cooked on an open fire. A complete ban on the lighting of fires in the open air on very hot, windy days was seen as too disruptive for daily life, and Victoria in 1946 was the first to impose a ban.

Thrift ruled the small tourist industry. Travel agents were almost unknown in the suburbs and large country towns, and shops specialising in luggage were rare. After all, a family usually needed only one or two suitcases, and they might rest on top of a bedroom cupboard for a whole year without once being used. Cruise ships did not exist. Air travel was for the wealthy, and the cheaper tourist-class seat was created in Australia only in 1955. For some years such passengers were in a minority. To book a holiday in New Zealand, let alone Europe, was not common until air travel became cheaper. Meanwhile in an aircraft most amenities were absent, including a radio for each passenger and a radar by which the pilot could foresee stormy weather. As the typical aircraft usually flew at only half of the present height, the turbulence could be severe. Even the short hop between Hobart and Launceston was notorious for airsickness.

Qantas became bold in its choice of long-distance routes. In January 1958, using Super Constellation aircraft, it opened a round-the-world service, with one plane flying east to San Francisco and New York and the other west to Asia and Rome. It was already planning to buy the Boeing 707, for its cruising speed of 885 kilometres an hour – almost twice as fast as the Constellation's – would cut flying time on the main 'kangaroo route' to England from about fifty hours to thirty. That it could carry eighty-four passengers was a bonus, but the noise level and the black fumes emitted by the pure-jet engines were a surprise to spectators who saw the first Boeing land in Australia. With cheaper and faster air travel, most Australians who went abroad in 1958 chose for the first time aircraft rather than ship.

It was necessary for planes on the Australia–England route to land frequently in order to take on fuel: the latest Boeing had a range of only 5600 kilometres. When we first flew overseas in December 1964 the Qantas plane left Melbourne for Sydney and Darwin, and then halted at Singapore, Calcutta, Karachi, Beirut, Rome and London. The word 'jet' was unknown to the traveller, and the slow journey had advantages. In daylight we looked out the windows at the scenery below, for no television set was present to divert us, and in a narrow plane everyone could sit near a window.

Curiously the television stations relied heavily on the fastest aircraft to bring them the latest overseas news and pictures, for no efficient method existed yet for transmitting moving pictures to a faraway city. When the Olympic Games were held in Melbourne in 1956 the newsreels of the main athletic events were rushed to the airport by van and sent by plane to Sydney for the evening news and then by planes across the world to the waiting television stations. A decade passed before events on one side of the world could be seen 'live' on the other side.

Aircraft flying on the shorter internal Australian routes were smaller and slower, and their accident rate was perturbing. The crash of Trans Australia's Fokker Friendship plane into the sea near Mackay in 1960, with the death of twenty-nine people, mostly schoolchildren, led indirectly to the compulsory fitting of a rugged black box. Now a worldwide device for recording voices in the aircraft's cockpit, it had been invented by David Warren in the aeronautical research laboratory in Melbourne and adopted first in the United States. Major aircraft accidents remained frequent. In the 1960s a Vickers Viscount airliner dived into Botany Bay, another crashed near Winton in western Queensland, and a third crashed at Port Hedland. In contrast in the following decade in Australia no crash caused so many deaths, though the passenger traffic was soaring.

In this excitingly prosperous era the annual holiday became longer for the typical worker, and that encouraged long-distance tourism. In 1968 about 250 000 Australians made short-term visits to the United Kingdom compared to a mere 5000 in 1938. The airports could not cope, and Tullamarine was opened at Melbourne and Kingsford Smith International at Sydney in 1970. The jumbo jet was about to inaugurate an era of cheap travel to foreign lands. Since the beginning of the human history of Australia all migrants had come by sea, but now more came by plane than by ship.

6

A new type of suburban house, arriving in the 1920s, was envied. Called the California bungalow, it was more likely to be of brick than weatherboard and its chimneys were fewer. Its roof, usually made of terracotta tiles in bright colours, was not so steep as the earlier roofs of slate, and the ceiling was lower. Fresh air was in favour – tuberculosis was still feared – and the veranda of many new houses enclosed a sleep-out where one or more of the children slept behind the privacy of canvas blinds or latticework. In the spacious backyard might stand a small building that served as a sleep-out for an older child. The bathroom was notable because the shower was used more than the bath.

A typical suburban house now occupied a wider frontage, thus enabling space at one side of the house to be used for a concrete driveway consisting of two narrow parallel paths, with a strip of lawn separating them; the various patches of lawn were cut regularly by 'the man of the house' who pushed along a simple mower without the help of an engine and inflated rubber tyres. Until such time as a car was bought, the garage was used for storage or as a dry spot where on a rainy day the washing could be hung on a rope clothesline.

In the 1960s, seven out of every ten Australians lived in houses that they or their family owned. This increase would have been impossible but for the high level of employment. That in turn ensured families earned a regular income from which they could month by month make the payment due on their house purchase. A home-owning family, it was believed, was likely to be more content and socially more responsible.

Flats or apartments were not yet in favour though they were multiplying in a few inner-city suburbs. A common objection to life in a flat was that it possessed no private garden at a time when the relatively large home garden was one of the differences between an Australian and a European city. The Victa motor mower – invented in the Sydney suburb of Concord in 1952 – made the keeping of a garden much easier.

In the four decades after the Second World War, food preferences and fads changed. New migrants as well as medical research altered the shopping habits. Butter was challenged by margarine, grain breads challenged the white loaf. Ice-cream, now much cheaper, became an everyday rather than a twice-a-year item in many families. The eating of lamb and pork products soared; the average person's consumption of chicken increased by four in the years 1965–85, but beef was eaten less often. Cheese became far more popular but the eating of jam and golden syrup declined dramatically, and the teeth of children were less decayed. Fluoride, added to the drinking water, saved teeth. By 1968, Sydney, Perth, Canberra and Hobart imbibed fluoride from their water taps. In the following decade the craze for fast food made obesity rather than tooth decay a cause for concern. A decade later vegetarianism – part of the green movement and the heightened sanctity of animal life – won converts among the young. The era was coming when the organiser of a grand dinner had to ask in advance whether any of the guests had implacable dietary fears.

Tea was the traditional Australian drink. It was in the weekly food allowance given to every shepherd in the 1840s, and half a century later was in the billy that boiled in the opening verse of 'Waltzing Matilda'. Tea was the common drink of the Australian soldiers at Gallipoli and, in the Second World War, in North Africa and New Guinea.

Coffee had been a minor beverage in 1900. Its main drinkers were in South Australia, the most German of the states, and they imported their coffee beans from Java and Ceylon; but a typical Australian could live to old age without once tasting what is now called real coffee. If they did drink coffee they drank it in the form of an essence or syrup. To the thick syrup were added hot water and often milk and several teaspoons of sugar.

Coffee gained popularity after American soldiers arrived in the early 1940s. With the 'instant coffee' made first by Nestlé in 1947, a strong and true cup of coffee, piping hot, could be made with slightly less trouble than a pot of tea. Within twenty years half of the coffee drunk was 'instant coffee'. As more migrants arrived from coffee-drinking countries in continental Europe the demand soared for an even truer drink: brewed coffee. The coffee shops and cafes multiplied, each with an espresso machine. The habit, once unimaginable, of sitting on a chair on the side of the pavement on a cold morning and drinking strong coffee turned into a craze. When coffee overtook tea as the favourite drink, in about 1980, it was one of the most unexpected culinary changes in our history.

Migrants from Italy, Greece and most parts of continental Europe liked wine, which began to challenge beer as the favoured form of alcohol. Before the war much of the wine drunk in Australia was port, muscat, sherry and the fortified wines, but now table wines were grown in districts where not one vineyard existed in 1950. Even Tasmania produced wine, and soon it was highly praised.

The consumption of alcohol increased partly because prosperity was widespread. A large segment of Australians, who had been teetotallers because their churches spoke out against alcohol, tasted 'strong drink' for the first time. The anti-alcohol crusade, so vigorous from the 1880s onwards, lost its zest. In the mid-1960s both Victoria and South Australia, which for half a century had closed their hotels at 6 p.m., permitted longer drinking hours. Soon began the astonishing growth of cafes and restaurants, which was a cultural marker of the era.

In mid-century the tax on imported tobacco was low, and no major church frowned on the habit of smoking – unless it was a woman who smoked. In 1940, and for decades previously, most Australian men had rolled their own cigarette from a pouch of ready-rubbed tobacco or smoked a pipe filled with strong tobacco, whereas cigarettes bought in a packet were a more expensive addiction. Smoking was so widespread, especially among men, that on a windless day at a big football match the haze of tobacco smoke hovered above the crowd like a halo. At a dinner party in a house or a restaurant, half or more of the guests lit a cigarette at table before the first course was served. From the 1960s, medical research linking tobacco smoke to lung cancer began to check the habit of smoking, though not among poorer people and teenage girls.

Alcohol and tobacco were the only drugs most people knew until the late 1960s, when marijuana attracted the younger generation. It foreshadowed more dangerous and addictive drugs such as heroin and crystal methamphetamine.

7

Few postwar changes seemed more revolutionary than in counting and measuring. The pound – no longer worth the same as the English pound – was replaced by the dollar in February 1966, each pound now being converted into two dollars. Sir Robert Menzies had initially preferred the name 'royal' for the new unit of the decimal currency, but the chosen word 'dollar' reflected the pervading American influence on daily life. Rapid inflation, setting in during the 1970s, was to dilute the value of the currency, and the original coins of one and two cents were almost worthless. The first $50 note was printed in 1973 and the $100 note in 1984.

Chequebooks were challenged, slowly at first, by credit cards. Tourists carrying a credit card to foreign lands no longer had to produce a folder full of 'travellers' cheques' which they signed – in the presence of a witness – when they paid the bill at their hotel or cafe. At home the credit card also altered indirect ways of borrowing money such as hire-purchase, a method by which two of every three refrigerators were bought. A simpler method called time-payment or lay-by was favoured for Christmas presents. The customers chose the electric toaster or alarm clock, which was then stored at the back of the shop until the weekly or monthly instalments had been completed.

The imperial weights and measures that Governor Phillip brought to Australia in 1788 were about to be discarded. Though they are now said to be complicated, most native-born Australians easily understood them, and measured their height in inches (12 inches to each foot, and 3 feet to the yard) and their weight in stones and pounds (14 pounds to each stone). But the metric system, more logical, prevailed in much of the world. Keith Laught, a senator from South Australia, chaired the select committee which recommended that it be adopted here. Actually the nervous official prediction that Australia would lose commerce unless it quickly converted to metrics was far-fetched.

The metre came in slow steps and shuffles. The first big project to use metric units was the long railway from Tarcoola to Alice Springs, planned first in 1970. Wool and nearly all other Australian produce except gold were first measured in kilograms instead of pounds in 1971. Next year horseracing and most other sports abandoned feet, yards and furlongs, and the weather bureau announced that a very hot day was 38.2 degrees Celsius, which was very close to the old 100 degrees Fahrenheit. In 1974, road signs throughout Australia were altered, and speeding and dangerous driving were no longer measured in miles an hour but were translated into the new terminology. Real estate in 1987 became the last profession to fall into line, the auctioneers having preferred to use the acre in listing a property for sale.

Those who savoured English words and their sounds did not necessarily like the new terms, for the ancient words were shorter, pithier and rich in folklore, songs and literary memories. It sounded cumbersome and pretentious to report that a climber was reaching the steep summit millimetre by millimetre rather than inch by inch. Even so, the nation's transition to the metric system was carried out with skill by lawmakers, bureaucrats and all who obeyed them.

The adoption of decimal currency and metrics pointed – like the conveying of news – to a world that was shrinking. When Abraham

Lincoln was assassinated in the United States in April 1865, about ten weeks passed before the news reached most Australian towns. Fifty years later, at the storming of the cliffs and ridges of Gallipoli, Charles Bean was the nation's only correspondent present; but after the wartime censors intervened in his first report, tapped out by his fingers on a Corona typewriter, it did not reach the newspapers until more than a fortnight had passed. In contrast Paul McGeough, the *Sydney Morning Herald*'s correspondent in New York on the infamous day of 11 September 2001, was to transmit report after report, hour after hour, simply by tapping his mobile phone.

8

Australia was probably the first nation in the modern world to be obsessed by spectator sport; and the obsession arose when international fixtures were rare and Australia's isolation further restricted its participation. The Olympic Games, reborn in Athens in 1896, were initially no more than an amateur contest attended by a small fraction of the world's best athletes. Tennis was becoming an international sport but audiences were small and only wealthier players could afford to travel and play. When Australia first played in the Davis Cup in the Edwardian era, its team consisted of Anthony Wilding of Christchurch and Norman Brookes of Melbourne who combined under the name of Australasia. Sculling or professional rowing was able to flourish here as a crowd-pleasing international sport partly because the team consisted of only one man, and so travelling expenses were light compared to cricket.

As late as 1900 a truly international football match, little known in Europe, was rarer here. What could be called Australia's first really international test on its own soil was played in 1903 – against New Zealand in rugby union. At that time Australia's most popular international sport was Test cricket, but the arrival of an overseas Test cricket team was a long-awaited event. England's team sailed to Australia once in every four or more years; and a century ago South Africa's was the only other cricket team to have toured Australia, first playing in the summer of 1910–11.

For its size Australia began to enjoy unusual successes in international sport. In the 1950s and 1960s the success was startling, particularly in international tennis and the Olympic Games. But at the end of that period Australia's natural advantages of prosperity, cheap land, ample leisure and a favourable climate were no longer enough to withstand the sheer weight of public and private money that rich or populous nations such as the United States and the Soviet Union, and even little East Germany, showered on its sporting elite. In 1976, day after day, the Australian public was shocked when the dismal results of the Montreal Olympics came through. In Canberra a solution was proposed by a federal minister, previously a leading Sydney barrister, Robert Ellicott, who against many objections guided through federal cabinet a simple but expensive plan to finance the Australian Institute of Sport, an elite training college which was opened by Malcolm Fraser, the prime minister, in 1981.

The humiliation at Montreal, followed by larger federal and state cheques, and a fast-growing population, was the spur to another era of sporting success. But the former triumphs were not fully equalled.

One Australian tradition is to cut down the elite and the successful. It had its roots in the era of convicts who naturally opposed those in authority. This levelling or egalitarian tradition continued to flourish on the goldfields in the 1850s when the unusual mining laws gave everyone an opportunity to find gold, and the tradition was accentuated around 1900 by the rising trade unions. The attitude was one of the spurs to Australian democracy. Somehow spectator sport suits this tradition, for it is attractive only if the stronger team sometimes loses. Even if the champions, whether Bradman in cricket or Lindrum in billiards, reign for an exceptionally long time, their ultimate decline and retirement are inevitable. Compared to business and science, the reign of nearly all champions in sport is brief.

The long-time Australian fascination with sport is mixed with nationalism. To defeat a major country at sport, especially Britain, has long been an ambition. And yet the Australian game that attracts the largest crowds is, even more than American baseball, confined to its native soil. An old game, founded in gold-rush Melbourne in the late 1850s, the original clubs of Australian Rules are older than any senior football club in Europe or South America or even those in the English Premier League. Even in the 1880s the game drew huge crowds by world standards, and the crowds grew. In September 1970 the grand final between teams from the adjacent suburbs of Carlton and Collingwood attracted 121 696 people to the Melbourne Cricket Ground.

Saturday was the traditional day of sport, and its afternoon and evening newspapers revelled in it, but by 1990 those papers no longer existed. Television was king, to be joined soon by mobile phone and website, and the whole weekend at home was turning into a continuous festival of spectator games.

CHAPTER TWENTY-THREE

The dancing partners: wilderness, paradise and religion

In the last third of the century, basic institutions and faiths were challenged and even undermined. Religion and its influential reign were attacked. Marriage and the family were attacked, and the dominance of men in public life. Even the concepts of civilisation and progress were confronted by the new green movement. These challenges were linked. To attack the family and the sanctity of marriage was indirectly to attack Christianity. To challenge the dominance of men was to challenge most of the Christian churches and not least the papacy. To defend nature vigorously was to attack economic progress, which had almost been the motto of Australia since 1788. To enthrone nature, in the style of some green leaders, was also to establish a new God and replant the Garden of Eden.

2

When the Commonwealth of Australia was formed in 1901, it gave more emphasis to religion than did the secular founding document of the United States of America. Australia's constitution, in its pre-amble, even included the prayer, 'humbly relying on the blessing of Almighty God'. At the same time the document emphasised that no religion was officially seen as superior to others. After the first federal politicians assembled in Melbourne in 1901, they resolved that each day's proceedings should begin with prayer. The Lord's Prayer is still recited but not with the strong support of all parties.

At the end of the Second World War, Christianity remained strong. Nearly every house kept a copy of the Bible, and a cook-ery book too. One in three people over the age of forty had read the Bible within the past week. Protestants were more likely than Catholics to read the Bible, and the old read it more than the young. The practice of saying grace before a family's meal – 'Bless this food' – persisted in one in every three households, especially those of nonconformists such as Baptists, according to the gallup poll in 1951. Who actually said the grace while the family closed its eyes? It was more likely to be a child than the father or mother. As for attending a church regularly, Catholics were the most diligent. They even shouldered the financial burden of running a vast system of schools without government aid.

Most marriages and funerals were still conducted in churches. Of the marriages celebrated in the early 1960s, Catholic and Anglican clergymen each blessed 27 per cent of them, followed by Methodist and Presbyterian pastors each with about 12 per cent. Even then the civil or secular marriage ceremonies were increasing, and were most frequent in Canberra. That city, really a country town, was already showing that it was a distinctive little nation inside a nation, with its high ratio of both Catholic and secular weddings.

By present standards the knowledge of Christianity among the general public was impressive. In a test conducted in the early 1960s among new army recruits, more than six in every ten said they knew where Jesus was born, and also named the event that Good Friday celebrated. Only 19 per cent, however, could write out the Lord's Prayer correctly. In the 1960s – and probably in every following decade – the young knew less about religion than the middle-aged and the old.

Many Australians who had faint interest in religion did not admit it publicly. They were not hostile to the church – they just walked past it. The atheists, agnostics, rationalists, freethinkers and secularists – they had much in common – were critical of Christianity but most were silent in public. Their main concern was the Christians' concept of heaven and hell. Even mainstream Protestants, however, were losing or loosening their belief in hell. Therefore the dividing wall between the atheists and a large section of modern Christians was not as high as is sometimes imagined. Many atheists opposed Christian dogma but supported Christian principles, praising most of the Ten Commandments.

For two decades the intellectual who probably was best known to the average newspaper reader was Walter Murdoch, a former professor of English, whose Saturday column was widely read. Occasionally he expressed a secular view of life and death: 'Quickly the night wind sweeps us away, and the traces of us. We serve the purposes of the day, and if we have served that purpose faithfully, we must be content to be forgotten tomorrow.' The death notices in the daily newspapers often disagreed, and reminded readers that 'in my Father's house are many mansions'. The sayings and metaphors of the Bible were still understood, being central to semi-popular culture.

3

Before 1950 it was hard to name a leading politician who was widely known to be an open agnostic. One was John Latham, member for the famous Liberal electorate of Kooyong, deputy prime minister under Joseph Lyons from 1932 to 1934 and later chief justice of the High Court; he had been the head of Melbourne's rationalists when young. Like all prominent rationalists he knew his Bible: he had to, in order to argue persuasively. Old friends, when he died in 1964, were surprised to read that his funeral service was to be held in a Methodist church – the creed of his youth.

John Curtin was the first prime minister – and still one of the few – to pass through a strong freethinking background. At what age he moved away from the Catholic church to a secular stance is not certain, for there is some evidence that as a youth he played a part in a large Salvation Army band in the Melbourne industrial suburb of Brunswick. Eventually his only link with the Salvationists was in the hotels where those 'lassies' selling their *War Cry* newspaper must have seen him swaying under the influence of alcohol. With the strong help of his wife, Curtin eventually gave it up, and at the height of his political power he preferred to stay at a temperance hotel or coffee palace, away from temptation. In his last years, in the early 1940s, Curtin came again to believe in an afterlife, and added 'God bless you' to the end of his nation-inspiring speeches. To the surprise of many he was buried with Presbyterian rites.

The Christian churches remained a hub of social activity, and the majority of people still married somebody of their own denomination. A Catholic married a Catholic, a Jew married a Jew, and a Lutheran a Lutheran. Probably they first met at a church activity. While the church was vigorous it was also becalmed. Churchgoing was a habit more than an infectious habit, and did not increase.

And yet some organisations that lived under the umbrella of Protestantism flourished. Between 1920 and 1954 the number of Freemasons' lodges in Australia trebled. The increase in the churches' tennis and cricket and basketball teams was even faster. A host of scouts and guides, cubs and brownies were attached to churches and met in their halls or under them. Those adults who did not attend church could hear it on the radio every Sunday in the 1930s. When television arrived in 1956 its daily program usually ended with a prayer or short religious talk.

4

Religion flavoured politics, as never before. B. A. Santamaria was in his mid-twenties when at his inner-suburban home he held a small meeting that is now remembered as a call to arms. The son of Sicilian migrants, his father a greengrocer, Santamaria had studied at several of the best Catholic schools and at Melbourne University, where even as a student he pointed to the perils of communism in Russia and to the danger that militant atheism would spread across Europe. Already in Australia, the communists – a tiny political party – ran vital trade unions, and at the peak of their influence in 1946 their particular unions held about four of every ten trade unionists in the country. Santamaria believed that those unions could be captured from communist control by careful generalship, by the collecting of useful knowledge about the enemy, and by systematically enlisting the support of Catholic workers in vital industries. He formed or moulded a chain of organisations – the Catholic Social Studies Movement, the 'industrial groups', and later the National Civic Council – and was a brilliant speaker and broadcaster who selected powerful and memorable words for his message. His view of communism came primarily from his religion: he was a devoted Catholic.

In Melbourne many parish priests spread his political message from the pulpit. Archbishop Mannix himself became a firm supporter and financier after he was visited by young Santamaria in his neat suit, a visitor only one-third of the age of the archbishop. Arthur Calwell – later the dedicated enemy of Santamaria – legally used his ministerial position in wartime Canberra to allocate scarce newsprint that enabled a weekly Santamaria newspaper to arise in 1943. The left wing that controlled the Labor Party in Victoria did not fully realise what a formidable young opponent they were facing.

An emphatic speaker with an urgent voice, small compelling eyes, an unhalting flow of words, and a touch of the scholar (some unkindly said 'a madman') in the way he argued, Santamaria won lifelong converts. His 'industrial groups' gained more and more influence within left-wing unions. When the communists overplayed their hand in 1946 by organising dislocating strikes in Victoria, Santamaria's status grew. The Cold War boosted him.

He did not wish to stand for parliament: he had no need to. He was exercising more influence than all but a few politicians in the land, and it is unlikely that he even belonged to a party. But then he himself was a political party. Left-wing Labor leaders were one by one toppled from the executives or committees on which they sat. He and his supporters controlled or supervised the Labor Party in Victoria and even nationally to some degree by the mid-1950s, thanks partly to the misjudgements of their opponents who retaliated. In 1955 at a conference in Hobart the politicians who supported him were expelled from the Labor Party. It was a suicidal step. Santamaria and his allies formed their own party, soon to be called the Democratic Labor Party. Already, before the next federal next election was called, it held nine federal seats and almost double that number of seats in the Victorian parliament.

Victoria was the heartland of the split, which virtually kept Labor from again winning power federally until 1972. Cardinal Norman Gilroy helped to prevent the split from spreading in New South Wales where the Labor Party was as Catholic as in Victoria. Gilroy had been an Anzac who became the bishop of Port Augusta at the age of thirty-seven and archbishop of Sydney at forty-three, the first Australian native to reach such eminence. He saw Santamaria as too much a Victorian and his movement as so controlled by laymen that it was 'almost Protestant in texture'. Gilroy was close, at times, to the NSW Labor Party. It was the Catholic poet James McAuley – a Santamarian in sympathies – who wittily wrote that Gilroy with his 'right hand blessed the victims of his left'.

The split in Labor was largely a contest between Catholics and others. But it was also a split inside scores of Catholic parishes where the resentment, anger and even hatred destroyed lifelong friendships. 'There is not a parish anywhere in Victoria where this division in families and parishioners does not exist,' wrote Calwell privately in 1956. Calwell was soon to become leader of the federal Labor Party and a persisting target for Santamaria's arrows. These two enemies, each so derided, can now be seen as commanding figures in their nation's story.

Sectarianism was not a simple nor unbroken strand in Australian history. In some decades and in some states the disputes within churches and sects were more intense than the disputes between Catholic and Protestant. At one time or other every Christian denomination in Australia had its dangerous divisions. In many towns and suburbs there was courteous disagreement between Catholic and Protestant. One elderly Catholic priest, born in 1911, said of the town of Bacchus March, which lay west of Melbourne: 'I've seen no sign of bigotry here whatsoever.' One significant snippet of political history we tend to overlook is that Australia was far more willing than the United States and the United Kingdom to elect or re-elect Catholics as leaders of the nation.

The decline of Christianity accelerated from the late 1960s. Suburbs spread out, with few churches. The attendance at Protestant Sunday schools declined rapidly – the young either rebelled or were quietly allowed to abandon the long-standing religious timetable that partly filled their Sunday. More families owned a car, which absorbed them on Sunday afternoon, and television, which held their attention that evening; Sunday service at 7 p.m., once so popular, faded and then ceased. Spectator sport, essentially a Saturday fixture, invaded Sunday afternoon. In 1970 the nation's most popular football competition, the Victorian Football League, played its very first match on a Sunday.

The decline of active church membership can easily be interpreted as simply a decline in religion, but by the end of the century it was clear that all kinds of organisations – churches, trade unions, political parties, Freemasons, service groups such as Rotary, Apex and Lions, the YMCA and YWCA, and school mothers' clubs – were losing members. The Catholic Church temporarily resisted the trend. In about 1986 it was to become the largest in the nation, but partly because so many of the postwar migrants were Catholics. For the first time in centuries numerous Catholic priests and nuns gave up their religious vows; many married each other. In Catholic schools the number of teaching priests, nuns and brothers decreased rapidly. The increasing revelations, after 2000, that Catholic priests had sexually abused children in their care damaged their vocation and the reputation of their church. That the same abuses had occurred in government institutions did not yet receive much publicity.

Leaders who were not Christian came to the fore. Gough Whitlam, prime minister from 1972 to 1975, did not go out of his way to disown Christianity. The news that he was an infidel was slow to reach the nation's kitchen tables and the ears of some of his admirers. Sir Fletcher Jones, a returned soldier from the First World War and a keen Christian, was one admirer. The creator of a large clothing factory in Warrnambool – his brand of trousers was bought nationwide – he was seen as an ideal employer. In May 1935 in the local town hall he staged a welcome for the Japanese Christian-socialist Toyohiko Kagawa, and then a year later visited him in Japan and imbibed his enthusiasm for the principle of profit sharing, eventually applying it to his Victorian factory. Retaining his Labor loyalties, Jones presumably rejoiced when Whitlam won the federal election in 1972. Later he began to hear whispers that Whitlam was an agnostic. That stunning revelation ended his life-long support for Labor.

Bob Hawke of the Labor Party in 1983 became the first prime minister to publicise his religious doubts. The son of a Congregational clergyman in Perth, he had travelled in an ocean liner as a young man to a Christian conference in South India where his concerns about poverty and social justice triggered his loss of faith. On his way home he was influenced in Sri Lanka by a few days spent in a Buddhist household whose atmosphere was 'very peaceful and unbelievably gentle'. He found Buddhism more logical than Christianity – this was a step in his journey to agnosticism. Later, as the nation's political leader, Hawke did not foreshadow a swing to the secular. In the quarter-century after his resignation in 1991, all but one of his successors were either strongly sympathetic to Christianity or regular churchgoers.

The rise of Asian migration quickly altered the religious makeup. In 2011 – the latest census for which figures are available – the Buddhists, Muslims and Hindus formed 7 per cent of the population whereas Christianity held about 63 per cent. The remainder were non-believers or refused to disclose their religion. A close examination of the census returns shows that these so-called Eastern religions were not entirely linked to Asia. The Buddhist temples or writings attracted many people of European descent, while the Christian churches attracted a large minority of recent Vietnamese, Filipino and Indian immigrants. In Victoria, which is a recent goal for Indians, 36 per cent are Christians. A sign of the new complexity was that many Australians worshipped nature, which owned no churches but displayed the characteristics of a major religion.

5

As late as 1945, women were not widely treated as first-class citizens in work or politics. Their tenure in many occupations was fragile. A male public servant could keep his job when he married, whereas a woman, just before her wedding day, usually had to resign. In 1918 a royal commission on the federal public service had suggested that women clerks were not quite as capable as men. It was also alleged or rumoured that unmarried women in their twenties and thirties – the death toll of soldiers had indirectly increased their percentage – did not quite 'stand the strain and pressure of work'. With the coming of full employment after the Second World War, there could be no complaint that women were stealing men's jobs. More women gained professional qualifications, and the rollcall of those who went to university or other tertiary colleges trebled between 1955 and 1965. As they were paid less than men – normally receiving only 75 per cent of a male salary – they rejoiced in 1969 when the Commonwealth Arbitration Commission took their side. It was decreed they should receive the same pay as men for the same kind of work, the reform to be phased in during the following three years. Of course many self-employed women earned more than men, especially in shops.

Occasionally the working roles and rules were turned upside down by new technology. In 1950 most of those capable of working a typewriter were women, and typist was a major female occupation. By 2016 most men – even chairmen of directors – could type on the computer with varying degrees of skill. The typing pool – the name for a room or hall where numerous typists assembled for work – had been one of the crowded places in the business world, but now the pool was emptying.

Women were slow to enter federal politics.. The remoteness of Canberra was one obstacle. The first woman to win a seat in the House of Representatives, Dame Enid Lyons of Tasmania, owed much to the fact that her late husband had been an honoured prime minister. As mother of twelve children she had also learned to organise her days. On 29 September 1943 her maiden speech, heard with deep respect on all sides, expressed her Catholic faith that every politician and citizen should have their 'vision of the City of God'. Enid Lyons and her generation – and Catherine Spence before her – did not necessarily feel that women lost influence by being unrepresented in parliament. They believed that a million God-fearing women staying at home and accepting responsibility for bringing up a family might have more influence on a nation's future than would a parliament packed with career-focused women.

While women could vote, they suffered from a dearth of other political and economic rights. They were rarely appointed to the influential, unpaid post of justice of the peace. Their right to sit on a jury was first granted, and only in Queensland, in 1923. New South Wales postponed their admission to juries until 1951, and one reason ingenuously offered for the delay was the absence of separate lavatories for women. The fact that in the same courtroom the witnesses and the spectators sat on the same lavatory seat, irrespective of gender, showed that logic was not entirely on the side of the people's guardians.

The Australian tradition of mateship was one-sided, wrote Judith Wright the poet, because 'it left out of account the whole relationship with women'. A revolution, 'a festival of the oppressed', was needed, wrote Germaine Greer, once a convent schoolgirl in Melbourne. To the National Press Club in 1972 she announced that 'Women's liberation is sexy, it's exciting, it's all kind of things. And it's here to stay.' In that same decade women were succeeding in professions where, in their grandmother's day, not one could be seen. They were judges, professors, industrial managers, engineers and ministers of religion. More women sat in parliament, and more became ministers, while others headed government departments. In 1974 Ruth Dobson became the first female ambassador, to Denmark. In 1976 Elizabeth Evatt became the chief justice of the new Family Court. Year after year a prestigious post for the first time was filled by a woman. It was in 1986 that General Eva Burrows, the eighth child of officers in the Salvation Army in Newcastle, became the worldwide head of that church – possibly the world's highest ecclesiastical position then held by a woman. One year later Mary Gaudron, once a small-town girl in northern New South Wales, became the first female judge in the High Court. She recalled that she first heard of the federal constitution, of which she was now a custodian and arbiter, when she listened eagerly to Dr H. V. Evatt, Labor's leader, speaking from the back of a blue utility truck in her hometown of Moree.

For feminists it was galling that the very highest political prizes eluded talented women. At last in 1990 Carmen Lawrence, a psychologist by profession, became premier of Western Australia and Joan Kirner, a schoolteacher, the premier of Victoria. The last rung of the political ladder remained out of reach. On that day in 2010 when Julia Gillard, who had arrived in Adelaide as a young Welsh migrant, became prime minister, her career was said to crown that long democratic campaign in which Australia once led the world. She left office, however, proclaiming that women were still on probation in the opinion of powerful misogynist men.

6

Marriages had been permanent in the era of the horse and cart. Western Australia in the early 1890s averaged only one divorce annually. Not until 1920 did the whole of Australia record 1000 divorces in a year; half were in New South Wales, which had recently laid down an easier path to divorce. In 1929 the nation's divorces passed 2000 for the first time but then fell away. The world Depression encouraged neither marriage nor divorce, both being expensive procedures for the average person. By then a divorce, slightly easier, could be granted not only on the grounds of adultery but also desertion and drunkenness. The difficulties of gaining a divorce in Australia lured a few wealthier individuals to California where they married new spouses under Californian law.

Celebrities became prominent in divorce cases in Australia, as in the United States. Thus Nellie Melba the soprano, Charles Kingsford Smith the aviator and Jack Davey the radio star were each divorced. In public life, however, divorce still carried a stigma. It is hard to think of a successful Australian politician who, in the century 1875 to 1975, was a divorcee. As a rule such pillars of society as judges, clergymen, bank managers, well-known school principals and heads of government departments did not divorce.

Divorce was widely judged by most outsiders to be a matter of guilt, shame or misfortune. Nearly all churches obeyed the maxim of Saint Mark: 'What therefore God hath joined together, let no man put asunder.' This maxim was known by heart in hundreds of thousands of homes. Anglican and Catholic bishops refused to allow a divorced person to remarry within the church, but other clergy stepped forward to tie the knot.

The Second World War – and the lives it overturned or changed – multiplied the occasions and desires for divorce. The divorces were increased by the onset of exceptional prosperity, and the slow decline of religion. Canberra in 1959 tried to make divorce easier as well as introduce uniform laws across the nation. The federal fathers had found this task too controversial, as had a succession of prime ministers; but a Liberal backbencher, Percy Joske, who was one of Melbourne's leading barristers and divorce lawyers, stepped forward. Menzies as prime minister encouraged him, and after much consultation with the states a bill was prepared under the name of the Matrimonial Causes Act. In parliament it was introduced by Sir Garfield Barwick, who was a Methodist – a sect slightly more sympathetic to the dissolving of marriages. Conceding that in a perfect world nearly all marriages should be permanent, Barwick admitted that we were not all quite perfect, and that was one reason why marriages failed. How could we possibly choose, 'often in years of immaturity', a lifelong partner with wisdom? Nor was it easy 'to bear with resignation and fortitude the maladjustments and torments of a faulty choice'. With his tactful approach to divorce, Barwick was in keeping with the basic Christian idea of original sin.

The Catholic Church trembled at the bill likely to be passed by federal parliament. In its view a loyal Catholic should not be a friend of a divorcee. Most churches were perturbed that a sacred institution was about to be sabotaged by legislators meeting in that secular city of Canberra whose citizens were already said to be the most reformist and leftist – and wealthiest – in the land. For many federal politicians the decision on how to vote was painful, and some Catholics ignored their church's teaching, and some Liberals did not follow their leader. It was one of the rare occasions when members were not compelled to vote along party lines, the topic being so thorny.

The new law, moderate in spirit, did not, as its critics had sensationally predicted, publicly unlock the 'floodgates of sexual passion'. A married couple could now be divorced if adultery or a similar fault was proved. A marriage also could legally end after five years of separation – a law borrowed from Western Australia. It was a revolutionary step to initiate a form of divorce in which no blame was pinned on one or more of the marriage partners. In 1975 the Whitlam Government, with Senator Lionel Murphy as the pilot, resolved to reduce the five years of separation to one. Moreover adultery or other events no longer entered the legal picture. Once again, in voting on divorce reforms, the federal politicians could cast a free or conscience vote – without it the bill might have foundered. After the Family Law Act came into force in January 1976 the long-expected flood appeared, and nearly 70 000 divorces were granted in that year.

Marriages lasting less than seven years became common though they were not yet typical. After a period of turbulence the divorce rate became stable. The modern one-parent family was partly the result of easy divorce or a reluctance to marry formally. At the end of the twentieth century it constituted one in five of all families, and usually a woman was the head. While the single-parent family seemed to be a revolution, it had been common in Australia in the nineteenth century, mainly because of the early death of the husband while of working age, or the death of a wife, often in childbirth. The need to remarry had been an economic necessity. Welfare payments to one-parent families were not introduced until 1973.

The ancient Aboriginal custom of polygamy was more and more confined to remote communities and even there was modified. The young tended to dislike the idea of one husband married to many wives. Almost certainly that ancient Aboriginal custom, favouring old men over young, lowered the status of women. Increasingly came evidence that the maltreating of women was widespread in modern Aboriginal society, but whether it was widespread in traditional Aboriginal society was not easily assessed.

Once the spirit of questioning and reform is in the air, many kinds of relationships are examined. Thus the abuse of women is now discussed, in public and perhaps in private, more than in 1950. Premiers, executives of sporting leagues, human-rights commissions deplore it and call for action. It was as if a giant searchlight was circling the nation in search of new grounds for a crusade.

7

South Australia was the first to legalise abortion, in 1969. The age-old ban on abortion once had strong religious backing, but overpopulation was now a pervasive concern in some intellectual circles, along with an emphasis on personal liberty. Similarly the law and public opinion had long frowned on homosexuality but the cultural revolution beginning in the late 1960s removed part of the frown. Homosexual activity ceased to be a criminal offence, South Australia in 1972 being the first to change the law whereas Tasmania waited another quarter-century. In everyday speech and in the smaller Sydney bars and cafes the word 'gay' blossomed, but for several decades the newsreaders remained wary of describing a prominent person as gay. If a biography of Patrick White the novelist had been written in 1971, just before he won his Nobel prize for literature, it would probably have skimmed over his sexual preferences; but twenty years later David Marr's *Life* of him did not skim.

This half-revolution in the family – including parenthood and childhood, marriage and divorce – was controversial. Perhaps fifty or 100 years will pass before the defenders of Western civilisation can reach a balanced opinion of how beneficial was this cluster of unpredicted changes, or how beneficial to the individuals who welcomed or doubted them. Certainly they opened windows and unlocked doors. They liberated talents. In some ways they were a mirror of Western societies, which tended, more than ever before, to enthrone change. The changes reflected a society that, being at peace, could emphasise individual rights rather than rights that previously were believed to knit society together and, if necessary, to defend it. In part these reforms reflected a loss of faith in mainstream Western civilisation and the religious precepts and social customs that had underlain it.

8

At one time a host of Australians vowed that nature must not stand in the way of progress. In their rush to open up the land, settlers had to trample on nature. The dispersing of sheep and cattle over a huge area began to alter the native grasses and the flow of creeks. Woodcutters in their thousands felled native forests with axe and saw. From the 1850s, goldminers spoiled creeks, and the flow of silt impaired the habitat of native fishes and the drinking water of towns further downstream. The clearing of scrub to make way for the plough caused dust storms in a few semi-arid regions, but dust storms must have been familiar to ancient Aborigines too.

Black coal was a popular fuel in the big cities and by the 1880s visitors to Melbourne and Sydney thought the sky was unusually black or hazy on windless days. Smelters could sometimes corrode the landscape. A place of desolation was Mount Lyell in western Tasmania where in 1896 the brilliant metallurgist and notable art collector Robert C. Sticht had built copper smelters employing a novel technique that became famous. It was a scientific and technical triumph, providing many thousand jobs directly and indirectly in a time of high unemployment. But the chimneys normally released, day and night, a cloud of sulphur fumes that prevented the regrowth of vegetation on the steep hills that were being denuded by the firewood cutters and blackened by bushfires. Heavy rain on the hills led to drastic erosion of the soil, peat and clay, until only the bare yellow and brown rocks were exposed. A barren and gloomy sight in the dull weather, though sometimes magical in the slanting shafts of winter sunlight, Mount Lyell by 1960 was waiting to become an object lesson, an ignominious exhibit, when the first professional ecologists arrived.

Among the new Australian migrants, more women than men were impressed by the wildflowers, the distant blue ranges, the tree blossoms and native birds. But in the nineteenth century even the female enthusiasts disliked many Australian landscapes. Louise Meredith, a skilled writer and watercolour artist, happily depicted native berries and wildflowers in watercolour, but she was disheartened by segments of Tasmania's landscape. 'Our way lay through the forest, dark, dismal, and dreary as ever,' she wrote. Other travellers were disappointed because – we now know – nearly all the perennial native plants were evergreens, thus depriving Australia of the rich coloured autumn they had known at home. In the words of a professor of botany, Australia had only one 'truly deciduous, autumn-colouring tree', the stately southern beech or *Nothofagus*, still be seen by hikers in the wet mountains of Tasmania.

An earlier nature movement had enlisted artists and intellectuals. Signposts of that crusade were the birth of the Boy Scouts in 1907 – its success in Australia was spectacular – and the new but minority respect for the art of Arnhem Land. The choice of the Southern Cross as the emblem on the Australian flag in 1902 was partly a statement of respect for the majesty of the heavens and the night sky. In that same decade many primary schools in Victoria and New South Wales, by instructing children about native birds, discouraged the boys' sport of stealing eggs from nests. The Gould League of Bird Lovers, with Alfred Deakin as its president in Victoria, gained a large junior membership spread across much of the nation. Schoolteachers, the most formidable green advocates, were essentially 'light greens', believing that certain gems of nature must be preserved but that economic development must also have priority.

In the period from 1880 to 1920, birds especially needed human guardians. Feathers became favoured ornaments on women's hats in the Western world. A wedding party or formal fete displayed a tiny forest of feathers of many colours. Australia was a big exporter of birds' feathers, whole flocks being killed for their plumage, while its colony in Papua sent each year to European milliners tens of thousands of gaudy feathers from birds of paradise. Nature lovers, denouncing this carnage, tried to persuade the singer Nellie Melba to curb her appetite for feathered hats. Though she refused, she explained that she loved native birds and even in childhood knew their distinctive melodies. On Bird Day in 1911 – a new celebration adopted from Oil City in Pennsylvania – Melba exclaimed to the children of Australia her delight in 'the chatter and song of birds'. The feathers in her hat were seen to nod gravely as the spoke.

Other threats arrived unexpectedly. Teams of camels, imported as carriers but replaced in the 1920s by motor trucks, were abandoned in the dry outback where they multiplied as roaming pests. Cane toads imported into Queensland sugarcane farms in the 1930s to solve one problem became themselves the problem; and in the next seventy years they walked west across the continent until finally they reached the huge Ord River reservoir. The African boneseed plant and its vivid yellow flower – with five to eight petals – became a pest in one district while the serrated tussock, a South American native first identified in the Yass Valley near Canberra in 1935, became noxious in another. The crown-of-thorns starfish, its population exploding occasionally, was endangering the coral in parts of the Great Barrier Reef. Albatrosses, those graceful ocean birds, were soon to be endangered by Japanese fishing-line techniques in the Southern Ocean.

9

Lists of endangered or rare species were a product of the twentieth century. Two dinosaur ants, found near the Great Australian Bight in Western Australia in 1932, were believed to be the most primitive ants in the world. Dark honey in colour, they were thought to resemble the very ancient ants that had slowly evolved from the wasps about 100 million years ago. For almost half a century a search for more dinosaur ants was a failure. It seemed that finally the species had died out. At last, in the 1970s, another tiny colony of dinosaur ants was found at Poochera, in the South Australian wheat belt. They resembled at first glance a glossy earthmoving machine; and in their humble way they are earthmovers. To scholars of the ant they are the most intriguing living species in the world, to be kept alive at almost any cost. As this land possessed, because of its long physical isolation, a unique mix of flora and fauna, the number of potential extinctions was very high in 50 000 BC and is still high.

In the late 1960s fresh voices offered high praise for nature. They proclaimed that it was ancient, pure, mysterious and majestic, like a god. Campaigns to save 'the environment' arose almost monthly. When in 1969 the Little Desert in western Victoria was about to be converted into farms, a blast of public criticism halted a scheme that would have been praised ten years earlier. In Tasmania plans to create large hydroelectric schemes and turn valleys into dams aroused indignation. There, separate crusades attempted to save the beautiful little Lake Pedder in the early 1970s and the raging Franklin River one decade later. Those protesting against the submerging of the freshwater lake and its beaches formed Australia's first green political party which, fighting an election in Tasmania in 1972, lost heavily.

The new woodchip industry provoked protesters into chaining themselves to bulldozers or a tree about to be felled. From the oil-searchers the Great Barrier Reef, a world treasure, had to be protected. Further south the mining of rare minerals on Fraser Island was prohibited in order to protect the exotic lakes sitting in the sand dunes. The hunting of whales – an industry commencing in the convict era – was now denounced as cruel and pointless. The last whaling station, at Cheyne Beach near Albany, was closed in 1978. Australia held the world's largest reserves of rich uranium, but most schemes to extract the uranium were officially banned. New dams were said to be harming the environment unduly, and a notable era of dam building came to an end in the 1980s. The highly variable climate of Australia soon challenged the wisdom of a ban on new reservoirs.

The Snowy Mountains Scheme, the engineering pride of the nation when completed in 1974, was now regarded in some circles with suspicion, for in the spirit of the time it had been designed without seeking the official advice of even one overall expert on the environment. The waters of mighty rivers had been diverted without a thought for the future of native wildlife and vegetation sustained by the flowing waters. By 2001 these neglected rivers had won new friends. A plan was afoot to rob irrigation townships in the interior of a percentage of the water they had 'stolen' from the Snowy River.

Somehow the idea spread, especially to the United States, that kangaroos would soon be extinct. An estimate is now made annually of red and the eastern grey kangaroos, and in 2011 the population reached 34 million without counting those in Victoria and Tasmania. In short, there were more kangaroos than people. As if to deepen the blame on modern Australians, the Aborigines were enthroned as perpetual nature lovers. David Suzuki, the Canadian ecologist, in wild words described Australia since 1788 as not 'a heroic history' but a sordid, greedy tragedy, and an arrogant contrast to the older Aboriginal cultures 'so exquisitely evolved to live in rich harmony with the land'.

The wilderness, once a word expressing fear or scorn, became one of praise. Gravely deficient in national parks and nature reserves in 1900, Australia was on its way to becoming a huge nature reserve by the end of the century, if the Aboriginal-owned lands are added in. The largest wildlife reserve, the Tanami Desert Wildlife Sanctuary, covered 3 753 000 hectares and had the rare advantage that it was 'ungrazed by cattle or sheep and relatively free of rabbits, foxes and feral cats'.

Green political parties, under various names, flourished. As in Germany, they readily held a foothold in those Australian parliaments that were elected by a system of proportional representation rather than by single-member electorates. Thus, Tasmania was the first nursery for Green politicians. In 2010 the Greens gained, and held for three years, the balance of power in Canberra.

While some crusades in Australia were local, the whole world was sometimes in peril. The fear, mistakenly disseminated by the

Club of Rome in the early 1970s, that the world was quickly running out of minerals and even adequate food boosted the green movement. From the mid-1980s, the fear of global warming and climate change became widespread. As Australia's prosperity relied partly on coal and iron ore, and as some of the world's largest steelworks and coal-fired power stations imported their raw materials from Australia, any decision to reduce fossil fuels and the emissions of carbon dioxide had deep economic and political effects. On this question, as shown in the federal elections of 2007, 2010 and 2013, the people were more divided in Australia than in any European nation.

CHAPTER TWENTY-FOUR

Wide spaces and
deep silences

In 1940, no Aborigine was famous nationally, and the few who were talked about within a state were usually sports players. Public spending on them was small compared to that spent on the original peoples of New Zealand, the United States or Canada. In the published histories of Australia few pages were devoted to them, and their arrival in this land was believed to be recent.

Few politicians spoke about their plight. In the wartime parliament in Canberra the only resolute advocate of a new deal had been Dr Archie Grenfell Price, a South Australian geographer and historian who was a loyal supporter of Menzies. After losing his seat in the landslide victory by Labor in the election of 1943, Price penned a short national history, a wartime paperback in which he deplored 'the destruction of native pride of life, ambition, religion, culture and customs'.

In national life the Aborigines were just a footnote. While the bright national goal of 'postwar reconstruction' filled report after report in Canberra, Aborigines were rarely mentioned.

Ever since the 1850s many Aborigines were entitled to vote but after 1901 the laws were less welcoming, even in sympathetic states such as South Australia and Victoria. At Australian polling booths the Maori generally were the more welcome. Some Aborigines were legally allowed to vote, but could not confidently enter a polling booth if they were inhabitants of Western Australia, Queensland or the Northern Territory. But after the Second World War the franchise was liberalised, step by step. Aboriginal ex-servicemen won the right to vote federally in 1949, as did adult Aborigines living in the four states where they were already enfranchised for state elections. Nearly all adults who had no vote at federal elections were granted it in 1962.

2

In the first half of the twentieth century the Aborigines were not united nor easily defined. One small group consisted of those who had not yet seen a white face or seen one only in the last thirty years. Their nomadic way of life was doomed but they were no longer doomed as a people: by the 1930s the nation's Indigenous population was increasing after a long decline. A second group lived in government reserves or on Christian mission stations. Most were fed and clothed by their custodians, but often lacked freedoms. They tended to preserve facets of their traditional culture and crafts, and even their spiritual beliefs though they mingled them with Christianity. Many of those living on missions were formally educated, and some of the new generation of articulate Aboriginal leaders gained from this schooling.

A third group – possibly the largest – contributed to the Western-style economy. Many of those in the tropics worked on vast pastoral properties and mustered the cattle or drove them long distances to the nearest port or mining town. Their pay was low but often their whole extended family received free flour, tea, sugar, beef and one or two of the other Western items that Aborigines liked. In Australia's temperate zone they could be counted in the tens of thousands. They worked as shearers, fence-builders, rabbit trappers, kangaroo-hunters, and pickers of fruit and peas and other summer crops, but less than half worked the whole year. Seasonal work was their speciality.

A host of people who today call themselves Aborigines would not have been so called in 1960. They were well along the road to assimilation, partly because they lived close to European families, worked alongside them and often married into them. Many had the rights of the typical Australian citizen. Today, similar people gladly identify as Aborigines.

3

Could so-called 'primitive' people produce 'great' works of art? In the wartime years of 1941–43 the appreciation of Aboriginal art increased after a small exhibition mainly of bark paintings toured the United States and Canada. Melbourne, too, was organising the most comprehensive collection of Aboriginal art so far seen in a public museum or art gallery, and it included one of those Wandjina figures that now spark wonder among tourists in the Kimberley. The aesthetic qualities of Aborigines were praised in the catalogue written by a Jewish refugee from Nazi Germany, Leonhard Adam.

The word 'primitive', still used to label such art, was to alter its meaning and become gilt-edged. Albert Namatjira became the first star in the modern story of Aboriginal art. An initiated member of the Western Arrernte people, he was baptised as a Lutheran at

Hermannsburg mission and nurtured later as an artist. Under the tuition of a visiting Victorian Rex Battarbee, the talented Namatjira learned to paint with watercolours. His purple-headed mountains bathed in brilliant light became so popular in public galleries that in 1954 he was flown from Alice Springs to Canberra to meet Queen Elizabeth II during her initial royal tour. Perhaps his work was liked because it seemed more accessible and less traditional in style, but in fact he tended to paint places that had spiritual significance for his kinsfolk.

About 150 kilometres from Hermannsburg was Papunya, and the two outback places had personal Aboriginal as well as Lutheran ties. A few women and men at Papunya were artists – Billy Stockman painted boomerangs and sold them to visiting American servicemen in the war – long before a young schoolteacher, Geoffrey Bardon, arrived from Sydney in 1971. He taught local people to use acrylic paint and canvas boards instead of the traditional ochres and pipeclays, and he fostered a school of painting that eventually invaded city art markets. At the Aboriginal settlement of Yuendumu, women raised so much money by selling their paintings that their new four-wheel-drive truck, ideal on the rough roads, was the envy of many. Eventually in the Northern Territory, more Aborigines than other people were making a satisfying living by selling their art.

4

Australia for the first time had a powerful federal politician, Paul Hasluck – by profession a journalist, historian and diplomat – with personal knowledge of the varieties of Aboriginal life. From 1951 to 1963, under Menzies as prime minister, Hasluck had ministerial charge of Papua New Guinea as well as the Northern Territory, where the percentage of Aborigines in the total population was higher than in any other Australian region. Hasluck's policy – the sympathetic assimilation of Aborigines – was surely right for the time, though much criticised later by activists who enthusiastically put forward their own formula, only to see it falter or fail.

It was towards the end of Hasluck's reign that the campaign for land rights found a persuasive voice. At the western end of the Gulf of Carpentaria, on an Aboriginal reserve near the Methodist mission at Yirrkala, plans were made to quarry bauxite as the basis for a big aluminium industry. In August 1963, in protest at the plans to exploit their land, thirteen leaders of the Yolngu people sent a petition to the federal parliament in the form of two bark paintings. Vividly decorated in ochres by experienced local artists, the Marika family of Yirrkala to the fore, the bark displayed the local sand dunes, tropical clouds, and such totemic creatures as snakes, goannas, possums, night birds, fish and dugong, all of which might be dislodged by the opening of a big bauxite mine. Attached to each strip of bark were petitions typed on white paper. Now prized as vital documents in the nation's history, the bark messages are displayed alongside a rare copy of Magna Carta in a ceremonial hall in Parliament House in Canberra.

Another significant claim for land was organised on the other side of the continent. In 1967 many of the Gurindji people went on strike at a British-owned cattle station at Wave Hill, about 600 kilometres south of Darwin. Led by the likeable Vincent Lingiari, they formally laid claim to part of Wave Hill, 'of which we were dispossessed in time past, and for which we received no recompense'. The strikers were soon depicted while planting their own garden at nearby Wattie Creek so that they could be self-sufficient while the strike went on. The publicity was persuasive on world television, though the garden itself would hardly have fed forty hens. Their claim – supported by the federal Labor Party, then in opposition – eventually succeeded, and Aborigines throughout the nation rejoiced.

Sometimes people become more radical when their conditions actually begin to improve. The irritant that had led to the strike at Wave Hill was a decision of the Arbitration Commission that promised equal pay to black stockmen within three years. For some thousands of outback people it proved to be a mottled victory. Most cattle stations in that difficult terrain, unable to afford such an increase in wages, cut back their worforce, and replaced them with employees who could use motorbikes, helicopters and other machines. Likewise the long semitrailers or 'road trains' carried to market the cattle that had once been driven – a few kilometres a day – by drovers with their horses and dogs.

Torres Strait Islanders adapted more easily to a Western way of work. Many moved to mainland Queensland and others galvanised a Western Australian mining region. In 1968, in one of the biggest railway projects in the nation's history, six teams were laying a long railway from Port Hedland to the new iron-ore mine and township at Mount Newman. To meet the deadlines each team worked a ten-hour day and used the most mechanised methods of laying down the sleepers and the steel rails. One team of 137 men – mostly migrants from Italy, Yugoslavia, Greece and Portugal and including forty or more Torres Strait Islanders – recorded an amazing day. On 8 May 1968 they laid, spiked and anchored 7 kilometres of new track – far above the previous record made in the United States. The Islanders were a vital part of that team.

The campaign for land rights was paralleled in New South Wales by a call for civil rights. In 1965 young people from Sydney set out on a bus tour designed to expose the inferior status of mixed-race Aborigines living on the fringe of country towns. Many of these people – unemployed for most of the year – knew the inside of the local gaol whenever they were declared to be drunk and disorderly. In some towns Aborigines were confined to a section of the local picture theatre, and excluded from the town's main swimming pool. It was a mild version of apartheid, though it was accompanied by a welfare system unknown in South Africa.

Individual Aborigines were jumping over barriers. In the mid-1960s, Lionel Rose won a world boxing championship, Pastor Lazarus Lamilami from the Goulburn Islands became the first Indigenous ordained minister in the nation's Methodist Church; and David Malangi, a Yolngu man, made the distinctive Aboriginal design, chosen (at first without his knowledge) for the inaugural $1 note, on which the Queen's portrait also stood. In 1966 Margaret Valadian in Brisbane and Charles Perkins in Sydney were the first Aborigines to graduate from university, and each was to become influential in national affairs two decades later. Valadian courageously warned in 1989 that the policy of allowing Aborigines to depend largely on the welfare state was intensely damaging to their physical health and morale. 'Collectively,' she said of her former Brisbane community, 'we are much worse off than we were even twenty years ago.' They had been indoctrinated into feeling that they were sheer victims, with no future. Her diagnosis, now respected, was then far ahead of its time.

5

Canberra began to pursue reforms. The Liberal government led by Harold Holt resolved that the Commonwealth constitution should be changed to allow Canberra, rather than the states, to be the main financier and legislator in Aboriginal affairs. A referendum to alter the constitution was held on 27 May 1967. People in each of the six states voted overwhelmingly for the 'yes' case. Aboriginal leaders rejoiced, seeing it as a vote of confidence. It is still hailed by most newspapers and history textbooks as a triumphant day in Australia's history, and in a real sense it was.

The referendum might not have succeeded if the voters had glimpsed what could flow from their verdict. As is the practice, all voters received in the post an official statement explaining why they should vote yes. It is fair to say that the statement, looked at more closely, was not very accurate. Moreover they received no arguments as to why they should think of voting no. They did not realise, nor had they been told officially, that the 'yes' vote might increase other powers and duties of the Commonwealth at the expense of the states. It could increase them not only in Aboriginal affairs but also in the control of mines, lands and rural industries – a control that would certainly be opposed in the big resource-rich states such as Western Australia. This suggests that if most voters in 1967 could have foreseen or glimpsed the long-term outcome, they might have hesitated to vote yes.

In essence the people's verdict on the main question was wise. It was vital that the Commonwealth should become involved in Aboriginal affairs. The missing questions were: how much should it be involved, and in what ways?

Another unexpected effect of the referendum emerged after several years. The more traditional definition of an Aborigine – held firmly in the minds of most Australians who voted in 1967 – was later widened by the federal bureaucracy and by most judges in the major courts. Henceforth Australians with a small fraction of Aboriginal ancestry – though a 'trivial' part was sometimes excluded – could declare themselves to be Aborigines, so long as they identified with and were accepted by one of the hundreds of Aboriginal communities.

On the same referendum day the people voted emphatically in favour of deleting another controversial section in the constitution, which, in the eyes of many commentators, seemed to state or imply that since 1901 Aborigines were not worthy of being counted as 'real' Australians. Why this section or clause, no. 127, should have been so interpreted is a puzzle. It had been originally inserted in the constitution mainly to solve a question of how to apportion 'surplus' federal revenue among the states. In fact Aborigines had been counted, often with difficulty, again and again in national censuses, including one count conducted less than six years before the 1967 referendum.

After the war the ranks of Aborigines, for long in decline, were growing quickly. In 1961 the national census had counted 79 000 full-blood and half-caste Aborigines, divided almost equally between the two categories. Another 10 000 were 'out of contact' on the week of the census and presumably were not included. The 5200 Torres Strait Islanders were counted separately. With the new definition prevailing, and with growing ethnic pride, the official Indigenous population was to soar, passing half a million early in the new century. It is now about 3 per cent of the total Australian population.

6

The 1960s witnessed an Aboriginal renaissance. Archaeologists and allied researchers enjoyed a golden age. Rhys Jones, a Welsh migrant, sparked the study of the Tasmanian Aborigines, and John Mulvaney the archaeologist completed the first ancient history of the people of this land. Jim Bowler, a scientist from a farming family in Gippsland, discovered at Lake Mungo in New South Wales the remains of a young Aboriginal women who had been ceremonially cremated so long ago that the date at first was unbelievable. Bowler next found the remains of an ancient Aboriginal man who had been ceremonially buried, also near Lake Mungo. So the history of Australia in the space of a few years was pushed back to 30 000 and even 40 000 years, and is now seen by many scholars as closer to 60 000 years.

In August 1971, amid the excitement fanned by Lake Mungo, Senator Neville Bonner, a Liberal, became the first Indigenous person to sit in the federal parliament. His mother was Aboriginal and his father was an English migrant who eventually returned home. Bonner's birthplace was just south of the Queensland border, near the mouth of the Tweed River. It was, he recalled, 'under a palm tree that still stands among the lantana bushes in the blacks' camp, that my mother gave birth to me'. His mother's bed was a government-issued blanket spread on the earth.

Events in the United States stirred Aboriginal leaders. In Washington the Rev. Dr Martin Luther King seemed to speak on behalf of Australia's 'Deep North' as well as his own 'Deep South'. His message eventually stirred young people in the Sydney suburb of Redfern. Erecting a 'tent embassy' on the lawns fronting Parliament House in Canberra in 1972, their clever gesture publicised their call for land rights. Here too flew the new Aboriginal flag, in black and red and yellow, devised by Harold Thomas, an Aboriginal painter who admired Goya, Delacroix and other Western artists. Gough Whitlam, soon to be prime minister, visited the Tent Embassy with his wife, Margaret, just when he was finalising his plan of handing to Aborigines 'their lost power of self-determination in economic, social and political affairs'. In his three years in high office (1972–75) Whitlam also laid plans – implemented by his Liberal successor – to confer vast areas of the Northern Territory on local groups.

By the 1980s a new Aboriginal freedom of choice was visible. More families had moved from cattle stations to the fringes of towns, while others, returning to their traditional homelands, had created several hundred townships in the Northern Territory and the remote parts of Western Australia. There was no economic basis, however, for these small townships that were among the most isolated in the land. And who was to provide for a mere fifty or 300 inhabitants the social services and professional skills, let alone the fresh water, electricity, police station, airport and roads?

The pace of change, including the new freedom, was exciting or bewildering. Max Griffiths, watching the revolution unfolding in remote settlements and camps, marvelled at the high expectations aroused. To give people 'within the space of a few short years and in unparalleled measure' such a set of roles, duties and challenges, and to think that they could quickly absorb and shape them was, 'to use a contemporary expression, a "big ask"'.

In 1991 a royal commission reported on the chaos in many of these remote settlements, both new and old. The poor health and the wasted lives of many inhabitants – and the high suicide rate if they went to prison – were documented in some 5000 pages. The report disproved the accusation that Aborigines were likely to die in prison as the result of 'foul play' by prison warders or police. In fact an abnormal number of Aboriginal prisoners died in prison – of sickness or suicide – simply because they formed an abnormal proportion of Australia's prison population. Many of their crimes were not minor but involved violence, especially against their own women.

The health of many Aborigines remained appalling. They were especially prone to kidney disease and rheumatic heart disease, cancer, pneumonia, bronchitis, and ear and eye diseases. Diabetes became widespread – perhaps it did not exist in the continent

2000 years ago. Scabies – painful rashes of the skin caused by a mite – were common. Many people were overweight because of their fatty and sugary diet; their old way of life based on hunting and gathering fresh food each day had given them a more balanced diet, and required mental and physical energy. The rash of diseases and disabilities owed much to malnutrition in infancy and early childhood.

Many Aboriginal babies were underweight, and remained malnourished in their first crucial years. Without a refrigerator it was impossible to preserve milk and other fresh foods in such a hot climate. In the crowded living conditions 'many of the bacterial infections were sustained indefinitely', wrote Professor John D. Mathews of Darwin, a dedicated researcher in this field. Moreover outback schools, despite heavy spending, were marked by absenteeism and poor results. In India it was realised that to educate the potential mothers was to improve the health of their babies and young children. This gateway to better health was rarely open in Aboriginal townships.

Success created failure. People could afford more cigarettes than before, and heavy smoking impaired their lungs – and half of the pregnant women were smokers. Unlimited freedom to drink alcohol, recently conferred, led to alcoholism and to more domestic violence. Fortunately some Aboriginal women took the lead, and by the year 2000 the heart of the temperance movement in the nation had moved from prosperous suburbs in big cities to certain Aboriginal townships where 'prohibition' was the local rule, though not easy to enforce.

A quiet revolution in health was initiated at townships in the arid north-west of South Australia, where the women of Nganampa Health Council began systematically to improve nutrition and infant health, with Dr Paul Torzillo of Sydney guiding them.

A vital precaution against infectious diseases was to give each baby twelve different immunisations in its first two years. In most remote and small townships, however, the amenities in health and education were poor. Labor's minister for health, Graham Richardson, after touring five remote hovel towns in 1995, was dismayed: 'they would barely be tolerated in a war-ravaged African nation, let alone here'.

Indigenous people still have a lower life expectancy than other Australians. Those living in Western Australia and the Northern Territory have the poorest health, and their life expectancy at birth is about the same as that of India and Papua New Guinea, though superior to that of nearly all African nations. In contrast in New South Wales, which has the largest Indigenous population in the nation, Aboriginal children born this year can expect to live much longer. Their life expectancy, while not impressive, is higher than those of Russia and the Ukraine. It is also higher than that of the typical white Australian child born in 1975, such is the advance of medical knowledge. The typical Aboriginal family did not live in these remote places. Most lived in cities or the larger towns – 40 000 lived in Sydney. They might be proudly Aboriginal but most married outside their race and culture and knew no Indigenous language. With scant knowledge of a traditional Aboriginal religion, they were as Christian or secular as the mainstream Australian families.

The campaign for land rights, moving rapidly in the 1970s, was most successful in the Northern Territory and South Australia. The Hawke Government, in power from 1983 to 1991, promised land rights to Aborigines across the nation but soon feared the loss of political influence in Western Australia and Queensland if it carried out the promise.

Then the High Court of Australia intervened: in the opinion of radical lawyers it had to intervene to solve a national crisis that parliament itself would not tackle. It was not the first entry of the High Court into what was essentially parliament's domain, but it was a more spectacular entry than any made in the first century of federation.

A dispute in the Torres Strait Islands, where Eddie Mabo was the symbolic claimant to land, provided the opportunity. The High Court, in confirming his right to land under what became known as 'native title', extended that same principle to mainland Australia. One judge, Sir Daryl Dawson, dissented from the other six, and even those six tended to disagree on several of the main reasons for their decision, while agreeing emphatically and sometimes eloquently that land must be granted or returned. According to two of the written judgements, the dispossessing of Aborigines from their land was the most shameful act in the nation's history.

In most regions of Australia, Aborigines initially cheered at the High Court's decision. It was one of the proudest days in their history.

After the High Court had made its judgement, the prime minister, Paul Keating, had to act, but first he spoke. On 10 December, in Redfern Park in Sydney, he addressed mainly an Aboriginal audience but the whole nation eventually heard his message. Keating seemed to pour the entire blame on mainstream Australians for the Aborigines' plight today: they were the only guilty ones. But his speech, written in crisp, persuasive prose by the historian Don Watson, ended positively: 'We are beginning to learn what the Indigenous people have known for many thousands of years – how to live with our physical environment. Ever so gradually, we are learning how to see Australia through Aboriginal eyes, beginning to recognise the wisdom contained in their epic story. I think we are beginning to see how much we owe the Indigenous Australians and how much we have lost by living so apart.'

In the following year, after listening to leading Aborigines, he began to push through the federal parliament a Native Title Act. The opposition parties fought against all its clauses. In the history of the Senate no previous Act had been debated for so many days and nights. Near midnight, on 21 December 1993, it was passed. Outside and inside, loud cheering could be heard. Across the nation the cheering – and the voices of protest – went on for months.

Another vast area of Australia was opened up for Aborigines as claimants. By 2015 at least 33 per cent of the nation's land was owned or part-owned by Aborigines under recent laws and titles. Most of the land returned to them under native title was poor and much was valueless under present economic conditions, but some was potentially rich in minerals. Perhaps 100 000 Aborigines had an interest in one or other of these lands, but no single portion could be subdivided or sold. Fortunately the new laws did enable a scattering of Aboriginal groups to gain royalties from a local mine, once it was producing, and also well-paid jobs and even business contracts.

Disappointed were those whose Aboriginal ancestors had once owned the sites of the capital cities and the vast fertile plains but – being the first to be uprooted – had lost contact with their original land. They gained little from the new law. In contrast the winners were those who still inhabited the far outback and retained continuing links with their ancestral lands. Their advantage was to have been conquered last. The inequity and complexity fed a lawyers' picnic.

For several decades there had been a widespread and learned opinion in favour of Aborigines reclaiming significant areas of land. But the question of how to identify and then make use of these lands was perplexing. It had not been solved by the High Court when it presented to parliament a communal and rigid system of land tenure that was not useful for the twenty-first century.

Amid the initial jubilation the clock, supposedly put forward, perhaps had been stopped or even turned back. Gary Johns, one of Paul Keating's ministerial colleagues, examining the outcome of native title after two decades, concluded that it had created exceedingly high expectations. On the whole, however, the new law had so far 'failed to deliver on these expectations'.

The expectations of reshaping Indigenous life, once so low, were now high. The thought arose – an unimaginable idea a century ago – of offering the 'The First People' a humble apology. Perhaps the whole nation should apologise for all the wrongs and hurt and even for the good intentions derailed; and yet a national apology could sometimes slide into self-righteousness and become a veiled attack on a nation's earlier leaders and citizens. Furthermore the making of grand sermonical speeches was less an Australian than an American passion. It was Rose Scott, an elderly feminist who watching in Sydney the unveiling of her portrait by Sir John Longstaff in 1922, had remarked that 'we Australians are a great people for liberty, for wide spaces and deep silences'.

Towards the very end of the century the call for a national speech of apology became loud, but John Howard as prime minister offered his own reasons for making no official apology, though he had expressed his 'sorry' personally, and the individualist Indigenous leader Noel Pearson had even praised Howard's gesture. But on 13 February 2008, in Parliament House in Canberra, Kevin Rudd as new prime minister delivered on behalf of the Australian nation a long apology. 'Words alone are not that powerful,' Rudd said late in his speech. Actions count, he insisted. It is time for 'new approaches to enduring problems'. It is surely time 'for fresh ideas to fashion the nation's future'. And yet most of the fresh ideas – it was observed – had already been tried.

Indigenous grievances and disadvantages still permeated the media. The main political parties were willing to pour in more money in the hope of solving or easing them. Less visible on the television were the successes. Most Aborigines did not live in the outback but inhabited provincial towns and big cities and increasingly belonged to mainstream Australian life. In cities and regional areas – but excluding the Northern Territory and far interior – four in every ten Indigenous families owned their house or were in the process of buying it. Even in Canberra with its expensive real estate, four in every ten were house owners. In the nation as a whole large numbers belonged to the teaching, legal, medical and other professions, worked in the public service, sat on countless government committees and boards and presided over major institutions. At least 11 000 – and possibly 14 000 – Indigenous students are enrolled in universities. In parliaments and public debate, in visual arts and literature, Indigenous names now stand out. Aborigines are celebrated participants in various major sports, and possibly the most admired athlete in the nation is Cathy Freeman, who won the 400 metres race at the Sydney Olympics in 2000. While assimilation is an unfashionable word, it goes on and on.

CHAPTER TWENTY-FIVE

Sails and anchors

The population has trebled since the Second World War, growing at a quicker pace than any nation in Europe. A frequent prediction is that it will double to fifty million before the century is over. Not for the first time has such optimism prevailed. The faith in the merits and likelihood of a high population were widely held in 1890, but then wavered or faded for half a century.

The rise and fall of national prosperity followed a similar pattern. By 1890 the typical Australian had for many years enjoyed the highest standard of living in the world. In the following half-century Australia lagged, and would not return to a very high place on that international ladder until after the Second World War. In the early 2000s Australia prospered even more, with an astonishing price for its coal and its iron ore shipped to China. Only after that spectacular surge of prosperity disappeared did Australians fully awake to the sense of how fortunate they had been.

Australia is now more than a middle-sized power. 'Our economy is the twelfth largest in the world,' argues one authority on international affairs. 'Our people are the fifth-richest.' They are also a major supplier of food to the world and have created one of the three largest and most diverse mineral industries. Huge bulk-carriers ply the sea routes from Australia, which now operates some of the world's largest cargo ports, measured by tonnage of cargo handled each year.

From time to time Australians have envisaged their nation becoming a second United States. That was a dream during the boom of the 1880s. Four decades earlier the German-born explorer Ludwig Leichhardt, after first seeing Sydney, decided that 'this rich country' would reward able migrants: 'And it is through them that a powerful state will gradually arise, a state which may possibly consign old Europe to oblivion.' To see Australia rivalling Europe in the far future was a breathtaking prediction.

Despite the rapid growth of population Australia remains sparsely settled. Huge areas are semi-desert, and deserted too. The Northern Territory is a rival to Greenland as one of the most thinly peopled regions on the globe.

2

The nation's two big cities are surprisingly large. If inserted on a population map of the British Isles, they will fill second and third place, though well behind London. Few pairs of rival cities, anywhere, have competed so closely for so long as Sydney and Melbourne. Since 1850, on the eve of the gold rushes, the two cities have often run neck and neck, and are still close rivals. In June 2014 Sydney held 4.6 million people and Melbourne 4.2 million, Sydney having recently lost part of its lead because the statisticians decreed that the Central Coast was not yet part of Sydney's urban sprawl. Melbourne is now growing the faster. One competitive advantage is that its outer suburbs, not so hemmed in by rugged mountain ranges, have valuable land to spare. Both cities, founded as tent villages, have become home to clusters of skyscrapers and high apartment buildings. Despite the multiplying of traffic jams in the last ten years, they are still classed among the world's ten most liveable cities. In coming decades that honour is more likely to be captured by Adelaide or Perth or Hobart or Canberra, for smaller cities tend to be more liveable.

Most Australians, except perhaps Indigenous peoples, usually want a large population. From 1840 to 1970 it was almost an axiom. Today a sizeable minority, articulate and politically active, wish for a smaller population. They dream of a Green Australia.

The population is overwhelmingly anchored to the coastline. The largest inland city, Canberra, holds fewer than 500 000 people. Australians are also overwhelmingly inhabitants of the southern half of the continent, where all the large cities stand. Tropical Australia – with four-tenths of the land area – has only recently acquired a cluster of middling cities, none of which approaches 200 000 people. Townsville, the largest, is followed by Cairns and Darwin, Mackay and Rockhampton. Four of the five are in Queensland, all are ports, and most now grow at a faster pace than Sydney.

Minerals and tourism have boosted tropical Australia in the last half-century, but the huge region holds only a tiny fraction of the nation's people. While it is closest to Asia it does not attract Asian migrants; they prefer the big cities further south. While tropical Australia is now the home of most of the large mines, a fresh mining town – compared to those of the nineteenth century – attracts few permanent residents.

An Australian scholar who has long lived overseas believes that one day his homeland will 'be a major, unique force in Asia', but first it must try to populate the crucial points on its long, empty northern coastline. 'We cannot', adds Ross Terrill, 'extend our role in Asia until our north is dotted with cities, railways, natural-gas pipelines, and world-class holiday resorts.' For Australia and its civilisation, the time is still 'early morning'.

Australia's future for much of the twentieth century seemed to lie in manufacturing, essentially a city and town activity. But the high tariff on imports was slowly pulled down after the 1960s, and the long-protected economy has been flung open and globalised, and the billboards and placards proclaiming 'Buy Australian' have disappeared. Newcastle, north of Sydney, was the showplace of that old smokestack nation, and an appealing scene at night for those who applauded the sight of furnaces glowing. There the extensive Broken Hill Proprietary steelworks were closed in 1999, a sentimental and symbolic event contrasting the pride surrounding their opening in 1915.

The main artery of the nation is the Hume Highway, linking Sydney and Melbourne and offering a short detour to Canberra. New South Wales and Victoria have long been the hub of political power, but now are challenged by the resource-rich states of Queensland and Western Australia, which together occupy more than half of the continent. In 1860 they held the smallest white population and the largest black population in the six colonies. By 1900 they were glamorous, though in the following forty years they did not quite fulfil their promise. Since 1945 they have usually been pacemakers, growing steadily even when minerals are not booming. Today, their combined population almost equals that of New South Wales. If they maintain that pace of growth, they could well contain almost half of Australia's population in the lifetime of children now starting school.

The nation has become strikingly cosmopolitan in the last forty years. Most migrants in 1950 had come from the British Isles; most migrants in 1970 came from continental Europe, and in 1990 they increasingly came from Asia. At the 2011 census the largest group of overseas-born inhabitants – they formed 21 per cent – were from the United Kingdom, followed by New Zealand with 9 per cent. China and India each was the birthplace of about 6 per cent, with Italy and Vietnam occupying the next rung of the ladder.

Today five of the eight states and territories accept more migrants from India and China than from any other country. China is also the main source of tourists and sends the most foreign students to Australian universities. It is a vital stimulus for the booming building industry in the bigger cities, and absentee Chinese often outbid young Australians at the auctions of houses and apartments. This is one reason why the powerful national dream – to own one's own home – is fulfilled less often than in 1950.

China was slow to become a big buyer of Australian goods. It passed Japan in 1993 as the main buyer of Australian wool, and by 2000 it was also an important buyer of minerals, though far behind Japan. China became the dominant market for Australian minerals just before the global financial crisis arose in 2008. Nothing did more than the Chinese market to cushion Australia in the global downturn that followed.

In many facets of our life China now occupies the place that Britain long occupied. Britain has ceased to be the main source of migrants and tourists, the main trading partner and foreign investor, and the main ally and protector in time of war. It has long ceased to be the main source of new technology. No longer is London the head office of even one major Australian bank: instead Melbourne, for nearly thirty years, was the head office of two banks operating in the British Isles. The enduring political ties with the British Isles were untied, one by one. The last of the governors-general to arrive from Britain, Baron de L'Isle, completed his term of office in 1965.

After Britain's empire ceased to be worldwide, its defence forces and especially its navy were rarely seen east of Suez. After Britain was admitted to the European Union in 1973 most Australian travellers arriving at British airports were, to their dismay, treated as second-class visitors and relegated to a slow-moving queue – in sight of a faster queue occupied in part by citizens of Britain's wartime enemies. Most British visitors suffered the same loss of face after landing at Australian airports. Soon the Whitlam Government set up Australia's own honours system, the Order of Australia, and Whitlam's successors in office – Malcolm Fraser and Bob Hawke – replaced the English national anthem with the nineteenth-century Sydney song 'Advance Australia Fair', the words being officially added to the tune in 1984. Two years later the High Court of Australia became all-powerful, the right of appeal to the Privy Council in London having been abolished.

Our national flag was increasingly criticised as no longer appropriate, for it enclosed a miniature British flag. The critics did not realise that most of the admired flags of the world were also out of date, the white in the flag of the Republic of France, for example, being the colour of the monarchy long since deposed. It was Paul Keating who as prime minister resolved to cut one of the oldest of the remaining ties by making Australia a republic. Already it really was a de facto republic, a crowned republic, for the Queen held only the ceremonial power, but in the eyes of Malcolm Turnbull and the other leaders of the young republican movement even that ceremonial power was outmoded and an affront to an independent nation making its mark in Asia.

Keating's plan seemed to sink when he lost the 1996 federal election to John Howard, a Liberal who was not a republican. But

Howard was willing to keep the topic alive. In the old Parliament House in Canberra in February 1998 was held a major convention that attracted more of Australia's political leaders than were ever assembled at the federal conventions in the 1890s. The more numerous republicans led by Turnbull clearly won the contest. The federal parliament basically endorsed their formula for an Australian republic. Finally in 1999 the formula had to be voted on by the people.

Nearly all newspapers and nearly all Labor politicians supported a republic. Influential Liberal politicians, but not the prime minister, approved. For several years the opinion polls indicated that a republic was almost inevitable. The republicans, however, were increasingly divided, and many seceded from the official crusade because they believed the people and not the politicians should elect the proposed president. Moreover the traditional supporters of the constitutional monarchy were underestimated because they inhabited those regions far removed from Sydney and Melbourne. To many political observers the result of the referendum in November 1999 was a shock. A majority of people in each of the six states voted no. While the republic is no longer a burning topic, the flame is not snuffed.

3

Australians, like most peoples of the world, valued social cohesion. They saw themselves as part of a European civilisation, tied heavily to the English language, law and institutions. Having created one of the world's oldest continuous democracies, they sensed that democracy relied on shared values. In times of crisis the nation's main allies, Britain and then the United States, had shared the same values. On the other hand in Canberra one version of 'multiculturalism' sometimes favoured diversity with the claim it led to unity.

As more and more immigrants came from a wide range of lands, and many came from undemocratic regimes or were members of a less tolerant religious faith, social cohesion could be challenged.

A few European nations showed puzzling evidence of fragmentation. In France, Belgium, Holland and Britain, where Muslim migrants were more numerous than in Australia, it became clear that a tiny, radical and unpersuadable segment of Islam did not believe in toleration. Margaret Thatcher, no longer prime minister of Britain, affirmed in 1995 a belief that would soon become common among the more conservative political leaders: 'If there is now a threat approaching the gravity of the Cold War, it is that of Islamic fundamentalism.' While she respected most of the values of Islam as a religion – it was one of the world's great religions and now the second-largest – she saw grave danger in those small cells of Muslims who did not respect the values of the West. The concepts of toleration and freedom were despised by terrorists, though they made full use of them when necessary.

By the 1980s Muslim migrants from the Middle East had settled in noticeable numbers in a few outer suburbs in Sydney and Melbourne. The smaller mosques were soon packed, giving way to grander buildings. By Australian standards an unusual proportion of the newcomers were unemployed and lived on social welfare; many came as refugees from dysfunctional states or simple rural societies and had few skills that were employable in a nation where the workforce in factories and farms was declining rapidly.

A few important Muslim leaders regretted that Australian society, as they experienced it, defied their beliefs and preachings. In their eyes it was decadent and irreligious. And yet one century earlier, a host of Australian churchgoers would have agreed with the mainstream Muslim suspicion of alcohol, drugs, pornography, party-going, scantily clad women, blasphemous language, suicide, homosexuality and the Sabbath. It was the Christians who, in the following four generations, relaxed their views on these social questions. They became more tolerant at a time when sections of Islam were becoming less tolerant.

The comforting and prevailing belief was that most Muslims would eventually fit, in their own way, into the Western way of life, and it is probably true. But the exceptions, the haters of Western civilisation in its modern form, proved to be formidable.

4

On 11 September 2001 the attack on New York and Washington by hijacked aircraft marked a new step in the offensive conducted by a radical wing of Islam. Australia's prime minister, John Howard, was then visiting Washington. On the previous day he had lunched with President George W. Bush at the White House, and the conversation made 'no mention of terrorism'. On the following morning, about to conduct a press conference, Howard was told by one of his staff that an aircraft had crashed into one of the twin towers at the World Trade Centre in New York. There was even then no thought of terrorism, and Howard thought 'it was probably an accident' until a few minutes later he was told that a second aircraft had hit the other tower. After he had completed the press conference and the room's curtains were opened, smoke could be seen rising from the direction of the Pentagon building, the scene of the third aircraft attack. It was 'the most significant assault on the American homeland since Pearl Harbor', Howard later wrote, and the casualties were even higher in New York and Washington than at the scene of the Japanese attack in 1941.

Howard had to return quickly to Australia, but was told that a complete ban had been imposed on any commercial aircraft leaving the United States. Finally he and his wife, Janette, were permitted to fly in an American military aircraft to Hawaii – 'the first flight from US airspace since the attacks'.

In October 2001 Australia was an ally of the United States when it sent forces to Afghanistan in an attempt to defeat quickly the Taliban. That war, though not fought continuously by Australians, is already the longest in the history of the nation's armed forces. Meanwhile in March 2003 Australian naval vessels, aircraft, helicopters and commandos joined the American-led forces that went to war against the dictatorship in Iraq, on the widely held assumption – later proved to be mistaken – that weapons of mass destruction were concealed there.

The war in Afghanistan provided Islamic sects with an additional justification for attacks on Western civilians. In Bali, the Indonesian holiday island where Muslims form only a minority of inhabitants, Australian tourists became a target. On 12 October 2002, bombs were exploded by Muslim terrorists – followers of al-Qaeda. The death toll of 203 included eighty-eight Australians, in whose honour Prime Minister Howard went to Bali to make a memorable speech. Three years later, at the same resort, fifteen Indonesians, four Australians and one Japanese were killed in another attack by Muslim terrorists. In every raid the wounded outnumbered the dead, and squads of Australian medical specialists were called upon to advise or operate.

Even on local soil some mainstream Muslim migrants or their Australian-born sons planned terrorist attacks. Their secret scheme to trigger an explosion in the crowded Melbourne Cricket Ground at the football grand final between West Coast and Sydney in 2005 was nullified by the authorities and also by the group's inexperience as terrorists. In the same city the busy Crown Casino was a target, once again the attack being thwarted.

Presumably the overwhelming majority of Muslims in Australia did not sympathise with such plans and plots. Thus in December 2014 the tragic capture of innocent Australians, as hostages in a cafe at Martin Place in the heart of Sydney by a murderous extremist, was aided not by fellow Muslims living in that city but directly and indirectly by a chain of mistakes and misjudgements from a range of Australian officials of goodwill who, in positions of authority over many years, gave this potential terrorist numerous benefits of the doubt. Even the senior police at one crucial time on the day and night of the siege gave him, rather than the hostages, special consideration.

The fear, puzzlement and indignation aroused by these attacks and thwarted plans were exceptional. Cities in Australia were very secure, by world standards. History attested to that. Aborigines were relatively safe in early Sydney and Melbourne after they became sizeable towns. The bushrangers of the nineteenth century did not ride on horseback into the cities. No civilian had been killed in a big Australian city by a wartime shell or bomb.

5

For years an intense dispute raged on the question of how to handle humanely but realistically the unexpected arrival of asylum seekers and illegal migrants in aircraft and by ship. The inflow, at first slow, was followed by sudden surges. Eventually many Australians questioned or feared the idea of many refugees and other migrants sidestepping an orderly, relatively generous system of migration and trying to come ashore on a remote coastline or reef, unannounced.

Of the waves of uninvited migrants who arrived in boats since 1976, the first, from Indochina, were small and manageable. In the three years 1999–2001, however, the refugees and others arrived in their thousands. In all, 180 boats conveyed them to the north-western coast or to offshore Australian territories. Most passengers in these frail or unseaworthy vessels were refugees from Iraq and Afghanistan, while others had fled civil war in Sri Lanka. Increasingly the majority were Muslims.

The migration episodes fired heated arguments. The welcomers insisted that Australia had a moral duty and international obligation to accept all refugees. On the other hand Australia was, in relation to the size of its population, already one of the top three welcomers in the world, and willing also to spend heavily on helping refugees year after year to make a new life.

In the second half of 2001, with unauthorised migrants increasing, Howard resolved to intercept and deter such boats. In effect he halted the inflow. The second-longest-serving of all the prime ministers, he was defeated at the 2007 federal election, and his successor, Kevin Rudd, a former diplomat, reversed the policy. Unwittingly he invited such an armada of frail boats, and many deaths at sea, that new deterrents and obstacles had to be devised.

'Stop the boats', one of the most debated slogans in our political history, later appeared in Europe. In 2015 and 2016, the large-scale migration of Middle Eastern and North African refugees and welfare seekers across the narrow seas into the southern ports of the European Union and, at almost the same time, the deadly attacks by Muslim terrorists in Paris, Brussels, Nice and other cities made many European observers think that Howard and one of his likeminded successors, Tony Abbott, had shown political courage and realism in tackling a deepening international dilemma. On such judgements there cannot be unanimity. Democracy is not only government by debate but a necessary incitement to debate.

In Australia it is easy to forget that immigration, or who actually should be selected to come, has been a divisive topic since at least the 1830s when the choice between admitting mainly British convicts or mainly free migrants aroused prolonged debate. That controversy produced the first informal and popular national flag, featuring the stars of the Southern Cross. Designed for the Anti-Transportation League and stitched by Launceston women in 1849, it proclaimed that British convicts must no longer be sent to this inviting land. Debates provoked by Chinese gold-seekers in the 1850s and the fear of an inflow of Japanese and Chinese half a century later, and the more recent arrivals, fit into a long tradition.

One fact of the last seventy years is irrefutable. Though Australia admits annually a high number of migrants, more wish to come than can possibly be provided with jobs, houses, schools, sickbeds, roads, parks, electricity and other amenities. It is one sign of the success of our modern history that, for all its faults, people crave to come here. A nation whose way of life had more faults than merits would not inspire such hope and excitement in the outside world.

6

In 1948, when young, I chanced to be a spectator in the public gallery of the old Parliament House in Canberra. There I looked down with a sense of wonder at the oldest member, the silver-haired Billy Hughes, once prime minister, who had sat in the first federal parliament, which met in 1901. I did not know that then he had often sat close to William Groom, a senior Queensland politician – the 'father of the house' who, as a young English convict in the 1840s, had been transported to Australia for a term of seven years. It shows the brevity of our phase of Australian history that through good fortune I was able to watch a living politician whose parliamentary colleague belonged to the convict era in which the first British settlement at Sydney was created.

Living archaeologists can bridge far wider gaps in time. On Australian soil they uncover the bones of animals and the eggshells of birds that lived twenty or forty thousand years ago and are now extinct, and they can touch the ochres painted on long-dead bodies and unveil rock art originally carved or painted before the last rising of the seas. Such excitement is open to few scholars.

The Indigenous history, unimaginably old, is at least 250 times as long as the British history of Australia. The two histories, however, hold much in common. Both endured or enjoyed relative isolation from the dynamic centres of the wider world. Both the ancient and the modern peoples were vulnerable to a variable climate and to long droughts, but attempted to adapt to them. The sparse peopling of the land was also common to both.

The early people, like the later, were explorers. The first people discovered the land, explored every region, named the distinctive plants and animals and insects, and then came the Europeans who explored it afresh, occupying it, renaming swathes of it and developing new resources and using them not only to benefit themselves but the outside world. That was one startling difference. The land, which in AD 1000 fed and sheltered few, was feeding a host of people in AD 2000. It was also, as an inheritor of Western civilisation and technology, able to afford amenities and lifesaving and pain-killing remedies not imaginable in earlier times.

Much do the two peoples and their history have in common. But when they confronted each other in 1788, and long after, they were far apart. Rarely if ever in the long history of the same land were two peoples so different in cultures, languages, religions, kinships, weapons and economic and social life. And yet it is, for both peoples, a continent of hope and opportunity.

ACKNOWLEDGEMENTS

While researching and writing this book I was helped by many people. Some are specifically mentioned in the 'Notes' that follow. Directly or indirectly some influenced the narrative in other ways. To John Day of Wangaratta, as always, I am grateful for his positive arguments about many themes in this book.

I am indebted to scholars at universities: Jim Bowler, William Coleman, and John Mulvaney of the Australian National University; the late John Hirst of La Trobe University; Bob Birrell, Graeme Davison and Malcolm Kennedy of Monash University; Jeff Borland, John Castles, Katrina Dean the university archivist, Marie Fels, Frank Lees, David Floyd Smith, and the late Stephen Murray-Smith of Melbourne University; and Jim Davidson and Rob Pascoe of Victoria University. For insights and information on a variety of themes I express gratitude to Gideon Haigh, the late S. E. K. Hulme, Q.C., Barry Jones, Peter Jonson, Stuart Kells, Anna Blainey Warner, Tim Warner and Peter Yule of Melbourne; and Paul Kelly, Deryck M. Schreuder and Keith Windschuttle of Sydney. To my wife Ann, I offer special thanks.

For discussions of certain Aboriginal customs, I express gratitude to the late Wandjuk Marika of eastern Arnhem Land, the late Dick Roughsey of Mornington Island in the Gulf of Carpentaria, and Richard Walley of Perth.

On Australian history and current events, I happened to write – during the last forty years – regular columns or frequent articles for newspapers and journals. It is likely that sentences from those writings reappear in this book. I thank the editors of *The Age*, *The Australian* and its weekend supplements, *Australian Book Review*, *Australian Business Monthly*, *Australian Financial Review*, *The Bulletin*, *Melbourne Herald* and *Herald Sun*, *National Times*, *Quadrant*, and *Times Literary Supplement*.

To the team at Penguin Random House I express my gratitude – to my publisher Ben Ball, editors Rachel Scully and Katie Purvis, proofreaders Hilary Reynolds and Amanda Martin, designers John Canty, Alex Ross and Samantha Jayaweera, cartographer Guy Holt and indexer Fay Donlevy. To Rachel Scully I give special thanks.

Geoffrey Blainey
Melbourne, September 2016

NOTES

Abbreviations

ADB	*Australian Dictionary of Biography* (18 vols, Melbourne, 1966–2012, ed. Douglas Pike, Bede Nairn, Geoffrey Serle, John Ritchie, Diane Langmore et al.)
ADBS	*Australian Dictionary of Biography: Supplement, 1580–1980* (2005)
AIA	*Documents on Australian International Affairs 1901–1918* (West Melbourne, 1977, eds Gordon Greenwood & Charles Grimshaw)
AIBR	*Australasian Insurance and Banking Record* (Melbourne, 1877–97)
AND	*The Australian National Dictionary* (Melbourne, 1988, ed. W. S. Ramson)
CEHA	*The Cambridge Economic History of Australia* (Port Melbourne, 2011, eds Simon Ville & Glenn Withers)
CHA	*The Cambridge History of Australia* (2 vols, Melbourne, 2013, eds Alison Bashford & Stuart Macintyre)
CYB	*Official Year Book of the Commonwealth of Australia.* An annual, first published in 1908. The formal title varies slightly.
DAQ	*The Dictionary of Australian Quotations* (Melbourne, 1984, ed. Stephen Murray-Smith)
Fullilove	Michael Fullilove (ed.), *Men and Women of Australia! Our Greatest Modern Speeches* (Melbourne, 2014)
HS	*Historical Studies* (journal, Melbourne, 1940–)
Knight's	*Knight's Cyclopedia of the Industry of All Nations* (London, 1851)
Meaney	Neville Meaney (comp.), *Australia and the World: A Documentary History from the 1870s to the 1970s* (Melbourne, 1985)

NCMH	*The New Cambridge Modern History* (Cambridge, 1967–79)
OCAH	*The Oxford Companion to Australian History* (Melbourne, 1998, eds Graeme Davison, John Hirst & Stuart McIntyre)
SAH	*Sources of Australian History* (London, 1957, ed. Manning Clark)
SDAH	*Select Documents in Australian History 1788–1900* (2 vols, London, 1950, 1955, ed. C. M. H. Clark)
THRA	*Tasmanian Historical Research Association: Papers and Proceedings* (Hobart, 1951–)
VHJ	*Victorian Historical Journal* (Melbourne, 1975–)
VPP	Victorian Parliamentary Papers
Warhaft	Sally Warhaft (ed.), *Well May We Say . . .: The Speeches that Made Australia* (Melbourne, 2014)

In the following notes the very long titles of articles and books are sometimes shortened. Place of publication is not given for books published by mainstream publishers in Australia, and details of publications are not always given in full when they appear in these notes for a second or third time.

1: RUSH TO THE GOLDFIELDS

Beechworth gold: G. Blainey, *The Rush that Never Ended* (2003), p.10.

Californian waterwheel: G. Blainey, 'Gold and governors', *HS*, May 1961, p.345.

Lewis on gold: P. L. Brown (ed.), *Clyde Company Papers* (London, 1963), vol. 5, pp.136, 172.

Gold licence: G. Blainey, 'The gold rushes: the year of decision', *HS*, May 1962, pp.136–9.

Clippers: G. Blainey, *The Tyranny of Distance* (1966), pp.183–6.

Three girls: William Howitt, *Land, Labour, and Gold* (London, 1855), vol. 1, pp.343–6, 352, 386–9.

Price inflation: *CYB*, 1919 (p.1090), 1951 (p.395), 1964 (p.434); W. H. Archer, *Statistical Register of Victoria* (1854), esp. pp.404–6.

Hotham and African slaves: M. C. Hunter, 'The hero packs a punch', *Mariner's Mirror*, August 2006, pp. 287ff.

Guerilla war: Hotham's dispatch, Eureka Documents, Public Record Office Vic., Part 1, n.d., p. 4.

Murder of Scobie: Weston Bate, *Lucky City* (1978), pp. 58–9.

Ballarat's grievances: W. B. Withers, *The History of Ballarat* (2nd edn, Ballarat, 1887), ch. 5; Justin J. Corfield, Dorothy Wickham and Clare Gervasoni (eds), *The Eureka Encyclopaedia* (Ballarat, 2004).

Deaths at Eureka: Geoffrey Serle, *The Golden Age* (1963), p. 168.

Liberal constitutions: *SDAH*, pp. 348–9, 374–5.

Advantage of secret ballot: John Hirst, *Looking for Australia: Historical Essays* (2010), pp. 115, 120; Serle, *The Golden Age*, pp. 208–10, 257.

Patrick Leslie: Eric C. Rolls, *Sojourners* (St Lucia, Qld, 1992), p. 65.

Robe arrivals: Blainey, *The Rush*, pp. 87–8.

Acupuncture: K. M. Bowden, *Goldrush Doctors at Ballarat* (Balwyn, Vic., 1977), ch. 10.

Opium and gambling: Rev. W. Young, 'Report on the Condition of the Chinese Population in Victoria', VPP, 1868, no. 56.

Chinese pride and prejudice: Jean Gittins, *The Diggers from China* (Melbourne, 1981), esp. ch. 1, 2.

Red-headed savages: Mrs Quong Tart (comp. and ed.), *The Life of Quong Tart* (Sydney, 1911), p. 5.

Optimism: Blainey, *Australian Economic History Review*, July 2010, p. 210.

Health and diseases: Alan Atkinson, *The Europeans in Australia* (1997), vol. 2, p. 269; Anthea Hyslop, 'Epidemics', *OCAH*, p. 220; Serle, *The Golden Age*, p. 80.

Tin discoveries: Blainey, *The Rush*, pp. 130–1, 207–9.

Later gold rushes: ibid., ch. 7.

Barrow and France's ambitions: Gerald S. Graham, *Great Britain in the Indian Ocean: A Study of Maritime Enterprise 1810–1850* (Oxford, 1967), esp. p. 424.

2: A NEVER-NEVER LAND

Origins of Never-Never and parallel names: *AND*, esp. pp. 194, 430, 452; William Fairfax (ed.), *Handbook to Australasia* (Melbourne, 1859).

Water for Sturt's horses: Malcolm J. Kennedy, *Hauling the Loads* (1992), p. 63. Kennedy's book is an outstanding practical guide to the explorers' needs and troubles.

Land explorers after 1850: Kathleen Fitzpatrick, *Australian Explorers: A Selection from Their Writings* (London, 1958); Bessie Threadgill, *South Australian Land Exploration 1856 to 1880* (Adelaide, 1922).

Discovery of Uluru: W. C. Gosse, *W. C. Gosse's Explorations, 1873* (Adelaide, 1973).

Forrest in Adelaide: John Forrest, *Explorations in Australia* (London, 1875), esp. ch. 6.

Giles' dreams: Ernest Giles, *Australia Twice Traversed* (London, 1889), vol. 1, p. lv.

Eating baby wallaby: ibid., vol. 2, p. 42.

Stuart and Aborigines: John Bailey, *Mr Stuart's Track* (2006), p. 156.

Advantage of horse and revolver: Kennedy, *Hauling the Loads*, pp. 72–4.

'If they had been Europeans': Bailey, *Mr Stuart's Track*, p. 163.

Smart black boy: *S. W. Silver and Co.'s Australian Grazier's Guide, no. II – Cattle* (London, 1881), p. 91.

Nat Buchanan: H. M. Barker, *Droving Days* (Adelaide, 1966), esp. pp. 41–2.

Droving: E. S. Sorenson, *Life in the Australian Backblocks* (London, 1911), pp. 162–4, 177, 179; Kennedy, *Hauling the Loads*, esp. pp. 129–30; Bobbie Hardie, *West of the Darling* (Brisbane, 1969), pp. 84–5.

Boring machines in outback: Hardie, ibid., p. 180; *Official Year Book of New South Wales*, 1905–06, p. 29.

Wire fences: G. L. Buxton, *The Riverina 1861–1891* (1967), pp. 41, 246; *Australian Handbook*, 1881, p. xxiii.

Wire fence and kangaroos: Donald Macdonald, *Gum Boughs and Wattle Bloom* (London, 1887), pp. 13–15.

Overland telegraph: Blainey, *The Tyranny of Distance*, ch. 9.

Breaks in telegraph cable: K. T. Livingston, *The Wired Nation Continent* (1996), pp. 96–7.

3: RABBITS, WATTLES AND PATERSON'S CURSE

What Gordon did not see: Edith Humphris and Douglas Sladen, *Adam Lindsay Gordon and His Friends in England and Australia* (London, 1912), pp. 260–1.

Gordon and Latin: ibid., pp. 258–60.

Fewer than 100 copies: F. M. Rodd (ed.), *Poems of Adam Lindsay Gordon* (1946), p. liii.

Gordon's suicide: Geoffrey Hutton, *Adam Lindsay Gordon* (1978), pp. 179–81.

Imported weeds: J. H. Willis, 'Weeds', *Australian Encyclopaedia* (Sydney, 1977), vol. 6, pp. 275–9.

Vineyards in Victoria: David Dunstan, *Better than Pommard! A History of Wine in Victoria* (Kew, Vic., 1994).

Fauna decimated on grasslands: *Letters from Victorian Pioneers* (Melbourne, 1898), esp. pp. 33–5, 237; W. K. Hancock, *Discovering Monaro* (Cambridge, 1972), p. 65; J. M. Powell, *Environmental Management in Australia, 1788–1914* (1976), esp. pp. 30–2; H. J. Frith, *Wildlife Conservation* (1973), esp. pp. 307 (tree-rat) 104, 272 (kangaroos), 228 (squatter pigeon).

Rabbits imported from Liverpool: Eric C. Rolls, *They All Ran Wild* (1969), p. 19.

Exterminating rabbits: *Royal Commission into Schemes for Extermination of Rabbits* (Sydney, 1890), esp. pp. 63–4, 66, 199; jam recipe in *The Victorian Settlers' Guide* (1905), p. 75; C. E. W. Bean, *On the Wool Track* (1945), pp. 71, 311.

Rabbit-proof fences: Rolls, *They All Ran Wild*, pp. 119–31.

Rabbit exports in 1906: *CYB*, 1909, pp. 340–1.

Cobar flock-owner: Evidence from George Frew in *Royal Commission on Western Lands*, NSW, 1900.

The Austins: Margaret Kiddle, *Men of Yesterday* (1961), pp. 279, 320–2; P. L. Brown in *ADB*, vol. 1, pp. 43–4.

4: THE LONG HONEYMOON

Growth of Australian cities: F. J. B. Stilwell in I. H. Burnley (ed.), *Urbanization in Australia* (Cambridge, 1974), p. 39; Lionel Frost, *CEHA*, ch. 11; Sean Glynn, *Urbanisation in Australian History, 1788–1900* (West Melbourne, 1975); W. A. Sinclair, *The Process of Economic Development in Australia* (Melbourne, 1976), pp. 106–9.

The statistician: T. A. Coghlan, *A Statistical Account of the Seven Colonies of Australasia, 1897–8* (Sydney, 1898), p. 60.

Cricket match: K. S. Inglis, *The Australian Colonists* (1974), p.126.

'Sydney asleep': Alfred Deakin, *The Federal Story* (Melbourne, 1944), pp.14, 101.

Charles Rasp: R. Maja Sainisch-Plimer in William D. Birch (ed.), *Minerals of Broken Hill* (Broken Hill, 1999), pp.14–33.

US experts at Broken Hill: Blainey, *The Rush*, ch. 14.

Australian Rules football: G. Blainey, *A Game of Our Own* (Melbourne, 1990), ch. 8.

Unhealthy cities: T. A. Coghlan, *The Wealth and Progress of New South Wales* (no. 1, 1886–87), pp.172, 177; Proceedings of Victorian Institute of Engineers, vol. 4, pp.137–43; Graeme Davison, *The Rise and Fall of Marvellous Melbourne* (1978), p.233.

5: CUTTING DOWN THE TALL POPPIES

Censorship in Europe: *NCMH,* vol. 10, pp.123–8.

The Seekamps: Anne Beggs Sunter in *ADBS*, pp.355–6.

Sydney hunger for news: Inglis, *The Australian Colonists*, p.221.

Brisbane flood: *Brisbane Courier*, 10 February 1893; Harry Gordon, *An Eyewitness History of Australia* (Adelaide, 1976), p.135.

Syme on the press as educator: D. Syme, *Representative Government in England* (London, 1881), p.122.

Power of press: James Bryce, *Modern Democracies* (London, 1921), vol. 2, p.248; Michael Cannon, *Who's Master? Who's Man? Australia in the Victorian Age* (Melbourne, 1982), vol. 3, pp.122–4.

The Murdochs: Elizabeth Morrison, *David Syme: Man of the Age* (Clayton, Vic., 2014), pp.383–4.

At Ercildoune: J. A. Froude, *Oceana* (London, 1894), pp.104–6.

Wilson and aristocratic marriages: Paul de Serville, *Pounds and Pedigrees: The Upper Class in Victoria 1850–80* (South Melbourne, 1991), p.236.

'Neighbourhood of connections': ibid., p.168.

The young Spence: Coral Lansbury and Bede Nairn, 'W. G. Spence' in *ADB*, vol. 6, pp.168–70.

Creswick union: W. G. Spence, *Australia's Awakening* (Sydney, 1909), p.51.

Tom Roberts paints Spence: Vance Palmer, *National Portraits* (1940), p.149.

Aboriginal shearers: Buxton, *The Riverina*, p.265.

Rise of shearers' union: Spence, *Australia's Awakening,* esp. pp.69–70, 81–2; W. G. Spence, *History of the AWU* (Sydney, 1961).

Notable shearing tallies: Sorenson, *Life in the Australian Backblocks*, p.242.

Shearing machines: G. P. Walsh, 'Frederick Wolseley' in *ADB*, vol. 6. pp.431–2; H.B. Grimsditch, 'Herbert Austin', *The Dictionary of National Biography: 6th Supplement* (1941–50); F. Wheelhouse, *Digging Stick to Rotary Hoe* (Melbourne, 1966), ch. 8.

London dock strike: P. F. Donovan, 'Australia and the Great London Dock Strike: 1889', *Labour History*, November 1972.

'Fire low': J. A. La Nauze, *Alfred Deakin: A Biography* (1965), vol. 1, pp.131–2.

Maritime Strike: T. A. Coghlan, *Labour and Industry in Australia* (London, 1918), vol. 3, pp.1591–1607.

Strikes of 1890–91: J. A. Merritt, 'W. G. Spence and the 1890 Maritime Strike', *HS*, April 1973, p.595; F. S. Piggin, 'New South Wales pastoralists and the strikes of 1890 and 1891', *HS*, September 1971; Humphrey McQueen, *A New Britannia* (1975), pp.214–16.

Collapse of union membership: Melissa Bellanta in *CHA*, vol. 1, p.229.

Charles Don: S. Merrifield, 'C. J. Don' in *ADB*, vol. 4, p.82; Serle, *The Golden Age*, pp.271, 294.

Rise of Labor Party: John Rickard, *Class and Politics* (Canberra, 1976), esp. ch. 1; J. B. Hirst, *Adelaide and the Country 1870–1917* (1973), pp.153–4; Spence, *Australia's Awakening,* pp.597–8 for Labor's first platform.

Georgites: Airlie Worrall, 'The Single Tax Movement in Eastern Australia', MA thesis, University of Melbourne; D. S. Garden, 'W. H. Gresham' in *ADB*, vol. 4, pp.297–8; L. F. Crisp in *Labour History*, May 1979, pp.32–4.

Career of Dawson: D. J. Murphy et al. (eds), *Prelude to Power* (Milton, Qld, 1970), pp.85–6 and 236–8; Ross Fitzgerald, *Seven Days to Remember: The World's First Labor Government* (St Lucia, Qld, 1999).

Assessing the Labor Party's achievement: John Faulkner and Stuart
Macintyre (eds), *True Believers: The Story of the Federal Parliamentary
Labor Party* (Sydney, 2001).

6: IN HOT PURSUIT OF A 'PURE WORLD'

She-oak: E. E. Morris, *A Dictionary of Austral English* (Sydney, 1972),
p. 413; *The Australian Encyclopaedia* (1926), vol. 2, p. 454.

Bishop Barker beer: Sidney Baker, *The Australian Language* (Milsons
Point, NSW, 1978), pp. 228–9.

Divorce statistics: Coghlan, *A Statistical Account 1897–8*, pp. 119–22.

Melbourne merchant: William Westgarth, *The Colony of Victoria*
(London, 1864), p. 398.

Disenfranchised men: *An Act to Amend the Electoral Law*, NSW, 1858,
no. 20.

Nellie Melba: Ann Blainey, *I Am Melba* (2008); Jim Davidson, 'Melba'
in *ADB*, vol. 10, pp. 475–9.

Women in universities: W. J. Gardner, *Colonial Cap and Gown*
(Christchurch, 1979), ch. 3.

Women armed with brooms: Philip Payton, *Making Moonta* (Exeter,
2007), p. 114.

Rise of the WCTU: Anna Blainey, 'The Fallen Are Every Mother's
Children: The WCTU's Campaign for Temperance, Women's
Suffrage etc.', Ph.D. thesis, La Trobe University, 2000.

Catherine Spence as public speaker: *Catherine Helen Spence:
An Autobiography* (Adelaide, 1910), esp. pp. 15, 45, 53.

New Zealand campaign: Patricia Grimshaw, *Women's Suffrage
in New Zealand* (Auckland, 1972), esp. ch. 4 and 5.

Catherine Spence as feminist: Susan Magarey, *Unbridling the Tongues
of Women* (Adelaide, 2010), explores the complexity of Spence's
attitudes towards women as politicians.

Schools in NSW: Coghlan, *The Wealth and Progress 1886–87*, pp. 86–7,
437–8.

Lawson's old bark school: Colin Roderick (ed.), *Henry Lawson:
Autobiographical and Other Writings* (Sydney, 1972), vol. 2, pp. 180–4.

A Catholic view of pagan schools in July 1870: R. B. Vaughan, *Pastorals*

and Speeches on Education (Sydney, 1880), printed in *SAH*, pp.368–72;
A. E. Cahill, 'Vaughan' in *ADB*, vol. 6.

Signing marriage register: Coghlan, *A Statistical Account*, (1891), p.261.

Chifley's marriage: D. B. Waterson, 'Chifley' in *ADB*, vol. 13, p.413.

Clarke's funeral: Michael Clarke, *Clarke of Rupertswood* (Collingwood, 1995), pp.319–21.

John West: Patricia F. Ratcliff, *The Usefulness of John West* (Launceston, 2003), p.403.

Missionaries: G. Blainey, *A Short History of Christianity* (2011), pp.517–19.

Birth and death statistics in NSW: *Official Year Book of New South Wales*, 1905–06, pp.234–44.

Women's work at home: Beverley Kingston, *My Wife, My Daughter, and Poor Mary Ann* (1975), esp. ch. 1–3.

7: RICH AND POOR: THE ECONOMIC WHIRLPOOL

Lives of Usher and Williams: Alexander Sutherland, *Victoria and Its Metropolis* (Melbourne, 1888), vol. 2, p.745, where brief biographies of the two nomadic businessmen are set out.

Storekeeper Menzies: A. W. Martin, *Robert Menzies: A Life* (1993), vol. 1, pp.4–5.

Destitute asylums: Marie-Louise Geyer, in Wilfrid Prest (ed.), *The Wakefield Companion to South Australian History* (Kent Town, SA, 2001), pp.147–8; Joan C. Brown, *Poverty Is Not a Crime* (Hobart, 1972), esp. ch. 3, 4.

Tasmanian charity houses: G. Blainey, *THRA*, December 1968, pp.85–6; Brown, *Poverty Is Not a Crime*, esp. ch. 3, 4.

Relief funds sent overseas: J. H. Heaton, *Australian Dictionary of Dates and Men of the Time* (Sydney, 1879), part 2, p.97.

The kind 'Giraffe': C. Roderick (ed.), *Henry Lawson: Letters* (Sydney, 1970), p.248.

Outback hospitality: Baker, *The Australian Language*, p.107; Kiddle, *Men of Yesterday*, p.298.

Burial of the Creole cook: J. O. Randell (ed.), *Adventures of a Pioneer* (Carlton, Vic., 1978), p.222.

Pinba the Aborigine: *Port Augusta Dispatch* (sic.) article, reprinted in

South Australian Advertiser, 21 December 1885; Robert Foster, 'Logic' in *ADBS*, pp.237–8; *Adelaide Observer*, 9 and 16 January 1904.

The hanging of Ritson: *The Age*, 4 August 1869.

House-ownership: Davison, *Rise and Fall*, esp. pp.180–1.

Popularity of life assurance: A. C. Gray, *Life Insurance in Australia* (Melbourne, 1977), esp. pp.37, 44–5, 51, 60–1; W. I. Spratt, 'Lessons learned', *AIBR*, 1968, esp. pp.132–4.

The gigantic AMP Society: G. Blainey, *A History of the AMP: 1848–1988* (1999), p.140.

New income taxes: *CYB*, 1908, pp.670–85.

Income tax and the Devil: Stephen Mills, *Taxation in Australia* (London, 1925), p.66.

Newcastle coal: A. Sutherland, *A New Geography for Australian Pupils* (Melbourne, 1885), p.61.

Albury railway banquet: Anon., *The Union of the Railway Systems* (Government Printer, Sydney, 1883), pp.42–3, 80–2.

Typewriter: Gideon Haigh, *The Office: A Hardworking History* (2012), p.65.

Head of AMP on women: Blainey, *A History of the AMP*, pp.159–60.

Australia's role in the combine harvester: A. G. Thompson in *Tools and Tillage*, vol. 2, 1977, pp.67ff.

Spectator sport and crowds: W. F. Mandle, 'Games people played', *HS*, April 1973, p.512; G. Blainey, 'History of leisure in Australia: the late-colonial era', *VHJ*, February 1978, p.15.

Heavy loads carried: G. Blainey, *Black Kettle and Full Moon* (2003), pp.310–11.

Tempo of work: Sir Richard Tangye, *Notes on My Fourth Voyage to the Australian Colonies* (Birmingham, 1886), pp.38, 40–1, 50.

8: SUGAR, PEARLS AND 'THE COMING OF THE LIGHT'

Independence for Port Phillip: A. C. V. Melbourne, *Early Constitutional Development in Australia*, esp. p.356; A. B. Keith (ed.), *Selected Speeches and Documents on British Colonial Policy, 1763–1917* (London, 1918), vol. 1, pp.199–200.

Cattle horns in commerce: *Knight's*, pp.1030–1; Blainey, *A History of the AMP*, pp.78–80.

Sugar-cane labourers: G. C. Bolton, *A Thousand Miles Away* (Brisbane, 1963), pp. 144–5.

Petition to Queen Victoria: *SDAH*, pp. 220–3.

North Queensland and secession: Bolton, *A Thousand Miles Away*, esp. ch. 9; G. L. Buxton in F. K. Crowley (ed.), *A New History of Australia* (1974), pp. 201–2.

Flinders sees outrigger canoes: Geoffrey C. Ingleton, *Matthew Flinders: Navigator and Chartmaker* (Guildford, UK, 1986), p. 201.

London Missionary Society arrives: C. Hartley Grattan, *The Southwest Pacific to 1900* (Ann Arbor, 1963), pp. 491–2.

Islanders' political rights: Jeremy Beckett, *Torres Strait Islanders: Custom and Colonialism* (Cambridge, 1987).

Torres Strait Islands and the monarchy: George Mye, *Report of the Constitutional Convention* (1998), vol. 3, p. 73.

Torres Strait warnings: *Australia Pilot*, vol. 3, 1916, p. 217.

Cosmopolitan Thursday Island: *Australian Handbook*, 1897, pp. 439–40.

Germans in New Guinea: Grattan, *The Southwest Pacific*, pp. 492–5.

Annexation of Papua: Blainey, *The Tyranny of Distance*, pp. 225, 388.

Chalmers the missionary: Grattan, *The Southwest Pacific*, p. 492.

9: THE BANKS CRASH

Inrush of British capital: Sinclair, *The Process of Economic Development*, pp. 127–8; Rodney Maddock in *CEHA*, p. 274.

Activities of big banks in 1880s: S. J. Butlin, *Australia and New Zealand Bank* (London, 1961), esp. ch. 11, 12; R. F. Holder, *Bank of New South Wales: A History* (1970), vol. 1, esp. ch. 25, 26; Anon., *A Century of Banking* (Sydney, 1934), ch. 10.

Multitude of branches: E. A. Boehm, *Prosperity and Depression in Australia 1887–1897* (Oxford, 1971), pp. 210–11.

Russian war scare: G. Blainey, *Gold and Paper* (Melbourne, 1958), p. 128.

Bank of VDL closes: ibid., p. 284.

Fall of Bank of South Australia: Butlin, *Australia and New Zealand Bank*, pp. 290–3.

Melbourne in crisis: Blainey, *Gold and Paper*, pp. 158–63; Holder, *Bank of New South Wales*, vol. 1, pp. 450–55.

The Dibbs brothers in Sydney: Boehm, *Prosperity and Depression in Australia*, p.314; Michael Cannon, *The Land Boomers* (1995), pp.127–8.

NSW government intervenes in banking crisis: T. A. Coghlan, *Labour and Industry in Australia*, vol. 3, pp.1675–80.

The drama of boom and crash: *AIBR,* esp. pp.1888–93.

Divine punishment: J. Watsford, *Glorious Gospel Triumphs* (London, 1900), p.292; F. F. Goe in *SAH*, pp.416–17; Davison, *Rise and Fall,* p.249.

Severity of 1893 banking disaster in Australia: My comparison with other bank crashes is based on evidence culled from Milton Friedman and A. J. Schwartz, *A Monetary History of the United States, 1867–1960* (Princeton, 1963) and a variety of European economic histories.

10: RETREAT FROM PARADISE

Empty skyscrapers: E. M. Clowes, *On the Wallaby: Through Victoria* (London, 1911), p.128; evidence from W. Zeal in *Parliamentary Standing Committee on Flinders Street Railway Station*, VPP, 1899, p.51.

Population exodus: *Victorian Year-Book*, 1910–11, pp.552–4; and other statistical registers and yearbooks.

Village settlements: Coghlan, *Labour and Industry*, esp. vol. 4, pp.1987–91, 2084–5; L. J. Blake, 'Village settlements', *Victorian Historical Magazine,* November 1966.

Life at Leongatha colony: *Report from Select Committee on 'Leongatha Labour Colony'*, VPP, 1900, esp. 'Minutes of Evidence'.

Lane's colonists prepare for Paraguay: Gavin Souter, *A Peculiar People: The Australians in Paraguay* (1968), pp.63–5.

Mary Gilmore in Paraguay: Barrie Ovenden in Dymphna Cusack, T. Inglis Moore and Barrie Ovenden, *Mary Gilmore: A Tribute* (Sydney, 1965), pp.34–7.

Friction in Cosme: Souter, *A Peculiar People*, pp.178–80.

Goldfields water pipeline: G. Blainey, *The Golden Mile* (1993), pp.59–71; G. Evans, *C. Y. O'Connor* (Crawley, WA, 2001), ch. 19.

'After the long day': Randolph Bedford, *Naught to Thirty-Three* (Melbourne, 1976), p.189.

Three rich goldmines in WA: Blainey, *The Golden Mile*, p.77.

Exports of frozen meat and butter: Boehm, *Prosperity and Depression in Australia*, pp.110–17.

11: A FEARFUL DROUGHT

Climate theories and agriculture in South Australia: D. W. Meinig, *On the Margins of the Good Earth* (Chicago, 1962), esp. pp.59–60.

A Victorian board: *Papers Relating to Forest Conservancy*, VPP, 1874, esp. pp.11, 24–5.

The Scottish forester: Richard Refshauge on the forester J. E. Brown in *ADB*, vol. 3, p.261.

Russell and his theories: H. C. Russell, *Climate of New South Wales* (Sydney, 1877), esp. pp.182–9.

Lake George: Russell, *Climate of New South Wales*, pp.29–33.

Hayter's optimism: H. H. Hayter in *Report of the Australasian Association for Advancement of Science*, 1890, pp.578–9.

Pattern of rainfall: J. C. Foley, *Droughts in Australia* (Commonwealth Bureau of Meteorology, 1957), Bulletin 43.

Protector of Aborigines and one emu: H. M. Tolcher, *Drought or Deluge* (1986), p.211.

Christison's sheep: M. M. Bennett, *Christison of Lammermoor* (London, late 1920s), ch. 25, 26.

Barton's sheep: R. D. Barton, *Reminiscences of an Australian Pioneer* (Sydney, 1918), ch. 21.

Drovers' hazards: Sorenson, *Life in the Australian Backblocks*; H. M. Barker, *Droving Days* (1966), esp. ch. 8.

Long drought: H. A. Hunt et al., *The Climate and Weather of Australia* (Melbourne, 1913), p.84 for dust storms; R. L. Heathcote, *Back of Bourke* (1965), pp.148, 153–7, 165.

Two driest years since 1900: information from Bureau of Meteorology, 2011.

Farmer Coote and drought: unpublished diaries of C. W. Coote, in University of Melbourne Archives.

Change in weather from the 1880s: C. H. B. Priestley et. al., *Report of a Committee on Climatic Change* (Canberra, 1976).

The Priestley report: This is tentative on some facets of the change
   in weather from the 1880s, but my private correspondence with
   Dr Priestley confirmed that the implications of the report for
   historians was profound. Parts of this chapter appeared in
   G. Blainey, *National Times*, 31 October – 5 November, 1977.
Elliott reminiscence: *The Land of the Lyre Bird* (Clayton, Vic., 1966), p.197.
Artists' attitude to summer: R. H. Croll (ed.), *Smike to Bulldog* (Sydney,
   1946), pp.14, 21–2, 124.
Attitudes to climate: A. Matzenik in *The Poems of Dorothea Mackellar*
   (Adelaide, 1971); G. Blainey, 'Climate and Australia's history',
   Melbourne Historical Journal, 1971, pp.8–9.
Emigration of Australian artists: Bernard Smith, *Australian Painting,*
   1788–1970 (London, 1978), ch.5.

12: THE ROCKY ROAD TO FEDERATION

Intercolonial clock times: Blainey, *Black Kettle and Full Moon*, pp.171–3.
Anthony Trollope on Australian disunity: P. D. Edwards and R. B. Joyce
   (eds), *Anthony Trollope: Australia* (St Lucia, Qld, 1967), pp.183, 544.
The objection to the Chinese: *Intercolonial Conference Held at Sydney,*
   January 1881, VPP, 1880–81, pp.61–3.
General Edwards' report: A. J. Hill in *ADB*, vol. 4, p.130.
Ivory-carving craft: *Knight's*, p.1075.
Parkes' careers: A. W. Martin, *Henry Parkes: A Biography* (1980).
Parkes' far-away expression: Alfred Deakin, *The Federal Story*
   (Melbourne, 1944), p.25.
'The crimson thread': Martin, *Henry Parkes*, p.391.
Choice of name 'Commonwealth': Helen Irving, *To Constitute a Nation*
   (Cambridge, 1997), pp.76–8.
John Quick's career: Michele Maslunka in *ADB*, vol. 11, pp.316–17.
Quick's formula accepted: J. A. La Nauze, *The Making of the Australian*
   Constitution (1972), p.90.
Six long-standing premiers of 1890s: By selecting long-standing
   premiers in 1856–1901 (listed in Ernest Scott, *A Short History of*
   Australia, 1943, pp.xxvi–xxviii), it was obvious how many flourished
   in the 1890s.

Strong 1898 pro-federal votes: G. Blainey in *HS*, 1950, pp.224–36.

Who voted for federation?: Irving, *To Constitute a Nation*.

'A series of miracles': Deakin, *The Federal Story*, p.173.

Division of powers in federal system: La Nauze, *The Making of the Australian Constitution*, ch. 17.

The Hopetoun blunder: La Nauze, *Alfred Deakin*, vol. 1, pp.204–10.

Political life of Barton: Geoffrey Bolton, *Edmund Barton* (2000).

13: A FRAIL SMALL SHIP

Australians fighting in Boer War: Craig Wilcox, *Australia's Boer War* (2002).

W. H. Groom's maiden speech: *Commonwealth Hansard*, 21 May 1901.

Rise of unionism after 1901: Tim Hatton and Glenn Withers in *CEHA*, pp.363–4.

Senator McGregor the veteran: G. C. Grainger in *ADB*, vol. 10, pp.275–6; Gavin Souter, *Lion and Kangaroo* (1976), p 73.

Deakin's cycling: La Nauze, *Alfred Deakin*, vol. 1, p.146.

Barton on racial differences: Gavin Souter, *Acts of Parliament* (1988), p.63.

Operations of Immigration Restriction Acts 1908–15: G. Greenwood and C. Grimshaw (eds), *AIA*, pp.418–22.

Bakhap the politician: Ann Millar (ed.), *The Biographical Dictionary of the Australian Senate* (2000), vol. 1, pp.252–6.

Kanakas and sugar: Geoffrey Sawer, *Australian Federal Politics and Law: 1901–1929* (1972), pp.23, 43.

New Guinea coffee and sheep: *Australasian Handbook*, 1906, p.359.

Infant Papua: La Nauze, *Alfred Deakin*, vol. 2, pp.456–7.

The wellbeing of Papuans came first: ibid., pp.474.

'Glorified curiosity-shop': ibid., p.460.

Aurora departs Hobart: *Mercury*, 4 December 1911.

To the Antarctic in search of weather forecasts: Alison Bashford and Peter Hobbins in *CHA*, vol. 2, pp.266–7.

Mawson's long ordeal: Philip Ayres, *Mawson: A Life* (2003).

Australia acquires huge chunk of Antarctic: Stephen Murray-Smith, *Sitting on Penguins* (Surry Hills, NSW, 1988), p.342.

BHP resolved to make steel: G. Blainey, *The Rise of Broken Hill* (1968), pp. 77–8; Roy Bridges, *From Silver to Steel* (1920), ch. 40–43.

Building the steelworks: Edith. M. Johnston-Liik, George Liik and R. G. Ward, *A Measure of Greatness: The Origins of the Australian Iron and Steel Industry* (1998), p. 358.

14: GALLIPOLI

Statistics of German pre-1914 dominance: W. O. Henderson, *The Rise of German Industrial Power 1834–1914* (London, 1975), pp. 130–43.

German colonies: ibid., pp. 224–8.

Birth of Australian navy: A. W. Jose, *The Royal Australian Navy 1914–1918* (1928), pp. xv, xli.

Australian navy captures Rabaul: ibid., ch. 3.

Trek to Port Davey: L. F. Giblin, 'Port Davey in wartime' in Douglas Copland (ed.), *Giblin: The Scholar and the Man* (Melbourne, 1960), pp. 121–7.

Military stalemate in France in 1914: G. Blainey in *The Great War: Papers of the Winter Conversazione* (Melbourne, 2014) pp. 16–18.

Motives of the Gallipoli campaign: G. Blainey, *A Short History of the 20th Century* (2005), pp. 74–8.

Churchill and the Gallipoli plan: Robin Prior, *Gallipoli* (Sydney, 2009), esp. pp. 8–31.

Billy Sing the sniper: John Hamilton, *Gallipoli Sniper* (2009).

Single-men soldiers: Les Carlyon, *Gallipoli* (2001), p. 121.

British-born Anzac soldiers: Robert Rhodes James, *Gallipoli* (London, 1999), p. xiv.

Cowardice or indiscipline of some Australian soldiers: ibid., p. xiii.

Hymns and poetry at Gallipoli: Michael McKernan, *Padre* (1986).

Prediction by von Tirpitz: cited in C. F. Aspinall-Oglander (comp.), *Military Operations: Gallipoli* (London, 1932), vol. 2, p. 375.

Hamilton and 'our warships': Ian Hamilton, *Gallipoli Diary* (London, 1920), vol. 2, p. 274.

Evacuating Gallipoli: Peter Stanley, *Quinn's Post* (2005), ch. 11; Carlyon, *Gallipoli*, ch. 32.

D-day organisers learned from Gallipoli: Field Marshal Earl Wavell,

in *NCMH*, vol. 10, pp.272–3; Henry Michel, *The Second World War*
(London, 1975), pp.620ff. In addition James in *Gallipoli*, p. xiv,
reported how the British forces fighting in the Falkland Islands
in 1982 gained from his book, written seventeen years previously.

15: THE SCYTHES OF WAR

W. M. Hughes becomes prime minister: L. F. Fitzhardinge, *The Little
   Digger 1914–1952* (1979), ch. 3.
Statistics on Australia's contribution to war effort: Arthur B. Keith,
   War Government of the British Dominions (Oxford, 1921), pp.106–7.
Women and conscription: Stephen Garton and Peter Stanley in *CHA*,
   vol. 2, pp.53–4.
Soldiers denounce cowards at home: Philip Payton, *Regional Australia
   and the Great War* (Exeter, UK, 2012), pp.76–7.
Mannix on Protestants and war: *SAH*, pp.546–7.
Germans in Australia: Walter Phillips in *OCAH*, p.280.
Monash at Hamel: Les Carlyon, *The Great War* (2006), pp.734–5.
Role of the naval blockade in defeating Germany: Robert Tombs,
   The English and Their History (New York, 2015), pp.639–40.
Life of Monash: Geoffrey Serle, *John Monash: A Biography* (1982),
   is the classic life of this soldier.
Australian forces in postwar Russia: Jose, *The Royal Australian Navy*,
   pp.238–30.
Australian enlistments and overseas contingents: Peter Stanley in John
   Connor, Peter Stanley and Peter Yule, *The War at Home* (2015), p.178,
   revises the traditional statistics.
Tally of war casualties: Wray Vamplew (ed.), *Australians: Historical
   Statistics* (Broadway, NSW, 1987), pp.413–16.
Shell shock and trauma: Richard Lindstrom, 'The Australian
   Experience of Psychological Casualties in War 1915–1939', Ph.D.
   thesis, Victoria University, Melbourne, 1997, p.25. In discussions with
   Lindstrom in 2014, he expressed his debt to Alistair Thomson and
   Marilyn Lake who had earlier grasped the importance of this topic.
The statistician: Copland, *Giblin*, p.128.
Hughes demands Germany pay for the war: Robert Skidelsky, *John*

Maynard Keynes (London, 1983), vol. 1, p.356.

On the greatness of Japan: Hughes, cited in Fitzhardinge, *The Little Digger*, p.468.

16: SKY AND EARTH: THE 1920s

Bruce's car in Dieppe: Cecil Edwards, *Bruce of Melbourne* (London, 1965), p.54.

Kingsford Smith's plane: Smith's *Southern Cross*, well preserved, can be seen at Brisbane Airport.

Dangerous flight to Fiji: Ian Mackersey, *Smithy* (London, 1998), p.144.

Landing in park at Suva: personal visit to site in February 2012.

Kingsford Smith the aviator: information from Ann Blainey of Melbourne, who is completing a biography of Smith.

Call for a flying doctor: Max Griffiths, *Angels in the Outback* (Kenthurst, NSW, 2012), pp.106–7, 115, 119–30.

Prime ministers converse by radio: Ann Moyal, *Clear Across Australia: A History of Telecommunications* (1984), p.140.

Long-distance phone to Perth and Hobart: ibid., p.144.

Melba's broadcast: Ann. Blainey, *I Am Melba*, p.320.

The ABC and music: K. S. Inglis, *This Is the ABC* (1983), p.27–8.

Bill Bowyang and Dad and Dave: John Ryan, *Panel by Panel: An Illustrated History of Australian Comics* (Stanmore, NSW, 1979), pp.35–7, 43.

Clydesdales and other heavy horses: Kennedy, *Hauling the Loads*, esp. p.6.

Amos Howard and sub clover: David F. Smith, *Natural Gain: In the Grazing Lands of Southern Australia* (Sydney, 2000), p.91.

Clover in Western Australia: ibid., pp.107–9.

Rise of farmers' parties: B. D. Graham, *The Formation of the Australian Country Parties* (1965); Don Aitkin, *The Country Party in New South Wales* (Canberra, 1972); G. Blainey, Earle Page Memorial Lecture, Townsville, 1999.

Relative aid for farms versus factories: M. Butlin, R. Dixon and P. J. Lloyd in *CEHA*, pp.578–80.

Bloody Sunday: Frank Crowley, *Australia's Western Third* (London, 1960), p.185.

Rural subsidies: Sawer, *Australian Federal Politics and Law*, vol. 1,
pp. 228–31.
Bruce and maritime union: Souter, *Acts of Parliament*, pp. 203–4; Sawer,
ibid., vol. 1, pp. 237–9.
Italians needed no passport: *CYB*, 1935, p. 563.
Kalgoorlie–Boulder riots: Charles Price, *Southern Europeans in Australia*
(Melbourne, 1963), pp. 207–11.
Sidney Myer and his emporium: Alan Marshall, *The Gay Provider*
(Melbourne, 1962).
The Watens kept their bags packed: Judah Waten, *Alien Son* (1952), p. 1.
Seeking a federal capital: Souter, *Acts of Parliament*, pp. 209–11.
Choosing a federal capital: Sawer, *Australian Federal Politics and Law*,
vol. 1, p. 41.
'Lamentable' choice of Canberra as capital: *The Age*, 12 March 1913.
Lionel Logue and Canberra speech: Robert Rhodes James, *A Spirit
Undaunted: The Political Role of George VI* (London, 1998), pp. 98–9.
The brilliant film *The King's Speech* alters the chronology of the
Duke's increasing command of his stutter.

17: THE WORLD DEPRESSION

Unemployment high in 1920s: Connor, Stanley and Yule, *The War at
Home*, p. 77.
Singing 'The Red Flag': L. F. Crisp, *Ben Chifley* (1960), p. 40.
Australia's economic crisis: E. A. Boehm, *Twentieth Century Economic
Development in Australia* (1971), pp. 21–2.
Devaluation of Australian pound: Blainey, *Gold and Paper*, pp. 329–31.
Federal treasury an infant: Colin White, *Mastering Risk* (1992),
pp. 190–1.
Few houses built in June 1933: *CYB*, 1935, pp. 555, 565.
Distress in Western Australia: Geoffrey Bolton, *A Fine Country to
Starve in* (Nedlands, WA, 1972), pp. 196–204.
Camping grounds: Kylie Tennant, *Tiburon* (1972). Tiburon is no specific
town, but 'a composite of many Australian places', wrote the author
in 1935.
Sustenance: Don Fraser, *Working for the Dole: Commonwealth Relief*

During the Great Depression (Canberra, 2001), pp. 47, 83. Fraser's
  research was based largely on the National Archives.
Financial fear in Sydney in 1931: Blainey, *Gold and Paper*, pp. 334–5.
Low point in Depression: C. B. Schedvin, *Australia and the Great
  Depression* (Sydney, 1988), p. 212.
Governments' policy in Depression: Ian W. McLean, *Why Australia
  Prospered* (Princeton, 2013), p. 164.
Granite for Sydney's harbour bridge: Peter Lalor, *The Bridge* (2005),
  pp. 137, 158–62.
Ugly steel of the bridge's arch: Robin Boyd, *The Australian Ugliness*
  (2010), p. 35.
Bridge like 'Pillar of Hercules': *Sydney Morning Herald*, 20 March 1932.
Bradman: Gideon Haigh, *Inside Out* (2008), pp. 81–136, esp. p. 87 for
  'quietness'.
Celebrities and amateur sports players: Gideon Haigh, 2012 Bradman
  Oration, Melbourne, accessed at www.espncricinfo.com/australia/
  content/story/587974.html
Lasseter's reef: Barry McGowan, *Fool's Gold* (2006); Blainey, *The Rush*,
  ch. 27.
Perth's isolation: Crowley, *Australia's Western Third*, pp. 278–9.
Secession for Western Australia: ibid., pp. 272–7.

18: SKELETONS IN THE NATION'S CUPBOARD

Gilgandra murders: G. P. Walsh on Jimmy Governor in *ADB*, vol. 9.
Murder of the Mawbeys: Eric Rolls, *A Million Wild Acres* (1981),
  pp. 227–9.
Erasing footprints: ibid., pp. 203, 230.
Homesteads deserted: ibid., p. 231.
Fate of Jimmy and Ethel Governor: Walsh in *ADB*, vol. 9, p. 62.
Frequent arrests for cattle thieving.: W. E. Roth, *Royal Commission on
  the Condition of the Natives* (PP no. 5, Perth, 1905), pp. 13–14. Evidence
  came from forty-two witnesses.
Aborigines' work on cattle stations: G. H. Knibbs (ed.), *Federal
  Handbook* (Melbourne, 1914), p. 114.
Aborigines as rural workers: Fred Cahir in *VHJ*, June 2014, esp. pp. 18–24;

Ann McGrath, *Born in the Cattle: Aborigines in Cattle Country* (1987). McGrath, cited in Cahir's article, is an expert on the history of Aboriginal workers in the northern half of the continent.

'Sharp as needles': George Riddoch cited in Douglas Sladen, *Adam Lindsay Gordon* (London, 1934), p.450.

Spear-carrier standing at door: H. M. Barker, *Camels and the Outback* (Melbourne, 1964), pp.113–14.

The Cahills and Aborigines: John Mulvaney, *Paddy Cahill of Oenpelli* (Canberra, 2004). See p.122 for curiosity about the First World War.

Next generation of Aborigines: Paul Hasluck, *Shades of Darkness: Aboriginal Affairs 1925–1965* (1988), p.143.

Gribble: Marian Aveling (ed.), *Westralian Voices* (Nedlands, WA, 1979), pp.152–5; anon., 'John B. Gribble' in *ADB*, vol. 4, p.299.

Hermannsburg mission: W. F. Veit on Carl Strehlow in *ADB*, vol. 12, p.122.

Newcomers at Hermannsburg in 1927: Paul G. E. Albrecht, *From Mission to Church 1877–2002* (Hermannsburg, NT, 2002), pp.303–6.

Dharug words: G. Blainey, *Sea of Dangers* (2008), p.272.

Changed spelling of 'billabong': *AND*, p.51.

Didgeridoo: ibid., p.199.

Moore River Settlement: Hasluck, *Shades of Darkness*, p.64.

June 1934 census of Aborigines: *CYB*, 1934, p.565.

Aborigines and numbers: Margaret S. Bain, *The Aboriginal–White Encounter* (Darwin, 1992), pp. lx, 1.

The confusing two-letter word *if*: ibid., pp.150, 228.

Aborigines and humour: Barker, *Camels and the Outback*, pp.104–5.

Maori seats in parliament: James Bellich, *Making Peoples: A History of the New Zealanders* (Auckland, 1996), p.265.

Murders at Caledon Bay: Alan Powell, *Far Country* (1982), p.180.

Caledon Bay trial: Ted Egan, *Justice All Their Own: The Caledon Bay and Woodah Island Killings* (1996); Humphrey McQueen, *Social Sketches of Australia 1888–1975* (1978), pp.146–7.

William Cooper's working life: Diane Barwick in *ADB*, vol. 8, pp.107–8.

William Cooper and day of mourning: Richard Broome, *Aboriginal Victorians* (2005), pp.300–5.

Sir Douglas Nicholls: Richard Broome in *ADB*, vol. 18, pp.219–21.

Stanner's warning: J. C. G. Kevin (ed.), *W. E. H. Stanner: Some Australians Take Stock* (London, 1939), p.10. This was three decades before Stanner gave his famous Boyer Lecture on the same topic.

19: 'THAT REDDISH VEIL': THE PACIFIC WAR

Crisis in Europe: Alfred Stirling, *Lord Bruce: The London Years* (1974), pp.96–7.

Last months of Lyons: Anne Henderson, *Joseph Lyons: The People's Prime Minister* (Sydney, 2011).

Decline of Australian army: John Robertson, *J. H. Scullin: A Political Biography* (Nedlands, 1974), p.215: Jeffrey Grey, *A Military History of Australia* (1988).

Threat of Japan in 1930s: Souter, *Acts of Parliament*, pp.302–3.

Curtin advocates a referendum on war: Paul Hasluck, *The Government and the People 1939–1941* (Canberra, 1952), pp.84–5.

Holyman and his ANA: Peter Yule, *The Forgotten Giant of Australian Aviation* (South Melbourne, 2001).

Hudson bombers: W. S. Robinson, *If I Remember Rightly* (1967), p.184.

Lewis and BHP: G. Blainey, *The Steel Master* (1971), ch. 9.

Loss of French fleet impairs Singapore's defences: Michel, *The Second World War*, pp.392–3.

Menzies fears defeat of UK in war: Christopher Thorne, *Allies of a Kind* (London, 1978), p.72.

Japanese said to be not air-minded: G. Blainey, *The Causes of War* (3rd edn, 1988), ch. 16.

General Blamey sees Middle East as main danger zone: John Hetherington, *Blamey, Controversial Soldier* (Canberra, 1973), p.190.

Curtin's appeal to Americans for help: Graham Freudenberg, *Churchill and Australia* (2008), p.340.

Japan's complete command of air: Grey, *A Military History of Australia*, p.167.

Bowden's gloom: Freudenberg, *Churchill and Australia*, p.338.

Patriotic music from the ABC: Inglis, *This Is the ABC*, pp.97–8.

Fear of invasion of Australia: Gavin Souter, *Company of Heralds* (1981), p.213.

Japanese submarine near Australian ports: David Jenkins, *Battle Surface! Japan's Submarine War Against Australia 1942–44* (1992), p.130.

Sinking of HMAS *Perth*: Mike Carlton, *Cruiser: The Life and Loss of HMAS Perth and Her Crew* (2011).

The influence of MacArthur: D. M. Horner in *ADB*, vol. 15, pp.150–2.

Victory of Wirraway: Brian L. Hill, *Wirraway to Hornet* (Bulleen, Vic., 1998), p.44.

David and the Boomerang aircraft: ibid., pp.67–70.

War on Kokoda Trail: David Horner, *Strategic Command: General Sir John Wilton and Australia's Asian Wars* (2005), p.75.

War correspondents recalled: Souter, *Company of Heralds*, p.213.

Thwarted by malaria and terrain: Grey, *A Military History of Australia*, pp.175–8.

Ford tackles malaria: Hetherington, *Blamey*, pp.275–7.

Fairley and tropical medicines: Frank Fenner on Fairley in *ADB*, vol. 14, pp.128–30; D. P. Mellor, *The Role of Science and Industry* (Canberra, 1958), pp.619–25.

Australian penicillin: Mellor, ibid., p.634.

Medical research of Florey and Gregg: Blainey, *A Short History of the 20th Century*, pp.393–4; P. A. L. Lancaster on Gregg in *ADB*, vol. 14, p.325–6.

Air-war casualties: Grey, *A Military History of Australia*, p.188.

Sinking of *Centaur*: Chris Milligan and John Foley, *Australian Hospital Ship Centaur* (Hendra, Qld, 1993).

Rationing: *CYB*, no. 38, 1951, p.1240.

Wartime economic controls: John K. Wilson in *CEHA*, pp.345–9.

Roosevelt visit: Hazel Rowley, *Franklin and Eleanor* (2011), pp.294–5.

Curtin's qualities: Lloyd Ross, *John Curtin* (1977), pp.384–8.

Comparison of casualties in two world wars: my calculation is based on statistics in Connor, Stanley and Yule, *The War at Home*, pp.78–9.

20: ACROSS THE SEA ROLLS THUNDER

Chifley's voice: Crisp, *Ben Chifley*, pp.97–9.

Chifley and communist unions: ibid., esp. pp.362–5.

Liberals and 1940s welfare payments: F. K. Crowley, *Modern Australia in Documents* (Melbourne, 1973), vol. 2, pp.36, 40, 90.

The 'sons of convicts': *DAQ*, p.184.

Liberal Party lauds women: John Howard, *The Menzies Era* (2014), pp.60–1.

Gallup polls: Meaney, pp.546–7.

Fear of nuclear war and of Soviet Union: Peter Edwards, *Crises and Commitments: The Politics and Diplomacy of Australia's Involvement in Southeast Asian Conflicts 1948–1965* (1992), p.4.

If Japan becomes 'aggressive': Meaney, p.571.

ANZUS Treaty: ibid., pp.583–92.

Menzies' reliance on USA: Edwards, *Crises and Commitments*, pp.380–1.

North West Cape base: ibid., p.233.

Jewish migrants to Kimberley: Arthur A. Calwell, *Be Just and Fear Not* (Hawthorn, Vic., 1972), p.116.

Australians' birthplaces: *CYB*, 1964, p.287.

Migrants from Greek islands: Price, *Southern Europeans in Australia*, p.134.

'There are many Wongs': Calwell, *Be Just*, p.103.

Calwell and PNG Chinese: Mary E. Calwell, *I Am Bound to Be True* (Preston, Vic., 2012), p.75.

Changes in migration policy: A. C. Palfreeman, *The Administration of the White Australia Policy* (1967), p.100.

'Coolies' versus educated Asians: Peter Edwards, *Arthur Tange* (2006), p.77.

Asian entry: Palfreeman, *The Administration of the White Australia Policy*, p.99.

Female missionaries killed in China: G. Blainey, *The Blainey View* (1982), p.58.

Hancock's defence of White Australia policy: W. K. Hancock, *Australia* (London, 1930), pp.79–80.

Hancock's second thoughts: W. K. Hancock, *IPA Review*, July–September 1968, p.91.

21: WOOMERA, MIGRANT FLEET AND SPACESHIP

To the disgust of Menzies: Martin, *Robert Menzies*, vol. 2, pp.422–3.

Communism in Indonesia: Edwards, *Crises and Commitments*, p.247.

Australian conscripts: Howard, *The Menzies Era*, pp.415–16.

Australia versus Indonesia: Meaney, pp.664–5; Edwards, *Crises and Commitments*, pp.329–31.

Washington's mistakes in Vietnam: Niall Ferguson, *Kissinger* (New York, 2015), vol. 1.

Holt on Chinese communists: Crowley, *Modern Australia in Documents*, vol. 2, p.506.

Holt's funeral: Howard, *The Menzies Era*, p.492.

Wilton on hands-tied crisis in Vietnam: Horner, *Strategic Command*, p.290.

Deaths in Vietnam War: David Lowe, *CHA*, vol. 1, pp.510–11.

The 'wellspring' of dissent: Paul Strangio in *CHA*, vol. 2, pp.140–1.

Pop music: Shaun Carney, in Steve Foley (ed.), *Reflections* (2004), pp.266–7.

Menzies' sleepless nights: Edwards, *Arthur Tange*, p.76.

Whitlam and China: Gough Whitlam. *The Whitlam Government* (1985), pp.19–21.

Fat lambs challenge wool: Richard Allen and Kimbal Baker, *Great Properties of Country Victoria* (2015).

Rural population: Simon Ville in *CHA*, vol. 2, p.388.

Iron ore in the Pilbara: David Lee, *Journal of Australasian Mining History*, vol. 11, 2013, pp.61ff.

Australia's recent mining bonanza: Blainey, *The Rush*, ch. 31, 32.

Fraser's and Hawke's migration policy: 'Asian migrants 1980–2000' in Australian Bureau of Statistics, 'Overseas arrivals and departures, Australia', cat. no. 3401.0 (http://www.abs.gov.au/ausstats/abs@. nsf/mf/3401.0); Mark Lopez, *The Origins of Multiculturalism in Australian Politics 1945–1975* (2000), p.10; Marion Lê in *The Alfred Deakin Lectures* (Sydney, 2001), p.126; Katharine Betts, *Ideology and Immigration* (1988) pp.173–5, 213.

22: CARS, COFFEE SHOPS AND BLACK BOX

Refrigerators in Sydney: Robin Walker and Dave Roberts, *From Scarcity to Surfeit* (Kensington, NSW, 1988), p.142.

Dorothy Hewett's kitchen: Nicholas Jose (ed.), *Macquarie PEN*

Anthology of Australian Literature (2009), p.713.

Rural phone exchanges: Moyal, *Clear Across Australia*, p.185.

Howard as petrol boy: Paul Kelly, *The March of Patriots* (2009), p.8.

Cars multiply: Graeme Davison in H. Bolitho and C. Wallace-Crabbe (eds), *Approaching Australia* (Cambridge, Mass., 1998), p.166.

Round Australia Trial: Pedr Davis, *Rear Vision* (South Hurstville, NSW, 2010), p.112.

First motels: Davison in *Approaching Australia*, p.167.

Shopping towns: speech by G. Blainey at Sydney Town Hall, May 2010; information from Frank Lowy.

Boeing aircraft: John Gunn, *High Corridors* (1988), pp.124, 153–5.

Air travel defeats sea: Agnieszka Sobocinska and Richard White in *CHA*, vol. 2, p.481.

Black box: *Technology in Australia 1788–1988* (Australian Academy of Technological Sciences and Engineering, 1988), p.516.

Overseas travel: Carl Bridge in *CHA*, vol. 2, p.532.

Suburban houses: Robin Boyd, *Australia's Home* (2nd edn, 1978), pp.81–5.

Home ownership: Shurlee Swain in *CHA*, vol. 2, p,286.

Food preferences: Walker and Roberts, *From Scarcity to Surfeit*, p.221.

Cheese: ibid., p.123.

Tea: Blainey, *Black Kettle and Full Moon*, pp.359–66.

Germans and coffee: ibid., p.367.

Hire-purchase: Howard, *The Menzies Era*, p.377.

Metrics: *Metrication in Australia* (Canberra, 1992); *Technology in Australia 1788–1988*, p.378.

Paul McGeough's mobile phone: *The Big Picture* (2005), p.292.

History of Australian sports: John Arlott (ed.), *The Oxford Companion to Sports and Games* (London, 1975).

Grand-final crowd: John Ross (ed.), *100 Years of Australian Football* (1996), p.254.

23: THE DANCING PARTNERS: WILDERNESS, PARADISE AND RELIGION

Religion in the constitution: Irving, *To Constitute a Nation*, pp.165–7.

Strong religious strand in Australia's history: Stuart Piggin, *Evangelical*

Christianity in Australia, 1996; and *Journal of Religious History*, September 2012.

Bible: A. F. Davies and S. Encel (eds), *Australian Society* (1965), p.47.

Canberra marriages: *CYB*, 1963, p.316.

Army recruits and religion: K. S. Inglis, 'Religious behaviour' in Davies and Encel, *Australian Society*, p.50.

'Quickly the night wind': *DAQ*, p.195.

Masons: Graeme Davison in *CHA*, vol. 2, p.226.

Santamaria: The best biography of Santamaria is Gerard Henderson, *Santamaria: A Most Unusual Man* (2015).

Santamaria on Gilroy: B. A. Santamaria, *Santamaria, Against the Tide* (1981), pp.169ff.

Calwell on 'division in families': Calwell, *Be Just*, p.172.

'No bigotry': Geoffrey Camm (comp.), *Bacchus Marsh by Bacchus Marsh* (Bacchus Marsh, Vic., 1986), pp.197, 202.

Fletcher Jones and Whitlam: John Lack in *ADB*, vol. 14, pp.579–81; and private knowledge.

Hawke the young Christian: Blanche d'Alpuget, *Robert J. Hawke* (Melbourne, 1982), pp.43–8.

Women in public service: Norman MacKenzie, *Women in Australia* (1962), p.227.

Equal pay for women: Tim Hatton and Glenn Withers in *CEHA*, pp.366–7.

Dame Enid Lyons' speech: Fullilove, pp.212–14.

Juries exclude women: MacKenzie, *Women in Australia*, p.253.

Greer 'sexy': Fullilove, p.218.

Divorce rates: Vamplew, *Australians: Historical Statistics*, pp.47–8.

Barwick: Crowley, *Modern Australia in Documents*, vol. 2, pp.380–2.

One-parent families: Shirlee Swain in *CHA*, vol. 2, p.293.

Polygamy: Law Reform Commission, *The Recognition of Aboriginal Customary Laws*, Report no. 31 (Canberra, 1986).

Homosexuals: Katie Holmes and Sarah Pinto in *CHA*, vol. 2, pp.326–7.

Meredith on sad landscape: Vivienne Rae Ellis, *Louisa Anne Meredith* (Sandy Bay, Tas., 1979), p.138.

Southern beech tree: *The Heritage of Australia* (1981), p.37.

Birds of paradise: Richard Schodde in Peter Ryan (ed.), *Encyclopaedia of Papua New Guinea* (1972), vol. 1, pp.88–9.

Melba's birds: Atkinson, *The Europeans in Australia*, vol. 3, pp.375–6.

Dinosaur ants: South Australian Museum display case, April 2015.

Early Green campaigns: Gregory Barton and Brett Bennett in *CHA*, vol. 2, pp.468–9.

Kangaroo census: Australian Government Department of the Environment, 'Kangaroo population estimates', 2011.

David Suzuki: foreword to William Lines, *Taming the Great South Land: A History of the Conquest of Nature in Australia* (Berkeley, 1991).

Tanami Desert Wildlife Sanctuary: *The Heritage of Australia*, p.47.

24: WIDE SPACES AND DEEP SILENCES

Price's paperback deplores: A. Grenfell Price, *Australia Comes of Age* (Melbourne, 1945), p.66.

Aborigines' franchise: Sawer, *Australian Federal Politics and Law*, vol. 2, p.193.

Aboriginal art exhibited: Philip Jones in Peter Sutton (ed.), *Dreamings: The Art of Aboriginal Australia* (1988), pp.168–70.

Namatjira: ibid., pp.169–72.

Acrylic paint: Chris Anderson and Françoise Dussart in Sutton, ibid., pp.95–9.

Yirrkala protest: www.australia.gov.au/about-australia/australian-story/bark-petitions-indigenous-art (accessed 25 August 2016).

Wave Hill and cattle industry: Anna Haebich and Steve Kinnane in *CHA*, vol. 2, pp.346–7; Whitlam, *The Whitlam Government*, p.463; Peter Nixon, *The Peter Nixon Story* (Ballan, Vic., 2012).

Mild version of apartheid: Gillian Cowlishaw, *Black, White or Brindle: Race in Rural Australia* (Cambridge, 1988); John Hirst, *Sense and Nonsense in Australian History* (2005), pp.280ff.

Margaret Valadian: Gerard Henderson, *Australian Answers* (1990), p.315.

Canberra the financier: Frank Brennan, *Sharing the Country* (1991), p.41.

Definition of Aborigines: Henry Reynolds, *Nowhere People* (2005), p.10; Australian Law Reform Commission, report no. 96 (2003).

Counting Aborigines in census: *CYB*, 1918–19, pp.88–9.

Census of 30 June 1961: *CYB*, 1964, p.307.

History of ancient Australia: John Mulvaney, *The Prehistory of Australia* (London, 1969), p.177.

Tent Embassy: Anna Haebich and Steve Kinnane in *CHA*, vol. 2, p.349.

A 'big ask': Max Griffiths, *Aboriginal Affairs 1967–2005* (Dural, NSW, 2006), p.55.

Death of Aboriginal prisoners: Peter Walsh, *Confessions of a Failed Finance Minister* (1995), pp.116–17.

Violence against Indigenous women: Marcia Langton, 'Two victims, no justice', *The Monthly*, July 2016, pp.36–9.

Mathews' research: John D. Mathews, 'Historical, social and biological understanding is needed to improve Aboriginal health', in *Recent Advances in Microbiology*, vol. 5, 1997, pp.257–334; see pp.307, 311–12 for overcrowding.

Richardson on hovel towns: Griffiths, *Aboriginal Affairs*, p.13.

Aboriginal life expectancy: *Mortality and life expectancy of Indigenous Australians: 2008 to 2012* (AIHW, 2014; cat. no. IHW 140); Australian Historical Population Statistics 2008 (ABS, cat. no. 3105.0.65.001).

Critics of 1992 Mabo judgement also disagreed: Francesca Dominello, 'The politics of remembering and forgetting', *Cosmopolitan Civil Societies Journal*, vol. 1, no. 3, 2009, p.31; S. E. K. Hulme, 'The High Court in Mabo', *Proceedings of the Samuel Griffith Society*, vol. 2, ch. 6, 1993; G. Blainey, *A Shorter History of Australia* (rev. edn, 2014), pp.272–4.

Redfern speech: Warhaft, pp.369–74.

Native Title Act of 1993: Kelly, *The March of Patriots*, p.206.

Aboriginal lands equalled 33 per cent of all: Jon Altman and Nicholas Biddle in *CEHA*, pp.548–54.

High expectations not satisfied: Gary Johns, 'Native title 20 years on', *Proceedings of the Samuel Griffith Society*, vol. 24, ch. 8, 2014, esp. p.201.

Rose Scott on silences: Warhaft, p.452.

Pearson on Howard: ibid., p.378.

Rudd's apology: ibid., pp.65, 68.

Owning homes: 'Indigenous Home Ownership Paper', endorsed by council of housing ministers, 28 March 2013, p.26. Tasmania was the highest at 52 per cent.

Aborigines in universities: Don Aitkin in *Quadrant*, September 2016, p.93.

25: SAILS AND ANCHORS

Australia's wealth: Fullilove, *A Larger Australia*, p.59.

Leichhardt in 1842 on a future Australia: *DAQ*, p.158.

Terrill on Australia's north: Ross Terrill, *The Australians* (2000), p.4.

National honours system and anthem: Whitlam, *The Whitlam Government*, pp.141–6.

Thatcher on radical Muslims: Margaret Thatcher, *The Path to Power* (London, 1995), p.535.

September 11 terrorism: John Howard, *Lazarus Rising* (2010), pp.379–85.

Boat arrivals: J. Phillips and H. Spinks, *Boat Arrivals in Australia since 1976: Statistical Appendix Updated 23 July 2013* (Parliamentary Library, Canberra).

Federal parliament in 1948: G. Blainey's reminiscence in *Weekend Australian*, 21 February 2015.

INDEX

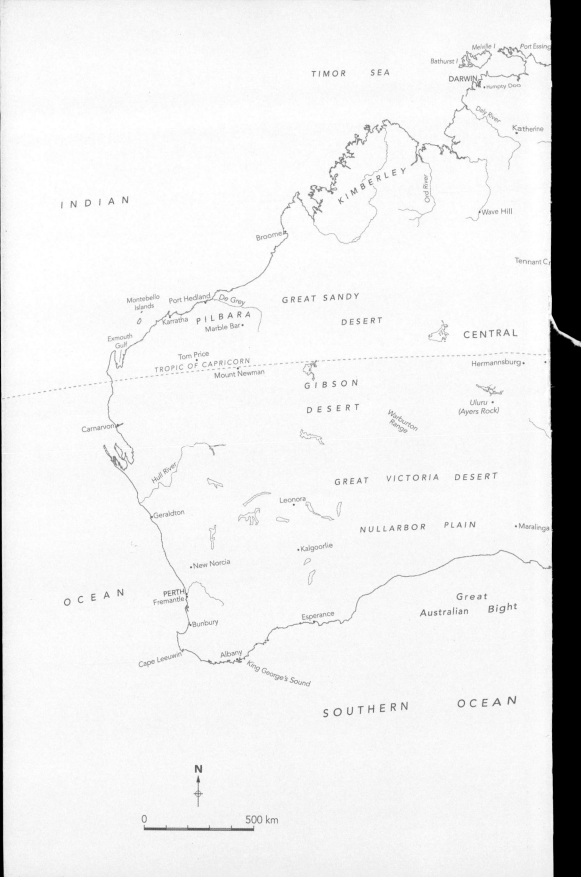